89616

FUNCT

D1461907

... be ... d on or before

**This book is to be returned on or before
the last date stamped below.**

16. NOV. 1993

3 0 NOV 1993

3 0 JAN 1996

COMPUTER SCIENCE TEXTS

COMPUTER SCIENCE TEXTS

Elements of
Functional Languages

MARTIN C. HENSON

BSc, MSc
Department of Computer Science
University of Essex
Wivenhoe Park
Colchester
Essex

BLACKWELL SCIENTIFIC PUBLICATIONS

OXFORD LONDON EDINBURGH

BOSTON PALO ALTO MELBOURNE

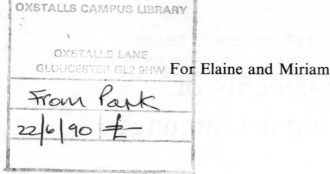
For Elaine and Miriam

© 1987 by
Blackwell Scientific Publications
Editorial offices:
Osney Mead, Oxford OX2 OEL
  (*Orders*: Tel. 0865 240201)
8 John Street, London WC1N 2ES
23 Ainslie Place, Edinburgh EH3 6AJ
52 Beacon Street, Boston
  Massachusetts 02108, USA
667 Lytton Avenue, Palo Alto
  California 94301, USA
107 Barry Street, Carlton
  Victoria 3053, Australia

First published 1987

Set by Macmillan India Ltd
Printed and bound
in Great Britain

DISTRIBUTORS

USA and Canada
  Blackwell Scientific Publications Inc
  P O Box 50009, Palo Alto
  California 94303
  (*Orders*: Tel. (415) 965–4081)

Australia
  Blackwell Scientific Publications
  (Australia) Pty Ltd
  107 Barry Street,
  Carlton, Victoria 3053
  (*Orders*: Tel. (03) 347 0300)

British Library Cataloguing in Publication
Data

Henson, Martin C.
  Elements of functional languages.—
  (Computer science texts).
  1. Electronic digital computers—
  Programming
  I. Title   II. Series
  005.1   QA76.6

  ISBN 0–632–01739–2
  ISBN 0–632–01506–3 Pbk

Library of Congress Cataloging-in-
Publication Data

Henson, Martin C.
  Elements of functional languages.

  (Computer science texts)
  Includes bibliographies and index.
  1. Functional programming
languages.   I. Title.
II. Series.
QA76.7.H46   1987   005.13   87–792
ISBN 0–632–01739–2
ISBN 0–632–01506–3 (pbk.)

Contents

Preface

About the book

This book is an introduction to functional languages, functional programming and those aspects of software science which, it is often claimed, functional languages can successfully address. These aspects include program structuring, program verification, program transformation, programming language semantics and programming language implementation.

The problems a serious student of functional languages may encounter include the rapid rate at which the subject is developing (with the consequence that much material is scattered throughout the literature or has the status of 'folklore') and the, possibly unfamiliar, background material which it is necessary to master. I hope that this book will help such a student by virtue of the two main aims I have been guided by during the writing of it.

The first of these is to provide the basic material and to discuss the major techniques which are necessary for understanding the significance of functional languages both computationally and theoretically. The second is to expound some of the more specialized material (some quite recent at the time of writing) which is both exciting and important for the future development of the subject.

These aims spawn more specific objectives which, to a great extent, are covered by the individual chapters of the book.

After an introductory chapter, I introduce the lambda notation, as a language of functions, and topics from the lambda calculus as an operational model of computing with functions. This second chapter provides the groundwork for much of the rest of the book. To this end it plays both a tutorial role and the role of a reference for later study.

In (the long) Chapter 3 I concentrate on functional programming and program verification. Of particular significance are the roles of lazy evaluation, higher-order operators and various inductive techniques for program verification.

In Chapter 4 I turn to program transformation. This is a fascinating and very important topic. I have chosen to describe the basic techniques and, as a more adventurous topic, selected continuation-based methods from a number of contenders. This chapter, in particular, could be extended into a book itself given the wealth of material which is available. I hope that once the material of this chapter has been mastered the reader will be able to approach the literature with confidence.

In Chapter 5 I look at the recent work on FP systems as originally conceived by John Backus. This complements much of the material of Chapters 3 and 4 by showing some alternative approaches to programming, verification and transformation. For internal consistency I have introduced the FP system as an extension of the language used everywhere else in the book; however, the style of presentation is in all but one respect that used by Backus and his colleagues in the literature.

Chapter 6 is dedicated to topics in programming language implementation. I have included a short section on conventional implementation strategies (at a rather abstract level) for the purpose of comparing and contrasting them with alternative methods. The majority of this chapter consists of what one might call the essential prerequisites for understanding the current development of compilers, typecheckers, interpreters, and machines for functional languages.

Chapter 7 consists of material of a more theoretical nature. Some of this material (on data types) ties up loose ends from Chapter 2 and contrasts the more operational approach taken in this earlier presentation. We develop a mathematical theory of data based on sets equipped with rather special relations. This allows us to solve recursive function equations denotationally and solve recursive-type equations.

The final chapter, Chapter 8, is an extended worked example in functional programming. The topic I have chosen is the derivation of a compiler from a functional description of a small imperative programming language. This topic allows me to present some elementary material on the Scott–Strachey approach to denotational semantics and to use many of the techniques developed elsewhere in the book on a larger example.

About the exercises

The text of this book is scattered, liberally, with exercises. Some of these simply tie up loose ends whilst others are designed to reinforce new ideas or to involve more substantial project work. It is not necessary to do all the exercises to understand the book. Indeed, I have avoided placing any critical material in these contexts. Proofs of theorems which are beyond the scope of the book are indicated as such and suitable references are provided; they are not left as exercises! At the end of the book there is a section entitled, *solutions to exercises*. This contains, for many exercises, sufficient information and material to render them trivial or else indications to places in the literature where solutions may be found. It does not, however, work through the solutions in complete detail.

Exercises along with definitions, propositions, theorems, examples and so on are terminated by a square: ■. This allows me to nest exercises within long examples and so on without confusion. If such a box follows the statement of a proposition (theorem, corollary, . . .) then the proof is omitted; otherwise the box indicates the end of the proof.

About the bibliographic notes

At the end of each chapter I have included bibliographic notes. One aim of the book is to place the reader into a context where he or she can investigate the subject further. These notes include references to both current and historical literature, for, in many cases, the roots of a topic can be traced back to the dawn of computer science itself. Two important abbreviations used in the references are: LNCS (*Lecture Notes in Computer Science*, Springer, Berlin) and ACM (Association of Computing Machinery).

About the audience

It will be an advantage for the reader to be aquainted with a modern, high-level, imperative programming language such as PASCAL, MODULA 2, ALGOL 68 or ADA. Now and again the exercises will suggest that a program be written in PASCAL. I have used PASCAL in these contexts purely as a generic, imperative, programming language. The reader, inclined to do these exercises, may attempt them in his or her own favourite imperative language.

For those coming to this book from a mathematical rather than computing background I have included an appendix outlining the basic terminology employed for programming languages and a brief sketch of the Von Neumann architecture which is often mentioned in this book and the research literature which I reference.

For those readers with less mathematics than computer science I have included an appendix detailing some of the mathematics I should otherwise take for granted. Most readers will find it worthwhile to glance at this appendix in order to fix the notation which I have adopted. The other mathematics required is introduced in the text along with the other material. Again, references to appropriate elementary and advanced literature appears in the bibliographic notes.

I have taught the content of this book, alongside other material, in courses on functional languages, implementation methods, programming language semantics, and foundations of software science for several years at the University of Essex. These courses have been addressed to final year undergraduates and postgraduate students. Some of these students have had little mathematics or little computer science (although rarely – at least intentionally! – neither) but they have had a great deal of enthusiasm for both subjects and a desire to see how they may can be employed and explored to develop a computer science worthy of the name. It is to this audience that the book is addressed.

About the programming language and semantics

The programming language which I have used throughout the book is based on the languages KRC and MIRANDA designed by David Turner at the University of Kent.

The choice of a programming language for a book on computer science (particularly one essentially *about* languages) is one of the most difficult decisions facing an (certainly this) author. One can select a well-known and widely available language (which would probably have meant LISP for this book) but this can have real disadvantages. These include notational obscurities and, in particular, a lack of semantic expressiveness. This is to say that some perfectly innocent concepts can become either bafflingly complicated or virtually impossible to express within the framework. On the other hand the introduction of (yet) another didactic programming language has the disadvantage of being unavailable for general use and, unless it is *very* carefully described, somewhat semantically ambiguous. The advantage of such a policy is the avoidance of semantic preconceptions on behalf of the reader. It is also my intention to develop some of the consequences which follow from various semantic descriptions of the language. KRC and MIRANDA have a fixed semantics (which I have called the *canonical semantics*) but I have made it quite clear at certain points in the text which semantics is being investigated. MIRANDA is a typed language and it will be useful most of the time, for various didactic reasons, to adopt a typed system (rather than the untyped KRC). My notation for types, however, differs from that of MIRANDA.

Computer scientists, along with mathematicians in general, know the significance of good notation. Excellent notation, however, rarely arises spontaneously; it is invariably the result of careful semantic analysis. Such study is able to reveal and isolate structure and form and can freeze this in some new syntax. This is the essence of good semantics. Chapter 8 of this book, with its introduction to Scott–Strachey semantics exemplifies just one example of this enterprise. The syntax of the programming languages KRC and MIRANDA are clear and concise because they are based on firm semantic analysis. They form (although occasionally thoroughly abused!) the programming backbone of the book.

By emphasizing semantic principles over the syntactic form I hope that any reader who has grasped an idea in this book, in my 'KRC-like' notation, will be able to apply it, in turn, in other languages with equanimity.

Acknowledgements

It is, first and foremost, a great pleasure to acknowledge those computer scientists whose research over the years has generated the material on which this book is based. Without them, and many others, there would be no subject and no book.

John Backus, Richard Bird, Rod Burstall, Alonzo Church, Haskell Curry, John Darlington, Peter Henderson, John Hughes, Stephen Kleene, Peter Landin, John McCarthy, Robert Milne, Alan Pritchard, John Reynolds, Barkley Rosser, Dana Scott, Guy Steele, Joseph Stoy, Christopher Strachey, Gerry Sussman, David Turner, Phil Wadler, Mitch Wand, John Williams.

I would also like to thank all my colleagues at Essex but especially Ray Turner (for any number of fruitful conversations), Mike Sanderson, Roland Backhouse and Sam Steel for their help in the preparation of this book. The referees, especially Simon Peyton Jones, have also given me sound advice and many useful suggestions.

Finally, thank you Ann and Marisa for struggling through the manuscript (over and over again!).

Martin C. Henson
'Warlin' Bulmer
Sudbury Suffolk

Chapter 1

Functional languages

1.1 Introduction

In this first chapter we will try to outline what functional languages are, how they differ from conventional programming languages and why we might prefer to program in them.

We shall see that whilst conventional languages are based primarily on a hidden store of named locations processed by sequences of assignment statements, functional languages are based on the composition of functions and the application of these to data. In particular, programs written in functional language compute *values* and not *store changes*, which is the aim of a program written in a conventional language.

We will outline some reasons why functional languages might be suitable for the formal study of various important topics in software science. These include, for example, verifying that programs possess certain properties, transforming programs into more efficient forms without compromising their correctness, and so on. Furthermore, we will suggest that functional programs generally exhibit more inherent parallelism than conventional programs. This suggests that they might be suitable candidates for new computer architectures which are composed of many separate processors which can communicate and co-operate with one another.

In the next section we will spell out some of the distinguishing features of both conventional and functional languages and then, in a further section, we will begin to explore, rather generally and superficially for the time being, why functional programming languages might be a good idea.

1.2 What?

Even though there appear to be a large number of different programming languages to choose from, it is surprising to learn how similar, in certain crucial respects, they are to one another. If we trim away the (significant) differences between FORTRAN, BASIC, PASCAL, ALGOL 60, ALGOL 68, SIMULA 67, and ADA we will find that they are all built upon a similar *computational substrate*. This is formed from two important notions.

1

The first of these is *assignment*. In a large number of languages this is signified by a colon and an equals sign, that is: ':='. Although the expressive power of assignments in the languages mentioned above varies considerably they do all share the same basic semantics and this is described, informally, rather like this:

When we write:

$$e := e'$$

the intention is that the *value* of e' is to be stored in the *reference* (address, location, . . .) computed from e.

The second notion is usually known as *sequencing*. Sequencing is, in many of the languages above, indicated by a semicolon. Thus, if c and c' are two commands then we can combine them by sequential composition, into the single, compound command which is written:

$$c\,;\,c'$$

In some languages (such as FORTRAN for example) sequencing is essentially implicit; there is no special symbol for it – it is simply the significance of the 'carriage return' or the 'end of card'.

We wish to stress the *form* in which sequencing has been described above. That is, we view it as a binary operator (or connective) which, when given two commands, yields a command as a result. This algebraic view makes the semicolon into an operator in much the same way that addition (of expressions) is usually viewed as a binary operator. If this seems at all strange then this is probably because the *properties* which sequencing possesses are rather different (in particular a certain asymmetry which we explore below) from those of 'ordinary' operators. To reinforce this let us consider three putative properties.

Example 1.2(i) Associativity

Addition is both commutative and associative. That is, for any numbers n, n' and n'' we have:

$$n + n' = n' + n$$

and

$$n + (n' + n'') = (n + n') + n''$$

Does sequencing enjoy these properties? For example, given three commands,

c, c' and c'' are the program fragments:

$$(c \; ; \; c') \; ; \; c''$$

and

$$c \; ; \; (c' \; ; \; c'')$$

equivalent? The answer seems to be yes. Now in arithmetic the associativity of addition allows us to write expressions like: $n + n' + n''$ without bracketing. This is also what we do when we write: $c \; ; \; c' \; ; \; c''$ and so on. Later on we will provide a formal proof that sequencing is associative but not until almost the end of the book.

■

Example 1.2(ii) Commutativity

On the other hand it is perfectly clear that the program fragments $c \; ; \; c'$ and $c' \; ; \; c$ are *not* in general equivalent. Sequencing is not commutative. This is obvious; the whole point is to utilize the semicolon to schedule simple commands sequentially and to exploit the control and data dependencies that this introduces. When two commands such as $x := 7$ and $y := 8$ do not share any control or data dependencies then the fragments $x := 7; \; y := 8$ and $y := 8; \; x := 7$ *are*, after all, equivalent. ALGOL 68 actually introduced a special command connective (indicated by a comma instead of a semicolon) called *collateral evaluation*. The idea is that the fragment $x := 7, \; y := 8$ may be executed as either sequence above. This decision is left to a compiler which can exploit the choice to introduce code optimizations. Moreover, a compiler could arrange, for a suitable target machine, for the commands to be executed concurrently.

■

Example 1.2(iii) Strictness

Consider program termination. Let W stand for a command (or an expression) which, when executed, enters an infinite loop. Note that $W + n$ is equivalent to W for any expression e. That is, $W + e$ is also an infinite loop. Since addition is commutative it follows that $e + W$ is equivalent to W too.

An operator with this property of *preserving non-termination* is called *strict* and we will be introducing this concept rather more formally in the next chapter.

Let us now turn to sequencing again. It is pretty obvious that any sequence of commands which begins with a command equivalent to W will itself be equivalent to *W*. That is: *W* ; *c* is equivalent to *W* for any command *c*. Now sequencing is not commutative, so we cannot establish immediately that *c* ; *W* is equivalent to *W*. We will need to think about this fragment on its own merits. To see that *c* ; *W* is not, in general, equivalent to *W* it suffices to demonstrate a counterexample. Consider the sequence: **goto** *L*; *W*. This avoids the sub-command *W* by means of a jump.

It is this asymmetry we alluded to earlier. It is indeed this property which makes it rather more difficult to view sequencing as a binary connective like addition.
■

Exercise 1.2(iv)

Many programming languages include a *conditional command*. A typical example of this might be:

$$\textbf{if } x = 0 \textbf{ then } y := 6 \textbf{ else } x := 7$$

View this as a ternary operator (that is one taking three arguments).
(a) Is the conditional strict in any of its arguments?
(b) Does sequencing *distribute* over the conditional on the left? That is, are *c* ; **if** *b* **then** *c'* **else** *c''* and **if** *b* **then** *c*; *c'* **else** *c*; *c''* equivalent?
(c) Does sequencing distribute over the conditional on the right?
■

The fact that sequencing delays evaluating its second argument until after the first argument has been completed gives the connective great power to avoid unnecessary computations. This will be developed later in the book.

The roles played by sequencing and assignment in the languages mentioned above make them essentially command oriented. That is, at some level, programs are sequences of commands to be obeyed. In this respect they resemble the underlying machine on which they run. We will refer to this class of conventional programming languages as *imperative* languages. The aim of an imperative program, then, is to effect changes in the store of a computer by suitable sequences of assignment statements.

The languages which are studied in this book are rather different from the imperative languages. They are not based on the same computational substrate of sequencing and assignment. Instead they are based on the single binary operator known as *application*. For this reason they are known as *applicative languages*. This class of languages is distinguished by its lack of a mechanism for programming assignment statements. In this book we concentrate exclusively on the special case in which application is interpreted to mean *functional application*, that is, the application of a function to its arguments. More generally the applicative languages include the *logical* languages (such as PROLOG) in which application is essentially *relational* application. The aim of an applicative program, then, is to compute some *value* (functional languages) or *set* of values (relational languages) rather than to effect changes in some notional store.

These functional languages grew out of the language LISP which in turn grew out of a theory of functions called the *lambda calculus*. This calculus is so important, and has remained so influential, that we devote the most part of the next chapter to its description and development. In fact, certain design decisions led to LISP being, in the early years, rather different to the lambda calculus. This came about for a variety of reasons which will become apparent rather later in the book. In particular most LISP (Winston & Horn, 1981) dialects are actually imperative languages for they include both sequencing and assignment. More recently descendants of LISP, for example SCHEME (Abelson & Sussman, 1986) and LISPKIT LISP (Henderson, 1980), have become more or less reconciled with the lambda calculus, although SCHEME still retains some notion of assignment.

Can we treat PASCAL as an applicative language by avoiding the use of assignment and sequencing? After all PASCAL has a sublanguage of expressions and functions. There is a sense in which we can. However the programs we would write would be limited in form and tortuous in style because application is not seen to be central to the language design and the language of expressions and functions is very limited. The programs would also execute very inefficiently.

Now at this stage the reader may see that functional languages are based on rather different principles to the imperative languages. However, the question we must now address is exactly why we wish to exorcize assignment and sequencing from our programming languages. A proper answer to this is, in a sense, what the book is about. Ultimately it is up to the reader after studying this book, and the literature, to decide to what extent the reasons are valid.

At this stage, however, we can outline an answer. We can draw some analogies, and state some conjectures which many computer scientists now hold. These can and should be borne in mind for future reference. Debates over the form of programming languages have always raged. At the time of writing it seems that the arguments over functional and imperative languages are the most passionate and exciting.

1.3 Why?

However informally the process of program construction proceeds certain elements are always present. Firstly, we will have some notion of the task we wish to program; in other words, a specification of the problem. Secondly, we use our knowledge of the lexical and syntactic components of the language, together with an idea of what they stand for (their semantics) according to some programming methodology (top down, step-wise refinement, . . .) to achieve the goal. We will further attempt to convince ourselves that the final program meets the specification, and will probably deploy some simple transformations or optimizations which, while maintaining the meaning of the program, improve its efficiency by exploiting special properties of the programming language implementation and machine.

These concepts of specification, semantics, programming methodology, verification, and program transformation may not be consciously considered during the program development; they may be vague and highly informal. For example, our grasp of semantics may be nothing more than a rough description of what the various programming language features do to the state of the machine at run-time. Nevertheless these concepts are discernible in the activity of programming itself and they have become some of the central concerns of software science.

It cannot be claimed that there are any definitive answers to these topics but it is at least certain that we need to study them formally and explicitly. This has become more urgent and more obvious during the last fifteen years or so as the costs of software development (particularly in relation to hardware costs) have risen dramatically, and the reliability and robustness of much software is quite often miserable.

It is the intense interest in the issues of software science which we introduced above which provides much of the motivation for the exploration of functional languages. One reason for this is the semantic clarity of functional notations which allows them to be manipulated and studied more easily than their imperative counterparts. In particular, formal investigation of destructive control commands (GOTO commands and the like) and destructive data commands (like assignments) have revealed that they are, semantically, very complex and possess few useful mathematical properties. This is described in an introductory fashion in Chapter 8 and can be investigated more thoroughly in the texts on denotational semantics which are referred to in the bibliographic notes.

One of the most important properties of a mathematical notation is known as *referential transparency*. There are a number of slightly different definitions of this concept but we will take it to mean that it is always reasonable to *substitute equals for equals.* Thus, in a context in which *x* is 3, and given the expression: f(9) we may reasonably substitute for the argument any expression which is equal to 9. Therefore all the following should be equivalent to f(9):

$$\mathbf{f}(1+(2*4)), \quad \mathbf{f}(\mathbf{square}\,(x)), \quad \mathbf{f}(x+x+x), \text{ and so on.}$$

Of course, we probably need to be more precise. What do we mean (exactly) by 'substitute'? What do we mean by 'equals'? These topics are addressed in the next chapter where we take a (syntactically) simple functional language called the lambda calculus and define precisely the concepts of substitution and equality.

In general, though, we do expect 'equality' to be an equivalence relation. In particular we would expect it to be reflexive. This means that identical objects are equal. In PASCAL, however, this is certainly not obvious: If f is a function then it is not always the case that f(3) = f(3). This occurs because functions may do 'side effects'. That is, they may make global assignments to variables. These in turn can affect the computation of future calls to the function f.

Exercise 1.3(i)

Write a PASCAL function f taking a single integer argument for which the call f(3) *never* returns the same value as any previous call of f(3).
∎

This has serious implications for any mathematical investigation of programs. At the heart of any system for program transformation (for example) we will need a way of asserting that two programs are equal. This equality is not, it seems, going to be easy to articulate. Indeed the subject of formal semantics is motivated to some extent by a desire to find a notion of equality of programs and to show when a programming language is, after all, referentially transparent. The results of formal semantics showed that the language in which the programming language has to be described and the sense of 'equality' required are quite far removed from the programming language itself. This is perhaps unfortunate; we might hope that programs and mathematical manipulation of programs can be carried out in the same, or at least similar, notation.

Now functional languages are exciting because this division between programming language and the language required for formal investigation is negligible or even non-existent. We might say that functional languages wear their semantics on their sleeves.

It is important to be careful with our claims. It is often suggested that imperative languages are semantically intractable and, even, that they are not referentially transparent. Neither is true. Indeed much work has been done, particularly in program verification, with imperative programming languages and the reader ought to be aware of this. References to some texts dealing with this topic are provided in the bibliography associated with Chapter 3.

Even within the ambit of imperative languages, some moves have taken place which restrict the power of arbitrary assignment-based programming. These changes have been motivated by the desire to improve the language for the purposes of program verification. In particular, in EUCLID, which is closely related to PASCAL but was designed with formal verification in mind, GOTO is absent and global assignments are banned. However, EUCLID also bans functional arguments, which play a major role in functional programming as we will see later.

Quite apart from the issues of software science there are some other reasons why functional languages are generating so much interest. These have to do with programming language implementation and machine architecture.

Until relatively recently the underlying principles of machine architecture have been based on the Von Neumann machine. This is the classic mono-processor architecture consisting of a store connected to a processing unit. This paradigm is now under serious threat. The massive advances in hardware science, particularly in fabrication of very high density integrated circuits, has made it possible to contemplate machines which consist of very large numbers of processors which can co-operate by communication with each other, or with shared global memory. In the 1970s some architectures consisting of many processors were investigated. In these the processors were designed to operate on the same instructions in parallel. These are quite useful for large vector calculations but less useful in exploiting the parallelism (or more properly, concurrency) which is inherent in general-purpose programs. Some research went into the study of FORTRAN programs to see if it was possible to extract implicit parallelism from them but this met with limited success. This seems, in retrospect, quite understandable. FORTRAN was designed to map tasks onto the Von Neumann architecture; at some point it is necessary to break up the program into a sequence of small transactions between the processor and the store. FORTRAN is designed to remove explicit parallelism from problems. Indeed this is the reason for assignment and sequencing playing such a crucial role in so many programming languages; at some point we need to break the problem down into a sequence of alterations to the store of the machine because this is how the machine is designed to operate.

If we reject the Von Neumann architecture then this raises the question of exactly how we program the new machines. It seems to stand to reason that a machine consisting of many processing elements will perform better than a single processor but in order to take advantage of any concurrency we will need to isolate it in our programs. That is, we need to be able to detect circumstances under which various parts of a larger problem can be concurrently executed.

In a sense it should not come as a surprise that conventional languages are inappropriate for these new architectures. These languages were developed to get the best out of an architecture which is fundamentally different from those now envisaged. In particular, corollaries of forcing sequentiality on programs are strong data and control dependencies between individual commands. We are back to the non-commutativity of the sequencing operator again. It is not often possible to execute a pair of commands in either order (let alone simultaneously). This follows because of assignments which alter the context (the store) in which commands are executed. There is, therefore, little exploitable concurrency in a sequence of commands. Indeed the only parts of a conventional program which look amenable to concurrent evaluation are the (side-effect free) expressions. This is so because the operators and primitive values which go to make up an expression do not impose any sequential data and control dependencies upon one another.

Some form of explicit manipulation of concurrency is available in some languages. We mentioned the collateral evaluation in ALGOL 68 earlier, but this is rather a trivial example. In ADA, for example, it is possible to set up objects called *tasks* which can be executed concurrently. They can communicate by means of the *rendezvous* concept. More recently, the language OCCAM, which is based on work on concurrency due to Hoare, has become important as a vehicle for programming systems built from a number of processors called transputers. Whilst this seems exciting for the manipulation of a modest number of processing elements it is debatable whether the explicit manipulation of concurrency is a possibility when we consider hundreds or even thousands of processing elements.

It has been suggested that the implicit concurrency inherent in functional languages makes them suitable for exploiting these new multiprocessor architectures. This has provided yet greater motivation for their study and development.

It may not be too harsh a judgement to claim that the drive for execution efficiency has dominated the desire for software reliability in the design and production of computer software. Functional languages, it is claimed, can address both these topics. By rejecting destructive data operations (just as we were encouraged to avoid destructive control operations in the 1970s) we can begin to develop programming languages which are amenable to mathematical manipulation *and* capable of exploiting the power of multiprocessor architectures.

Ultimately, it is up to the reader to decide to what extent these claims are true or are likely to become true in the future.

1.4 Bibliographic notes

There are a number of books and papers which contain some consideration of the issues raised in this brief chapter. In particular Dijkstra's (1972) excellent critique of some conventional languages and more specifically (because Dijkstra is not advocating a functional language in his paper) the polemical paper of Backus (1978) are suitable material to complement this chapter.

Several of the papers in Darlington *et al.* (1982) and, for example, the paper by Turner (1981) contain a discussion of the *software crisis*, the impact that functional languages can make on formal software science and the contribution they can make to exploit the potential of recent trends in hardware science.

Abelson, H. & Sussman, G. J. (1986) *The Structure and Interpretation of Computer Programs*. MIT Press, Cambridge, Mass.

Backus, J. (1978) Can programming be liberated from the Von-Neumann style? *Commun. ACM*, **21**, 613–41.

Darlington, J., Henderson, P. & Turner, D. (eds) (1982) *Functional Programming and its Applications*. Cambridge University Press, Cambridge.

Dijkstra, E. W. (1972) The humble programmer. *Commun. ACM*, **15**, 859–66.

Henderson, P. (1980) *Functional Programming: Application and Implementation*. Prentice-Hall, Englewood Cliffs, NJ.

Turner, D. A. (1981) The future of applicative programming. In *Trends in Information Processing Systems*, *LNCS*, Vol. 123, pp. 334–48, Springer Verlag, Berlin.

Winston, P. H. & Horn, B. K. P. (1981) *LISP*. Addison-Wesley, Reading, Mass.

Chapter 2

Lambda and combinatory calculi

2.1 Introduction

We will begin with a look at functions, since they are clearly at the heart of our enterprise. In this chapter we will develop two topics: the *lambda calculus* and the *classical calculus of combinators*. Both have made a significant impact on functional programming languages from theoretical and practical perspectives. The lambda calculus in particular can be said to have had a major impact on computer science itself. The reader will be able to judge the enormity of this contribution by observing the extent to which these calculi play a role, in one form or another, in the rest of the book.

Until Section 2.4 our treatment will be entirely syntactic or formal. Up to then we will be inclined to use these calculi as a means for presenting some intuitions regarding the nature of functions and how they interact. In Section 2.4 and Chapter 7 we will concern ourselves with semantic issues and ask questions like: which functions (set theoretically) do lambda terms (or combinatory terms) actually stand for? For the present, then, such questions will be avoided.

2.1.1 Functions

Informally, functions of ordinary mathematics are formed from expressions which involve variables. Thus the expression $x^2 + 3$ of arithmetic would be converted into a function of x by writing something like:

$$\mathbf{f}(x) = x^2 + 3$$

In this case the domain of discourse is arithmetic but a similar process may be adopted in any area of mathematics where the operators may be quite different. For example, in vector calculus we might take the expression:

$$\nabla^2(A \times A)$$

and form the vector operator $\mathbf{f}$ of A written as:

$$\mathbf{f}(A) = \nabla^2(A \times A)$$

In order to remove the specificity of these different domains of mathematical discourse we can *treat all operators as functions*. By doing this we find that there is just one operation at work in these examples and that is the operation called *functional application*. This operator when given a function **f** and an argument x forms the expression **f**(x) which stands for **f** applied to x. In this way, our examples become:

$\quad$ **f**(x) = **add**(**square**(x), 3)
$\quad$ **f**(A) = **delsquare**(**cross**(A, A))

2.1.2 Currying functions

In the examples above we have functions such as **f**, **square** and **delsquare** which take one argument, and functions such as **add** and **cross** which take two. We can simplify these expressions still further by insisting that functions only take one argument. This can be done without banning **add** and **cross**. The process is called *currying* after a mathematician called Curry (but was actually introduced by Schönfinkel). Currying allows functions such as **add** to take one argument at a time so that **add**(3, 4) is written (**add**(3))(4). The explanation is that **add**(3) is a unary function which will add three to its single argument. More formally, **add** $\in N \times N \rightarrow N$ is to be regarded as **add** $\in N \rightarrow [N \rightarrow N]$. Viewed in this way it is clear that to each integer **add** returns a function.

$\quad$ If we introduce currying our examples now look like this:

$\quad$ **f**(x) = (**add**(**square**(x)))(3)
$\quad$ **f**(A) = **delsquare**((**cross**(A))(A))

We are probably used to functions which take some simple values as arguments and return simple values as results. This naïve viewpoint has been challenged. One of our examples above provides a function (**add**) which, given an integer, returns an integer function as a result. In fact the arguments we can supply to functions can be functions themselves. Consider, for example, the function **apply** which applies its first (functional) argument to its second: (**apply**(**f**))(x) = **f**(x). **apply** is clearly an example of this kind.

$\quad$ In spite of these rather general ideas about expressions and combinations of functions we still need expressions to be *well formed* in some sense. In this context we mean that the domain of a function must match any argument it is given. It is surely clear that the following examples are not well formed in this respect:

$\quad$ **add**(true)
$\quad$ (**apply**(6))(**square**)

We shall be devoting a good deal of attention to the topic of type matching later in the book. For the time being, for simplicity amongst other reasons, we shall not pay too much attention to this issue.

2.1.3 Naming functions

There are two remaining inconveniences with the notation we now have for functions. The first is the rather excessive use of bracketing. This can be solved easily.

Firstly, we shall take *juxtaposition* as an indication of function application. Thus fx, **f** x, or (**f** x) if it is more perspicuous, is equivalent to the **f**(x) we are probably more familiar with. Secondly, we shall insist that *juxtaposition associates to the left*. Thus xyz is equivalent to $(xy)z$ and not $x(yz)$. Again, if it is clearer, we will write $(x\ y\ z)$ which is equivalent to $((x\ y)\ z)$ and not $(x\ (y\ z))$. Given these rules, we may rewrite our two examples from arithmetic and vector calculus more conveniently as:

> **f** x = **add** (**square** x) 3
> **f** A = **delsquare** (**cross**A A)

The second inconvenience is more subtle and will have very important repercussions. It concerns the need to *name* our functions. In

> **f** x = **add** (**square** x) 3

f is clearly the name of the function. This is perhaps a useful device to employ (if the function is to be used frequently in future expressions) but often the name is only present to provide and facilitate a mechanism for stating the parameter(s) of the function and their order.

This cannot be solved simply by omitting the left-hand-side reference to **f**. This is because:

> **add** (**square** x) y

may be any of the following functions (and many more):

> **f** x = **add** (**square** x) y (y is a free parameter)
> **f** x y = **add** (**square** x) y
> **f** y x = **add** (**square** x) y

Our question is basically this: how do we best convert an expression into a function of its variable(s)? This process is absolutely fundamental and is called *functional abstraction*. We shall, in the next two sections, investigate two very important techniques of functional abstraction. Before we do this we will finish this introduction by discussing a very important principle which relates functional abstraction to functional application.

The principle of abstraction

There is a naïve sense in which the process of *application* is inverse to the process of *abstraction*. Roughly speaking, abstraction converts an expression into a function, whereas application converts a function into an expression. This insight is actually not so naïve for it characterizes a property we wish these two operations to enjoy. In general terms let us write (**abs** x E) to stand for the function of x given by the expression E. Let (**apply** f x) stand for the process of applying the function f to argument x. At this stage we are not suggesting any particular form of abstraction or application. We are simply appealing to the general concepts.

The relationship we expect any particular process of abstraction and application to enjoy is captured by the following principle:

$$(\text{for all expressions } E)((\textbf{apply } (\textbf{abs } x\, E)\, x) = E)$$

In the sections which follow it will be possible to check that any proposal for functional abstraction actually satisfies this relationship.

2.2 Lambda calculus

2.2.1 Default naming

As a means of identifying *abstractions* (the term we shall now use to refer to what we have previously called functions) we introduce a sign λ, and we follow this with a variable to introduce a parameter. Thus, given the expression (**add** (**square** x) 3) we can write $\lambda x \cdot$ (**add** (**square** x) 3) and we say that prefixing "$\lambda x \cdot$" *abstracts the function* (*with respect to variable* x) *from the expression.*

Notice that we can now distinguish easily between the functions:

$\lambda x \cdot$ (**add** (**square** x) y)
$\lambda x \cdot \lambda y \cdot$ (**add** (**square** x) y)
$\lambda y \cdot \lambda x \cdot$ (**add** (**square** x) y)

which we discussed earlier.

For convenience we will shorten the last two of these to: $\lambda xy \cdot$ **add** (**square** x) y and $\lambda yx \cdot$ **add** (**square** x) y, respectively. We now have a notation for the various functions we might be interested in. In the absence of any explicit name for the function we can use the notation *itself* as a name. The notation, therefore, provides us with a *default naming convention*.

The process of forming functions which we have described is called *lambda abstraction* and the abstractions which result are *lambda forms* (or *terms*, or *expressions*).

For the rest of the chapter, and indeed the book, let us define exactly what the lambda forms are.

2.2.2 Lambda notation

Definition 2.2.2(i)

Let VAR be a set of variables with typical elements v, v', and so on. We define the set EXP of *lambda terms* as follows.

(a) $v \in VAR \Rightarrow v \in EXP$ *variables*
(b) $v \in VAR, E \in EXP \Rightarrow \lambda v \cdot E \in EXP$ *abstracts*
(c) $E, E' \in EXP \Rightarrow (E\ E') \in EXP$ *applications*
(d) $E \in EXP \Rightarrow (E) \in EXP$ *bracketing*
(e) nothing else is in EXP

(a) says that every variable is a lambda expression. (b) says that we can form a new expression $\lambda v \cdot E$ from any variable v and expression E: $\lambda v \cdot E$ represents a function or abstraction. (c) tells us that from any pair of expressions E and E', we can form $(E\ E')$, that is, E applied to E'. (d) allows us to bracket expressions however we please. (e) ensures that lambda expressions are formed only by lines (a)–(d). In an abstract $\lambda v \cdot E$ we will refer to v as the *bound variable* and E as the *body*. In an application $(E\ E')$ we will call E the *operator* and E' the *operand* or *argument*. When it is possible and convenient to do so we will write $(E\ E')$ simply as $E\ E'$ or even EE'.

■

Some simple examples of lambda expressions are $\lambda x \cdot x$, $\lambda x \cdot \lambda y \cdot xy$, xy, $(\lambda x \cdot x)y$. It will be clear that the set EXP of lambda expressions is somewhat more austere than the examples of abstracts we introduced above. In particular EXP does not contain constants such as **square**, **add**, and 3. These, it turns out, can be represented by lambda expressions as we shall see in Section 2.2.5. The reader interested in how this can be extended will find some direction in the bibliography.

We continue to employ the syntactic rules for application and λ-binding that we introduced above in order to avoid drawing in a mass of brackets. Furthermore a new syntactic rule is worth introducing in order to prevent excessive bracketing: *a lambda abstract finishes at the end of the expression or at the first unmatched right bracket* (*whichever is the sooner*). Thus $\lambda x \cdot xy$ is an abstraction $(\lambda x \cdot xy)$ and not $(\lambda x \cdot x)y$, which is an application.

What we have is a notation for expressing and combining functions. This lambda notation is used extensively in the rest of the book for describing functions and it is interesting to note that the language itself is often found at the core of many useful functional programming languages and machines (as we will see later).

2.2.3 Lambda conversion

A notation is all well and good but we might expect more of this λ-notation. For example, it seems as though $(\lambda x \cdot \mathbf{add}(\mathbf{square}\ x)3)4$ should be equivalent to 19. Furthermore $\lambda x \cdot x$ is a very simple abstract built from the single variable x; in our old notation we might write $f(x) = x$. It is clear that $\lambda x \cdot x$ is the *identity function*. Given this we might expect $(\lambda x \cdot x)y = y$.

This suggests a *calculus* of λ-terms which captures our intuitions about functions and the way they evaluate. To introduce this we will need to develop some more terminology.

The following two definitions express precisely when a variable in an expression is *free* and when *bound*. Loosely speaking these concepts are close to the terms *global* and *local variable* in a conventional programming language such as PASCAL. Thus, a bound variable v, in an expression, is controlled by some occurrence of "$\lambda v \cdot$" while a free variable is not so constrained.

Definition 2.2.3(i)

$v \in VAR$ *occurs free* in $M \in EXP$ iff
(a) $M = v$
(b) $M = (M1\ M2)$; $M1, M2 \in EXP$ and v occurs free in $M1$ or $M2$
(c) $M = \lambda v' \cdot M'$, $v' \in VAR$, $M' \in EXP$ and
          $v \neq v'$ and v occurs free in M'
(d) $M = (M')$ and v occurs free in M'
■

For any $M \in EXP$, let $FV(M) = \{v \mid v$ occurs free in $M\}$

Definition 2.2.3(ii)

$v \in VAR$ *occurs bound* in $M \in EXP$ iff
(a) $M = \lambda v' \cdot M'$, $v' \in VAR$, $M' \in EXP$, $v = v'$ or v occurs bound in M'

(b) $M = (M1, M2)$, $M1$, $M2 \in EXP$ and v occurs bound in $M1$ or $M2$

(c) $M = (M')$, $M' \in EXP$ and v occurs bound in M'

Examples 2.2.3(iii)

v occurs free in v, $(\lambda v \cdot v)v$, vw and $(\lambda w \cdot v)$ but not in $\lambda v \cdot v$ or in $\lambda v \cdot w$. v occurs bound in $\lambda v \cdot v$ and in $(\lambda v \cdot v)v$ but not in v, vw or $(\lambda w \cdot v)$. Note that free and bound variables are not opposites. A variable may occur free and bound in the same expression.

It is necessary to be this precise about free and bound variables because, as the reader will surely know, avoiding name clashes in programs is very important. Clashes can cause us problems if we are careless with our choice of identifiers. We shall see that this problem of name clashes occurs in the lambda calculus too.

Exercise 2.2.3(iv)

When is M a subexpression of N? (We will write this: $M \leq N$.) Give a formal definition.

A slightly more general concept is that of *free expression*.

Definition 2.2.3(v)

$M \in EXP$ occurs free in $N \in EXP$ iff

(a) $M \leq N$

(b) for all N' such that $M \leq N' \leq N$; $v \in FV(M) \Rightarrow v \in FV(N')$

In Chapter 6 we will need to use this notion of free expression. In particular we need to find the largest free expressions of any lambda form.

Definition 2.2.3(vi)

$M \in EXP$ is a *maximal free expression* of $N \in EXP$ iff
M is a free expression of N, and whenever M is a proper subexpression of M', M' is not a free expression of N.

This tells us that the maximal free expressions of a lambda expression cannot be extended to larger free expressions.

Exercise 2.2.3(vii)

Identify the free and maximal free expressions of $\lambda xy \cdot xzy(zwx)(wwzyw)$.
■

Let us return to the example above which suggested that $(\lambda x \cdot x)y$ is equivalent (or evaluates) to y. What we seem to require is the substitution of an argument (which, here, is y) for all occurrences of a bound variable in an abstraction (which, here, is x).

We are led to define a process of *substitution*. This has to capture the notion of replacing a variable in an expression by another expression. As a first approximation we might try:

Definition 2.2.3(viii)

$E[x \leftarrow E']$ (to be read E *where free occurrences of x are replaced by E'*) is defined as follows:

(a) $x[x \leftarrow E']$ $\qquad = E'$

(b) $y[x \leftarrow E']$ $\qquad = y$ $\qquad\qquad$ (for all $y \neq x$)

(c) $(\lambda x \cdot E)[x \leftarrow E']$ $\quad = \lambda x \cdot E$

(d) $(\lambda y \cdot E)[x \leftarrow E']$ $\quad = \lambda y \cdot (E[x \leftarrow E'])$ $\qquad$ (for all $y \neq x$)

(e) $(E_1 E_2)[x \leftarrow E']$ $\quad = (E_1[x \leftarrow E'])(E_2[x \leftarrow E'])$
■

This is 'almost' correct but fails to take into account the possible name clashes we alluded to earlier. Consider for example the function $\lambda x \cdot y$. Now $(\lambda x \cdot y)[y \leftarrow w]$ is $\lambda x \cdot w$ but $(\lambda x \cdot y)[y \leftarrow x]$ is $\lambda x \cdot x$. In the second, the free variable x (in $[y \leftarrow x]$) is captured by the bound variable x in $\lambda x \cdot y$. Now $\lambda x \cdot y$ is a constant function and $\lambda x \cdot x$ is the identity function. We do not wish these to be equivalent. This clash of interpretation follows immediately from the clash of variables. If the variable we substitute for y is w ($w \neq x$) then the clash does not occur and the variable is not captured by the λx. In order to solve this we need to complicate case (d) above.

Definition 2.2.3(ix)

$E[x \leftarrow E']$ is defined as follows:

(a) $x[x \leftarrow E']$ $\qquad = E'$

(b) $y[x \leftarrow E']$ $\qquad = y$ $\qquad\qquad\qquad$ ($y \neq x$)

(c) $(\lambda x \cdot E)[x \leftarrow E']$ $\quad = \lambda x \cdot E$

(d) $(\lambda y \cdot E)[x \leftarrow E']$ $\quad = \lambda y \cdot E[x \leftarrow E']$ $\qquad$ (if $y \neq x$ and y is not free in E' or x is not free in E)

(e) $(\lambda y \cdot E)[x \leftarrow E'] = \lambda z \cdot E[y \leftarrow z][x \leftarrow E']$ (if y is free in E' and z is not free in E' or E)

(f) $(E_1 E_2)[x \leftarrow E'] = (E_1[x \leftarrow E'])(E_2[x \leftarrow E'])$

Note carefully the bracketing in (d) and (e) above.

■

The reader may be forgiven for finding this less than simple. In the next section we shall see a way of doing without variables which simplifies things quite significantly.

We can now try to formalize our intuitions about functions and suggest some axioms which relate the lambda expressions.

Clearly, it does not matter unduly if we change the bound variable of an abstraction if we change all references to it too. This much is certainly obvious to all programmers for it is equivalent to claiming that the choice of a name for a formal parameter in a procedure is irrelevant. This is fine providing that we do not introduce a conflict with the name of any global variable referred to in the procedure. In such a circumstance the global variable would become local. Similarly, in the lambda notation, we must ensure that changes to bound variables do not accidently capture free variables. This suggests:

Axiom α

$$\lambda x \cdot E = \lambda y \cdot E[x \leftarrow y] \qquad \text{if } y \text{ does not occur free in } E$$

Now that we have defined substitution we can utilize it to capture the idea of evaluating the application of an abstract to an argument.

Axiom β·

$$(\lambda x \cdot E)(E') = E[x \leftarrow E']$$

Finally we shall take it that functions are characterized simply by the results they yield for all possible arguments. More formally this suggests the following definition of equality for functions:

Definition 2.2.3(x)

$$\mathbf{f}_1 = \mathbf{f}_2 \quad \text{iff} \quad (\text{for all } x)((\mathbf{f}_1 \, x) = (\mathbf{f}_2 \, x))$$

■

This is called the *extensional equality* of functions and suggests for the lambda notation the axiom:

Axiom η

$$\lambda x \cdot Ex = E \qquad \text{if } x \text{ not free in } E$$

The rules which follow are designed to make = an equivalence relation (which is surely what we intend) and to force = to respect the structure of terms.

Rules

$$E = E$$
$$E = E' \Rightarrow E' = E$$
$$E = E' \wedge E' = E'' \Rightarrow E = E''$$
$$E = E' \Rightarrow FE = FE'$$
$$E = E' \Rightarrow EF = E'F$$
$$E = E' \Rightarrow \lambda x \cdot E = \lambda x \cdot E' \text{ rule } \xi$$

The last rule is particularly important for it combines with axiom η to prove that the lambda calculus satisfies the extensionality principle, introduced above. This principle, cast in lambda terms, is

$$Ex = E'x \Rightarrow E = E'$$

These axioms and rules of inference constitute a theory of *lambda equality* and it is possible, therefore, to furnish formal proofs of the equality of two lambda expressions.

It is important to notice that by developing this theory we have achieved an aim discussed in the previous chapter which arose during the discussion of *referential transparency*. This was to have a precise notion of equality and substitution for a programming language. Notice too that the last three rules given above (which we might term the *congruence rules of equality*) ensure that we may substitute equals for equals in lambda forms.

The theory of lambda equality is of course rather *static*. What we lack are any *evaluation schemes* for lambda expressions which, hopefully, simplify complex forms into simple answers. It is to this we now turn. All our evaluation strategies are based on axioms β and η viewed as *rewrite rules*. Using an axiom as a rewrite rule means finding instances of one side of the axiom in an expression and replacing this instance with the corresponding instance of the other side.

When we treat the axioms as rewrite rules we will replace the "passive" symbol of equality, =, with the more "active" symbol, cnv, to emphasize *conversion*. We should stress that there is no formal difference between cnv and =.

If we restrict ourselves to rewriting axioms β and η from left to right we will use the symbol, red, rather than = or cnv (to emphasize the *reduction* of the number of abstractions which occur in the axioms). Notice that if E red E' then E cnv E' (equivalently $E = E'$) but if E cnv E' then it is not *necessarily* the case that E red E'. It is often useful to add the name of the axiom involved in a conversion or reduction as a subscript. This can be seen in the examples which follow:

Examples 2.2.3(xi)

(a) $(\lambda x \cdot \lambda y \cdot x(yx)y)z$ red$_\beta$
    $\lambda y \cdot z(yz)y$

Note that $\lambda y \cdot z(yz)y$ does not red$_\eta$ to $z(yz)$ because y is free in $z(yz)$.

(b) $(\lambda x \cdot (\lambda y \cdot y)z)x$ red$_\beta$
    $(\lambda y \cdot y)z$ red$_\beta$
    z

Notice that in this second example we could have proceeded in a different fashion:

(c) $(\lambda x \cdot (\lambda y \cdot y)z)x$ red$_\beta$
    $(\lambda x \cdot z)x$ red$_\beta$
    z

■

We need to introduce a little more terminology. If an expression may be reduced by axioms β or η then we say that it contains a *β-redex* or an *η-redex*, respectively.

In each of the examples we reached an expression when the only axiom we could apply is α-conversion. Since such a conversion does not substantially alter the expression we do not persist in rewriting it further.

We shall say that an expression is in *normal form* if it does not contain a β-redex or an η-redex. Clearly the expressions z and $\lambda y \cdot x(yx)y$ are normal forms.

The examples above serve to motivate and provoke some observations and questions. Do all expressions reduce to a normal form? In view of the second example we may also ask whether, when there are alternative redexes to reduce, it matters in which *order* the reductions are performed.

To see that, in fact, all expressions do *not* reduce to a normal form it suffices to show a common counterexample:

Example 2.2.3(xii)

Consider the expression:

$$(\lambda x \cdot xx)\lambda x \cdot xx$$

It can clearly be reduced by axiom β but when we substitute the argument $\lambda x \cdot xx$ for x in xx we obtain the result $(\lambda x \cdot xx)\lambda x \cdot xx$ which is the original expression (and therefore contains a β-redex). This process may be repeated *ad infinitum* but the expression will clearly not reach a normal form. The reader should note that the expression does not contain an η-redex (in either occurrence of $\lambda x \cdot xx$) because x is free in x.

■

There are, of course, many other examples we could examine for which the reduction rules fail to obtain a normal form. As exercises in reduction try:

Exercise 2.2.3(xiii)

(a) $(\lambda x \cdot xxx)\lambda x \cdot xxx$
(b) $(\lambda x \cdot xy)((\lambda z \cdot z)z)$
(c) $(\lambda x \cdot \lambda y \cdot xy)((\lambda x \cdot y(\lambda x \cdot x)x)z)$
(d) Verify the principle of abstraction for lambda abstraction.

■

So not all lambda expressions have normal forms. However, these normal forms are unique if they exist. This is a corollary of the following important theorem:

Theorem 2.2.3(xiv) (Church–Rosser I)

If E red E_1 and E red E_2 then there exists an expression F such that E_1 red F and E_2 red F.

This can be better appreciated diagrammatically (see page 23).

The proof of this is rather combinatorial and is beyond the scope of this book. The interested reader is referred to Appendix 1 of Hindley & Seldin (1986).

■

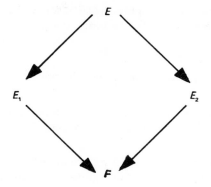

Corollary 2.2.3(xv)

If E has normal forms E_1 and E_2 then E_1 and E_2 are equivalent (up to α-conversions).

Proof. The Church–Rosser theorem gives us an F for which E_1 red F and E_2 red F. Since E_1 and E_2 are normal forms they contain no β- or η-redexes. Thus F is obtained from E_1 and from E_2 by an α-conversion so E_1 may be obtained from E_2 by an α-conversion.
■

We must be careful in drawing conclusions from this result. It is certainly true that if two different (reduction) sequences take an expression into two normal forms then the normal forms are (essentially) the same. However, we must beware of concluding that the reduction strategy is irrelevant. The theorem does *not* say that any sequence of reductions will provide the normal form if it exists; just that it will be unique if it is found.

Indeed, the reduction strategy adopted *can* make a difference. Again, a simple example reinforces this very clearly.

Example 2.2.3(xvi)

Consider the expression $X = \lambda x \cdot xx$. We have already seen in example 2.2.3(xii) that XX red XX. Now consider the expression $(\lambda x \cdot y)(XX)$. If we take the leftmost β-redex of this expression and reduce it we obtain the sequence

$$(\lambda x \cdot y)(XX) \qquad \text{red}_\beta$$
$$y$$

which is a normal form.

If we reduce (or attempt to reduce) the argument to normal form before doing the leftmost reduction we obtain the sequence

$$(\lambda x \cdot y)(XX) \text{ red}_\beta \, (\lambda x \cdot y)(XX) \text{ red}_\beta \ldots$$

which is a non-terminating sequence of reductions.
■

This evidence, then, raises another question regarding the power of reduction strategies, i.e. their ability to produce the normal form of an expression if it exists.

There are many possible ways to reduce an expression. A number of the systematic strategies have important implications for program verification and programming language implementation.

Definition 2.2.3(xvii)

A reduction sequence is a *normal order reduction sequence* if at every stage the leftmost redex is reduced. The leftmost redex of MN is identified by the beginning of the operator M. Thus, the leftmost redex of $(\lambda x \cdot (\lambda y \cdot y)x)z$ is that with operator $(\lambda x \cdot (\lambda y \cdot y)x)$ and operand z.
■

Definition 2.2.3(xviii)

A reduction sequence is an *applicative order reduction sequence* if at every stage the leftmost redex free of internal redexes is reduced.
■

Going back to example 2.2.3(xvi) we see that in $(\lambda x \cdot y)(XX)$ the leftmost redex is the β-redex with $\lambda x \cdot y$ as operator and (XX) as operand. Thus a normal-order reduction takes this to y and immediately to normal form.

Writing the expression in full as $(\lambda x \cdot y)((\lambda x \cdot xx)\lambda x \cdot xx)$ we see that the leftmost redex which contains no inner redexes is the β-redex with $\lambda x \cdot xx$ as operator and $\lambda x \cdot xx$ as operand. Thus an applicative-order reduction sequence takes this expression to $(\lambda x \cdot y)((\lambda x \cdot xx)\lambda x \cdot xx)$ and it is clear that the applicative reduction does not terminate with the normal form y. Indeed it does not terminate at all.

In fact, there is an important theorem regarding normal-order reductions, again due to Church and Rosser:

Theorem 2.2.3(xvix) (Church–Rosser II)

If E red E' and E' is a normal form then the normal-order reduction sequence starting with E terminates with E'.
■

This tells us that normal-order reduction will find the normal form of an expression if it has one. In view of the first Church–Rosser theorem, and the evidence of the previous example, it follows that applicative-order reduction will produce the same normal form if it terminates but it is not capable of bringing all expressions with a normal form into normal form.

These reduction strategies are related (but by no means equivalent!) to parameter passing mechanisms in conventional programming languages such as ALGOL 60. One, rough, correspondence is between normal-order reduction and the call-by-name mechanism in which arguments to procedures are not evaluated until they occur in the body of the procedure. The other rough correspondence is between applicative-order reduction and call-by-value in which the arguments are evaluated before the body of the procedure is evaluated. These correspondences are indeed very rough, for the equivalent of the Church–Rosser theorems in ALGOL 60 do not hold. For example, in elementary texts on ALGOL 60 programming one is encouraged to use the combined power of assignments and call-by-name parameters to produce a procedure in which a parameter evaluates to a *different* value each time it occurs in the text of the procedure. We shall return to these issues later.

Although normal-order reduction is 'safer' than applicative-order reduction it is often the case that a normal-order reduction is much longer than the corresponding applicative reduction. The reason is not hard to find: in applicative reduction the argument of an application is reduced to normal form once and once only before substitution for the bound variable. However, the argument is substituted (maybe many times) into the operator of an application in its *unreduced* form in a normal-order reduction. Therefore it may be necessary to reduce it many times during the subsequent stages of the reduction. An elementary example will serve to make this clear.

Example 2.2.3(xx)

Consider the following expression $(\lambda x \cdot xyxx)((\lambda z \cdot z)w)$ and the following reduction sequences:

Applicative order

$(\lambda x \cdot xyxx)((\lambda z \cdot z)w)$	red$_\beta$
$(\lambda x \cdot xyxx)w$	red$_\beta$
$wyww$	(normal form)

Normal order

$(\lambda x \cdot xyxx)((\lambda z \cdot z)w)$	red$_\beta$
$((\lambda z \cdot z)w)y\,((\lambda z \cdot z)w)((\lambda z \cdot z)w)$	red$_\beta$
$wy\,((\lambda z \cdot z)w)((\lambda z \cdot z)w)$	red$_\beta$
$wyw\,((\lambda z \cdot z)w)$	red$_\beta$
$wyww$	(normal form)

∎

Although reducing the argument as often as it occurs is often a considerable luxury there are occasions when the arguments need *never* be evaluated.

When the argument has no normal form and the abstract makes no use of it in its body we have the precise situation where normal order reduction succeeds when applicative order fails. This might seem like a rather unusual, even artificial, situation. It is *not* and we shall see why not when we turn later to recursion.

Head reduction and head normal forms

Apart from the two reduction strategies we have discussed already there are many other interesting and significant systematic reduction schemes.

Of particular importance is the notion of head normal form and its associated reduction strategy which is known as head reduction.

Definition 2.2.3(xxi)

A lambda expression M is in *head normal form* (HNF) iff it has the form:

$$\lambda x_1 \ldots x_n \cdot yN_1 \ldots N_m$$

for some $n, m \geq 0$. Note that the N_i do not need to be in either HNF or NF.
∎

Examples 2.2.3(xxii)

(a) $\lambda z \cdot zxy$ is a HNF and a NF.
(b) $\lambda z \cdot z((\lambda x \cdot x)y)$ is a HNF but not a NF. It does of course have a NF which is $\lambda z \cdot zy$.
(c) $(\lambda zx \cdot xz)(XX)$ (where $X = \lambda x \cdot xx$ as before) has a HNF and this is $\lambda x \cdot x(XX)$. It has no normal form.
(d) $(\lambda xz \cdot zx)y(XX)$ has no HNF and no NF.
(e) Let $Y' = AA$ where $A = \lambda xy \cdot y(xxy)$.

$Y'(\lambda xy \cdot yx)$ has a HNF but no NF since the expression $Y'(\lambda xy \cdot yx)$ reduces through $(\lambda xy \cdot yx)(Y'(\lambda xy \cdot yx))$ to $\lambda y \cdot y(Y'(\lambda xy \cdot yx))$. Y' is a very important expression which is used to describe recursion as we will see in the next section.
∎

These examples serve to illustrate that head normal forms are weaker than normal forms. Many expressions which do not have normal forms do have head normal forms.

Definition 2.2.3(xxiii)

$(\lambda x \cdot M)N_1$ is a *head redex* of E iff:

$$E = \lambda x_1 \ldots x_n \cdot (\lambda x \cdot M)N_1 \ldots N_m$$

for some $n \geq 0$ and $m \geq 1$.
∎

Definition 2.2.3(xxiv)

A reduction sequence is a *head reduction sequence* if at every stage the head redex is reduced.
∎

Theorem 2.2.3(xxv) (Wadsworth)

If M has a HNF, N, then the head reduction sequence of M terminates with N.
∎

Proposition 2.2.3(xxvi)

(a) $\lambda x \cdot M$ has a HNF if and only if M has a HNF
(b) If MN has a HNF then M has a HNF
∎

The proofs of these can be found in Barendregt (1984).
 The idea of a HNF divides the class of expressions which have no NF into two. It turns out that those with no HNF (and therefore no NF) are really 'meaningless'. This means we can add an extra rule to those given earlier:

$$E \text{ and } E' \text{ have no HNF} \Rightarrow E = E'$$

Intuitively, this makes all expressions without HNF equally meaningless.
 The consistency proof for the theory of lambda equality with this extra

axiom scheme is beyond the scope of this book. The interested reader can consult Barendregt (1984, section 16.1).

It is interesting to add that in the early development of the lambda calculus it was believed that *all* expressions without NF were meaningless. This is not the case. If we add the rule:

E and E' have no $\text{NF} \Rightarrow E = E'$

then it is possible to show that *all* lambda expressions are equivalent. Not a very useful theory of functions!

Proposition 2.2.3(xxvii)

If the rule:

E and E' have no normal forms $\Rightarrow E = E'$

is added to the theory then the theory becomes inconsistent, that is, $E_1 = E_2$ for all lambda expressions E_1 and E_2.

Proof. Let $M = (\lambda x \cdot x(\lambda xy \cdot x)(XX))$ and $N = (\lambda x \cdot x(\lambda xyz \cdot xz(yz))(XX))$ where $X = \lambda x \cdot xx$ as before. Neither M nor N have normal form. Let us assume that the rule: $E = E'$ when neither E nor E' have normal form, is added to the calculus. We reason that: $\lambda xy \cdot x = M(\lambda xy \cdot x) = N(\lambda xy \cdot x) = \lambda xyz \cdot xz(yz)$. Now if $\lambda xy \cdot x = \lambda xyz \cdot xz(yz)$ then we can show that $\lambda x \cdot x = E$, for all E, as follows:

$$\lambda x \cdot x = (\lambda x \cdot x)\lambda x \cdot x = (\lambda xy \cdot x)(\lambda x \cdot x)((\lambda xy \cdot x)E)(\lambda x \cdot x) =$$
$$(\lambda xyz \cdot xz(yz))(\lambda x \cdot x)((\lambda xy \cdot x)E)(\lambda x \cdot x) =$$
$$(\lambda x \cdot x)(\lambda x \cdot x)((\lambda xy \cdot x)E)(\lambda x \cdot x) =$$
$$(\lambda x \cdot x)E = E$$

Now, if $\lambda x \cdot x = E$, for all E, then $E = E'$ for all E and E' by transitivity.
∎

Let us write W to stand for a prototypical expression with no HNF and let us interpret W as "undefined". Clearly, for all M, we have $WM = W$ since WM has no HNF if W does not [proposition 2.2.3(xxvi)(b)]. Moreover $\lambda x \cdot W = W$ by Proposition 2.2.3(xxvi)(a). Using W we can define the notion of a *strict* expression M. We will say that M is *strict* if $MW = W$. Essentially this says that MN has no HNF if N has no HNF. Clearly if M is strict it does not matter whether we reduce MW applicatively or by normal order. In both cases the result is a non-terminating reduction sequence. This fact is very important in justifying the evaluation strategies of certain reduction machines we will be examining in Chapter 6.

2.2.4 Representations

Essentially our lambda expressions have been construed as *trees*. Substitution effects the replacement of certain *leaves* (bound variables) by expressions. The tree structure reflects explicitly the *grammatical structure of lambda expressions*. For example the reduction:

$(\lambda x \cdot xyxx)((\lambda z \cdot z)w)$ red_β
$((\lambda z \cdot z)w)y((\lambda z \cdot z)w)((\lambda z \cdot z)w)$

is construed to be:

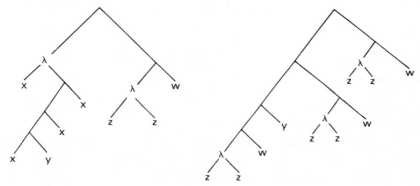

Fig. 2.2.4(i)

However, there are other possible ways of representing explicitly the grammatical structure of expressions. One such representation treats them as *directed acyclic graphs*. In this case the above reduction would look a little different:

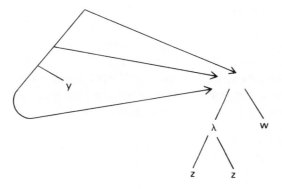

Fig. 2.2.4(ii)

The advantage of this representation of expressions is that occurrences of bound variables share, and so when substitutions are effected there is just one *copy* of the argument. Thus, whenever a subexpression is reduced, several occurrences may feel the benefit. For example, if we now do a reduction on the graph above we obtain:

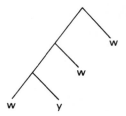

Fig. 2.2.4(iii)

which is a normal form.

This reduction strategy, which is called *normal-order graph reduction*, combines the benefits of both normal-order and applicative-order evaluation. This means that it terminates with a normal form as often as normal-order reduction and, like applicative reduction, reduces expressions (at most) once.

2.2.5 Constructions within the lambda calculus

In this section we shall see how to *code up* certain concepts in the lambda calculus. In particular, we will explore compound data (in the form of a *pairing* operator and its associated *selectors*), truth values, a conditional expression, numerals and some arithmetic.

Pairing

When is a value p the pair of values x and y? Presumably when there are two selection operators **h** (head) and **t** (tail) which, when applied to p, will result in x and y, respectively. This is coded up quite easily:

$$\textbf{pair} = \lambda xyz \cdot zxy$$
$$\textbf{h} = \lambda p \cdot p\,(\lambda xy \cdot x)$$
$$\textbf{t} = \lambda p \cdot p\,(\lambda xy \cdot y)$$

Let $p = (\textbf{pair }x\,y) = \lambda z \cdot zxy$. We claim that p is the pair of values $x\,y$. Now p, as a lambda abstract, is ready to accept a selection function z to which the component values x and y will be supplied. A quick look at **t** and **h** above should be enough to see that the pair p is given a lambda abstract designed to extract either the first component or the second component of a pair of objects x and y. More formally note that:

$$\begin{aligned}
\mathbf{h}(\mathbf{pair}\, xy) &= \mathbf{h}(\lambda z \cdot zxy)\\
&= (\lambda z \cdot zxy)\lambda xy \cdot x\\
&= (\lambda xy \cdot x)xy\\
&= x
\end{aligned}$$

and

$$\begin{aligned}
\mathbf{t}(\mathbf{pair}\, xy) &= \mathbf{t}(\lambda z \cdot zxy)\\
&= (\lambda z \cdot zxy)\lambda xy \cdot y\\
&= (\lambda xy \cdot y)xy\\
&= y
\end{aligned}$$

as required.

This strategy for representing pairs is an example of a powerful functional programming style and we will be discussing it further in Chapters 3, 4 and 8.

Before moving on to other derived operations let us examine the *strictness* properties of the three we have defined so far. Recall that we may extend the notion of equivalence of lambda expressions so that $M = N$ if neither M nor N have a HNF. We introduced the notation W to stand for the prototypical term with no HNF. An expression M is strict if it preserves W under application.

Consider $\mathbf{h} = \lambda p \cdot p(\lambda xy \cdot x)$. If we form $(\mathbf{h}\, W)$ we get the expression $W(\lambda xy \cdot x)$. We observed earlier that WM has no HNF and so is equivalent to W. Thus **h** is a strict operation. The same goes for **t**, as the reader may quickly verify.

Now let us take the pairing operation $\mathbf{pair} = \lambda xyz \cdot zxy$. This has three arguments. The first two are for the objects we wish to pair. The third is for a selector abstract which will be supplied when the pair is interrogated. Note first that $(\mathbf{pair}\, x\, y\, W) = (W\, x\, y) = W$. **pair** is therefore strict in its third argument. However $\mathbf{pair}\, W = \lambda yz \cdot zWy$ and $\mathbf{pair}\, x\, W = \lambda z \cdot zxW$. These are HNFs. Consequently we can conclude that **pair** is not strict in its first and second arguments.

What are the intuitive consequences of this? We can illustrate this by a simple example. Consider $\mathbf{h}(\mathbf{pair}\, x\, W)$. This reduces to x. Thus a pair can be well defined even though one component is meaningless. Providing we extract a defined component we need not be troubled by other undefined subcomponents. Clearly if we request the second component by means of $\mathbf{t}(\mathbf{pair}\, x\, W)$ we will obtain W. If **pair** were strict in its first two arguments, $\mathbf{h}(\mathbf{pair}\, x\, W)$ would then be $(\mathbf{h}\, W)$ and we know this is W because **h** is strict.

Indeed there can be no strict pairing in the lambda calculus for if **pair**
$W = W$ and **pair** $x\ W = W$ then neither of the axioms governing pairing, namely
h(**pair** $x\ y$) $= x$ and **t**(**pair** $x\ y$) $= y$, would be satisfied.

These deliberations will bite in Chapter 3 when we discuss lazy data
construction and also in Chapter 6 when we need to develop a correct
interpretation for data constructors and selectors on a reduction machine.

Truth values and conditional expressions

We define:

> T(true) to be $\lambda xy \cdot x$
>
> F(false) to be $\lambda xy \cdot y$

If this seems arbitrary and strange then the following should support these
definitions. Notice that $T\ M\ N = M$ and $F\ M\ N = N$. This allows us to define
conditionals rather easily:

> **if** B **then** M **else** N is defined to be $B\ M\ N$

If B does not have T or F as a normal form then $B\ M\ N$ is unconstrained.
If B is restricted to a *proposition* (a lambda term with normal form T or F) then
this definition works well.

Exercise 2.2.5(i)

Show that the conditional is strict in its first argument and non-strict in its
second and third.
■

Numerals and arithmetic

There are a large number of different ways of representing numerals in the
lambda calculus. The different choices make operations over them more or less
difficult to represent.

A *numeral system* consists of a lambda term c_n for each numeral n and two
operations **succ** and **zero** which satisfy the axioms:

> **succ** $c_n = c_{n+1}$
>
> **zero** $c_0 = T$
>
> **zero** $c_n = F$ when $n > 0$.

The numeral system devised by Church (see Barendregt, 1984) is defined as follows:

$$c_0 = \lambda fx \cdot x$$
$$c_1 = \lambda fx \cdot fx$$
$$c_2 = \lambda fx \cdot f(fx)$$
$$c_n = \lambda fx \cdot f^n(x) \quad \text{where } f^n(x) \text{ is } f(f(\ldots f(x)\ldots))(n \text{ times})$$

The successor operator is given by **succ** $= \lambda xyz \cdot y(xyz)$.

Note that **succ** c_n

$$= (\lambda xyz \cdot y(xyz))\lambda fx \cdot f^n x$$
$$= \lambda yz \cdot y((\lambda fx \cdot f^n x)\, y\, z)$$
$$= \lambda yz \cdot y(y^n z)$$
$$= \lambda yz \cdot y^{n+1} z$$
$$= c_{n+1} \text{ as required.}$$

zero is a little more tricky:

$$\textbf{zero} = (\lambda x \cdot (\lambda x \cdot x\ T)\ (x\ (\lambda y \cdot \textbf{pair}\ F\ y)(\lambda x \cdot x)))$$

Now **zero** $c_0 =$

$$(\lambda x \cdot x\ T)((\lambda fx \cdot x)(\lambda y \cdot \textbf{pair}\ F\ y)(\lambda x \cdot x))$$
$$(\lambda x \cdot x\ T)(\lambda x \cdot x) =$$
$$(\lambda x \cdot x)\ T = T \qquad \text{as required}$$

and **zero** $c_n =$

$$(\lambda x \cdot x\ T)((\lambda fx \cdot f^n(x))(\lambda y \cdot \textbf{pair}\ F\ y)(\lambda x \cdot x)) =$$
$$(\lambda x \cdot x\ T)((\lambda y \cdot \textbf{pair}\ F\ y)^n (\lambda x \cdot x)) =$$
$$(\lambda x \cdot x\ T)(\textbf{pair}\ F((\lambda y \cdot \textbf{pair}\ F\ y)^{n-1}(\lambda x \cdot x))) =$$
$$(\textbf{pair}\ F((\lambda y \cdot \textbf{pair}\ F\ y)^{n-1}(\lambda x \cdot x)))\ T =$$
$$T\ F(\textbf{pair}\ F((\lambda y \cdot \textbf{pair}\ F\ y)^{n-1}(\lambda x \cdot x))) =$$
$$F \text{ as required.}$$

Exercise 2.2.5(ii)

Let **add** $n\,n' = \lambda xy \cdot nx(n'\ x\ y)$

times $n\,n' = \lambda x \cdot n(n'\ x)$

exp $n\,n' = n'\,n$

Show that

(a) **add** $c_n c_{n'}$ $= c_{n+n'}$

(b) **times** $c_n c_{n'} = c_{n \times n'}$

(c) **exp** $c_n c_{n'}$ $= c_e$ where $e = n^{n'}$

(d) Why is η-conversion important in (c)?

∎

Exercises 2.2.5(iii)

(a) Given an expression, F, which satisfies $F M = F$, show that adding the axiom $F = \lambda x y \cdot x$ makes the lambda calculus inconsistent (i.e. $M = N$ for all $M, N \in EXP$).

(b) Let $S = \lambda x y z \cdot x z (y z)$.

Find the normal form of $(S\ S\ S\ S\ S\ S\ S)$.

∎

2.2.6 Recursive definitions

Recursive definitions are, of course, central to computing in general and of particular importance in functional languages. Our experience of recursive definitions in conventional languages suggests that the circularity of these definitions is achieved by the use of the function *name* itself. It may be of some surprise that recursion can be expressed indirectly without explicit reference to the idea of naming. Indeed since a lambda abstraction is to be regarded (itself) as a default name it would seem impossible to achieve the circularity by means of ordinary name reference in the lambda calculus.

Let us consider the recurrence formula which defines the famous *Fibonacci sequence*:

$$\mathbf{f}(0) = 1$$
$$\mathbf{f}(1) = 1$$
$$\mathbf{f}(n+2) = \mathbf{f}(n) + \mathbf{f}(n+1) \text{ when } n \geq 0$$

Written in a more conventional programming notation we might have:

$$\mathbf{f}(n) = \text{if } n = 0 \text{ or } n = 1 \text{ then } 1 \text{ else } \mathbf{f}(n-2) + \mathbf{f}(n-1)$$

or in the lambda notation we might have:

$$\mathbf{f} = \lambda \mathbf{n} \cdot \text{ if } n = 0 \text{ or } n = 1 \text{ then } 1 \text{ else } \mathbf{f}(n-2) + \mathbf{f}(n-1)$$

If we abstract the function **f** of the right-hand side of this definition we get the expression:

$$\mathbf{F} = \lambda g \cdot \lambda n \cdot \text{if } n = 0 \text{ or } n = 1 \text{ then } 1 \text{ else } g(n-2) + g(n-1)$$

Note that $\mathbf{F}(\mathbf{f}) = \mathbf{f}$. We say that **f** is a *fixpoint* of the expression **F**.

In all these deliberations note that we are dealing with *equations* and not *definitions*. We require, of course, a solution to these equations. So far we have reduced the problem of solving the original equation for **f** to that of finding a fixpoint of the operator **F**.

Indeed all such recursive equations can be reduced to this problem for if we have $f = E$ for some lambda expression E, involving f, we can set $F = \lambda f \cdot E$ and then since $(\lambda f \cdot E)f = E$ (by the principle of abstraction) we see that $F(f) = f$.

The following theorem is of fundamental value in our present enterprise.

Theorem 2.2.6(i)

Every lambda term F has a fixpoint.

Proof. Let $M = \lambda x \cdot F(xx)$. Let $V = MM$.
Now

$$
\begin{aligned}
V &= \\
(MM) &= \\
((\lambda x \cdot F(xx))\lambda x \cdot F(xx)) &\text{ cnv} \\
F((\lambda x \cdot F(xx))\lambda x \cdot F(xx)) &= \\
F(MM) &= F \, V
\end{aligned}
$$

so V is a fixpoint of F.
∎

Now if V is a fixpoint of a particular expression F we can immediately set $Y = \lambda F \cdot (\lambda x \cdot F(xx))\lambda x \cdot F(xx)$ which generates a fixpoint of an *arbitrary* abstraction F. Thus Y is a *fixpoint finder*.

If we go back to our original expression for the Fibonacci sequence we see that $\mathbf{f} = YF$ where $\mathbf{F} = \lambda g \cdot \lambda n \cdot \text{if } n = 0 \text{ or } n = 1 \text{ then } 1 \text{ else } g(n-1) + g(n-2)$.

Now $\mathbf{f} = YF = \mathbf{F}(YF) = \mathbf{F}(\mathbf{f})$. If we apply **f** to 1 we get: $\mathbf{f} \, 1 = \mathbf{F}(\mathbf{f})1 = 1$. It is important to see how the internal term $\mathbf{f} = \mathbf{F}(\mathbf{f}) \ldots$, which has no normal form, can be ignored if we reduce the conditional first. If we insist on reducing the internal instances of the recursive calls first the reduction simply fails to terminate. This again shows the importance of reduction strategy.

It is interesting to note that the *fixpoint finder* Y can itself be described by a recursive equation. Since $YF = F(YF)$ we have the equation $Y = \lambda F \cdot F(YF)$.

Now using the same technique as before we set $G = \lambda Y \cdot \lambda F \cdot F(YF)$. Fixpoints of G will be fixpoint finders. Given $Y = \lambda f \cdot (\lambda x \cdot f(xx))(\lambda x \cdot f(xx))$, which we know to be a fixpoint finder, we can construct YG which, therefore, is itself a fixpoint finder. Let us call it Y'. Interestingly, it is different from Y; i.e. Y does not convert to Y' given the axioms and rules of Section 2.2.3. Since Y' is a fixpoint finder we can produce a fixpoint of G using this too by writing $Y'G$. This is yet another, different, fixpoint finder. Fixpoints are not, therefore, unique in general. All this may seem rather strange, since conversion is based on a notion of equivalence, and these fixpoint operators certainly have equivalent properties in a precise sense. Here we are opening a door into the very rich world of the mathematics of the lambda calculus: an ambitious reader will do no better than to embark on the very comprehensive Barendregt (1984).

This approach to recursion raises a number of questions most of which we will dodge for the moment. For example, fixpoints are not unique; does this matter? Another very important question involves the structure of Y because it contains the subexpression xx which is an example of *self-application*, i.e. an expression applied to itself. Earlier in the chapter the reader may recall that we rather glibly cast off worries about the matching of the domain of a function to any argument it is applied to. We did this on grounds of simplicity but we now seem to be exploiting our lack of care on this point. Self-application is clearly a problem for if x is an element of a set A then, in the expression xx, the first x must be a function with domain A. Since both occurrences of x in xx are the same we would need the set A to be *equal* (in some sense) to the set $A \rightarrow B$ of functions from A to some set B of results. This leads to set theoretic difficulties which we will leave until Chapter 7. Indeed, we have developed a notation and calculus for formalizing our intuitions about functions but said *nothing* about which functions (set theoretically) the expressions are supposed to stand for. This topic we shall also take up later, in Section 2.4.

Exercises 2.2.6(ii)

(a) Find a lambda expression F such that $FM = F$ for all expressions M.
(b) Find all the fixpoints of $\lambda x \cdot x$. Which is generated by Y?
∎

2.2.7 Mutual recursion

It is quite easy to generalize our technique for solving recursive definitions to mutually recursive families of definitions. This is done by utilizing the pairing operation we introduced in Section 2.2.5.

How does pairing help in the description of mutual recursion? Suppose we have two definitions $f = E$ and $f' = E'$ such that the expressions E and E' have both f and f' as free variables. Without loss of generality we will also assume that p is not free in either E or E'.

First we form F and F' such that:

$$F = E[f \leftarrow (\mathbf{h}\, p)][f' \leftarrow (\mathbf{t}\, p)]$$
$$F' = E'[f \leftarrow (\mathbf{h}\, p)][f' \leftarrow (\mathbf{t}\, p)]$$

Now we set:

$$p = (\mathbf{pair}\ F\ F')$$

The expression $(\mathbf{pair}\ F\ F')$ has p as a free variable. The idea here is that p is the pair of functions f and f'. However, we have altered references to f to the first component of p and references to f' to the second such component. Now in the manner of simple recursion we define:

$$G = \lambda g \cdot (\mathbf{pair}\ F\ F')[p \leftarrow g]$$

then we have:

$$p = Gp \text{ as usual.}$$

The recursion is solved by means of the fixpoint finder: $p = YG$. Now to recover the functions f and f' we merely exploit the selectors:

$$f = \mathbf{h}(YG) \text{ and } f' = \mathbf{t}(YG).$$

Exercise 2.2.7(i)

Generalize the technique introduced in this section to allow the solution of n equations (of the form: $f_i = E_i$; $n \geq i \geq 0$).
∎

2.3 The calculus of combinators

One of the most frustrating aspects of the lambda calculus is the difficulty of avoiding the variable clashes that we discussed earlier. It is interesting, and probably quite surprising, that it is possible to work with a calculus of functions in which we do *without* variables. The key to this is a new way of abstracting a variable from an expression so that this variable does not occur in the resultant expression. The upshot of this is that by a sufficient number of abstractions we can form abstracts which are *variable free*. Of course we have to check that such a process is legitimate by ensuring that it obeys the principle of abstraction which we introduced earlier.

2.3.1 Variable-free abstraction

Let us start with a set of *applicative expressions* which consist entirely of variables and applications. This is just the largest subset of the lambda expressions which contains no abstractions. We hope to introduce abstractions in a new way.

We develop our abstraction process inductively on the structure of these applicative expressions and we shall write $[x]E$ to stand for the result of the process of abstracting x from E.

If E is the variable x then we are required to produce the identity function as we saw at the beginning of Section 2.2.3. Let us introduce a symbol I subject to the axiom: $Ix = x$ and add it as a constant to the set of applicative expressions. Given this we can set $[x]x = I$.

If E is a variable y which is different from x then we need to produce a constant function which ignores its argument and returns y. To this end we could introduce a symbol K_y such that $(K_y x) = y$ but since there are a countably infinite number of variables different from x it seems sensible to introduce a single symbol K subject to the axiom: $K\ y\ x = y$. Given this we can set $[x]y = K\ y$ and it is easy to see that $K\ y$ is exactly the *constantly y* function required.

This concludes our analysis when the expression E is a variable of any kind. Finally, we consider the case where E is an application $(E_1 E_2)$. The idea here is to work recursively on the subexpressions E_1 and E_2 by abstracting the variable x from each. Having done this we need to arrange that when the argument is given to the abstract $[x]E_1 E_2$ it can be steered into the subabstracts $[x]E_1$ and $[x]E_2$. To this end we introduce another symbol S subject to the axiom: $S f\ g\ x = ((f\ x)(g\ x))$. It is clear that this symbol steers the argument x to the two subexpressions f and g. Given this, we can set $[x]E_1 E_2 = S([x]E_1)([x]E_2)$. If I stands for *Identity* and K for *Konstant* (!) then perhaps the best pronunciation for S is *Steering* for its effect (as can be seen from the axiom) is to steer an argument x into two subabstracts. These new symbols are called *combinators*.

Let us summarize the above:

Definition 2.3.1(i)

$$(i) \quad [x]x \quad = I$$
$$(k) \quad [x]y \quad = K\,y \qquad (y \neq x)$$
$$(s) \quad [x]E_1 E_2 = S[x]E_1[x]E_2$$

∎

Definition 2.3.1(ii)

$$(i') \quad I\,x \quad = x$$
$$(k') \quad K\,x\,y \quad = x$$
$$(s') \quad S\,f\,g\,x \quad = f\,x\,(g\,x)$$

∎

It is, of course, our intention that the process we have defined is really an abstraction process. To see that it is admissible we can show that it obeys the *principle of abstraction.*

Proposition 2.3.1(iii)

For all applicative expressions E;

$$(([x]E)x) = E$$

Proof. The proof proceeds by induction on the structure of applicative expressions.

Base step

Case 1: $E = x$

$$(([x]x)x) = I\,x \qquad (i)$$
$$= x \qquad\quad (i')$$

Case 2: $E = y$ and $y \neq x$

$$(([x]y)x) = ((K\,y)x) \qquad (k)$$
$$= y \qquad\qquad\quad (k')$$

Induction step

$$(([x]E_1 E_2)x) = ((S[x]E_1[x]E_2)x) \quad (s)$$
$$= [x]E_1 x([x]E_2 x) \quad (s')$$
$$= E_1 E_2 \qquad\qquad\text{(induction twice)}$$

∎

2.3.2 Multiple abstraction

It is important to see that the expression which results from an abstraction operation is itself an applicative expression. Therefore, further abstractions may be performed if required. Let us take a simple example.

Example 2.3.2(i)

Consider the applicative expression $(x\,(y\,z))$. We can abstract the variables x, y and z by lambda abstraction to give the abstract $\lambda x \cdot \lambda y \cdot \lambda z \cdot x(y\,z)$, but we can also apply our new method of abstraction. In this case we need to evaluate $[x]([y]([z]x(y\,z)))$. Let us begin with just $[z]x(y\,z)$.

$$
\begin{aligned}
[z]x(y\,z) \qquad\qquad &= (s) \\
S[z]x[z]y\,z \qquad\quad\; &= (k, s) \\
S(K\,x)(S[z]y[z]z) &= (k, i) \\
S(K\,x)(S(K\,y)I)
\end{aligned}
$$

Next we need to abstract y from this expression.

$$
\begin{aligned}
[y]S(K\,x)(S(K\,y)I) \qquad\qquad\qquad\qquad\qquad\qquad &= (s) \\
S[y]S(K\,x)[y]S(K\,y)I \qquad\qquad\qquad\qquad\qquad\quad &= (s, s) \\
S(S[y]S[y]K\,x)(S[y]S(K\,y)[y]I) \qquad\qquad\qquad\;\; &= (k, s, s, k) \\
S(S(K\,S)(S[y]K[y]x))(S(S[y]S[y]K\,y)(K\,I)) \qquad &= (k, k, k, s) \\
S(S(K\,S)(S(K\,K)(K\,x)))(S(S(KS)(S[y]K[y]y))(K\,I)) &= (k, i) \\
S(S(K\,S)(S(K\,K)(K\,x)))(S(S(K\,S)(S(K\,K)I))(K\,I))
\end{aligned}
$$

The tenacious reader is invited to complete this example by abstracting x from the expression above to yield the variable-free form of the abstract $\lambda x \cdot \lambda y \cdot \lambda z \cdot x(y\,z)$.

■

The example demonstrates rather forcefully that the size of applicative expressions increase rather dramatically with iterated abstractions. A careful look at (i), (k) and (s) shows why. (k) introduces an application from a variable and (s) introduces two applications from the single application $(E_1 E_2)$. It should be fairly clear that the number of applications will rise exponentially with the number of abstractions performed. From a theoretical perspective such complexity is of little consequence. On the other hand, if we wish to utilize such an abstraction process in a practical fashion (and we shall) we do need to worry about this growth rate. Fortunately, even some quite elementary techniques can bring the growth factor down from exponential to quadratic and later in the book we shall discuss other techniques for improving still further the size complexity of expressions with respect to abstraction.

2.3.3 Optimizations

Definition 2.3.3(i)

In order to effect some optimization of expression size we introduce two new combinators. We assume that these new symbols are added to the applicative expressions.
(a) $B f g x = f(g x)$
(b) $C f x g = f g x$
∎

B is a *composition* combinator and C *swaps* a pair of arguments.

Proposition 2.3.3(ii)

$$\begin{align}
(01)\quad & S(K E_1)(K E_2) && = K(E_1 E_2) \\
(02)\quad & S(K E)I && = E \\
(03)\quad & S(K E_1)E_2 && = B E_1 E_2 \\
(04)\quad & S E_1(K E_2) && = C E_1 E_2
\end{align}$$

Proof

$$\begin{align}
01\quad & S(K E_1)(K E_2)x && = (s') \\
& K E_1 x (K E_2 x) && = (k', k') \\
& E_1 E_2 && = (k') \\
& K(E_1 E_2)x &&
\end{align}$$

$$\begin{align}
02\quad & S(K E_1)I\, x && = (s') \\
& K E_1\, x\, (I\, x) && = (s') \\
& E_1 x &&
\end{align}$$

$$\begin{align}
03\quad & S(K E_1)\, E_2 x && = (s') \\
& K E_1 x\, (E_2 x) && = (k') \\
& E_1\, (E_2 x) && = (b) \\
& B E_1 E_2 x &&
\end{align}$$

$$\begin{align}
04\quad & S E_1(K E_2)\, x && = (s') \\
& E_1 x\, (K E_2 x) && = (k') \\
& E_1\, x\, E_2 && = (c) \\
& C E_1 E_2 x &&
\end{align}$$

∎

Now it is easy to see that the right-hand sides of these equivalences contain fewer applications than the left-hand sides. Since they are equivalences it is possible to substitute right for left whenever we please. We should also note that any expression matching the left-hand side of 01 will also match 04 and any expression matching 02 will also match 03. In view of the number of applications involved in the corresponding right-hand sides we should tend to apply 02 in preference to 04. We utilize 01 rather than 03 because $(K (E_1 E_2) x)$ reduces to $(E_1 E_2)$ while $(B E_1 E_2 x)$ reduces to the more complex $(E_1 (E_2 x))$.

If we return to our example we can now see if these optimizations make any impact.

Example 2.3.3(iii)

Evaluate $[x]([y]([z]x(y\ z)))$.

Firstly, we recall from example 2.3.2(i) that $[z]x(y\ z)$ is

$$S(K\ x)(S(K\ y)I)$$

Now $S\ (K\ x)(S\ (K\ y)\ I) = (02)$
         $S\ (K\ x)\ y \qquad\quad = (03)$
         $B\ x\ y$

Now we proceed with $[y]B\ x\ y$:

$\quad\quad [y]B\ x\ y \qquad\qquad = (s)$
$\quad\quad S\ [y]B\ x[y]y \qquad\quad = (s, i)$
$\quad\quad S\ (S\ [y]B\ [y]x)\ I \quad\ = (k, k)$
$\quad\quad S\ (S\ (K\ B)\ (K\ x))\ I$

$\quad\quad$ Now $S\ (S\ (K\ B)(K\ x))\ I = (01)$
$\quad\quad\qquad\quad S\ (K\ (B\ x))\ I \qquad = (02)$
$\quad\quad\qquad\quad B\ x$

$B\ x$ is a rather simpler expression than the one we generated earlier!

$\quad\quad$ Finally $[x]B\ x \qquad\ = (s)$
$\quad\quad\qquad\quad S\ [x]B\ [x]x = (k, i)$
$\quad\quad\qquad\quad S\ (K\ B)\ I$

and it is possible to apply 02 to this to achieve the final expression B.
■

2.3.4 Combinatory reduction

In an arbitrary combinatory expression E a *redex* is a subexpression of the form $(S\ E_1\ E_2\ E_3)$, $(C\ E_1\ E_2\ E_3)$, $(B\ E_1\ E_2\ E_3)$, $(K\ E_1\ E_2)$, or $(I\ E)$. An expression *E* without redexes is in normal form. Normal-order and applicative-order reduction sequences are defined as for lambda expressions, and the Church–Rosser theorems follow for the combinatory calculus too. We will say that a combinator is *saturated* if it has sufficient arguments for its rewrite rule to be invoked.

Definition 2.3.4(i)

A combinatory expression *M* is in *head normal form* (HNF) iff $M = HN_1 \ldots N_m$ where *H* is a combinator and *H* is unsaturated in *M*.
∎

Definition 2.3.4(ii)

A combinatory expression *M* has a *head redex* iff *M* has the form $HN_1 \ldots N_m$ where *H* is a saturated combinator in *M*.
∎

Proposition 2.3.4(iii)

If *M* has HNF *N* then the head reduction sequence starting with *M* will terminate with *N*.
∎

There will be many occasions in the book where we shall need to use one or other calculus of functions. We shall utilize lambda notation as a general function notation very freely and we will discuss the problem of assigning functions to the notation in the final chapter. The combinatory calculus plays an important role in compilation and machine architecture for functional languages and so we will return in some detail to this topic in Chapter 6.

Exercise 2.3.4(iv)

In the lambda calculus it is easy to show that, for all expressions *M*;

$$FV(M) - \{v\} = FV(\lambda v \cdot M)$$

Show that, for all combinatory expressions *E*; $FV(E) - \{v\} = FV([v]M)$.
∎

2.4 The semantics of the lambda calculus

In this section we provide three interpretations for the lambda terms. The first is a *denotational semantics* which provides an interpretation for each expression in a rather special set of functions. The mathematical details of this set are quite deep and we will avoid such considerations until Chapter 7. This semantics expresses the meaning of expressions in a *compositional* fashion. That is to say it furnishes the interpretation of a given expression, *E*, in terms of the interpretations of the subexpressions of *E*. This gives the semantics a *declarative* style in which the meaning is given without reference to some notion of computation. On the other hand the second and third semantics we provide are *operational semantics*. They both stress, to a greater or lesser extent, the idea of attributing meaning to lambda expressions in terms of a *computation scheme*. The distinction between denotational and operational semantics is actually rather more precise than the rough distinction made here, but for our present purposes, however, it will suffice.

2.4.1 Denotational semantics

We have already argued that if we wish to interpret lambda terms *set theoretically* in some set of functions then this set will need to be rather special. This is because the lambda calculus does not distinguish between *levels of functionality*. In particular, the lambda calculus allows *self-application*. If, therefore, *V* is a set of values we hope to interpret lambda terms within we have seen that *V* must contain its own function space $V \to V$. Finding a set with this property is by no means trivial and we shall take up the story again in Chapter 7. For the time being let us suppose that we have a set $V = V \to V$. That is, *V* and $V \to V$ have the same elements.

In order to interpret lambda terms in *V* we will need to define a mapping which given an arbitrary lambda term will yield a value in *V*. This suggests that the mapping lies in the set $EXP \to V$. However, lambda terms, as we know, can contain *free variables* and so our interpretation of such terms will have to take place relative to the values that the free variables can stand for (these are, of course, the values in *V*). To this end we introduce the concept of a *binding environment*. These are the elements of the set $ENV = VAR \to V$. Elements of *ENV*, then, are functions which, given a variable as an argument, will yield some interpretation of this variable in *V*. Environments simply associate variables with values. Let *p* be an element of *ENV*. We will need, in a moment, a way to form a new element, $p' \in ENV$, in such a way that p' is exactly the same as *p* except that for a certain variable (*x* say) p' yields a particular value (say *v*). We introduce a way to achieve this with the following notation:

$p[x \leftarrow v]$ and this is the desired p'. This operation on environments is defined as follows: let x and y be variables. Let p be an environment and v be an element of V, then $p[x \leftarrow v]$ is given by:

$$(p[x \leftarrow v] \; y) = \begin{cases} v & \text{when } x = y \\ (p \; y) & \text{otherwise.} \end{cases}$$

Our semantic interpretation mapping takes a term and an environment (for the interpretation of free variables in the term) to a value in V. Therefore it has the following functionality: $EXP \rightarrow (ENV \rightarrow V)$. Note that we have curried this function as far as possible.

We will name our *interpretation function*, [ ], and we place the first argument (which is a term) within the brackets. [ ] is defined, by cases, over the set of terms EXP:

Definition 2.4.1(i)

> [ ] $\in EXP \rightarrow (ENV \rightarrow V)$
> $[x] \; p \quad = (p \; x)$
> $[\lambda x \cdot E] \; p \; = f \in V \rightarrow V$ where $f v = [E] \; p[x \leftarrow v]$
> $[E \; E'] \; p \; = [E] \; p \; ([E'] \; p \,)$

The first clause tells us that the meaning of a variable is just the value associated with that variable in the environment p. The second tells us that the meaning of an abstraction, $\lambda x \cdot E$, is, as expected, a function in $V \rightarrow V$. This function, when applied to a value v in V, yields the interpretation of E in an environment in which the bound variable x is associated to v. The third clause tells us that the meaning of an application, $E \; E'$, is to be found by applying the meaning of E to the meaning of E'. That is, syntactic application in the lambda calculus is interpreted as the functional application of values of V to functions of $V \rightarrow V$.

■

Armed with this interpretation we could ask some interesting questions: are the conversion rules correct with respect to this semantics? In particular is it the case that $[(\lambda x \cdot E)E']p = [E[x \leftarrow E']]p$ for all environments p and expressions $\lambda x \cdot E$ and E'? Fundamental to such questions is the following proposition:

Proposition 2.4.1(ii)

$$[E[x \leftarrow E']]p = [E]p[x \leftarrow [E']p]$$

for all p, x, E and E'.

Proof.   By induction on the structure of *E*. Once the reader has mastered the material on structural induction in the next chapter this proposition could then be attempted as an exercise.
∎

This property is often termed *substitutivity* and demonstrates an absolute connection between *syntactic substitution* of the form: $E[x \leftarrow E']$ and *semantic substitution* of the form: $p[x \leftarrow [E']p]$.

2.4.2 The SECD machine

The SECD machine is an abstract architecture for the applicative evaluation of lambda expressions. It was introduced in 1964 in a paper by Peter Landin which has, to this day, remained influential. In many ways, Landin developed ideas in the mid-1960s which were not fully recognized untill perhaps ten years later. It is an operational semantics and, indeed, it is so computational in flavour that it has formed the basis of some practical systems for the implementation of functional languages.

Before embarking on a detailed description let us take a look at one stage in the applicative reduction of a lambda expression.

Example 2.4.2(i)

Consider the expression $(\lambda x \cdot xx)((\lambda y \cdot \lambda x \cdot x)w)$ and let us imagine the point at which the argument redex $((\lambda y \cdot \lambda x \cdot x)w)$ is to be reduced. At this stage, the body being evaluated is $\lambda x \cdot x$. Should this contain instances of the bound variable *y* (as it happens, it doesn't) we need to know, somehow, the expression with which it has been associated. In this example, *y* has at this moment been associated with *w*. Whilst all this is going on we need to remember or record the fact that this small reduction is happening in the context of the larger expression. In other words, we need to know what to do with the result of $(\lambda y \cdot \lambda x \cdot x)w$ when we have completed its reduction. Finally, when this inner reduction is complete we will need to record the result as a partial result so that we can associate it with the bound variable *x* prior to processing the body *xx*.
∎

Abstracting a little from this example we see the need for four data structures. Firstly, a place for partial results; secondly, a place for recording the bindings of bound variables to arguments; thirdly, a place to record the body of the abstract being reduced; and, finally, a place to preserve the wider context of the evaluation, i.e. a means of preserving the structure of enclosing expressions whilst an internal redex is being reduced.

These four data structures are called the *stack*, the *environment*, the *control* and the *dump*, respectively. It is the initial letters of these quantities which give the SECD machine its name.

Finally, before the formal definition, let us consider how we ought to represent abstractions as values in the machine. A typical abstract might be $\lambda x \cdot yx$. Notice that this has y as a free variable. The above rather rough description suggests that we have a data structure called the environment whose responsibility it is to provide the values which are associated with variables. Probably, the abstract above is a subexpression of a larger term; for example, $(\lambda y \cdot \lambda x \cdot yx)w$. The moral seems to be that to provide all the information necessary to capture the meaning of the abstract we need to form a composite value consisting of the abstract and an environment which provides values for any free variables the abstract contains. Which environment should we associate with the abstract? There seem to be two main contenders. Should it be the environment active when the body of the abstract (yx in our example) is evaluated or should it be the environment active when the abstract itself is first considered? This is essentially the same problem we had when we defined substitution in Section 2.2.3. There it was clear that we should take it that variable associations are fixed by the static structure of the expression and not by some accidental name associations occurring dynamically during the evaluation. This ensures that *the meaning of an expression is independent of the particular variables of which it is composed.*

To facilitate this we arrange that, as soon as an abstract is encountered, we form a package which consists of the abstract together with the current environment. This package essentially closes the expression with respect to its free variables and, for this reason, is often called a *closure*.

Definition 2.4.2(ii)

First we define some sets. The reader who is not familiar with the set operations we use may like to consult Appendix A.

Let EXP be the set of lambda expressions as defined by Definition 2.2.2(i).

$$
\begin{array}{lll}
S & = V* & \text{stacks} \\
E & = (VAR \times V)* & \text{environments} \\
C & = P* & \text{controls} \\
D & = M & \text{dump} \\
M & = S \times E \times C \times D & \text{states} \\
P & = EXP + \{\mathbf{ap}\} & \text{programs} \\
V & = APP + CLO & \text{values} \\
CLO & = VAR \times EXP \times E & \text{closures}
\end{array}
$$

APP is the largest subset of *EXP* containing no abstractions.
∎

Notice that the stack can store applicative expressions or closures. The environment is represented by a list, or sequence of pairs, associating variables with values. The control mainly consists of a sequence of expressions to be evaluated but the special signal **ap** can also occur on the control. This indicates the moment when the reduction of an application is to begin. The machine state consists of a stack, an environment, a control, and a dump. Finally, a dump, as a suspended evaluation, is itself a machine state.

Definition 2.4.2(iii)

Now we introduce a function called **transform** which indicates how the state is to change, given the control, to a new state. **transform** is often thought of as a function from M to M and this is quite natural. For clarity of presentation we will define it as:

$$\textbf{transform } P \rightarrow [M \rightarrow M]$$

The intention is that

$$\textbf{transform } [p]\langle s, e, c, d \rangle = \langle s', e', c', d' \rangle$$

specifies the transition of the state $\langle s, e, \langle p, c \rangle, d \rangle$ to the state $\langle s', e', c', d' \rangle$.

We can now spell out the details of **transform**. We do this by considering the various possible entities which can occur on the control stack.

$$\textbf{transform } [x]\langle s, e, c, d \rangle = \langle \langle (\textbf{lookup } xe), s \rangle, e, c, d \rangle$$

In this first case we place the value associated with x in the environment e onto the stack of partial results. The function **lookup** is given by:

$$\textbf{lookup } x \langle \langle x, v \rangle, e \rangle = v$$
$$\textbf{lookup } x \langle \langle y, v \rangle, e \rangle = (\textbf{lookup } x \ e)$$
$$\textbf{lookup } x \langle \ \rangle \qquad = x$$

It should be clear that the value associated with x is given by the first occurrence of a pair $\langle x, v \rangle$ in e. Also note that the variable has itself as a value if it is not present in the environment e.

$$\textbf{transform } [\lambda x \cdot E]\langle s, e, c, d \rangle = \langle \langle \langle x, E, e \rangle, s \rangle, e, c, d \rangle$$

When we are presented with an abstraction we form a closure with the current environment and place it as a partial result on the stack.

$$\textbf{transform } [(E \ E')]\langle s, e, c, d \rangle = \langle s, e, \langle E, E', \textbf{ap}, c \rangle, d \rangle$$

This clause simply rewrites the control field. We split the application into two constituents E and E' and place them separately on the control. The tag **ap** is placed last so that when E and E' are evaluated the application can proceed. Notice that it is here that applicative evaluation is forced. We will have to pass all the internal redexes of E and E' before we get to the token **ap**. In the original description Landin placed E' before E. This means that his machine reduces the *rightmost* redex free of internal redexes first. We have changed things simply to coincide with our discussions in Section 2.2.3.

> **transform** $[\textbf{ap}]\langle s, e, c, d\rangle = \langle s', e', c', d'\rangle$

> where $s' = \langle\ \rangle$ (the empty stack)
> $\qquad e' = (\textbf{extend}\ e''\ x\ v)$
> $\qquad c' = E$
> $\qquad d' = \langle s'', e, c, d\rangle$
> and
> $\qquad s = \langle v, \langle x, E, e''\rangle, s''\rangle$

This is the most complicated case. For the moment we assume the stack has the form given above, that is, the values of some pair of expressions E' and E'' are present. Usually the value of E' will be a closure as indicated. The reduction of the body of the closure is now to be undertaken so the control in the new state becomes the body (E). The stack can be cleared for partial results and the environment is extended. Notice that, as the discussion earlier suggested, it is the environment e'' from the closure that is extended. Naturally the extension to e'' binds the bound variable of the closure (x) to the value of E'' (v). The function **extend** is given by:

> **extend** $e\ x\ v = \langle\langle x, v\rangle, e\rangle$

Finally, notice how the new dump d' contains everything contained in the old state (which was $\langle s, e, \langle \textbf{ap}, c\rangle, d\rangle$) except that which is being dealt with in the new state. That consists of everything except the two values of the top of s, and the application token **ap** on control. When this new evaluation is complete we hope to return a result to the suspension now being placed in the dump.

> **transform** $[\textbf{ap}]\langle s, e, c, d\rangle = \langle\langle(xy), s'\rangle, e, c, d\rangle$
> if $s = \langle y, x, s'\rangle$

Here we indicate how to transform the application if the stack value is not a closure. The application is irreducible and we simply return it to the stack.

> **transform** $[\ \ ]\langle s, e, \langle\ \rangle, d\rangle = \langle\langle v, s'\rangle, e', c', d'\rangle$
> where $d = \langle s', e', c', d'\rangle$ and
> where $s = \langle v, s''\rangle$

This indicates that when the current control becomes empty we have completed the current reduction. The result of this is on the stack. We can now reactivate the suspension in the dump remembering to return the value v to the old stack.

∎

When is an evaluation finished? Presumably when both control and dump are empty. We can finish this description by defining an iterating function I which, given an SECD state, will reduce it using **transform** until both control and dump are empty.

Definition 2.4.2(iv)

$I \in M \to M$

$I \langle s, e, \langle \ \rangle, \langle \ \rangle \rangle = \langle s, e, \langle \ \rangle, \langle \ \rangle \rangle$

$I \langle s, e, \langle p, c \rangle, d \rangle = I \ (\textbf{transform} \ [p] \langle s, e, c, d \rangle)$

Clearly I is a *partial function* for we know full well that many lambda expressions have non-terminating reductions.

∎

Example 2.4.2(v)

There is really no substitute for working through a number of examples in order to informally understand the way in which the SECD machine implements applicative reduction. We will introduce some simple notation which will make our examples a little less opaque.

The empty stack we will write as **empty**. The empty environment we will write as **arid**. The empty control we will write as $\langle \ \rangle$ (as usual). The empty dump we will write as **finish**. If $\langle x, E, e \rangle$ is a closure then we will write it $[x \ E \ e]$. If $\langle x, v \rangle$ is an identifier value pair in the environment we will write it $[x \to v]$ to emphasize the association of x with v. In order to avoid overlong expressions we will often replace the dump by a (meta) variable (like $d1$) by a declaration (like: **where** $d1 = \ldots$). Finally, if $\langle s, e, c, d \rangle$ is an SECD machine state and $\langle c_1, c_2, \ldots, c_n \rangle$ is an SECD machine control then we shall write these as $s \ e \ c \ d$ and $[c_1 \ c_2 \ \ldots \ c_n]$, respectively.

We will reduce the expression $((\lambda x \cdot x)(\lambda y \cdot y))((\lambda w \cdot w) \ v)$ into normal form.

> **empty arid** $((\lambda x \cdot x)(\lambda y \cdot y))((\lambda w \cdot w) \ v)$ **finish**
> **empty arid** $[((\lambda x \cdot x)(\lambda y \cdot y)) \ ((\lambda w \cdot w) \ v) \ \textbf{ap}]$ **finish**
> **empty arid** $[\lambda x \cdot x \ \lambda y \cdot y \ \textbf{ap} \ ((\lambda w \cdot w) \ v) \ \textbf{ap}]$ **finish**
> $[x \ x \ \textbf{arid}]$ **arid** $[\lambda y \cdot y \ \textbf{ap} \ ((\lambda w \cdot w) \ v) \ \textbf{ap}]$ **finish**

[*y y* **arid**] [*x x* **arid**] **arid** [**ap** ((λ*w*·*w*) *v*) **ap**] **finish**
empty [*x*→[*y y* **arid**]] *x d*1
   (where *d*1 = **empty arid** [((λ*w*·*w*) *v*) **ap**] **finish**)
[*y y* **arid**] [*x*→[*y y* **arid**]]⟨ ⟩ *d*1
[*y y* **arid**] **arid** [((λ*w*·*w*) *v*) **ap**] **finish**
[*y y* **arid**] **arid** [λ*w*·*w v* **ap ap**] **finish**
[*w w* **arid**][*y y* **arid**] **arid** [*v* **ap ap**] **finish**
v[*w w* **arid**][*y y* **arid**] **arid** [**ap ap**] **finish**
empty [*w*→*v*] *w d*2
   (where *d*2 = [*y y* **arid**] **arid ap finish**)
v [*w*→*v*] ⟨ ⟩ *d*2
v[*y y* **arid**] **arid ap finish**
empty [*y*→*v*] *y d*3
   (where *d*3 = **empty arid** ⟨ ⟩ **finish**)
v [*y*→*v*] ⟨ ⟩ *d*3
v **arid** ⟨ ⟩ **finish**

And this is the final state of the machine. The normal form *v* is on the top of the stack.
■

This example shows in particular the role played by the dump in reducing lambda expressions. The next example is designed to illustrate how the environment incorporated in each closure enforces the correct association of variables with values.

Example 2.4.2(vi)

Our expression is to be:
(λ*x*·λ*v*·*vx*) *v* (λ*x*·*x*)

empty arid ((λ*x*·λ*v*·*vx*) *v* (λ*x*·*x*)) **finish**
empty arid [((λ*x*·λ*v*·*vx*) *v*) (λ*x*·*x*) **ap**] **finish**
empty arid [λ*x*·λ*v*·*vx v* **ap** λ*x*·*x* **ap**] **finish**
[*x* λ*v*·*vx* **arid**] **arid** [*v* **ap** λ*x*·*x* **ap**] **finish**
v[*x* λ*v*·*vx* **arid**] **arid** [**ap** λ*x*·*x* **ap**] **finish**
empty [*x*→*v*] λ*v*·*vx d*1
   (where *d*1 = **empty arid** [λ*x*·*x* **ap**] **finish**)

Remember that it is the environment **arid** in the closure [*x* λ*v*·*vx* **arid**] which has been extended by the binding [*x*→*v*].

[*v vx*[*x*→*v*]] [*x*→*v*] ⟨ ⟩*d*1

Notice how the closure formed has a non-trivial environment for the first time.

> $[v\ vx\ [x{\to}v]]$ **arid** $[\lambda x{\cdot}x\ \mathbf{ap}]$ **finish**
> $[x\ x\ \mathbf{arid}][v\ vx\ [x{\to}v]]$ **arid ap finish**
> **empty** $[v{\to}[x\ x\ \mathbf{arid}]][x{\to}v]\ vx\ d2$
> 　　(where $d2 =$ **empty arid** $\langle\ \rangle$ **finish**)

Again notice how the environment from the closure has been extended. This environment binds x to v. If we were to extend the current environment, which at this moment is **arid**, then x would be bound to x.

> **empty** $[v{\to}[x\ x\ \mathbf{arid}]][x{\to}v]\ [v\ x\ \mathbf{ap}]\ d2$
> $[x\ x\ \mathbf{arid}]\ [v{\to}[x\ x\ \mathbf{arid}]][x{\to}v]\ [x\ \mathbf{ap}]\ d2$
> $v[x\ x\ \mathbf{arid}][v{\to}[x\ x\ \mathbf{arid}]][x{\to}v]\ \mathbf{ap}\ d2$
> **empty** $[x{\to}v]\ x\ d3$
> 　　(where $d3 =$ **empty** $[v{\to}[x\ x\ \mathbf{arid}]][x{\to}v]\langle\ \rangle d2$)
> $v[x{\to}v]\langle\ \rangle d3$
> $x[v{\to}[x\ x\ \mathbf{arid}]][x{\to}v]\langle\ \rangle d2$
> $v\ \mathbf{arid}\langle\ \rangle$**finish**

This is the final state and the normal form is v.

Using the reduction rules of the calculus we have for this expression:

> $(\lambda x{\cdot}\lambda v{\cdot}vx)\,v\,(\lambda x{\cdot}x)$　　red_β
> $(\lambda w{\cdot}wv)(\lambda x{\cdot}x)$　　red_β
> $(\lambda x{\cdot}x)\,v$　　red_β
> v

Notice how the bound variable v in $\lambda v{\cdot}vx$ is altered to w (which is not free in vx or v) to avoid the capture of the free occurrence of v [in $(\lambda x{\cdot}\lambda v{\cdot}vx)v$] by the bound occurrence of v (in $\lambda v{\cdot}vx$).

∎

Exercises 2.4.2(vii)

(a) Reduce $(\lambda x{\cdot}xx)\lambda x{\cdot}x$ on the SECD machine.
(b) Reduce $(\lambda x{\cdot}xx)\lambda x{\cdot}xx$ on the SECD machine.
(c) Using the advice in Section 2.2.5 show how the Fibonacci program can be formulated entirely within the lambda calculus.
(d) Evaluate your answer to (c), with the argument 0, on the SECD machine. Explain what happens.
(e) Repeat (d) using (manual) normal order reduction.
(f) Implement the SECD machine in PASCAL (or whatever). How much do you like the language (**after**)?!

∎

2.4.3 Another operational semantics

It is possible to define another operational semantics for the lambda calculus which utilizes closures but which resembles more closely the style of the denotational semantics given in Section 2.4.1.

Let V' be some set of result values containing the special value Error and $CLO = VAR \times EXP \times ENV$, where $ENV = VAR \to V$ and $V = V' + CLO$.

$$[\ ] \in EXP \to (ENV \to V)$$

$$[x]\, p = (p\ x)$$
$$[\lambda x \cdot E]\, p = \langle x, E, p \rangle$$
$$[E\ E']\, p = \mathbf{apply}\,([\ E\ ]p)([E']p)$$

where

$$\mathbf{apply}\ v\, v' = \begin{cases} [E]p[x \leftarrow v'] & (\text{if } v = \langle x, E, p \rangle) \\ \text{Error} \end{cases}$$

The interpretation of a variable is, as before, given by the environment. The interpretation of an abstraction is a closure and the interpretation of an application is obtained by applying the meaning of the operator and the meaning of the operand to the auxilliary function **apply**. Notice that this function is only sensibly defined when its first argument is a closure. If **apply** is furnished with the closure $\langle x, E, p \rangle$ and the argument v, then the result is the interpretation of E in the closure's environment p updated so that the bound variable (kept in the closure) is associated to the actual parameter v.

Perhaps the most important point to stress here is that the meaning of the applications are given *via the entire semantic function*. Recall that, in the denotational semantics, application was interpreted by semantic application directly. For this reason the semantics we have just introduced is not compositional.

2.4.4 Conclusions

More questions arise now that we have several semantic descriptions of the lambda calculus. For example, are the semantics presented in Sections 2.4.1, 2.4.2 and 2.4.3 *equivalent* in some sense? It is perhaps better to ask if they are *congruent* because they each utilize different universes of interpretation and so cannot perforce yield equivalent results. In general, proofs of such congruence properties are rather difficult to answer and we are certainly not in a position to address them here although questions like these are addressed implicitly in Chapter 8.

Denotational semantics allows us to grasp the meaning of the expressions in a static, non-computational way. This has several benefits. Firstly, meaning is not dependent on some (even abstract) architecture. It is given in a way which is independent of arbitrary decisions regarding the way in which evaluations should proceed. Secondly, because the meaning is given in an entirely *syntax-directed* way it is possible to think about properties of expressions and their meanings without having to mentally consider their evaluation. This *declarative* reading is a very important aspect of functional languages in general and we will stress this reading in the next chapter both for analysing and, indeed, synthesizing programs.

On the other hand, operational semantics are interesting and important because they exhibit techniques for actually evaluating expressions. The essential concepts they introduce (for example the idea of *closures*) can be used in practical implementations. Furthermore, it is possible to analyse the time and space requirements of programs with respect to operational descriptions.

If we have both denotational and operational descriptions of our languages then we get the best of both worlds. On the one hand we have a way of thinking about (and, in particular, *reasoning* about) programs in a manner that is abstract and algebraic. On the other hand we have a mechanism for evaluating programs and ways of determining their expected performance. Of course, we also require a *congruence proof* along the lines of that described above to ensure that, from one perspective, our formal reasoning (using the denotational semantics) is actually borne out in practice (by the operational semantics). From another perspective this congruence proof ensures that the implementation of the language (given by the operational semantics) is correct, i.e. it agrees with our abstract requirements (as specified by the denotational semantics).

2.5 Bibliographic notes

For further study at a reasonable level, including details of the Church–Rosser theorem the reader might start with Hindley and Seldin (1986). The most comprehensive and modern treatment is the major treatise by Barendregt (1984). In spite of appearing rather awe-inspiring it is very well written and deserves the attention of the well-motivated reader. This text also contains an excellent account of the relationship between lambda calculus and computability and various numeral systems and other exotica.

For a more historical perspective the reader should consult Curry and Feys (1958) and Curry *et al.* (1972).

For pioneering work on the lambda calculus and programming the important historical literature includes the papers of McCarthy (1960, 1962, 1963) and those by Landin (1964, 1965, 1966a, 1966b). It is the first of these which introduced the SECD machine. Other machines for lambda reduction can be found in Wegner (1971).

We will be discussing the semantics of the lambda calculus again in Chapter 7. References for this topic are given there.

Barendregt, H. P. (1984) *The Lambda Calculus; Its Syntax and Semantics (Revised), Studies in Logic*, Vol. 103. North-Holland, Amsterdam.

Curry, H. B. & Feys, R. (1958) *Combinatory Logic*, Vol. 1. North-Holland, Amsterdam.

Curry, H. B., Hindley, J. R. & Seldin, J. P. (1972) *Combinatory Logic*, Vol. 2, *Studies in Logic*, Vol. 65. North-Holland, Amsterdam.

Hindley, J. R. & Seldin, J. P. (1986) *Introduction to Combinators and Lambda Calculus*, London Mathematical Society student texts 1. Cambridge University Press, Cambridge.

Landin, P. J. (1964) The mechanical evaluation of expressions. *Computer J.*, **6**, 308–320.

Landin, P. J. (1965) A correspondence between Algol 60 and Church's lambda notation. *Commun. ACM*, **8**, 89–101, 158–165.

Landin, P. J. (1966a) A lambda calculus approach. In *Advances in Programming and Non-numerical Computation*, pp. 97–141. Pergamon Press, New York.

Landin, P. J. (1966b) The Next 700 programming languages. *Commun. ACM*, **9**, 157–164.

McCarthy, J. (1960) Recursive functions of symbolic expressions and their computation by machine. *Commun. ACM*, **3**, 184–195.

McCarthy, J. (1962) Towards a mathematical science of computation. *Proc. IFIP 62*, pp. 21–28. North-Holland, Amsterdam.

McCarthy, J. (1963) A basis for a mathematical theory of computation. In *Computer Programming and Formal Systems*, pp. 33–70. North-Holland, Amsterdam.

Wegner, P. (1971) *Programming Languages, Information Structures and Machine Organisation*. McGraw-Hill, New York.

Chapter 3

Programming and verification

3.1 Introduction

In this chapter we introduce many of the styles and techniques of programming which are appropriate for functional languages. We also develop methods for showing that the programs we write possess various properties.

The language which is used in this chapter and in most of the rest of the book is a language of recursion equations over arbitrary data types. From time to time we will relax or restrict certain aspects of the notation for pedagogic reasons. In many respects it resembles the languages KRC (Turner 1982a, 1982b) and MIRANDA (Turner 1985) quite strongly but often this resemblence is somewhat strained. In particular we will wish to investigate the consequences of adopting various evaluation strategies (as we did in the last chapter for the lambda calculus).

The reason for this approach is our belief that it is semantic rather than syntactic issues which are central to computing and to programming and programming languages in particular. Usually, convenient, helpful notation follows from strong semantic foundations rather than vice versa. Our hope is that once important ideas have been grasped in our KRC-like notation they may be applied in the context of other programming languages with equanimity.

3.2 Data structures and recursion equations

3.2.1 Data structures

In the last chapter we saw how the lambda notation could be employed to represent data values such as truth values, natural numbers, and data pairs, together with appropriate operations. We also saw that the calculus ensures that the axioms we expect such data types to satisfy do indeed hold.

In this chapter we will adopt a different and more conventional approach by introducing data types directly as sets of values described by equations. These data structures (spaces, types – we use these terms synonymously) are formed by certain *type-forming operations* from a collection of primitive types.

We will assume the existence of some *primitive data types*, including:

$$N = \{0, 1, 2, \ldots\}$$
$$B = \{\text{"True"}, \text{"False"}\}$$
$$C = \{\text{"A"}, \ldots, \text{"Jasper"}, \ldots, \text{"Jenny"}, \ldots\}$$

These are, respectively, *natural numbers, truth values,* and *symbolic atoms.* Symbolic atoms are to be construed as an infinite collection of distinct tokens having no structure and no relation imposed on them except, of course, equality. Symbolic atoms will be denoted by alphanumeric sequences in quotations. We will introduce other primitive types (by enumeration) later.

Other more sophisticated data structures can be constructed from these primitives. As a first and simple example let us define a very useful collection of basic items, the *atoms*:

$$A = B + N + C$$

This describes the data structure A which consists of all the natural numbers, truth values, and symbolic atoms. Thus A is the *union* of C, B and N. The sign, $+$, here denotes a binary operation on data types called the *disjoint union*.

Types of this form are available in quite a variety of imperative languages. In ALGOL 68 we form the union of, for example, the types **int** and **char** by writing:

union(int, char)

An element of this type is either an integer or a character.

In PASCAL a rudimentary form of union typing is available via the *variant record* construction. SIMULA 67 offered a novel and very influential form of typing which includes union type construction by means of the *prefix class* concept.

We may also introduce compound data in the form of *tuples*:

$$P = A \times A$$

As in elementary set theory, the cross, $\times$, denotes a *product* operation. The data structure P consists of the collection of *pairs of atoms*. Thus, $\langle$"Jenny", "Jasper"$\rangle$ and $\langle$"Jasper", 5$\rangle$ are both elements of this data space. Sometimes it is useful to employ a *named* data constructor for tuple data rather than the anonymous angled brackets notation we are familiar with from set theory and which we have used in the examples above. We could, for example, decide to form elements of P with the name 'node'. Thus the elements introduced above would be written:

> node "Jenny" "Jasper"

and

> node "Jasper" 5

We might also write the constructor as an infix operator, indeed our next example of a product will do exactly this. The anonymous tuples are used in Chapter 5 where we specify a data type, O, of *objects*.

Tuple types are available in a very large number of imperative languages. In PASCAL this is achieved by way of the *record* facility. In ALGOL 68 one employs the **struct** operation and in SIMULA 67 the *class* can be used for this purpose.

We may introduce *functional* data spaces from two components A and B by writing:

$$F = A \rightarrow B$$

F is the data space of functions from the data space A to the data space B. **plus**, for example, is a member of the data type: $N \rightarrow N \rightarrow N$ (recall that we treat **plus** in its *curried* form and that the arrow associates to the right.

We will also allow our data type descriptions to be recursive as the next, and very important, example shows:

$$L = \{\text{"Nil"}\} + (A \times L)$$

This is the data type of *lists of atoms*. There are two components of the union which constitute L. The first of these is $\{\text{"Nil"}\}$ which is a primitive type consisting of the token "Nil" alone. This tells us that a simple example of a list is "Nil". The second component, which is $A \times L$, tells us that a list may be a pair whose first component is of type A and whose second is of type L. We will use an *infix colon* as a data constructor for the product $A \times L$. Thus "Telemusik":"Nil" is a list because "Telemusik" is an atom and "Nil" (we reasoned) is a list. Likewise: "Stockhausen":("Telemusik":"Nil") belongs to L because "Stockhausen" is an atom and (we reasoned) "Telemusik":"Nil" is a list. To avoid the bracketing we will take it that the data constructor associates to the right, thus, the example above can be written "Stockhausen": "Telemusik": "Nil".

As an aid to readability (we will be using this data structure a good deal) we will introduce and employ some syntactic sugar. We will write lists in square brackets with the following intention: [ ] stands for "Nil" and, for example: ["Jarrett", "DeJohnette", "Peacock"] stands for: "Jarrett": "DeJohnette":

"Peacock": "Nil" and so on. More exactly this notation is defined, recursively, as follows:

[ ]   is defined to be "Nil"
$[a, b, \ldots, z]$ is defined to be $a : [b, \ldots, z]$

The lists we will be programming with, it transpires, need not be limited to finite length and we can contemplate such lists as: $[1, 1, 1, \ldots]$, the infinite list of ones, and $[0, 1, 2, 3, \ldots]$ the list of natural numbers in ascending order. These, and other exotica (the partial lists) we will meet in Section 3.11:

Recursive types are also available in modern imperative languages such as PASCAL, MODULA 2 and ALGOL 68. In these languages, though, the recursion is set up indirectly through the notion of a *pointer* or *reference*. In PASCAL these pointer objects are introduced by means of a vertical arrow. Thus, if t is some type, then $\uparrow t$ is the type of *pointers to objects of type t*. The incantation in ALGOL 68 for this is **ref** t. Abstractly, if we followed these languages, we would have to define our lists by means of something like:

$$L = \{\text{"Nil"}\} + A \times (\textbf{ref } L)$$

The implementational intuition behind this kind of recursive type is that computers usually have words of fixed length. Consequently, it is not possible to store arbitrary objects in fixed fields. The common solution to this is to store, instead, the address (a pointer or reference) of the object. It seems, though, that this is a question of representation, and issues at this level do not properly belong to abstract descriptions. In our language, recursive types are specified directly as we indicated above.

Lists need not be composed of atoms. In Section 3.4.4 we will introduce entities called *substitution lists*, *SL*, whose elements are *substitution pairs*, *SP* by the type definition:

$$SL = \{\text{"Nil"}\} + SP \times SL \qquad \text{substitution lists}$$

Note that we will assume that the product construction binds more tightly than the union constructor.

We might entertain lists of numerals or lists of Booleans for one reason or another. These two types would be defined by:

$$LN = \{\text{"Nil"}\} + N \times LN \qquad \text{lists of numerals}$$
$$LB = \{\text{"Nil"}\} + B \times LB \qquad \text{lists of Booleans}$$

The reader can probably see that these are all rather similar in shape. This suggests that we parameterize the definition with respect to the list elements.

We introduce the concept of a *type variable*, that is, a variable over types (and not a variable over values of some type), and define the *type function*:

$$\text{List}(\alpha) = \{\text{"Nil"}\} + \alpha \times \text{List}(\alpha)$$

Given this we can obtain all our examples above by substituting for the type variable as follows:

$$L = \text{List}(A), \quad SL = \text{List}(SP), \quad LN = \text{List}(N), \quad \text{and} \quad LB = \text{List}(B)$$

Such type-generating functions are often called *generic types*.

Associated with the data spaces of atoms and lists are a number of primitive operations. We give these in Table 3.2.1(i) along with the data types to which they belong. Table 3.2.1(i) requires some explanation. The operator **eq** yields "True", if the two arguments are equal *atoms* and "False" otherwise. We will also write **eq** with an infix '=' in examples later.

Table 3.2.1(i)

Operation	Data type
eq	$L \to (L \to B)$
and	$B \to (B \to B)$
and other logical connectives . . .	
plus	$N \to (N \to N)$
and other arithmetic . . .	
le (less than or equal)	$N \to (N \to B)$
and other similar relations . . .	
numeric	$A \to B$
h (head)	$A \times L \to A$
t (tail)	$A \times L \to L$
cons (construct)	$A \to (L \to L)$

and, or, and **not** have the obvious semantics over the space B as do the arithmetic and logical operators over N.

numeric yields "True" if its argument lies in N and "False" otherwise.

h and **t** are the list destructor operations. We show them in un-curried form because they are defined over the second summand of L. The function **h** yields the first argument and **tail** yields the second. **cons** constructs a list by concatenating its first argument onto its second (which is a list). Note that **cons**, and indeed all multi-argument functions, have their types described in fully curried form and that the function type constructor, $\to$, *associates to the right*.

In this discussion of primitive operators we have presented the collection over L which is the type of lists of atoms. The operators **h**, **t**, and **cons** are actually available for *any* kind of list for *they do not make reference to the* *elements of which the lists are composed.* If we, again, let α stand for a type variable, then we wish to say that **h**, for example, has the type: $\alpha \times \text{List}(\alpha) \to \alpha$ for any type assigned to the type variable α. To capture this idea of *quantification over types* we write this type more succinctly as:

$$(\forall \alpha)(\alpha \times \text{List}(\alpha) \to \alpha)$$

using the sign $\forall$ (for all) from logic for this purpose. By the same token the function **t** has type:

$$(\forall \alpha)(\alpha \times \text{List}(\alpha) \to \text{List}(\alpha))$$

and the constructor **cons** has type:

$$(\forall \alpha)(\alpha \to \text{List}(\alpha) \to \text{List}(\alpha)).$$

Types such as these which quantify over all possible versions of a generic type are called *polymorphic types* and were first mentioned by Strachey (1967) who observed that there are many operations which have a large number of types each of which is given by some type scheme. It has been the rise of functional languages which have heralded the renewed interest in polymorphic types.

Our second example of a recursive data type is the collection of *s-expressions composed of atoms.* We usually refer to these simply as *sexpressions.* They are so called because they are essentially the data objects of the language LISP (Winston & Horn, 1981) as originally conceived by McCarthy in the late 1950s. It was he who coined the term sexpression as a shorthand for *symbolic expressions.*

This data structure is specified by the following equation:

$$S = A + (S \times S)$$

From this it is easy to see that an sexpression is either an atom, or it is a pair of sexpressions. We shall use an infix colon as a data constructor for this product as we did for lists. Given this, we can provide a few examples of sexpressions:

4, "Jasper":"Jenny", 4:3:2, ("True":4):5

Again, we shall take it that the colon ':' associates to the right. Thus, our third example above is equivalent to 4:(3:2) and not to (4:3):2. The sexpressions are, it seems, unlabelled, binary trees of atoms.

Exercise 3.2.1(ii)

Write down definitions of the following data types:
(a) sexpressions of numerals;
(b) sexpressions of Booleans;

(c) a type, Sexp, of *generic sexpressions*;
(d) how are the types (a) and (b) obtained from your solution to (c)?
∎

S comes equipped with the operations for atoms introduced above and some
others listed in Table 3.2.1(iii). **fst** and **snd** are the sexpression destructors. They
yield the obvious components of a pair of sexpressions. **pair** is the sexpression
constructor. It forms elements of the $S \times S$ component of *S* from two elements
of *S*. **atom** is a predicate which gives "True" just when its argument is an atom
and "False" otherwise.

Naturally, the operators **fast, snd**, and **pair** are available for any kind of
sexpression since they do not make reference to the type of the objects which
can appear as sexpression leaves. Therefore these operators are actually
polymorphic and have the following types:

> **fst** has type $(\forall\alpha)(\text{Sexp}(\alpha) \times \text{Sexp}(\alpha) \to \text{Sexp}(\alpha))$
> **snd** has type $(\forall\alpha)(\text{Sexp}(\alpha) \times \text{Sexp}(\alpha) \to \text{Sexp}(\alpha))$
> **pair** has type $(\forall\alpha)(\text{Sexp}(\alpha) \to \text{Sexp}(\alpha) \to \text{Sexp}(\alpha))$

Types are discussed again in some detail in Section 6.6 where we investigate
the task of ensuring that programs are *well formed* with respect to types. That
is, the process of typechecking. The inclusion of polymorphic types makes this
a more complex task than it is in most languages as we will see. Some of the
mathematics needed to explore these types precisely is outlined in Appendix B
on mathematics and in Chapter 7.

3.2.2 Patterns

In the majority of programming languages it is possible to denote an arbitrary
value of a data type by means of a variable. In our notation any alphanumeric
sequence, not in quotes (that is, not a symbolic atom) is a variable. Usually we
use lower-case letters for variables. We also allow variables to be subscripted
(as in v_1) or primed (as in v') for ease of presentation.

More recently it has been demonstrated that it is possible and desirable to
refer to more specific values of a data type by means of *patterns*. Patterns are

Table 3.2.1(iii)

fst (first)	$S \times S \to S$
snd (second)	$S \times S \to S$
pair	$S \to (S \to S)$
atom	$S \to B$

partially specified values and are built up from the constants, variables and data constructors for a given data type. If the data type is simple, like N for example, then the forms of patterns are also rather simple. Typical examples of patterns over N are 3, 9, 27 and n, n', n_1, etc. These examples are either completely specified values from, or simple variables over, the set N. The idea is that a pattern will, in general, only fit a subset of the data type on which it is defined. In the simple examples above the subsets picked out are singleton sets (for the constant patterns) and the whole data type (for the variables).

If the data type is complex, more interesting patterns can be formed. Taking the data type L of lists, the following are examples of patterns: [ ], l, [a, 3]. The first of these fits only the constant [ ] itself. The variable l fits any list value in L. The pattern [a, 3] matches only lists of length 2 whose second entry is 3. Thus [3, 3] and ["Elaine", 3] fit this pattern but [3, 4] and [3, 3, 4] do not.

When a function, or procedure, in a conventional language is called with an actual parameter it is usual to talk of the *binding* of the actual parameter to the formal parameter which is used in its definition. When the formal parameters are allowed to be patterns the process of associating the actual parameter to the formal becomes more complicated, in particular, the association may fail to occur as we saw in the examples in the previous paragraph. Some form of *matching* is required and we will describe this in detail later. Moreover, several variables may become bound in the process. In conventional languages there may be several, complicated ways in which values become bound to formal parameters when a function or procedure is called. For example, *call by name, call by value, call by reference*, and so on. In functional languages things are much simpler, as we will see.

Here is another example: the pattern [a, 3, b] contains the two variables a and b. The list ["Garbarek", 3, "Vitous"] matches this pattern with the variable a bound to "Garbarek" and b bound to "Vitous". Note that the pattern a:l matches any non [ ] list and so consequently matches the list ["Shorter", "Zawinul", "Pastorius"] with a bound to "Shorter" and l bound to ["Zawinul", "Pastorius"]. The pattern [ ] is just a constant and it matches only itself. As a result of this match no variables become bound.

Before we move on we should perhaps sound a terminological warning. In this section we have discussed variables becoming *bound* to values. The idea of variables becoming bound (by lambda abstraction) was introduced in Chapter 2. These are quite separate concepts and it is a pity that the usage is, in both cases, so standard as to make it impossible to rename one or other for convenience.

3.2.3 Recursion equations

A *recursion equation* (or *clause*) is a term of the form:

> **def f** $pl = E$

where **f** is the name of the function being defined, pl is a sequence of the patterns described above, and E is an expression. Quite often we will drop the prefix **def** when introducing equations. Usually, E will simply be an *applicative expression* (see Chapter 2) formed from variables (those occurring in pl), operators associated with data types, other user-defined functions, and, indeed, the function **f** itself. Occasionally, especially towards the end of this and the next chapter, we will also wish to include lambda abstracts in E. Finally, although we seldom need to resort to it, E may contain a *conditional expression*.

When E_1, E_2, and E_3 are expressions then:

> **if** E_1 E_2 E_3

is also an expression with the following informal semantics: the value of (**if** E_1 E_2 E_3) is the value of E_3 if the value of E_1 is "False" and the value of E_2 if the value of E_1 is "True".

Example 3.2.3(i)

Our first example is a very simple function of type $L \rightarrow B$:

> **def null** $l =$ **eq** l [ ]

This single equation defines the function **null** which is a predicate on lists, yielding "True" only when its argument is [ ]. In several respects this is a rather atypical function definition because it consists of just one equation (most will consist of more than one) and the formal parameter is a variable (mostly we will use more general patterns). In fact, there *is* an alternative definition of the function which does use patterns and two equations:

> **null** [ ] = "True"
> **null** $a:l$ = "False"

In general, then, a *function definition*, say of the function **f**, is that collection of recursion equations which begin: **def f** . . . .
■

Example 3.2.3(ii)

As our first major example let us write a program which, when given a list *l*, will determine its length, that is, the number of atoms it contains. This function, called **length** belongs to the data type: $L \to N$ although we will discuss this further in a moment.

> **def length** [ ] $= 0$
> **def length** $(a:l) = 1 + ($**length** $l)$

This program, as we see, comprises of two recursion equations. The pattern for the first clause is the constant list value [ ] which is the empty list. The first clause, therefore, specifies the value of **length** only for a single value. As we observed earlier, the pattern $a:l$, composed of the variables *a* and *l*, will match against any list which is not empty. The second equation, therefore, specifies the value of **length** for all other list values. We can say that this set of equations is *complete* because, for any list value *l*, there is an equation which specifies the value of the function for input *l*. Moreover, in this example, the equations are *disjoint*. This means that only one equation applies to any input list *l*. In fact most often a function over lists will comprise two equations; one for each of the two components of the disjoint sum used in the definition of the data type of lists. This is a useful guide and indeed aids in program construction too; we try to furnish one equation for each disjoint component of the data type over which our programs are written. This is, however, a guide and not a rule; we will see many examples where the functions do not follow the structure of the type definition so closely (notably in Section 3.4.3).

It is also instructive to note that the function **length** is in no way constrained to operate on lists composed of atoms, or indeed any particular type of list element. So, although our first reaction was to state that **length** belongs to the data type: $L \to N$, this is too restrictive. Given the generic description of lists of arbitrary elements, List, we more accurately say that **length** belongs to the data type:

"List(α)$\to N$ for all types α"

or in our notation outlined above:

$(\forall \alpha) (\text{List}(\alpha) \to N)$

Such functions whose type quantifies over all possible versions of a generic type we have called *polymorphic functions*. Interestingly, it is not possible to write such functions in languages such as PASCAL because they do not allow the definition of generic types. In such languages it is necessary to define **length** for as many kinds of lists as are needed. What is so frustrating in these languages is that all versions are identical *except for the type information* they introduce.

Our definitions are always complete but are occasionally not disjoint. This is because it is sometimes useful to exploit the following operational rule for recursion equations: *the equations are matched against the input value in the order in which they appear.* Thus, we would not introduce any ambiguity into the definition of **length** if we recast it as follows:

> **def length** [ ] $=0$
> **def length** l $=1+(\textbf{length}\ (\textbf{t}\ l))$

even though the constant list [ ] matches both clauses. It is clear that, in this case, it is actually disadvantageous to provide an *overlapping* (non-disjoint) set of equations but we shall see some occasions later when this is not the case. Moreover, we will shortly stress the advantages which accrue from avoiding, as far as is possible, recourse to operational considerations when constructing or reading programs. From this perspective, too, the use of overlapping clauses is not to be recommended.

A final, although trivial, point to note is the re-emergence of the use of infix operations which we carefully factored out of expressions in the previous chapter. For notational convenience we often adopt this technique (even for some functions which we define ourselves) with the understanding that (for example) $n+n'$ is just a variant of (**plus** $n\,n'$). The point we wish to stress is that a curried form of all our functions is available.
∎

Example 3.2.3(iii)

> **def length** [ ] $=0$
> **def length** $(a:l)=1+(\textbf{length}\ l)$

One of the great benefits of this style of presentation is that the programs may be considered *declaratively*. It is *not* necessary to attempt a mental execution of the program in order to understand what it 'does'. This is also often referred to as a *denotational* reading, and is to be contrasted with an *operational* reading which emphasizes execution or evaluation. In fact the word 'does' itself emphasizes the dynamic way in which programs are usually understood. We wish to adopt a more static approach in which it is more appropriate to ask what a program 'means' rather than 'does'.

Of course, this operational reading is critically important, for if there was none, then the programs could not be executed! However, it is of great benefit to be able to avoid operational considerations when one tries to understand a program. Indeed such a declarative style is of immense help in constructing programs too, as we will see.

Our example function, **length**, may be understood, or *analysed*, simply as follows:

'The length of an empty list is 0 and the length of a list beginning with an atom *a*, and continuing as the list *l*, is just one greater than the length of the list *l*.'

Alternatively we might take a more *synthetic* reading, stressing the way in which the program is discovered or constructed:

'As a firm basis we take it that the length of the empty list is 0. Suppose, though, we are given a non [ ] list of the form *a* : *l*. Suppose further that we can establish the length of the structurally simpler sublist *l*. The result we are looking for is found by incrementing that sub-length.'

The mathematically inclined reader may note a methodology akin to *inductive definitions* or *inductive proofs* in the synthetic description. We will shortly see that such an emphasis is deliberate and is utilized time and again in our program construction and verification.

Let us contrast these declarative readings with an operational description of **length**.

Consider, for example, the application (**length** [*A, B, C*]). The list [*A, B, C*] does not match [ ] in the first equation but does match the pattern *a* : *l* of the second with *a* bound to *A*, and *l* bound to [*B, C*]. The call reduces to 1 + (**length** [*B, C*]). The recursive call also matches in the second equation with *a* bound to *B*, and *l* bound to [*C*]. Thus the value of (**length** [*A, B, C*]) is 1 + (1 + (**length** [*C*])). This too matches the second equation and yields 1 + (1 + (1 + (**length** [ ]))) in a similar way. This recursive invocation of **length** is the final one since [ ] matches the first equation. This yields 0 as its result. Thus the original clause has value 1 + (1 + (1 + (0))) = 3 as expected.

∎

Of course neither the operational nor the denotational descriptions of the function amount to a proof that **length** terminates for all input lists. Termination *is* almost obvious in this case; later we will explain how this property is formally established.

Example 3.2.3(iv)

We now compare the pattern-directed program for **length**, given above, with one which utilizes predicates, selectors, and the conditional.

> **def length** $l=$ **if** (**null** l) 0 (1 + (**length** (**t** l)))

It is easy to see why the predicate **null** and the conditional are necessary and how **t** is used to obtain the appropriate sublist from l. We can classify the behaviour of this program into two components: *control computation*, which is effected by the selectors, predicates, and conditionals; and *data computation*, which actually computes the desired results. The pattern-directed approach removes this control computation from the program and relegates it (in a way we explain in detail in Chapter 6) to the evaluation mechanism. Moreover, the evidence of this control computation in the program interferes with the denotational reading of the program; it is really not possible to avoid some operational consideration when we read and understand the program.
∎

Example 3.2.3(v)

As an alternative notation to conditional expressions we will often use *guarded recursion equations*. Our example program, **length**, written in this form, would be:

> **def length** $l=0$ **when** (**null** l)
> **def length** $l=1+$ (**length** (**t** l)) **otherwise**

The expression which follows the "**when**" in such equations is called the *guard*. The meaning of these equations is quite straightforward: for a particular equation to match an argument we require that it satisfies the guard as well as fit the pattern. Semantically the indication: "**otherwise**" in the second equation, plays no active role and can be omitted.

Clearly, the pattern-directed version of **length** is rather more attractive than this definition. In more elaborate examples the use of guarded expressions can be quite elegant.

Suppose we introduce a program which determines the number of numbers in a list of arbitrary atoms. This program (which is very similar to **length**) might be written:

> **def numnum** [ ] $=0$
> **def numnum** $(a:l)=1+$ (**numnum** l) **when** (**numeric** a)
> **def numnum** $(a:l)=$ (**numnum** l) **otherwise**

∎

We also introduce some syntax which is designed to avoid repeated evaluations. Let **f** and **h** be functions. Rather than writing (**h** (**f** x) (**f** x)) we might be inclined to write either: (λv.**h** v v) (**f** x) or define another function: **def g** v = **h** v v and then set the original expression to (**g** (**f** x)). In both cases we avoid the duplicate computation of the value (**f** x).

In order to avoid introducing explicit lambda abstraction and extra function definitions we allow the following program forms:

> **let** v = (**f** x) **in** (**h** v v)   and also
> (**h** v v) **where** v = (**f** x)

The brackets can be omitted if the context is clear. Both of these expressions are equivalent to: (λv.**h** v v) (**f** x).

In fact we will allow v to be an arbitrary pattern rather than just a variable. Thus:

> **let** a:l = [2 3 4] **in** $a + a$

has the value 4.

Explaining these more general declarations in terms of lambda abstraction requires the concept of *lambda abstraction over a general pattern* which we will not explain in detail until Chapter 6. This syntax is rather attractive because it allows us to pay regard to some important operational concerns (the cost of incurring repeated computations) without compromising the declarative reading of the program.

3.2.4 Operational semantics

So much for the language in which we write our programs. In this section we consider their evaluation.

In Chapter 6, when we deal with programming language implementation techniques, we will describe, in detail, how this language can be compiled and evaluated. That is, we provide an *operational semantics*. Such a semantics, like the SECD machine for the lambda calculus, defines the meaning of the programming language in terms of an abstract machine and evaluation schemes. The description we provide commits us to a particular evaluation strategy (we will call this the *canonical semantics*) just as the SECD machine of Section 2.4 commits the lambda calculus to an applicative reduction strategy.

Now there are many functional languages and each has a specific reduction strategy underlying its operational semantics. KRC, for example, bases its operational semantics on the canonical semantics we describe later; this is essentially *head reduction* (see Sections 2.2.3 and 2.3.4). Languages such as FP, which we consider in Chapter 5, and (pure) LISP (Winston & Horn, 1981) (and some of its variants – Steele & Sussman, 1975; Abelson & Sussman, 1985) are based on applicative reduction.

Therefore, in order to describe aspects of functional languages in general terms it becomes necessary to study the ramifications of adopting a variety of evaluation strategies for our language of recursion equations. For example, we will see later that several programming techniques and transformation strategies make sense only under particular evaluation regimes.

Underlying the choice of reduction order is the notion of a generalized β-reduction for our recursion equations. We will not provide a formal definition of this for the details are fairly obvious and the problems (as usual regarding name clashes) have been well aired in the previous chapter. Moreover, the exact definition is given in Chapter 6.

We will be considering the three systematic reduction strategies of the last chapter (applicative, normal, and head reduction) along with the canonical semantics. A *redex* in a program is either a combinatory redex or a lambda redex (since both can occur in this language).

The canonical reduction strategy we adopt is, as we mentioned above, essentially head reduction. The need for the qualification arises because we take direct representations of our data objects and the primitive operations over them.

To see the problem this causes consider the expression (**fst** (**f** x)). The head redex has **h** as operator and (**f** x) as operand. Now because **fst** is a primitive operation over a direct representation of the sexpressions we have no rule which will reduce the **fst** operation on this argument. The impasse is avoided by undertaking the evaluation of the operand (**f** x). Now this is an applicative reduction step [although (**f** x) is reduced by the same canonical strategy]. If (**f** x) reduces (say) to the head normal form 6:(**g** x), then the **fst** operator can reduce this to 6.

This deviation from strict head reduction takes place whenever the head operator is a *strict primitive function*. This includes, for example, the first argument to the conditional operator **if**, which needs to determine which arm to yield on the basis of a direct representation of the Boolean values. For example: **if** (**eq** "*A*" "*B*") 3 "Miriam" evaluates to: **if** "False" 3 "Miriam" and then to "Miriam". Note that (**eq** 3 4) is not the head redex of the original expression.

Now we do not lose the termination properties of head reduction [see proposition 2.3.4(iii)] by this strategy for the simple reason that the operators which instigate non-head redex steps in the evaluation are *strict* as we noted at the close of Section 2.2.3.

Non-strict primitive operators, on the other hand, do not provoke this exceptional evaluation step. For example: **cons** $(\mathbf{f}\, x)\,(\mathbf{g}\, x)$ reduces to $(\mathbf{f}\, x):(\mathbf{g}\, x)$ which is a head normal form. The slogan for data construction is: '**cons** does not evaluate its arguments' (Friedman & Wise, 1976). We will return to this topic many times in the sequel.

We will refer to our canonical reduction strategy as *lazy reduction* or *lazy evaluation*. This terminology captures the most striking intuitive consequence of adopting this operational semantics which is the fact that evaluation proceeds *on demand*. This will become clear later when we have examined a number of example programs.

3.3 Induction on data types

When we begin to develop more ambitious programs in the next sections we will wish to show that programs possess certain properties. One such property, which we have already mentioned, is the property of *termination*.

Suppose that **f** is a program over a data type D which has d as a typical element. Let P be a predicate over D. If we wish to show that the property P holds of $(\mathbf{f}\, d)$, for all possible inputs d, we might write more formally:

$$(\text{for all } d \in D)(P\,(\mathbf{f}\, d))$$

How do we go about proving such a proposition? If D is a finite set we might simply undertake (a possibly laborious) case analysis on all elements of D.

Problems arise, however, if D is infinite. No amount of manual checking will suffice. This is reminiscent, in elementary mathematics, of problems such as establishing that, for all $n \in N$:

$$1 + \ldots + n = n(n+1)/2$$

In this case, too, checking particular values will never be sufficient. It is at this point we would turn to *numerical induction*. The reader who is not familiar with this will find the example above worked through in the appendix on mathematics.

Numerical induction works because the set of numbers is a *well-founded set* under the relation $<$ (less than). A well-founded set is one which contains no infinite decreasing sequence of elements (under the ordering). That is, there is no element, d, of the set for which $\{d_i \,|\, i \geq 0,\ d_{i+1} < d_i, d_0 = d\}$ is an infinite subset.

This means that every subset of a well-founded set has *minimal elements*. In the case of the natural numbers every subset has a single *least* element because the relation $<$ is a total ordering. In general the relation may only be a partial ordering, and so there may be many minimal elements.

Induction may be generalized to arbitrary well-founded sets. Numerical induction can then be seen as a rather special case. This is the content of the following proposition:

Proposition 3.3(i)

The principle of well-founded induction. Let A be a well-founded set under the partial order $\leq$. Then:

$$(\forall a \in A)((\forall a' \in A;\ a' < a)(P(a')) \Rightarrow P(a)) \Rightarrow ((\forall a \in A)(P(a)))$$

This tells us that we may conclude that $P(a)$ holds for all elements a of A if we can establish that $P(a)$ holds on the assumption that $P(a')$ holds for all $a' < a$.

Proof. Suppose, on the contrary, that the antecedent of the main implication above holds but $((\forall a \in A)(P(a)))$ fails because there is an $a \in A$ such that $P(a)$ fails. We can, in such a circumstance, construct a set $B = \{a | a \in A$ and $P(a)$ does not hold$\}$. This set is not empty given the assumptions above. Now A is well founded so B must have minimal elements. Select one of these and call it b. Now for all $a \in A$ with $a < b$ we have $P(a)$ holds (or else a would be in B). But we have assumed that whenever $P(a)$ holds for all $a < b$ we can conclude that $P(b)$ holds. Thus we arrive at a contradiction. B must be empty, that is, if the antecedent is true then $P(a)$ holds for all $a \in A$ as required.
∎

Example 3.3(ii)

Consider the well-founded set N totally ordered by $\leq$. The principle of well-founded induction, in this case, can be simplified to:

$$(P(0) \wedge (\forall n \in N)(P(n) \Rightarrow P(n+1))) \Rightarrow (\forall n \in N)(P(n))$$

$P(0)$ appears on the left-hand side because the principle requires us to show that $P(a)$ holds under the assumption that $P(b)$ holds for all $b < a$. However, there are no elements of N smaller than 0 so we have to show that $P(0)$ holds without help.
∎

Example 3.3(iii)

Consider the set of finite lists of atoms, L. This can be well ordered by the relation *is a sublist of.*

More formally the relation is defined as follows:

$$l \leq l' \text{ iff } (\exists n \geq 0)(l = (\mathbf{t}^n \, l'))$$

That is $l \leq l'$ if l is equal to some tail list of l'.
$(\mathbf{f}^n \, x) = (\mathbf{f}(\mathbf{f} \ldots (\mathbf{f} \, x) \ldots))$, the *n-fold* application of $\mathbf{f}$ to x.

Exercise 3.3(iv)

Check that this is a partial ordering on lists. What is the least element of L?
■

The principle of induction can be simplified, in this case to:

$$(P([\ ]) \wedge (\forall l)(\forall a)(P(l) \Rightarrow (P(a:l)))) \Rightarrow (\forall l)(P(l))$$

This is the *principle of list-induction*.
■

Example 3.3(v)

The set of finite sexpressions can be well ordered by the relation *is a subexpression of*.

Exercise 3.3(vi)

Provide a formal definition of the relation *is a subexpression of*.
■

The principle of induction can be simplified to:

$$((\forall a \in A)(P(a)) \wedge (\forall s_1, s_2 \in S)((P(s_1) \wedge P(s_2)) \Rightarrow (P(s_1:s_2)))) \Rightarrow$$
$$(\forall s \in S)(P(s))$$

This is the *principle of sexpression-induction*.

Exercise 3.3(vii)

Why do we have to establish $(\forall a \in A)(P(a))$ without assumptions?
■

■

Naturally, if we choose to program with the infinite data structures that we mentioned briefly earlier we will not have well-founded sets with respect to the relations provided above. This is because it is easy to form sets with no minimal elements, as the following example shows:

Example 3.3(viii)

Suppose L contains infinite lists. Consider the element ones $= [1\ 1\ 1\ 1\ \dots\ ]$ (the infinite list of ones) which is in L if $1 \in A$. Now consider the following subset of $L:\{l|l=t^n$ (ones) for all $n \geq 0\}$.

This set has no minimal element. The consequence of this is that the crucial step in the proof of proposition 3.3(i) (selecting a minimal element of a set) cannot be made and the induction principle cannot be established. It remains to be seen (in Section 3.11) how we prove properties of programs which are defined over these infinite data structures.

∎

3.4 Elementary programming

In this section we will provide a number of reasonably simple examples of programs which manipulate lists and sexpressions. The programming does not, however, occur in isolation. At every stage we will demonstrate that the functions we introduce behave as we expect them to. We show, for example, that they are *total*, they terminate for all possible inputs, and that they compute the intended results. Showing that functions produce intended results often amounts to showing that they interact with others in certain, precise, ways.

After the simpler examples we will move on to consider a more substantial problem called *unification*. This, and related topics, are covered in Section 3.4.4. We will develop a unification function and show that it is correct.

3.4.1 List programming

Example 3.4.1(i)

We will describe a program which, given two lists, will concatenate, or append them, into a single list.

Let us call this function **append**. As a basis we take it that appending an empty list (written simply: (**append** [ ])) is the identity function on lists. This suggests the equation: **append** [ ] = **id** or perhaps more clearly: **append** [ ] $l=l$. Suppose, however, we are to append $a:l$ to some list l'. Let us assume that we can form the subresult: **append** $l\ l'$. Presumably the result we want is formed by placing the atom, a, on the front of this list. As an equation, this suggestion reads:

    append $(a:l)\ l' = a : ($**append** $l\ l')$

In summary, we have formed the following pair of pattern-directed equations:

> **append** [ ] l $= l$
> **append** $(a:l)\, l' = a : ($**append** $l\, l')$

In terms of conditionals, predicates, and selectors we would obtain the more conventional looking, but less attractive, program:

> **append** $l\, l' =$ **if** (**null** l) l' (**cons** (**h** l) (**append** (**t** l) l'))

It would seem natural to view **append** as an infix operator. We will choose $*$ (which is also used for multiplication of numbers) for this and write, with even greater clarity:

> [ ] $* l = l$
> $a:l * l' = a: (l * l')$

(Recall that the data constructor, : , binds tighter than any other operation except functional application.)

∎

At first sight it seems that **append** has type (belongs to the data type) $L \rightarrow (L \rightarrow L)$. However, like the function **length**, this function does not depend in any way on the elements of which the lists it takes as arguments are composed. Therefore it is a polymorphic function of type: List $(\alpha) \rightarrow (\text{List}(\alpha) \rightarrow \text{List}(\alpha))$ for all possible instantiations of the type variable α. More succinctly:

> $(\forall \alpha)\,(\text{List}(\alpha) \rightarrow \text{List}(\alpha) \rightarrow \text{List}(\alpha))$

It is clear that, by definition, [ ] is a *left unit* for $*$. If our definition is correct we would certainly expect [ ] to be a right unit too. This requires a simple inductive proof.

Proposition 3.4.1(ii)

> $(\forall l \in L)(l * [\ ] = l)$

Proof. Let $P(l)$ iff $l * [\ ] = l$. We show, by list induction, that $(\forall l \in L)(P(l))$.

Base step

$P([\ ])$ holds since this is just $[\ ] * [\ ] = [\ ]$ which follows from the definition.

Induction step

To show $P(a:l)$ we may assume $P(l)$. $P(a:l)$ is equivalent to $a:l * [\ ] = a:l$. Now $a:l * [\ ]$ is by definition $a:(l * [\ ])$. The expression in brackets is just the left-hand side of the assertion $P(l)$ and thus we may assume that this is equal to l. Thus $a:l * [\ ] = a:(l * [\ ]) = a:l$ which is what we require.

∎

Proposition 3.4.1(iii)

$*$ ought to be *associative* too. To see that our definition satisfies this we show that $(\forall l \in L)\,(P(l))$ holds when $P(l)$ iff $(\forall l_1, l_2 \in L)$

$$(l * l_1) * l_2 = l * (l_1 * l_2)$$

Proof. (By induction on l.)

Base step

$$([\ ] * l_1) * l_2 = \text{(by definition } *)$$
$$l_1 * l_2 \qquad\ = \text{(by definition } *)$$
$$[\ ] * (l_1 * l_2)$$

Induction step

$$(a:l * l_1) * l_2 \ = \text{(by definition } *)$$
$$a:(l * l_1) * l_2 \ = \text{(by definition } *)$$
$$a:((l * l_1) * l_2) = \text{(by hypothesis)}$$
$$a:(l * (l_1 * l_2)) = \text{(by definition } *)$$
$$a:l * (l_1 * l_2)$$

and the proof is complete. Note that the crucial step is the one labelled 'by hypothesis' when we make use of the assumption that $P(l)$ holds. More explicitly $P(l)$ says that $l * (l_1 * l_2) = (l * l_1) * l_2$.

∎

append should also enjoy algebraic relationships with the program **length** we gave in example 3.2.4(i). In particular:

Proposition 3.4.1(iv)

For all lists $l_1, l_2 \in L$;
(length l_1**)** + **(length** l_2**)** = **length** $(l_1 * l_2)$

Proof. By induction on l_1.

Base step

> **(length** [ ]**)** + **(length** l_2**)** =
> **length** l_2 =
> **length (**[ ] * l_2**)**

Induction step

> **(length** $(a:l)$**)** + **(length** l_2**)**   =
> $(1 +$ **(length** l**))** + **(length** l_2**)** =
> $1 + ($**(length** l**)** + **(length** l_2**))** =
> $1 +$ **length** $(l * l_2)$ =
> **length** $(a:(l * l_2))$ =
> **length** $(a:l * l_2)$

∎

Exercise 3.4.1(v)

State the induction hypothesis more formally by defining a suitable property P of lists. Annotate the proof above, noting in particular when the induction hypothesis is assumed.
∎

Examples 3.4.1(vi)

Here are a number of other useful and simple recursive functions over lists.

1   We wish to write a program **member** such that **(member** $a\ l$**)** = "True" if the atom a is a member of the list l and "False" otherwise. We start with the base case: if $l =$ [ ] then **(member** $a\ l$**)** = "False".

> **member** a [ ] = "False"

If $l = a : l'$ for some list l' then **(member** $a\ l$**)** = "True".
If $l = a' : l'$ for some a' and l' (a not equal to a') then suppose by induction (on the structure of l) that we can form the value: **(member** $a\ l'$**)** then **(member** $a\ (a':l')$**)** holds, if and only if **(member** $a\ l'$**)** holds. This leads to the equations:

> **member** $a\ (a' : l) =$ "True"   **when** $a = a'$
> **member** $a\ (a' : l) =$ **(member** $a\ l$**)**   **otherwise**

We could combine these into a single clause and write:

member a $(a' : l) = (a = a')$ **or** (**member** a l)

At this point an operational consideration might interrupt this pleasant, declarative foray. Isn't it the case that we avoid computing the subexpression (**member** a l) in the original definition whilst incurring the costs of its evaluation in the combined equation *even when* $a = a'$? This, of course, turns on the operational behaviour of the operator **or** which we will take to be defined as follows:

or x $y =$ **if** x "True" y

Note that y is not evaluated if x evaluates to "True". Therefore, even though from a declarative point of view it matters not at all, we would not want to rewrite the combined equation for **member** as:

member a $(a' : l) = ($**member** a $l)$ **or** $(a = a')$

Other operations on Booleans can be defined in a similar way:

and x y = **if** x y "False"
not x = **if** x "False" "True"

Before we leave the function **member** let us enquire as to its type. As usual the first suggestion is: $A \rightarrow (L \rightarrow B)$. Is this too restrictive? Can we treat it as a polymorphic function whose type is:

$(\forall \alpha)(\alpha \rightarrow (\text{List}(\alpha) \rightarrow B))$?

There is a small problem here which concerns the equality test which **member** uses on the elements of the lists. If this is a specific equality (say on the atoms) then the function **member** is constrained to work on lists of atoms. We will assume that *every* type comes equipped with an equality predicate and that this can be referred to in the ordinary way, with an infix =. =, then, is a polymorphic function and so **member** can also be considered as polymorphic.

2   Our next task is to write a program which deletes all occurrences of an atom from a list.

Presumably we cannot delete anything from an empty list:

delete a [ ] = [ ]

Suppose that we wish to delete a from $a' : l$. We assume that we can form the list (**delete** a l). This is the result if $a = a'$. If a and a' are different then the result begins with a'. This suggests the following two equations:

delete a $(b : l) =$ **delete** a l **when (eq** a b)
delete a $(b : l) = b$:(**delete** a l)   **otherwise**

The type of **delete** can be established by a similar argument to that given above for **member**.

3   We now wish to describe a function which will, given a list, l, as an argument, form a list of the elements of l in reverse order. We will call this function **reverse** and it has type:

$$(\forall\alpha)(\text{List}(\alpha) \to \text{List}(\alpha))$$

As a base case note that [ ] is self reverse. This suggests the clause:

reverse [ ] $=$ [ ]

Next, we tackle the reverse of a list $a : l$ for some element a and list l. Assume by induction that we can already find the reverse of l. To form the reverse of $a : l$ we need to place the element a on the right of this. Lists as we have described them are not symmetrical; there is no primitive operator which places an element on the end of a list. We can, however, utilize one of our earlier operators, **append**, and use this to construct the desired result.

reverse $(a : l) = ($**reverse** $l) * [a]$

The use of **append** in this equation is very unpleasant because it increases the number of **cons** operations which are required to produce the result beyond that which we might have hoped for. We will discuss the costs of programming in the next section.

4   For all $i \geq 0$ we define an operator **listi** which takes i arguments. It places these arguments into a list. Thus:

list1 x $= [x]$ and (for example)
list3 x y $z = [x$ y $z]$
list3 has type $(\forall\alpha)(\alpha \to \alpha \to \alpha \to List(\alpha))$

Sometimes it is possible to avoid the numeral (which can be recovered from the context). However, since we can curry our functions we occasionally need it to avoid ambiguity.

5   Lists of atoms can be tested for equality by the program **lequal**:

lequal [ ] [ ] $=$ "True"
lequal $(a : l)$ $(a' : l') =$ (**eq** a a') **and** (**lequal** l l')
lequal l l' $=$ "False"

6   A very important program *filters* a list according to some property:

> **filter** p [ ] = [ ]
> **filter** p $(a:l) = a:$(**filter** p l)   **when** $(p$ $a)$
> **filter** p $(a:l) =$ (**filter** p l)   **otherwise**

Note that this is a higher-order function since its first argument is a function. This must have B as its co-domain and its domain must be the same type as the elements of the list. Thus the polymorphic type of **filter** is:

$$(\forall\alpha)((\alpha\to B)\to(\mathrm{List}(\alpha)\to\mathrm{List}(\alpha)))$$

Note, for example, that we may obtain the function **delete** from **filter** as follows:

> **delete** a $l =$ **filter** $(\lambda a' \cdot$ **not** $(a' = a))$ l

■

In our description of the construction of the functions introduced above we have utilized some of the language of induction proofs. We have, for example, talked of 'base steps' and 'by induction'. The close correspondence between recursion and induction is quite evident; we think of a recursive program as being explicitly defined on some primitive data (a base case) and then on other, more complex data, we construct a result on the assumption that we can solve the problem for 'simpler' data. This correspondence is particularly clear in languages like ours which use pattern-directed equations because we isolate the base cases and inductive cases in separate equations and we reveal the structure of the data in our patterns. The correspondence is there even in programs written in imperative languages but it is rather less easy to spot because these programs tend to obscure the inductive structure in the extra control computations and the 'secret' manipulations of the store. When we move on to some programs which manipulate 'infinite' lists we will see that the connection between recursion and induction is less obvious. The relationship is then a little more intricate and the techniques introduced for reasoning about such programs reveal this.

Exercise 3.4.1(vii)

(a) Show that, for all lists l; **reverse** (**reverse** l) = l.

   This, though necessary, is not a sufficient condition to characterize **reverse**. For example the identity function has this self-inverse property too. To capture the 'reversing property' we notice that if we split any list into two pieces and reverse each individually then the reverse of the entire list is given by gluing these two pieces back together in the reverse order. This property is rather better stated formally! That is, we need, for all lists l_1 and l_2:

(b) **reverse** $(l_1 * l_2) = ($**reverse** $l_2) * ($**reverse** $l_1)$

Prove that the definitions of **reverse** and **append** ($*$) enjoy this property.
∎

We have yet to discuss termination. All the functions we have described so far are *total* (defined for all possible inputs) but we have not shown this explicitly.

Proof by structural induction is a *total correctness* strategy; i.e. it provides equivalences which are not conditional on one or other expression terminating. A *partial correctness* strategy, on the other hand, can only tell us that a function computes the correct answer *if it terminates*.

However, structural induction cannot distinguish between different solutions to our recursive equations. This means it cannot be used to argue about certain *non*-termination properties. For example we might, foolishly, define the function:

f $x =$ **f** x

Every function satisfies this equation (of course!) although the one *computed* is the *completely undefined function* (it terminates for no arguments). This fact cannot be established by structural induction which is a method based on the structure of the data domain over which functions are defined and not on the form of the function **f** itself. For a more thorough discussion of the issues surrounding proof techniques for programs, and structural induction in particular, the reader is referred to Loeckx & Sieber (1984).

We *can* provide explicit proofs of the termination properties of many programs. Termination depends crucially on the structure of a program, in particular the recursive structure. It is, therefore, a good idea to investigate classes of programs (grouped by structure) rather than individual programs in this respect. Termination properties for specific programs can then be established by simply showing that they fit a particular *program scheme* for which termination is guaranteed. Most of the programs introduced so far fit into a simple program scheme which captures a general form of recursive programming over the *tail of a list*. Let us call them *list recursive* programs.

Definition 3.4.1(viii)

Let **G** and **H** be *program variables*. These are not part of the programming language. They are introduced so that we may describe classes of programs easily.

The following *program scheme* (we call any program involving program variables a program scheme) describes the list recursive programs:

f [ ] **= G**
f(*a*:*l*) **= H**(*a*:*l*)(**f** *l*)

A program conforms to this scheme if it can be formed from this scheme by instantiating the program variables to some data or functions. We will give some examples of programs which conform to this scheme in a moment.

■

Proposition 3.4.1(ix)

On the assumption that **G** and **H** are always defined, all list recursive programs are total.

Before we embark on the proof let us explain in more detail what this means. A function is *total* if it is defined for all possible input values. In general, as we know, computer programs need not be total; some enter infinite loops for certain input data. If the program variables are instantiated to simple, constant values then they are trivially 'always defined'. If they are instantiated to functions 'always defined' means, simply, that they are total functions. For the time being we do not consider programming with the infinite data structures we mentioned briefly earlier; we restrict ourselves to the finite lists. In Section 3.11 we will show how to reason about programs which do use these data objects.

Proof

Base step

> **f [ ]** = **G** which is defined by assumption.

Induction step

> **f**(*a*:*l*) = **H**(*a*:*l*)(**f** *l*)

since (**f** *l*) is defined (by induction) we see that **H** has two well-defined arguments, so by assumption, **H** is defined on them and therefore (**f**(*a* : *l*)) is defined.

■

Let us now see how some of our programs fit into this scheme.

Example 3.4.1(x)

1   Let $\mathbf{G} = [\ ]$ and $\mathbf{H} = \lambda(a:l)\ v\cdot v * [a]$

then the scheme of definition 3.4.1(viii) specializes to:

$$\mathbf{f}[\ ] \quad = [\ ]$$
$$\mathbf{f}(a:l) \ = (\mathbf{f}\ l) * [a]$$

which is just **reverse**.

2   Let $\mathbf{G} = \lambda l\cdot l$ and $\mathbf{H} = \lambda(a:l)\ v\cdot\lambda l'\cdot a:(v\ l')$

the scheme now specializes to:

$$\mathbf{f}[\ ] \quad = \lambda l\cdot l$$
$$\mathbf{f}(a:l) \ = \lambda l'\cdot a:((\mathbf{f}\ l)\ l') \qquad \text{but this is just}$$
$$\mathbf{f}[\ ]\ l \ = l$$
$$\mathbf{f}(a:l)\ l' = a:(\mathbf{f}\ l\ l') \qquad \text{which is } \textbf{append}.$$

3   Let $\mathbf{G} = \lambda a\cdot$ "False" and $\mathbf{H} = \lambda(a:l)\ v\cdot\lambda a'\cdot(\mathbf{eq}\ a\ a')\ \mathbf{or}\ (v\ a')$
The scheme now yields:

$$\mathbf{f}[\ ] \quad = \lambda a\cdot\text{"False"}$$
$$\mathbf{f}(a:l) = \lambda a'\cdot(\mathbf{eq}\ a\ a')\ \mathbf{or}\ ((\mathbf{f}\ l)\ a)$$

and this is more usually written:

$$\mathbf{f}[\ ]\ a \quad = \text{"False"}$$
$$\mathbf{f}(a:l)\ a' = (\mathbf{eq}\ a\ a')\ \mathbf{or}\ (\mathbf{f}\ l\ a')$$

and this is just **member** (with the arguments permuted).
■

Corollary 3.4.1(xi)

member, **append**, and **reverse** are all total functions.

Proof.   In (3) above $\mathbf{G}$ and $\mathbf{H}$ are defined for all defined inputs. In (2) the same observation is sufficient. In (1) we need the result that **append** is total to show that $\mathbf{H}$ is total. But we have just established this.
■

The idea of considering program schemes is an old and useful technique for examining classes of programs grouped in terms of their recursive structure. One of the benefits of a *higher-order* functional language is that such schemes can be realized directly as programs. Indeed the program scheme given in definition 3.4.1(viii) is nothing more than the program:

> **lrec** $g\ h\ [\ \ ] = g$
> **lrec** $g\ h\ (a:l) = h(a:l)\ (\textbf{lrec}\ g\ h\ l)$

lrec has the type:

$$(\forall\alpha,\ \beta)(\beta\to(\text{List}(\alpha)\to\beta\to\beta)\to\text{List}(\alpha)\to\beta)$$

Therefore, proposition 3.4.1(ix) can be construed as a proof that this program *preserves totality*. That is, it is a total function if its arguments are. Moreover, programs like **append** and **reverse** are now **defined** as instantations of this higher-order operator by those values for g and h, given in example 3.4.1(x).

This ability to handle program schemes within the language is a powerful and important consequence of adopting a higher-order language. We will spend some time in Sections 3.9 and 3.10, and Chapters 4 and 5 developing some of the consequences of, and discovering some of the benefits which accrue from, this ability to manipulate higher-order functions.

Showing that a program is total is very much like showing that a definition in mathematics in general is *well defined*. We are checking that the equations denote values for arbitrary inputs. In a sense, then, the proof that a function is total is a confirmation that the informal inductive language we use for its construction is valid.

Exercise 3.4.1(xii)

Define a program **sublist** taking two lists as input and yielding "True" if and only if the first list is a sublist of the second.

Prove that **sublist** is a total function. Show that **sublist** imposes a partial ordering on lists. That is, prove the program satisfies the axioms of a partial order.

Define a program which establishes the common 'tail list' of two lists. That is, for example:

> **comtaillist** $[1, 2, 3, 4, 5]\ [6, 7, 3, 4, 5] = [3, 4, 5]$
> **comtaillist** $[1, 2, 3]\ [4, 5, 6] = [\ \ ]$

Prove that your program does indeed generate a list which is sublist of both arguments.

∎

3.4.2 Sexpression programming

We now move on to some elementary examples of programs over the set of sexpressions.

Example 3.4.2(i)

1   We start with an example which relates sexpressions and lists and which will reccur in this and later chapters as we develop techniques in program verification.

We wish to form a list of the atoms which occur as the leaves of an arbitrary sexpression. If the sexpression is a pair then suppose that we can form the fringes of the components of the pair. The result is simply these joined together by **append**. This leads to the following equation:

fringe $(s_1:s_2)$=(**fringe** s_1) ∗ (**fringe** s_2)

If the sexpression is just an atom then the fringe is just the singleton list containing this atom alone:

fringe a=$[a]$

The type of **fringe** is $S \rightarrow L$, or more properly, since we do not wish to restrict ourselves to finding the fringe of sexpressions of **atoms**:

$(\forall\alpha)(\text{Sexp}(\alpha) \rightarrow \text{List}(\alpha))$

2   A program of similar structure yields the *mirror image* of any sexpression.

The mirror of a pair of sexpressions is the mirror image pair composed of the mirror images of the components. If we assume that we can form these mirror images we are led to the following equation:

mirror $(s_1:s_2)$=(**mirror** s_2):(**mirror** s_1)

The mirror image of an atom is the atom itself:

mirror a=a

The type of **mirror** is just $(\forall\alpha)(\text{Sexp}(\alpha) \rightarrow \text{Sexp}(\alpha))$.

3   Next, a program to search for an atom in an arbitrary sexpression.

If the sexpression is a pair then it is in the entire expression if it is in either subexpression:

smember a $(s_1:s_2)$=(**smember** a s_1) **or** (**smember** a s_2)

An atom occurs in another atom only if they are equal. This leads to:

> **smember** $a\ a' = $ **eq** $a\ a'$

The type of this function is $A \rightarrow S \rightarrow B$ if **eq** is the equality predicate on atoms.
■

The program **mirror** (for sexpressions) is analogous to the program **reverse** (for lists). This statement can be made quite precise:

Proposition 3.4.2(ii)

For all sexpressions, s: **reverse (fringe** s) = **fringe (mirror** s)

Proof.   Clearly the principle we need to deploy here is that of sexpression induction. The base step consists in showing that the result holds for all atoms and the induction step allows for two assumptions (the **fst** and **snd** subexpressions) to be utilized.

Base step

> **reverse (fringe** a)   =
> **reverse** $[a]$ =
> (**reverse** [ ]) $* [a]$ =
> [ ] $* [a]$ =
> $[a]$ =
> **fringe** a =
> **fringe (mirror** a)

Induction step

> **reverse (fringe** $(s_1 : s_2)) =$
> **reverse** ((**fringe** s_1) $*$ (**fringe** s_2)) $=$
> [by exercise 3.4.1(vii) (b)]
> (**reverse (fringe** s_2)) $*$ (**reverse (fringe** s_1)) $=$
> (by induction hypothesis)
> (**fringe (mirror** s_2)) $*$ (**fringe (mirror** s_1)) $=$
> **fringe** ((**mirror** s_2):(**mirror** s_1)) $=$
> **fringe (mirror** $(s_1 : s_2)$) as required:

■

Exercise 3.4.2(iii)

The program **smember** (for sexpressions) is analogous to the program **member** (for lists). Justify this statement.
∎

Example 3.4.2(iv)

We have a primitive notion of equality on atoms but not on sexpressions. Exactly how equality should be defined on these more complex data structures depends crucially on applications. That is, it depends on what sexpressions are being used to model. In some cases it is necessary to respect the structure of the expressions, in others it is simply the atoms in the fringe which are important. Thus we may define:

$$\textbf{sequal } (s_1{:}s_2)\,(s_3{:}s_4) = (\textbf{sequal } s_1\ s_3)\textbf{ and }(\textbf{sequal } s_2\ s_4)$$
$$\textbf{sequal } s\ s' \qquad\qquad = \textbf{eq } s\ s'$$

which gives full structural equality. Notice that (**eq** $s\ s'$) yields "True" only if s and s' are equal *atoms* and "False" otherwise. This predicate has type $S \rightarrow (S \rightarrow B)$ (since **eq** is defined over atoms).

As an alternative we could define:

$$\textbf{cequal } (s_1\ s_2) = \textbf{lequal } (\textbf{fringe } s_1)\,(\textbf{fringe } s_2)$$

which gives a 'fringe' equality.

Exercise 3.4.2(v)

Show that, for all sexpressions s and s':

$$((\textbf{sequal } s\ s') = \text{``True''} \Rightarrow (\textbf{cequal } s\ s') = \text{``True''})$$

This may appear to be a rather inelegant way of expressing properties of programs which are predicates. We might prefer to write:

$$(\textbf{sequal } s\ s') \Rightarrow (\textbf{cequal } s\ s')$$

However, the values of the antecedent and consequent in this implication are *atoms*. We will, in spite of this, utilize the more perspicuous form on the understanding that it is a shorthand for the precise, although rather awkward, formulation given above.
∎

The program **cequal** deserves close attention for it has (under the different name **samefringe**) often been quoted by opponents of functional programming. Their argument goes something like this:

The aim of the program **cequal** is to determine whether or not two binary trees (sexpressions) have the same fringe. The program does this by forming the fringes of *s* and *s'* and then comparing them for (list) equality. Suppose that *s* and *s'* are large sexpressions (containing, say, 2000 atoms each) and suppose further that their leftmost atoms are different. In such a case an enormous amount of work is undertaken (to flatten *s* and *s'* to lists) only to discover that the heads of the lists are distinct. In an imperative language, the argument continues, one would certainly not need to do this unnecessary work. Pairs of atoms would be extracted from *s* and *s'* and the program would halt as soon as a distinct pair of atoms is encountered.

For some time this challenge remained open, but there are at least two well-known solutions. One depends on a programming technique known as *generalized arguments* and some program transformation strategies. These are covered in Sections 3.9 and 4.6, respectively. This solution applies when the operational semantics of the language is taken to be applicative. The other solution, given our canonical semantics, is simply that *the argument outlined above is fallacious*. Before continuing the reader might like to reread the argument and attempt to find the mistake!

The fallacy is contained in the implicit operational semantics assumed for the functional language in which **cequal** is written. This means that the informal description of the behaviour of the program is wrong. It is quite easy for a programmer experienced in a conventional language to assume that the operational semantics of a functional language is roughly the same as the functional subcomponent of their favourite imperative language. This is not the case. Our programming language does *not* form the fringe of *s* and *s'* and then compare the resulting lists. This would happen only if two conditions applied. Firstly, and quite clearly, if we evaluate our programs by applicative reduction then we should certainly reduce (**fringe** *s*) and (**fringe** *s'*) to normal form (a pair of lists) before embarking on the comparison. Secondly, and more subtly, even if we reduce the programs by normal order reduction we could still end up forming the fringes completely if our data construction operator is strict in both its arguments. This is a little harder to see but we will now run through an example evaluation (using the canonical semantics) in order to see why we do not form the entire fringes of *s* and *s'* of necessity.

Let $s = A : (B : C) : D$ and $s' = (B : A) : (C : D)$.

cequal $s\ s' =$ **lequal** (**fringe** s) (**fringe** s')

Now it is at this point at which things go wrong if **cons** evaluates its arguments.

In order to determine which clause of **lequal** applies we have to investigate the structure of the fringes somewhat. When **cons** is strict we simply form the fringes and then we press on with the list equality program. We have, however, formed the entire fringes after all. Now because **cons** follows the lambda definition of pairing, which we gave in Chapter 2, this complete evaluation of the fringes does not take place. We evaluate only enough to force a match on a clause of **lequal**. This leads to:

lequal A: (**fringe** $(B:C):D$) B:((**fringe** A) ∗ (**fringe** $C:D$))

which matches the final clause of **lequal** and reduces to:

(**eq** A B) **and** (**lequal** (**fringe** $(B:C):D$) ((**fringe** A) ∗ (**fringe** $C:D$)))

Now **and** is given by the definition: **and** b b' = **if** b b' "False". Thus the above reduces to:

if (**eq** A B) (**lequal** (**fringe** $(B:C):D$) ((**fringe** A) ∗ (**fringe** $C:D$))) "False"

The conditional is strict in its first argument position. Therefore the next reduction takes (**eq** A B) to "False" and then **if** takes the whole expression to "False". Notice that this happens without the subfringes being evaluated.

This goes to show that the program **cequal** does not represent a serious threat to functional programming. The naïve analysis of the operational behaviour was just wrong.

To be fair, however, this challenge was laid when most functional languages possessed a strict **cons** and applicative reduction rules. We will be taking this up again, and in more detail, in Section 3.11 and Chapter 6.

Exercise 3.4.2(vi)

The program **cequal** can be transliterated into PASCAL in an obvious way. This is *not* the program a competent PASCAL programmer would write because PASCAL functions are evaluated applicatively, i.e. they evaluate their arguments. Such a program would suffer the criticism made above.

Write the preferred PASCAL program for **cequal**. Notice it is the fact that *sequencing of commands* (*semicolon in PASCAL*) *is a binary operator which is strict in its first argument and non-strict in its second* that ensures that the entire fringes are not formed, or investigated.
∎

This exercise allows us to turn the tables on the critics. Languages such as PASCAL are to a large extent founded on the power and desirability of *procedural* (and *functional*) *abstraction*. It seems, however, that constraints

(regarding execution efficiency) can impose restrictions on the applicability of procedural abstraction. Thus the natural factoring of a problem into parts (**cequal** in terms of **lequal** and **fringe**, for example) is not compatible with normal standards of efficient programming. This issue of problem solving and program structuring versus efficient execution is a major theme in computing. As it stands there are still many problems which factor nicely into subproblems but yield inefficient computations in our language. We will see some examples of these later in this chapter and we will discuss some implementation techniques in Chapter 6 which help to make them more efficient.
■

Proposition 3.4.2(vii)

The number of atoms in an atom is just one, and in a pair of sexpressions is the sum of those in its components. The function, **countatoms** which we now introduce to compute this, has type $S \to N$ (although the same function could count the elements of an arbitrary sexpression; it would then have the type:

$$(\forall \alpha)\,(\mathrm{Sexp}(\alpha) \to N):$$
countatoms $(s_1 : s_2) =$ (**countatoms** s_1) + (**countatoms** s_2)
countatoms $a \qquad = 1$

This suggests that the following relationship holds: for all sexpressions, s:

length (**fringe** s) + (**countatoms** s)

Exercise 3.4.2(viii)

Prove this by induction.
■

For convenience, we will often write just **ca** for **countatoms**.
■

We can develop a program scheme for the ordinary "divide and conquer" style of recursion, natural for sexpression manipulation, as we have done for list recursion.

Definition 3.4.2(ix)

Let **G, H** be program variables as before. The following program scheme describes the structure of the *sexpression recursive* programs.

$$\mathbf{f}\,(s_1 : s_2) = \mathbf{H}\,s_1 : s_2\,(\mathbf{f}\,s_1)\,(\mathbf{f}\,s_2)$$
$$\mathbf{f}\,a \qquad = \mathbf{G}\,a$$
■

Proposition 3.4.2(x)

The sexpression recursive program scheme preserves totality.

Proof. This can be tackled by sexpression induction. We assume that **G** and **H** are total.

Base step

$$\mathbf{f}\, a = \mathbf{G}\, a \qquad \text{and this is defined by assumption.}$$

Induction step

$$\mathbf{f}\, s_1 : s_2 = \mathbf{H}\, s_1 : s_2\, (\mathbf{f}\, s_1)\, (\mathbf{f}\, s_2)$$

The two recursive calls are defined by the induction hypothesis and this is sufficient because **H** is total by assumption.
∎

Examples 3.4.2(xi)

(a) Setting $\mathbf{G} = \lambda a \cdot [a]$ and
$$\mathbf{H} = \lambda(s:s')v\, v' \cdot (v * v')$$
yields **fringe**.
(b) by setting $\mathbf{G} = \lambda a \cdot a$ and
$$\mathbf{H} = \lambda(s:s')\, v\, v' \cdot (v':v)$$
we obtain **mirror**.
(c) By setting $\mathbf{G} = \lambda a' \cdot \lambda a \cdot (\mathbf{eq}\, a\, a')$ and
$$\mathbf{H} = \lambda(s:s')\, v\, v' \cdot \lambda a \cdot (v\, a)\ \mathbf{or}\ (v'\, a)$$
we obtain **smember** (with its arguments reversed).
∎

Exercise 3.4.2(xii)

The sexpression recursive programs can be realized by a higher-order operator in much the same way that the list recursive scheme was realized by **lrec** in the previous section. Define an operator **srec** which does this. What is the type of **srec**?
∎

3.4.3 Other well-founded orderings

Consider the following function:

$$\mathbf{A}\,0\,y = y+1$$
$$\mathbf{A}\,x\,0 = \mathbf{A}(x-1)\,1$$
$$\mathbf{A}\,x\,y = \mathbf{A}(x-1)(\mathbf{A}\,x\,(y-1))$$

This is known as the *Ackermann function*; it has type $N \to N \to N$ and has an important role in the development of elementary computability theory. We are interested in it for a different reason.

Up to now it has been possible to use the natural well-founded ordering over the structure of one argument of a given function in order to prove various properties, most importantly, termination.

Inspection of the function **A** shows that neither argument is guaranteed to decrease from the left side of an equation to the right. The second argument for example actually *increases* in equation two and the first argument stays the same for the internal recursion of equation three. Any attempt to prove termination by numerical induction on either argument is bound to fail.

In such circumstances we have to construct a well-founded ordering on which to base an induction. More informally we have to discover a quantity which is genuinely being reduced at each recursion. The proof over this ordering can then show that $(\mathbf{A}\,x\,y)$ is given in terms of a finite number of applications of **A** to arguments which are lower in the ordering.

Note that, apart from the internal recursion of the third equation, the value of x *does* decrease uniformly. In the one case where it does not we can see that the value of y decreases. This suggests we define the following relation on pairs of natural numbers:

$$(n,m) < (n',m') \text{ iff } ((n < n')\,\text{or}\,(n = n' \text{ and } m < m'))$$

This is the *lexicographic* (or alphabetic) ordering.

It is easy to see that there cannot be any infinite decreasing sequences of pairs under this ordering. It is also clear that the pair $(0,0)$ is least since there are no pairs (n,m) for which (n,m) is strictly less than $(0,0)$.

Proposition 3.4.3(i)

We can now show that **A** is total:

$(\mathbf{A}\,n\,m)$ is defined for all $n,m \geq 0$.

Proof. By induction on the ordering defined above.

Base step

A $0\,0 = 1$ trivial.

Induction step

Given $(\mathbf{A}\,x+1\,0)$ we have (by the second equation) $(\mathbf{A}\,x\,1)$ but $(x, 1) < (x+1, 0)$ so the result follows by induction. If we have $(\mathbf{A}\,x+1\,y+1)$ then the third equation yields $(\mathbf{A}\,x\,(\mathbf{A}\,x+1\,y))$. Also $(x+1, y) < (x+1, y+1)$ so the internal call is defined by induction. Now $(x, (\mathbf{A}\,x+1\,y)) < (x+1, y+1)$ whatever $(\mathbf{A}\,x+1\,y)$ yields since $x < x+1$. Hence the right-hand side of equation three is defined by another appeal to the induction hypothesis.
∎

Example 3.4.3(ii)

Suppose that we wish to write a function which *rotates an sexpression into a right linear form*. Thus, for example, **rotate**, which is to have type $(\forall\alpha)(\text{Sexp}(\alpha) \rightarrow \text{Sexp}(\alpha))$, when applied to the first sexpression below would be equal to the second.

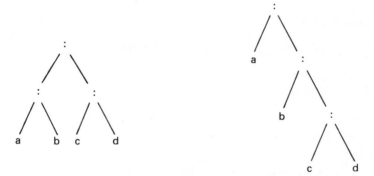

Fig. 3.4.3(i)   (Note: the result is *not* a list.)

A leaf is already rotated as far as possible to the right; this is the simplest case. If we apply **rotate** to a compound sexpression, $s:s'$, then there are two possibilities: firstly, $s = s_1:s_2$ for some s_1 and s_2. This will be rotated providing we can rotate the expression $s_1:(s_2:s')$ in which s_2 appears rotated to the right. If, on the other hand, s is a leaf then the expression will be rotated providing that s' is already rotated. Putting these together we obtain the following equations:

$$\textbf{rotate } ((s_1:s_2):s_3) = \textbf{rotate } (s_1:(s_2:s_3))$$
$$\textbf{rotate } (a:s) \qquad = a:(\textbf{rotate } s)$$
$$\textbf{rotate } a \qquad\quad = a$$

This seems to be, and indeed is, a more sophisticated program than those we have written for sexpressions before now. The intuitions which lead to the program seem to require some more justification. In particular we need to be sure that the function is *well defined*: is it total?

The problem here is the first clause. Using the ordinary structural notion of ordering on sexpressions we cannot claim that the argument on the right-hand side is structurally simpler than that on the left. We have to search for a well-founded ordering which is reduced by every clause. First we construct a formal counterpart to the informal idea of *making progress* which is implicit in the discussion which led to the program. This has to capture two sorts of *making progress*. The first is our usual notion of *structural progress* and the second might be loosely described as the *degree of rotation*. This degree of rotation is measured with reference to the structural complexity of the *left component, s*, of a compound sexpression $s:s'$.

Definition 3.4.3(iii)

In order to make this precise we define a function **z** as follows:

$$\textbf{z}(s_1:s_2) = (\textbf{ca}(s_1:s_2), \textbf{ca } s_1)$$
$$\textbf{z } a \qquad = (1,1)$$

We now set $s_1 < s_2$ iff $(\textbf{z } s_1) < (\textbf{z } s_2)$ in the lexicographic sense described above.

In fact we could be a little less pedantic about this and define the relation a touch less formally, as follows:

$s \leq s'$ iff s is a subexpression of s' or [s is not a subexpression of s' but (**fst** s) is a subexpression of (**fst** s')].

∎

Note, in particular, that $(s_1:s_2):s_3 > s_1:(s_2:s_3)$. The ordering is clearly well founded and atoms are the minimal elements.

Proposition 3.4.3(iv)

rotate is a total function.

Proof

Base step

rotate $a = a$ trivial.

Induction step

If we consider (**rotate** $(a:s)$) then this, by the second equation, is just $(a:$**rotate** $s)$. We can assume by induction that (**rotate** s) is defined (since s has one fewer leaf than $a:s$).

If we consider (**rotate** $(s_1:s_2):s_3$) then this, by the first equation, is just (**rotate** $s_1:(s_2:s_3)$). Although these have the same number of leaves we have fewer leaves in s_1 than in $(s_1:s_2)$ so the result follows immediately by induction.
∎

Exercise 3.4.3(v)

Let **fr** $s = $ **rotate** $[s]$.
Prove that, for all sexpressions s, we have (**fr** s) = (**fringe** s).
∎

We will be looking at several different ways of forming the fringe of an sexpression in the next few sections. **fr** is just the first of these.

Example 3.4.3(vi)

In this example we devise a program which will *balance* an sexpression whilst preserving its fringe. For $s_1:s_2$ to be *balanced* we insist that the number of leaves in s_1 and s_2 differ by no more than 1. Moreover, we require s_1 and s_2 to be balanced by the same criteria. This defines a predicate on sexpressions and suggests:

Exercise 3.4.3(vii)

Write a predicate called **balanced** of type $(\forall \alpha)(\text{Sexp}(\alpha) \to B)$ which determines when an sexpression is balanced.
∎

We now develop a function **balance** which is to have type $(\forall \alpha)(\text{Sexp}(\alpha) \to \text{Sexp}(\alpha))$. First, however, we need a program **unbal** which determines the imbalance in a sexpression in terms of those leaves contained in its left and right subexpressions:

> **unbal** $s_1 : s_2 = ($**ca** $s_1) - ($**ca** $s_2)$
> **unbal** $a \quad = 0$

Given this we can begin to develop the main program. The argument, we will see, is based on the degree of imbalance of s and on the structural complexity of s.

First, suppose that the degree of imbalance of s is at most 1. Then, there are two cases to consider. Firstly, s is a leaf. A leaf is, however, already a balanced sexpression and so we have nothing to do. Secondly, $s = s_1 : s_2$ for some sexpressions, s_1 and s_2, such that the number of leaves they contain differ by no more than 1. If we can assume, by induction on the *structural complexity* of s, that we can balance the subexpressions then we can balance the entire expression by pairing these together (since the difference in the number of leaves in s_1 and s_2 is satisfactory). This leads to the equations:

> **balance** $s_1 : s_2 = ($**balance** $s_1) : ($**balance** $s_2)$ **when** (**abs** (**unbal** $s_1 : s_2)) \leq 1$
> **balance** $a \quad = a$

abs here gives us the absolute value of any integer. In fact we will be making use of the operational rule regarding the order in which clauses are matched in this program. Given this, we really wish the second equation here to appear after those we are about to develop. The reason for this is that we avoid having to guard this clause with a predicate which ensures that the argument is in fact a leaf. Such a guard (. . . **when** (**atom** a) for example) would spoil the polymorphic nature of the program.

Now suppose that the degree of imbalance of s is $k + 1$ where $k > 0$. We may assume that **balance** is capable of balancing sexpressions with fewer leaves than s (this is an appeal to the *structural* complexity of s) or with imbalance at most k (this is an appeal to an *imbalance* complexity measure over sexpressions). Since s is certainly not an leaf we need to consider two cases:

(a) In the case that s_1 has more leaves than s_2 we shall suppose that s_1 can be reformulated as $s_3 : a$ for some sexpression s_3 and leaf a such that **fringe** $s_1 = $ **fringe** $(s_3 : a)$. Then **fringe** $(s_1 : s_2) = $ **fringe** $(s_3 : (a : s_2))$ and $s_3 : (a : s_2)$ has smaller imbalance than $s_1 : s_2$. We can compute s_3 and a from s_1 using a function **unroll** of type: $(\forall \alpha)(\text{Sexp}(\alpha) \rightarrow \text{Sexp}(\alpha))$ and which is given by:

> **unroll** $(s_1 : (s_2 : s_3)) = $ **unroll** $((s_1 : s_2) : s_3)$
> **unroll** $(s : a) \qquad = s : a$
> **unroll** $a \qquad = a$

and hence $s_1 : s_2$ can be balanced as follows:

> **balance** $(s_1 : s_2) =$ **let** $s_3 : a =$ **unroll** s_1 **in**
> **balance** $(s_3 : (a : s_2))$ **when** (**unbal** $s_1 : s_2) > 0$

(b) In the case that s_2 has more atoms than s_1, by a symmetric argument, we introduce the function **roll**:

> **roll** $((s_1 : s_2) : s_3) =$ **unroll** $(s_1 : s_2 : s_3)$
> **roll** $(a : s)$ $= a : s$
> **roll** a $= a$

The value of **roll** $(s_1 : s_2)$ is an expression of the form $(a : s_3)$ such that **fringe** $(s_1 : s_2) =$ **fringe** $(a : s_3)$. Thus $s_1 : s_2$ is balanced, in this case, by:

> **balance** $(s_1 : s_2) =$ **let** $a : s_3 =$ **roll** s_2 **in**
> **balance** $((s_1 : a) : s_2)$ **when** (**unbal** $s_1 : s_2) < 0$

Exercise 3.4.3(viii)
(a) Show that the programs **roll** and **unroll** terminate for all inputs.
(b) Show that **roll** and **unroll** preserve the fringes of their arguments.
∎

Exercise 3.4.3(ix)

(a) To show that **balance** is total we need an appropriate well-founded ordering. We constructed the program inductively and pointed out the sense in which progress is made by the recursions in an informal fashion. Turn these informal descriptions into a suitable ordering and show that **balance** is indeed total.
(b) To see that the program computes the correct result we need to show that for all sexpressions, s, both:

> **fringe** $s =$ **fringe** (**balance** s)   and
> **balanced** (**balance** s)

∎
∎

The program **balance** rather inefficiently recomputes the weights of subexpressions during balancing (by repeated calls to **ca**). There are a number of ways to improve matters, one of which is the technique of *memoing* which we will, briefly, mention in example 3.5(ii). We will deal with memoing in more detail in Section 6.7 and we will discuss **balance** again in example 6.7(vii).

3.4.4 Unification

In this section we devote ourselves to a single topic and introduce and verify many useful functions.

Ultimately we will define the *unification algorithm* (Robinson, 1979) which is a very important algorithm in computer science. In the context of functional languages it is used for *typechecking* purposes as we will see in detail in Section 6.6. To begin with we concentrate on some more elementary programs.

Example 3.4.4(i)

We begin by defining a function **substitute** of type $S{\to}A{\to}S{\to}S$ so that (**substitute** s a t) is identical to s except that occurrences of the atom a in s are replaced by t. The reader might like to compare this with substitution in the lambda calculus and the updating of environments in semantic descriptions. Both of these topics were introduced in Chapter 2.

If the sexpression s is equal to $s_1 : s_2$ for some sexpressions s_1 and s_2 then we assume, by induction, that we can achieve (**substitute** s_2 a t), for $i \in \{1, 2\}$, and then we pair these results together:

def substitute $(s_1 : s_2)$ a $s =$ (**substitute** s_1 a s) : (**substitute** s_2 a s)

If s is an atom then there are two cases: if the atom is the target of the substitution then the result is t; on the other hand if the atom is not the target then the function has no effect on s.

> **def substitute** a a' $s = s$ **when (eq** a a')
> **def substitute** a a' $s = a$ **otherwise**

■

Example 3.4.4(ii)

Slightly more complex are *multiple substitutions.*

We introduce a new data type of *substitution pairs* as follows:

$$SP = A \times S \times \{\text{"Nil"}\}$$

We include the component "Nil" so that a substitution pair is a certain kind of *two-list* and can be written using our conventions for lists in general.

For example: $[a, s]$ is a substitution pair when a is an atom and s an sexpression. Furthermore l is a *substitution list* when it is a list of substitution pairs. That is, the data type:

$$SL = \{\text{"Nil"}\} + SP \times SL$$

Now we can consider the problem of replacing occurrences of all atoms appearing in a substitution pair by their corresponding sexpressions. One solution might be based on the following reasoning:

We introduce a function called **substlist** of type $S \rightarrow SL \rightarrow S$. Consider the expression (**substlist** $s\ l$):

If l is [ ] then there are no substitutions to perform; the result is s.

def substlist $s\ [\ ] = s$

On the other hand, if $l = [a, s']:l'$ for some substitution pair, $[a, s']$, and substitution list, l', then we can assume, by induction, that we can achieve (**substlist** $s\ l'$) which is identical to s except that all the substitutions described by l' have been performed upon it. The result we want is achieved by simply replacing occurrences of a in this by s'. This leads to:

def substlist $s\ [a, s']: l = $ **substlist** (**substitute** $s\ a\ s'$)l

substlist, which belongs to the data type $S \rightarrow SL \rightarrow S$, is defined by recursion over the length of the substitution list which appears as the second argument.

Notice that, for a substitution list such as $[[a, s], [a', s']]$, we will replace occurrences of a' in s by s' with this definition. Often, however, it is necessary to simulate what is effectively a *simultaneous substitution* of the substitution pairs in a substitution list. Under these circumstances we do not wish to replace atoms in those sexpressions which appear in the substitution pairs by anything at all. This can be accomplished by defining **substlist** recursively over the *sexpression* rather than the *substitution list*.

A simultaneous substitution function, **subst**, of type $S \rightarrow SL \rightarrow S$, can now be defined: consider (**subst** $s\ l$). If $s = s_1 : s_2$, for some pair of sexpressions then we can assume by induction that we can achieve (**subst** $s_i\ l$) for $i \in \{1, 2\}$. These results can be paired to form the required answer:

def subst $(s_1 : s_2)l = ($**subst** $s_1\ l$):(**subst** $s_2\ l$)

If, on the other hand, s is an atom then we need to replace it by the expression to which it is associated in the substitution list l. This suggests an auxiliary function, called **extract** of type $A \rightarrow SL \rightarrow S$, which takes an atom and a substitution list as arguments:

def subst $a\ l = ($**extract** $a\ l$)

extract is easy to define by induction over its second argument:

def extract $a\ [\ ]\qquad = a$
def extract $a\ [a', s]:l\ = s$ **when** (**eq** $a\ a'$)
def extract $a\ [a', s]:l\ = ($**extract** $a\ l$) **otherwise**

Note that **extract** treats an atom which has no entry in a substitution list as if
the pair $[a, a]$ were, indeed, present.

■

Exercise 3.4.4(iii)

Suppose l is a substitution list such that whenever $[a, s]:l'$ is a sublist of l none
of the atoms appearing in the left field of a substitution pair in l' occur in s. We
will call these *clean substitution lists*.

(a) Write a program called **clean** of type $SL{\rightarrow}B$ which yields "True" of its
    single argument if, and only if, it is a clean substitution list.
(b) It seems likely that one might be able to show that for all substitution lists l
    we have: (**clean** l) $\Rightarrow$ (**substlist** s l) = (**subst** s l) but this is not so. What goes
    wrong? Can you alter the definition of **subst** so that the above becomes
    true?

■

Example 3.4.4(iv)

Substitution list structure *is* preserved by the binary list **append** operation.
However, this does not seem to be the correct way to combine substitution lists
in order to mimic iterated applications of **subst**. More formally, we require a
binary operator on substitution lists, ● of type $SL{\rightarrow}SL{\rightarrow}SL$, such that, for all
sexpressions s, and substitution lists l_1 and l_2 we have:

$$(\textbf{subst } (\textbf{subst } s \, l_1) \, l_2) = (\textbf{subst } s \, (l_1 \bullet l_2))$$

This operator cannot be **append** (specialized to lists of substitution pairs)
because the substitutions in l_1 and l_2 are undertaken *sequentially* on the left-
hand side. In other words, the sexpressions appearing in l_1 will "feel the
benefit" of substitutions in l_2. $l_1 \bullet l_2$ must yield a substitution list in which
sexpressions in l_1 have substitutions (determined by l_2) imposed on them. This
suggests we define:

$$\textbf{def } l_1 \bullet l_2 \qquad = (\textbf{sub } l_1 \, l_2) * l_2$$
$$\textbf{def sub } [\ \ ] \, 1 \quad = [\ \ ]$$
$$\textbf{def sub } [a, s]:l \ \ l' = [a, (\textbf{subst } s \, l')] : (\textbf{sub } l \, l')$$

■

Exercise 3.4.4(v)

Show that, given this definition, we have $(\textbf{subst } (\textbf{subst } s \, l_1) \, l_2) = (\textbf{subst } s \, (l_1 \bullet l_2))$

for all substitution lists l_1 and l_2 and all sexpressions s. Hint: how are extracting from l_1 and extracting from $l_1 \bullet l_2$ related?
∎

In example 3.4.4(iv) we specified a function by formulating a property which we required it to possess. This is a very natural and desirable feature of programming in functional languages. In the next chapter we will see how programs can, sometimes, be *derived* from these properties, by a process of *program transformation*. This transformation process ensures that the resultant program satisfies the required properties.

The operation $\bullet$ is a way of *composing* substitutions. It stands in relation to substitution lists very much as $*$ (**append**) stands in relation to ordinary lists. This suggests that we attempt the following:

Exercise 3.4.4(vi)

Show that:
(a) [ ], the *empty substitution list*, is a left and right identity for $\bullet$
(b) $\bullet$ is an associative operation on substitution lists.
∎

Substitutions are not, in general, commutative. Thus $l_1 \bullet l_2$ is rarely the same as $l_2 \bullet l_1$ although we have at least one exception to this non-commutativity in the exercise above.

Other instances of commutativity can be found by defining *powers* of substitutions.

Let l be a substitution list then we introduce **expsub** of type $SL \rightarrow SL$:

> **expsub** $l\ 0 = [\ \ ]$
> **expsub** $l\ n = (\textbf{expsub}\ l\ (n-l)) \bullet l$

Given this we can certainly solve:

Exercise 3.4.4(vii)

(a) For all n, m and substitution lists l:
   $(\textbf{expsub}\ l\ n) \bullet (\textbf{expsub}\ l\ m) = (\textbf{expsub}\ l\ m) \bullet (\textbf{expsub}\ l\ n)$
(b) Even the law of exponents holds:
   $(\textbf{expsub}\ l\ n) \bullet (\textbf{expsub}\ l\ m) = (\textbf{expsub}\ l\ (n+m))$
∎

Very occasionally substitutions can be *undone*. That is, given l_1 we would require an l_2 such that $l_1 \bullet l_2 = [\ \ ]$ (the identity substitution). The constraints on l_1 for this to prevail are quite severe.

We will call a substitution list, *l*, a *permutation list* just when *l* comprises of substitution pairs of atoms [*a*, *a'*] where all the *a'* are distinct and, indeed, whenever [*a*, *a'*] is a substitution pair in *l* then there is a pair [*a''*, *a*] in *l*.

Thus [["*A*", "*B*"], ["*B*", "*C*"], ["*C*", "*A*"]] is a permutation list but [["*A*", "*B*"], ["*B*", "*C*"]], and [["*A*", "*B*"], ["*B*", "*B*"]] are not. Inverses of permutation lists exist and can be generated by switching round all the pairs in the list.

From now on we will refer to substitution lists and permutation lists simply as *substitutions* and *permutations*.

Exercise 3.4.4(viii)

(a) Write a program **invert**, of type $SL \to SL$, which given a permutation will generate its inverse. Show that the program is correct.

(b) We can extend **expsub** to arbitrary integers for permutations by introducing **power** of type $SL \to SL$:

power $l\ 0 = [\ ]$
power $l\ n = ($**power** $l\ n+1) \bullet ($**invert** $l)$ **when** $(0 < n)$
power $l\ n = ($**power** $l\ n-1) \bullet l$ **otherwise**

Show that the rule of adding exponents generalizes for permutations under this definition.

∎

We now turn the tables on this substitution activity. Up to now we have essentially been asking for an expression generated from an expression and a substitution. That is: given *s* and *l* find the *s'* which results from applying the substitutions in *l* to *s*. This is undertaken by the function **subst**. Suppose, however, we say something rather different: given s_1 and s_2 find a substitution *l* such that s_2 results from the substitution of *l* in s_1. Even more generally we might ask for a substitution *l* which, given a series of expressions $s_1, s_2, \ldots, s_n$ (for some *n*) will make them the same. That is, some *s'* and *l* such that (**subst** $s_i\ l$) $= s'$, for all $1 \le i \le n$. Such a substitution is called a *unifier* and the process of finding *l* is called *unification*.

Example 3.4.4(ix)

The pair of sexpressions "*A*":"*B*" and ("*C*":"*D*"):"*E*" can be unified by the substitutions [["*A*", "*C*":"*D*"], ["*B*", "*E*"]]; [["*A*", "*C*":"*D*"], ["*E*", "*B*"]], and [["*A*", "*E*":"*E*"], ["*B*", "*E*"], ["*C*", "*E*"], ["*D*", "*E*"]] (amongst others).

The pair of sexpressions "A" and "B":"A" can be unified only by a substitution [["A" **infB**]] where **def infB** = "B": **infB**. It is conventional to avoid infinite expressions in unification processes so these two expressions would normally be considered non-unifiable.

■

We will now make life a little more interesting by enriching the expressions we are investigating. This makes the unification algorithm more interesting and generates other ways in which it occasionally fails to supply a useful answer.

We assume a program **var** which when given an atom yields "True" or "False". The idea is that **var** picks out a subset of atoms which we call *variables* (not to be confused with the variables of the programming language). These are the atoms which may be replaced in substitutions. Atoms for which **var** is "False" are considered to be constants and may not be substituted.

We might, for convenience, assume that the data type of symbolic atoms is given by:

$$C = NV + VR$$

where NV are the *non-variables* and VR are the *variables*. **var** just picks out the elements of C in VR just as the primitive **numeric** picks out the elements N of A (see Section 3.2.1). Thus we are led to redefine our data type of substitution pairs as follows:

$$SP = VR \times S \times \{\text{"Nil"}\}$$

Moreover our function **extract** now belongs to the data type:

$$VR \rightarrow (SL \rightarrow S)$$

This leads us to redefine substitution:

def subst $s_1 : s_2 \ l$ = (**subst** $s_1 \ l$) : (**subst** $s_2 \ l$)
def subst $a \ l$ = (**extract** $a \ l$) **when** (**var** a)
def subst $a \ l$ = a **otherwise**

Notice how constants are simply unaffected by substitutions.

For simplicity we will assume that (**var** a) holds if and only if a is a symbolic atom beginning with the letter V. Thus "$V1$", "Var", "$V139$", and "V" are unification variables for the purposes of this section.

Examples 3.4.4(x)

The sexpressions "V":"A" and "A":"V" are unified by the substitution [["V", "A"]]. However, "V":"A" and "B":"V" do not unify because "A" and

"*B*" are constants. "*V*":("*A*":"*B*") and "*V*":("*V*1":"*B*") can be unified by either
[["*V*", "*A*"] ["*V*1", "*A*"]] or [["*V*1", "*A*"]].
∎

Unifying substitutions do not appear to be unique, but they can be classified.
Let *C* be a set of sexpressions. We write $\langle C \rangle$ for the *set of substitutions which
unify the expressions in C*. Clearly $\langle C \rangle$ can be empty. Suppose that $\langle C \rangle$ is non-
empty, and that *l* is *any* substitution. It turns out that for every $l' \in \langle C \rangle$ we have
$l' \bullet l \in \langle C \rangle$:

Proposition 3.4.4(xi)

Let s_i, for $1 \leq i \leq n$ be sexpressions and *l* and *l'* be substitutions. If *l* unifies the
s_i then $l \bullet l'$ unifies the s_i.

Proof. This is just a corollary of exercise 3.4.4(iii). Suppose that *l* unifies
the s_i. Then there is an *s'* such that (**subst** s_i *l*)=s' for $1 \leq i \leq n$. To show that
(**subst** s_i *l* ● *l'*)=s'' for $1 \leq i \leq n$ and some *s''* we observe that (**subst** s_i *l* ● *l'*)
=(**subst** (**subst** s_i *l*) *l'*)=(**subst** s' *l'*)=s'' for some *s''* and $1 \leq i \leq n$.
∎

A rather deeper property of $\langle C \rangle$ is that, if it is not empty, it contains a
substitution *l* such that for any other substitution in $\langle C \rangle$, say *l'*, we have
$l \bullet l' = l'$. Just as [ ] is a left identity for *all* substitutions, *l* is a left identity for the
substitutions in $\langle C \rangle$. This substitution is called the *most general unifier* and is
produced by the unification program we are about to develop and study.
    We begin with a function which, when given two sexpressions, constructs a
list of differences between them. We will call this function **difference** and
it is to have type $S \rightarrow S \rightarrow$ List(Diff) where Diff$= S \times S \times$ {"Nil"} is the type of
differences.

> **def difference** $s_1 s_2$ =[ ] **when (sequal** $s_1 s_2$)
> **def difference** $(s_1 : s_2) (s_3 : s_4)$=(**difference** $s_1 s_3$) * (**difference** $s_2 s_4$)
> **def difference** $s_1 s_2$ =[[s_1, s_2]]

Note that, in the third clause, s_1 cannot be the same atom as s_2. Furthermore,
at this stage, we are not making any distinction between atoms which are
constants and those which are acting as variables.
    We are interested particularly in those lists of differences consisting of pairs
where at least one of the elements is a variable. This is because we can, for such
pairs, envisage replacing the variable in one expression by the other
component of the pair in the other expression, by a substitution. This would

tend to reduce the difference between the two expressions and so tend towards making them identical. To this end we define a predicate called **negotiable**, of type List(Diff)→B, which is true if and only if at least one element of each pair is a variable.

> **def negotiable** [ ]   = "True"
> **def negotiable** $[s_1, s_2]$:l = ((**var** s_1) **or** (**var** s_2)) **and** (**negotiable** l)

In example 3.4.4(ix) we noted that we do not wish to entertain substitutions involving infinite sexpressions. To prevent this it is necessary to extend the negotiable predicate so that it catches instances of difference pairs where the variable element occurs within the other element. This is called the *occurs check*. It suggests we extend the function as follows:

> **def negotiable** [ ]   = "True"
> **def negotiable** $[s_1, s_2]$:l = ((**var** s_1) **or** (**var** s_2))
>   **and** (**occheck** $s_1 s_2$)
>   **and** (**negotiable** l)
> **def occheck** $a\,a'$ = "False" **when** (**var** a) **and** (**eq** $a\,a'$)
> **def occheck** $a\,s$ = **not** (**smember** $a\,s$) **when** (**var** a)
> **def occheck** $s\,s'$ = "True" **otherwise**

Now for convenience we would like each pair of a negotiable list of differences to be ordered with a variable as first component and expression as second. This is easily achieved by means of **twist** of type List(Diff)→List(Diff).

> **def twist** [ ]   = [ ]
> **def twist** $[s_1, s_2]$:l = $[s_1, s_2]$:(**twist** l) **when** (**var** s_1)
> **def twist** $[s_1, s_2]$:l = $[s_2, s_1]$:(**twist** l) **otherwise**.

Note that **twist** is defined to act on negotiable lists of differences so if the second clause fails then s_2 (in the third clause) must be a variable.

It is easy to see that a *twisted negotiable list of differences is a substitution list*. The unification algorithm uses a single entry from this list to bring the original expressions closer together. We are actually now in a position to define the *unification algorithm*. The main program we call **unify** and it has type $S→S→SLF$. It is based on another function, **unify1** of type $S→S→SL→SLF$ which uses an extra argument (called an *accumulator*) which contains a contextual substitution list. The idea behind programs which use accumulators is described in Section 3.6. The type SLF is simply $SL+\{$"FAIL"$\}$, that is, the result of these functions may be either a unifying substitution or an indication of failure.

def unify $s_1 s_2$ = **unify1** $s_1 s_2$ [ ]
def unify1 $s_1 s_2$ l = l **when** (**eq** (**difference** $s_1 s_2$) [ ])
def unify1 $s_1 s_2$ l = **"FAIL" when (not (negotiable (difference**
                                          $s_1 s_2$)))
def unify1 $s_1 s_2$ l = **unify1** (**substitute** s_1 a s) (**substitute** s_2 a s)
                                          $[a, s]$:l
where $[a, s]$ = (**h** (**twist** (**difference** $s_1 s_2$)))

Note that "FAIL" is just an atom which we are using to indicate that two expressions cannot be reconciled by the algorithm.

In practice we might be inclined to write a simpler program **twist** taking just a pair as an argument. This would allow **h** and **twist** to be commuted in the definition above. Although this leads to a more efficient program we lose the correspondence above which is central to understanding the algorithm.

Proposition 3.4.4(xii)

For all sexpressions s_1 and s_2 (**unify** $s_1 s_2$) terminates.

Proof. It is clear that we need to begin by setting up a suitable well-founded order on which to base this proof. Notice that at each recursion a substitution is made which eliminates a variable from the expressions (recall the occurs check ensures that the substituted expression does not contain the variable it is to replace). Eventually the difference list becomes [ ] or becomes unnegotiable. It is this intuitive description of *making progress* which has to be formalized. We define a function to natural numbers as follows:

z $s_1 s_2$ = 0 **when (not (negotiable (difference** $s_1 s_2$)))
z $s_1 s_2$ = (**varsin (difference** $s_1 s_2$)) **otherwise**

Exercise 3.4.4(xiii)

varsin is a program which returns the number of distinct variables in a difference list. Provide a definition.
∎

Now we use this to order pairs of sexpressions:

$(s_1, s_2) \leq (s_3, s_4)$ iff ($\mathbf{z}\ s_1 s_2) \leq (\mathbf{z}\ s_3 s_4$)

This is well founded because ($\mathbf{z}\ s_1 s_2$) is always finite and ($\mathbf{z}\ s_1 s_2$) cannot be smaller than zero.

We can now show that **unify** terminates for all inputs by induction on this well-founded ordering.

Base cases

(**unify1** s_1 s_2 l) terminates trivially when (**difference** s_1 s_2) is [ ] or when it is not negotiable.

Induction step

To show (**unify1** s_1 s_2 l) terminates where (**difference** s_1 s_2) is negotiable (and not empty) we may assume that (**unify1** s_3 s_4 l') holds for any l' and $(s_3, s_4) < (s_1, s_2)$. Now it is sufficient for us to show that (**unify1** (**substitute** s_1 a s) (**substitute** s_2 a s)) terminates ([a, s] is the head of the negotiable difference list). We can conclude this immediately, providing ((**substitute** s_1 a s), (**substitute** s_2 a s)) $< (s_1, s_2)$. Since s_1 and s_2 generate a negotiable difference list the expressions (**substitute** s_1 a s) and (**substitute** s_2 a s) contain strictly fewer distinct variables because the substitutions remove a. Thus the new arguments to **unify1** are strictly lower in the ordering as required. From this we conclude that **unify1** terminates for all arguments. The termination of **unify** follows immediately.

∎

Project 3.4.4(xiv)

Show that if s_1 and s_2 unify then (**unify** s_1 s_2) yields the most general unifier.

This is quite involved so we provide a few notes for guidance. First show by induction that the following lemma holds:

Lemma 3.4.4(xv)

For any s_1 and s_2 which can be unified by l we have:
(a) (**negotiable** (**difference** s_1 s_2))
    for all [s_3, s_4] in (**difference** s_1 s_2):
(b) l unifies s_3 and s_4.

∎

Now let s_1 and s_2 be unifiable sexpressions. Recall that l is the most general unifier if and only if, for all unifiers l' of s_1 and s_2, we have $l \bullet l' = l'$. Now suppose (**unify1** s_3 s_4 l) is some stage in the evaluation of (**unify** s_1 s_2). Show that if l' unifies s_1 and s_2 then $l \bullet l' = l'$. Notice that l is not a unifier of s_1 and s_2 at an arbitrary stage in the evaluation; consider for example the initial stage: (**unify1** s_1 s_2 [ ]). [ ] is not a unifier of s_1 and s_2 (in general) but, clearly, [ ] $\bullet l' = l'$. Use the lemma above to reason that the difference lists remain negotiable and that termination occurs without failure. Note that when **unify1** terminates the substitution created **will** be a unifier.

∎

Project 3.4.4(xvi)

Extend the algorithm so that **unify** takes a single argument which is a list of sexpressions to be unified. Show that the algorithm terminates and correctly generates the most general unifier whenever possible.

∎

3.5 Counting the cost

Up to now we have tended to stress the declarative aspects of programming over the operational. This is because we have concentrated mainly on program construction and on program verification which are best addressed this way. Once or twice we did mention some operational considerations; for example, in example 3.4.1(vi) we debated the order in which the arguments to the function, **or**, should be supplied on purely operational grounds.

In this section we will spend a little more time thinking about program efficiency or, more properly, program complexity. Roughly, this concerns the computational costs incurred in executing computer programs. In particular we are interested in some measure of the time they require and the space they utilize for their complete evaluation.

We shall not be interested in measuring time in seconds or minutes, for such measures will be dependent on some rather special properties of the computer on which they are run. Rather, we will look for *relationships* between the execution lengths of programs on various *sizes* of input data. Such an enterprise might discover that, for a certain program, the time required for execution quadruples whenever the data size doubles, giving us a *square law* for its time complexity.

Complexity, like programming itself, can be undertaken at various levels of abstraction and detail. It is feasible, if absolutely necessary, to treat every primitive operation and every store access that a program makes with great precision; for example, we might differentiate between a local store access and a non-local store access (the latter, presumably, being slower). We will, however, not do this, preferring to work at a less detailed level. In fact we will simply assign an arbitrary constant to the time of such primitive computational units as variable accesses and primitive operations. For our purposes this approach will be entirely sufficient; we are hoping to investigate how the recursive structure of our functions affects time complexity and this can be done without resorting to highly precise timings for primitive transactions.

As far as *space* is concerned two separate contributions are significant.

Firstly, there is the space required to represent data structures which a program creates, either as results or simply as intermediate storage. Essentially this is measured by the number of *data constructor* operations which it utilizes. This space component is one we discuss most in this section.

Secondly, there is a space component associated with the program execution itself. In some sense each invocation of a function requires some space to represent its essential features. These include the values of actual parameters and local variables for example. We shall be rather vague about this component of space utilization because the contribution it makes to the overall space utilization can vary enormously according to the exact operational semantics we give the language.

Precise operational semantics for our language (under the canonical semantics) and for conventional languages is provided in Chapter 6. Both styles of language implementation introduce overheads in space due to function invocation and some details are discussed there. In practice the precise measures of these overheads can be very difficult to estimate (particularly in the so-called *combinator reduction strategies*: see Section 6.4) and we will tend not to spend much time in the present context discussing these contributions.

Example 3.5(i)

In this example we estimate the time costs for the program, **fact**, whose type is $N \rightarrow N$ and which computes the factorial of its input:

$$\textbf{fact } 0 \quad = 1$$
$$\textbf{fact } (n+1) = (n+1) * (\textbf{fact } n)$$

We will write $T_{\text{fact}}(n)$ for the time required for the program **fact** with input n. What we have to do is unpack this in terms of the structure of the algorithm. Taking the first equation first we set $T_{\text{fact}}(0) = a$ where a is some constant. The second equation gives rise to the formula $T_{\text{fact}}(n+1) = b + T_{\text{fact}}(n)$ where b is a constant which stands for the computation of the multiplication.

A little arithmetic will convince us that $T_{\text{fact}}(n) = b(n-1) + a$. It is easy to see that this function is a linear equation in n. We will adopt standard usage and write $O(n)$ for a time complexity which can be expressed as a linear function in n. In fact the terminology, $O(n)$, has a precise definition and the interested reader might like to follow up our brief excursion into elementary complexity by refering to Aho *et al.* (1974) where that definition can be found.

Let us now turn to the space requirement of **fact**. Since the program contains no data constructor it is tempting to assume that it executes in constant space, but we are also taking into account that space required by suspended recursive invocations of functions as well (note that multiplication is a strict primitive operator; so even under the canonical semantics this operation does not take effect until after the recursive invocations have produced a result). The equation for this is identical: let $S_{fact}(n)$ stand for the space requirement of this program at argument n. The first equation executes in some (small) constant space a; and the second in space $b + S_{fact}(n)$ where b is the space required to maintain the integrity of the partial result $n + 1$. Thus $S_{fact}(n)$ is also $O(n)$. This is already disappointing because the obvious iteration one would write in a conventional imperative language [whilst having time complexity $O(n)$] has space complexity $O(1)$ (that is it executes in constant space). We shall see in Section 3.6, and again in more detail in the next chapter, how we may obtain a program for **fact** with these improved characteristics.
■

Example 3.5(ii)

We now turn to a more complex program, of type $N \rightarrow N$, which computes the Fibonacci sequence:

> **fib** $0 = 1$
> **fib** $1 = 1$
> **fib** $n = ($**fib** $(n-1)) + ($**fib** $(n-2))$

Clearly $T_{fib}(0) = a$, $T_{fib}(1) = a$, and $T_{fib}(n+2) = c + T_{fib}(n+1) + T_{fib}(n)$.

The time complexity is essentially the Fibonacci sequence itself! In fact it is easy to see that in computing (**fib** n) we require (**fib** $n + 1$) function calls. Now the Fibonacci series is an exponential sequence. We conclude that this program has an exponential time complexity. Not a pleasant conclusion.

Suppose that once an invocation of **fib** completes the result produced is 'jotted down' (in some sense) for future reference. Suppose, further, that this is done in such a way that, if the program is ever evaluated at the same argument, the previously computed result can be accessed. Presumably this accessing can be done in constant time. Since (**fib** $n + 1$) will compute (**fib** n) as a subcomputation we may write $T_{fib}(n+2) = c + T_{fib}(n+1) + d$. This yields a linear time complexity for **fib**. This digression has introduced the concept of *memoization* (Michie, 1968; Hughes, 1985). We shall return to this topic again, in Section 6.7 in particular.

Let us turn to the space complexity of **fib**.

$$S_{fib}(0) \quad = a; \; S_{fib}(1) = a;$$
$$S_{fib}(n+2) = c + \mathbf{max}(S_{fib}(n+1), \; S_{fib}(n))$$

Note that all invocations involved in the computation of (**fib** $n+1$) are complete before the evaluation of the second recursive call. This gives rise to the **max** operation above.

Since $S_{fib}(n+1)$ is either equal to $S_{fib}(n)$ or contains the space required by (**fib** n) we may simplify this to $S_{fib}(n+2) = c + S_{fib}(n+1)$. This clearly yields a linear relationship and we can conclude that **fib** has space requirement $O(n)$. This is also the space requirement under memoization.

The obvious program written in, say, PASCAL executes with time complexity $O(n)$ and space complexity $O(1)$. Again, this is not very encouraging for the functional programming approach. We will show how to improve matters later, and in particular in Chapter 4.
■

Exercise 3.5(iii)

What is the "obvious" PASCAL program which computes Fibonacci with the complexity measures given above?
■

Finally we will examine a program which actually forms data structures and thus requires space for reasons other than just function invocation.

Example 3.5(iv)

In the last section we defined the program **reverse**, of type $(\forall \alpha)(\text{List}(\alpha) \to \text{List}(\alpha))$, and we commented that it needs to use extra construction operations in order to place an item on the end of a list.

$$
\begin{aligned}
&\textbf{reverse } [\ ] &&= [\ ]\\
&\textbf{reverse } (a:l) &&= (\textbf{reverse } l) * [a]\\
&(\text{recall that } [a] &&= a\text{:``Nil''})
\end{aligned}
$$

We aim to estimate the space required for data construction. There are essentially two components to this: the space required by the $*$ operator and that required by the expression $[a]$ in each recursion.

It is also easy to see from the definition of **append**:

$$
\begin{aligned}
&[\ ] * l = l\\
&(a:l) * l' = a:(l * l')
\end{aligned}
$$

that * requires space (for data construction) proportional to the length of the first argument (which determines the number of recursions required). It is perhaps more convenient, when discussing this form of space requirement, to think in terms of the actual number of data constructions required rather than the quantity of space required (these are, after all, directly proportional). Thus we can say that the space utilization (as determined by the number of **cons** operations) is **equal** to the length of the first argument.

Let us return to **reverse**. The first equation requires no constructions. At each recursion we will require one **cons** operation for construction of the structure $[a]$ and that alone implies a space requirement equal to the length of the argument.

However at each recursion we do an **append** operation. In total we will do n appends when the length of the list is n. Each of these recursive calls has a first argument of a particular size (length) ranging from 0 to $n-1$. Thus, given the space complexity of * we see that the number of **cons** operations required will be $(n^2 - n)/2$ for this aspect of the call. Adding in the contribution due to the expressions of the form: $[a]$, we have in total, $(n^2 + n)/2$ **cons** operations for an argument of length n.

Thus the total space utilization of **reverse** is quadratic in the length of the list. We conclude that the space complexity of **reverse** as defined above is $O(n^2)$.

■

Example 3.5(v)

Consider the program:

fringe $(s_1:s_2) = ($**fringe** $s_1) * ($**fringe** $s_2)$
fringe $a \qquad = [a]$

Let us investigate the space utilization of this due to data construction. Recall from our discussions above that * has a space requirement which is linear in its first argument.

For the sake of simplicity let us assume that the argument to **fringe** is a symmetrical expression with 2^n leaves, for some n. Essentially **fringe** replaces each atom by a **list** operation and each internal **cons** node by an **append** operation. This is perhaps best viewed diagrammatically (see Fig. 3.5 (vi)). The atoms will contribute 2^n constructions. Each of the * operators at the first level will take arguments of length $1(=2^0)$. There are 2^{n-1} such calls. At the next level there are 2^{n-2} calls of * where the first arguments will have length $2(=2^1)$. This continues until at the root we have $1(=2^0)$ calls of * with a first argument of length 2^{n-1}. At each of the n levels we have 2^{n-1} data

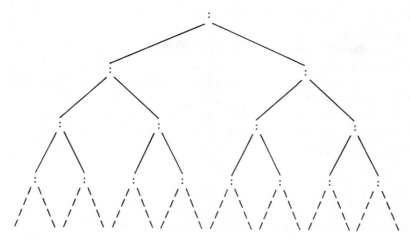

Fig. 3.5(vi)

constructions since at each level we have 2^{n-i} calls of $*$ with first argument length 2^{i-1}, for all i from 1 to n, and $2^{n-i} \cdot 2^{i-1} = 2^{n-1}$. Adding on the contribution of leaves we have, for a tree of 2^n leaves, a total of $n \cdot 2^{n-1} + 2^n$ constructor operators. Recasting this more conventionally, we see that given a tree of size n we require $\log n \cdot (n/2) + n$ constructors. The complexity is thus $O(n \log n)$.

∎

Exercise 3.5(vii)

Confirm that the *best case* behaviour of this function is $O(n)$ and in fact a tree of n leaves gives rise to $2n - 1$ constructors.

Confirm that the *worst case* behaviour is $O(n^2)$ and in fact a tree of size n requires $(1/2)n(n + 1)$ constructions.

∎

We conclude that the space complexity of this program lies between $O(n)$ and $O(n^2)$. This is not particularly encouraging. In the next section we shall see an alternative program which is always $O(n)$ in data construction and this is independent of the input shape. Indeed its space complexity with respect to data construction is always half that of the best case of the program above.

3.6 Accumulating results

The programming technique known as *adding an accumulator* is an old and well-used programming strategy and is especially useful in functional programming.

Essentially the technique consists of redefining a function in order to form a new one which takes one more argument; this extra argument is known as the *accumulator*. This is to hold the partial (and eventually the final) result of the computation. The new program is to be related to the original one in a precise way. Eventually this leads to a proof that the new program is correct (equivalent to the old program). To begin with the link is used to guide the program development.

Example 3.6(i)

Perhaps the simplest example of this is the extension of the program:

> **factorial** $0 \quad = 1$
> **factorial** $(n+1) = (n+1) * ($**factorial** $n)$

to the definition:

> **factorial** $n \quad =$ **f** n 1
> **f** 0 $m \quad = m$
> **f** $(n+1) m \quad =$ **f** n $((n+1) * m)$

In this definition **factorial** is defined by a function, **f**, of type $N \to N \to N$, and which has an accumulator as a second argument. The property we wish to impose on **f**, and which is used to guide the construction of **f**, is that:

> $($**f** n $m) = ($**factorial** $n) * m.$

Initially the accumulator is set to 1. This represents the trivial "partial result" of computing a factorial and the property above simplifies to the first equation for **f**. The second equation essentially tells us that, when the main argument is zero, the partial result is actually the final result. Again, this is a simple consequence of the property. The third equation shows how at each stage the partial result is extended toward the final value. This is the most interesting case. Note that, in view of our requirement that $($**factorial** $n) * m = ($**f** n $m)$, the equality specified by the third equation is justified. Furthermore the program appears to be making computational progress (by induction on the first argument). We will confirm this formally later. Indeed, in Chapter 4 we explain how the new program can be formally derived from the original with respect to the property by a process of program transformation.

Thus, for example, under applicative evaluation:

factorial 5 =
f 5 1   =
f 4 5   =
f 3 20   =
f 2 60   =
f 1 120   =
f 0 120   =
120

as expected. This should be contrasted to the original program which would evaluate as follows:

factorial 5 =
5 ∗ (**factorial** 4) =
5 ∗ (4 ∗ (**factorial** 3)) =
5 ∗ (4 ∗ (3 ∗ (**factorial** 2))) =
5 ∗ (4 ∗ (3 ∗ (2 ∗ (**factorial** 1)))) =
5 ∗ (4 ∗ (3 ∗ (2 ∗ (1 ∗ (**factorial** 0))))) =
5 ∗ (4 ∗ (3 ∗ (2 ∗ (1 ∗ 1)))) =
5 ∗ (4 ∗ (3 ∗ (2 ∗ 1))) =
5 ∗ (4 ∗ (3 ∗ 2)) =
5 ∗ (4 ∗ 6) =
5 ∗ 24 =
120

The reason for stressing the evaluation of the multiplication in the above is to indicate that the final value is computed after each recursion has completed. This occurs on the way back through the calling sequence. In contrast the accumulating parameter version computes the result as the recursive structure is being unfolded under applicative semantics.

The time complexity of the new algorithm is still $O(n)$ and it might seem that the space complexity (entirely due to the recursion structure) is also $O(n)$. This need not be so as we shall now see.
∎

So far we have split space requirements into two components: firstly, that space required for the data structures created and, secondly, that space required to maintain the integrity of the recursion.

In many cases, as we will see in detail in Chapter 6, implementations can have *self-optimizing properties* which can take advantage of many special cases.

One special case, which is exemplified by the current example is that of *tail recursion*. A tail recursion occurs when the final stage in the evaluation of an equation is a function call, in particular a recursive function call. This is important for if the call is the *last* computation in the equation there is no need to preserve any information relevant to the invocation of the current equation:

If we take the equation $\mathbf{f}(n+1)\,m = \mathbf{f}\,n\,((n+1)*m)$ we see that the recursive call is indeed a tail recursion. There is consequently no need to preserve the value of the arguments of the invocation $(\mathbf{f}(n+1)\,m)$ for these will never be used again.

Consider, however, the equation **factorial** $(n+1) = (n+1)*(\textbf{factorial } n)$. The recursion on the right-hand side is *not* a tail recursion for its result is to be multiplied by $n+1$ before the invocation of (**factorial** $n+1$) is complete. Thus the value of the argument $n+1$ needs to be preserved during the nested recursion. This naturally implies that the definition has space complexity $O(n)$.

In order to develop these ideas further we will need a more formal description of a class of functional programs. These are called the *iterative forms*.

Definition 3.6(ii)

Consider the following set of recursion equations:

$$\{f_i\,p_{ij_i} = e_{ij_i}\,|\,n \geq i \geq 1,\ m_i \geq j_i \geq 0\}$$

The f_i are n distinct function names. The p_{ij_i} are the argument patterns for the m_i equations describing f_i and the e_{ij_i} are the corresponding expressions for these equations.

We say that this system of equations is in *iterative form* if and only if for every equation $f_i\,p_{ij_i} = e_{ij_i}$ the expressions e_{ij_i} satisfy:

(a) e_{ij_i} is a simple expression consisting of no function calls (just primitive operations, variables and constants); or

(b) e_{ij_i} has the form $(f_k\,v)$ where $n \geq k \geq 1$ and v is a sequence of arguments composed only of simple expressions (as above); or

(c) e_{ij_i} is a conditional expression with a simple expression for its predicate part and whose arms satisfy these three conditions.

∎

We shall take it (although we cannot justify this until Chapter 6) that *iterative systems may be applicatively evaluated in constant space*. That is, their space requirement with respect to the recursion structure is $O(1)$. Remember, though, that this only accounts for part of the space requirement of a program.

Corollary 3.6(iii)

> **factorial** $n = $ **f** n 1
> **f** 0 m $\quad = m$
> **f** $n+1$ m $\quad = $ **f** n $(n+1) * m$

has space complexity $O(1)$ under applicative evaluation.

Proof. This forms a system of equations which satisfies the definition above. Equations one and three satisfy the second criterion and equation two satisfies the first. Furthermore, the program requires no additional space for intermediate data structures.

■

Example 3.6(iv)

We can apply the accumulation strategy to the program **reverse** by providing an extra argument in which to form the reversed list. The new function, **r** of type $(\forall \alpha)$ $(\text{List}(\alpha) \rightarrow \text{List}(\alpha) \rightarrow \text{List}(\alpha))$ is introduced via a constraint we hope to make it satisfy:

> $(\mathbf{r}\ l\ l') = (\mathbf{reverse}\ l) * l'$

Since the trivial partial result (the reversed list on nothing at all) is [ ] we are led to define:

> **reverse** $l = \mathbf{r}\ l$ [ ]

and it should be clear that this satisfies the constraint. Furthermore, if l is [ ] then we obtain the equation:

> $\mathbf{r}$ [ ] $l = l$

Finally we set:

> $\mathbf{r}\ (a:l)\ l' = \mathbf{r}\ l\ (a:l')$

by induction on the structure of the first argument.

The constraint will appear again later when we show that **r** is correct and in the next chapter when we derive the program **r** by transformation techniques. The transformational approach allows us to adopt a somewhat more formal connection between the introduction of the equations and the constraint which we impose on the new program.

To summarize we have:

> **reverse** $l = \mathbf{r}\, l\,[\ ]$
> $\mathbf{r}\,[\ ]\, l\quad = l$
> $\mathbf{r}\,(a{:}l)\, l' = \mathbf{r}\, l\,(a{:}l')$

This clearly has time complexity $O(n)$ as before. Since it is a system of equations in iterative form we conclude that the space complexity with respect to the recursive structure is $O(1)$ under applicative evaluation. This should be contrasted to the original program which had complexity $O(n)$ for this component of space utilization.

Finally, we must avoid thinking that iterative forms, or at least programs which use an accumulator only improve matters for applicative evaluators. After all, it is easy to see that the number of data constructions required in this new version of **reverse** is equal to the length of the original argument and so the space complexity of **reverse** with respect to data structuring is $O(n)$. This should be contrasted to the $O(n^2)$ we deduced for the original version.

■

Some languages evaluate applicatively but possess a data constructor (like **cons**) which is non-strict (does not evaluate its arguments). In such languages we can allow iterative forms to encompass those programs with equations whose right-hand sides are embedded in expressions involving data constructors and constants. The following is an example.

Example 3.6(v)

Consider the following program:

> **copy** $l = c\, l\,[\ ]$
> $\mathbf{c}\,[\ ]\, l = l$
> $\mathbf{c}\,(a{:}l)\, l' = a{:}(\mathbf{c}\, l\, l')$

This is an iterative form in the sense described above since the second equation introduces an acceptable expression ($\mathbf{c}\, l\, l'$) embedded in an expression consisting exclusively of data constructors and constants.

Such (extended) iterative forms can be applicatively evaluated in constant space (with respect to recursive structure) in languages with a non-strict data constructor.

■

Exercise 3.6(vi)

Define a version of **length** in iterative form by adding an accumulator.

Estimate the complexity values T_{length} and S_{length} for both original and new solutions.

■

The next example is a warning against the belief that adding an accumulator is guaranteed to improve the execution characteristics of arbitrary programs.

Example 3.6(vii)

Consider the program

> **member** a [ ]   = "False"
> **member** a $(a':l)$ = (**eq** a a') **or** (**member** a l)

We might be tempted to add an accumulator. This results in the following system of equations:

> **member** a l = **m** a l "False"
> **m** a [ ] v = v
> **m** a $(a':l)$ v = **m** a l ((**eq** a a') **or** v)

Strictly speaking the first version has space utilization $O(n)$ and the second version $O(1)$. It is, however, easy to rewrite the original program in iterative form using the definition: x **or** y = **if** x "True" y to obtain the system:

> **member** a [ ]   = "False"
> **member** a $(a':l)$ = **if** (**eq** a a') "True" (**member** a l)

This is an iterative form. The second equation satisfies the third criterion of definition 3.6(ii). This program too has space complexity $O(1)$.

On the other hand there is the question of time complexity. This is clearly $O(n)$ in both cases but there is something else to be said on this score. The worst case will occur when the atom is not in the list. In this circumstance both programs do the same work. In the average case we have to assume a probability that the atom is in the list and then average over the possible positions it can occupy in the list. We will do no more than assume that the atom is *sometimes* in the lists given as arguments. This implies that the worst case behaviour for the original definition is worse then the average case by some multiplicative constant. However, by moving the conditional inside the recursion in the second definition we see that the average and worst case behaviour are the same. We conclude that the accumulating parameter version is inferior to the original. In general the difference between two versions of an algorithm might be more serious than just a multiplicative constant. This certainly suggests that we take care in our programming.

■

Accumulation can also be applied to programs which compute with more complex data as the next example shows.

Example 3.6(viii)

Consider the program **fringe** of type $(\forall\alpha)$ $(\text{Sexp}(\alpha)\rightarrow\text{List}(\alpha))$:

> **fringe** $(s_1:s_2)=(\textbf{fringe } s_1) * (\textbf{fringe } s_2)$
> **fringe** $a \qquad = [a]$

It is our intention to establish an alternative version which builds the flattened list in an accumulator. We base this new function **f**, of type $(\forall\alpha)$ $(\text{Sexp}(\alpha)\rightarrow\text{List}(\alpha)\rightarrow\text{List}(\alpha))$, on the following property which takes into account a contextual list (such contexts will be investigated often, particularly in Section 4.7).

> **f** $s\, l = (\textbf{fringe } s) * l$

This leads us to the following initial equation:

> **fringe** $s = \textbf{f } s\, [\ ]$

We choose $[\ ]$ as an initial value because this stands accurately for the fringe of nothing at all. It is easy to see that this satisfies the property above.

> **f** $a\, l = a:l$

This simply says that if we have to flatten the leaf a, in a context l, then all we need do is place a on this list. Again, this follows from the property above.

What do we do, however, when faced with $(\textbf{f } s_1:s_2\, l)$? We should like this to be $(\textbf{f } s_1\, l')$ for some list l'. l' has to represent a context including s_2. In other words the context $(\textbf{f } s_2\, l)$. Thus the appropriate clause is:

> **f** $(s_1:s_2)\, l = \textbf{f } s_1\, (\textbf{f } s_2\, l)$

This equality is justified by the property although we have not yet shown that the equation makes computational progress. We will tackle this shortly. In summary then we have:

> **fringe** $s \quad = \textbf{f } s\, [\ ]$
> **f** $(s_1:s_2)\, l = \textbf{f } s_1\, (\textbf{f } s_2\, l)$
> **f** $a\, l \qquad = a:l$

This is clearly an accumulating parameter version but it is just as clearly *not* an iterative form. This is because we have a nested call to **f** in the right-hand side of the third equation. This is not that important because we have improved the space utilization due to data construction quite significantly by adding the accumulator. A quick glance at the definition shows that we do one data construction for each leaf in the list. If we measure the argument size in terms of the number of leaves it contains it is easy to see this has space complexity $O(n)$.

Under some regimes of applicative evaluation the improvement in space due to data construction might be outweighed by the space required to maintain the integrity of the recursive invocations. Under such circumstances we may be tempted to look for an iterative version of **fringe**. We will address this in Section 3.9.

■

Exercises 3.6(ix)

(a) Find an accumulating parameter form of the program:

    countatoms $(s_1 : s_2) = ($**countatoms** $s_1) + ($**countatoms** $s_2)$
    countatoms $a \qquad = 1$

(b) Can you find an accumulating parameter version of:

    mirror $(s_1 : s_2) = ($**mirror** $s_2) : ($**mirror** $s_1)$
    mirror $a \qquad = a$

(c) Can you draw any general conclusion from your two answers?
(d) Evaluate the accumulating argument version of **fringe** over the list $[1, 2, 3, 4]$ by canonical and applicative order reduction. Note that the role played by the accumulator is rather different in each case. Under the canonical semantics the accumulator maintains a *suspended* computation which is evaluated somewhat later. Under applicative reduction the accumulator acts as a placeholder for *partial results*. This is a very important distinction and we will make use of it often in the sequel.

■

3.7 Generalizing induction hypotheses

In the last section we introduced some programs which were designed to achieve the same results as earlier programs but by different computational routes. However, we did not show explicitly that this is the case. In this section we will rectify this matter and, in the process, demonstrate that forming appropriate hypotheses for induction proofs is not always easy.

Let us be more specific by considering the programs:

> **reverse** [ ]   =[ ]
> **reverse** $(a:l)$ =(**reverse** l) * [a]
> **reverse'** l =**rev** l [ ]
> **rev** [ ] l =l
> **rev** $(a:l)$ l' =**rev** l $(a:l')$

We want to know that, in spite of very different computational behaviour, these programs compute the same result for the same input. That is, they are extensionally equal, even though their *intensional* properties as programs are rather different.

Proposition 3.7(i)

(for all $l \in L$)((**reverse'** l) = (**reverse** l))

Proof attempt.   We will take $P(l)$ **iff** (**reverse'** l) = (**reverse** l) and try to show that $P(l)$ holds for all l by induction on the list l. This seems to be the obvious approach.

Base step

> **reverse'** [ ]
> **rev** [ ] [ ] =
> [ ]   =
> **reverse** [ ] =

Induction step

> **reverse'** $a : l =$
> **rev** $a:l$ [ ]   =
> **rev** l [a]

This is an impasse. We have no more detail about the argument to deploy and we cannot use the induction hypothesis. Perhaps we should try to establish this result from the other side of the equation:

> **reverse** $a:l$ =
> (**reverse** l) * [a] = (by hypothesis)
> (**reverse'** l) * [a]

but now what?

One way of overcoming this problem is to bridge the gap by conjecturing an appropriate relationship and then attempting to prove it. Here, for example, we might try to show:

Lemma 3.7(ii)

(for all $l, l' \in l$) ((**reverse′** l) ∗ l') = **rev** l l'

Exercise 3.7(iii)

Prove this.
∎
∎

However, this seems to be rather a lot of work for a simple enough problem. Let us try another tack. Recall that our impasse was reached when we obtained (**rev** l [a]) because we could not apply the induction hypothesis. Had this expression been (**rev** l [ ]) we could have applied the assumption because **rev** l [ ] = **reverse′** l and hence we could conclude that this is equal to (**reverse** l). The problem lies with the second argument to **rev**. The induction hypothesis itself refers to a specific constant [ ] whilst we seem to need an arbitrary list in this context. In other words the induction hypothesis is *too specific* to be of use. This is even more clear if we rewrite the original proposition as: $(\forall l \in L)((\text{\bf rev } l \ [\ ]) = (\text{\bf reverse } l))$. Suppose we generalize the left-hand side of this to (**rev** l l') for arbitrary l'. Certainly this is not going to be equal to (**reverse** l) in general. Presumably we need to rewrite the right-hand side as ((**reverse** l) ∗ l'). With this in mind let us restart our proof.

Proof. Let $P(l)$ iff $(\forall l' \in L)$ ((**rev** l l') = (**reverse** l) ∗ l').

Base step

> **rev** [ ] l' =
> l' =
> [ ] ∗ l' =
> (**reverse** [ ]) ∗ l'

Induction step

> **rev** ($a:l$) l' =
> **rev** l ($a:l'$)   = (by hypothesis)

(**reverse** l) $* (a : l')$ =
(**reverse** l) $* ([a] * l')$ =
(**reverse** $(a:l)$) $* l'$

and the induction step is complete.

Notice how the induction step utilized some elementary properties of **append** without discussion.

To obtain our desired result all we need to do is instantiate l' in the above to [ ], since **rev** l [ ] $=$ (**reverse**$'$ l) and (**reverse** l) $*$ [ ] $=$ (**reverse** l).
∎

This is our first example of a rather common situation. Often the 'obvious' induction hypothesis is not sufficient to obtain the desired result. This is a rather amusing situation, for in trying to establish any proposition, we shall not be inclined, at first sight, to attempt a more *general* result (for fear of it being too difficult). What we fail to take into account is that *in an inductive proof there comes a time when the inductive hypothesis may be deployed as an assumption.* At such a point, clearly, the hypothesis is working for us and the more general and powerful it is the better. Thus we conclude, rather fatuously, that we must not state too weak or too strong a hypothesis for we are likely to come to grief. What we have to do is to find one which is just right!

Before we move on it is instructive to note that the inductive hypothesis we eventually employed is the property we used for guidance in the program construction. This observation will surface again in Section 4.5.

Exercise 3.7(iv)

Establish that the solution you obtained to exercise 3.6(vi) is correct.
∎

It is also necessary to find more general hypotheses for programs like these which are defined over sexpressions.

Example 3.7(v)

We wish to show that:

(for all $s \in S$)((**fringe**$'$ s) $=$ (**fringe** s))

where **fringe**$'$ is the accumulator version [example 3.6(viii)] and **fringe** is the standard definition. If we rewrite this as: (for all $s \in S$)((**f** s [ ]) $=$ (**fringe** s)) we immediately see a specialization. If we take this as our induction hypothesis directly the induction step will fail as follows:

$$\mathbf{f}(s_1 : s_2) \, [\,] \quad =$$
$$\mathbf{f} \, s_1 \, (\mathbf{f} \, s_2 \, [\,]) \quad = \qquad \text{(by hypothesis)}$$
$$\mathbf{f} \, s_1 \, (\mathbf{fringe} \, s_2)$$

but now we cannot utilize the hypothesis again because the accumulator is not [ ].

The obvious approach is to prove: (for all $s \in S)(P(s))$ where $P(s)$ iff $(\forall \, l \in L)((\mathbf{f} \, s \, l) = (\mathbf{fringe} \, s) * l)$ and this is successful.

■

Exercises 3.7(vi)

(a) Complete example 3.7(v).
(b) Prove that your answer to exercise 3.6(ix) is equivalent to the original definition of **countatoms**.
(c) We remarked after example 3.7(iii) that the inductive hypothesis we utilized was based on the property we employed in the program construction. When we constructed **f** we avoided this approach. What property is being preserved by the construction of **f**?

■

It is time to draw a few tentative conclusions. The programs we introduced in Section 3.6 were constructed with the help of certain properties we hoped the new functions would satisfy. We remarked earlier, when we introduced the composition operator for substitution lists in Section 3.4.4, that it is quite usual in the functional style of programming to construct functions with respect to some property.

It is probably true to say that the constructions of programs in Section 3.6 have a more operational (and less obviously inductive) flavour to them than those we gave in Sections 3.4.1 and 3.4.2. This desirable characteristic of program construction for programs such as these are examined properly in Chapter 4 where, as we have remarked before, we derive these programs from their properties by transformation. At this stage it is, however, important to focus on one or two themes which are beginning to emerge.

Firstly, when we derive programs which satisfy a constraint or property we are basically establishing (informally) that the equations we introduce *preserve the property*. In other terminology we might say that the property is an *invariant*. It is the formal induction proof (like those given in this section) which actually gives us the certainty that the property or invariant is indeed preserved; after all, did we not notice that the *correct* hypothesis we required for our proofs was based on the properties we had introduced in the previous section? Thus, the construction and the correctness of the program turns on finding an *invariant property*.

Secondly, recall that ensuring that a function is total required us to find in fact a *variant* property. That is, a metric or measure on the data which we could be certain varied (indeed was 'reduced' in a strict sense) with each recursive invocation.

These two concepts of variant and invariant are ubiquitous in the formal study of programs and of functional programs in particular.

3.8 Homomorphisms

In Section 3.4 we found it useful to characterize classes of programs by program schemes in order to establish general properties like termination. In this section we see how certain higher-order programs can mimic program schemes within the language and give rise to very concise descriptions of a wide class of programs.

A large number of programs can be thought of as ways of replacing the nodes and leaves in some data structure (lists, sexpressions, numbers) by certain operations and then reducing the resulting expression. The operators which replace these structures do so in a way which is compatible with the shape of the data structure. Thus, in an sexpression, the leaves (having no substructures) can be replaced by a value (possibly dependent on the leaf concerned) and the internal nodes (having two substructures) by binary operations over these values.

If the data structure is a list then [ ] and leaves (having no substructure) are replaced by values, and an internal node (having two substructures) is replaced by a binary operation over these values. To see this forcefully it is best to take a few examples with which we are familiar and sketch out diagrammatically how they replace data by operations.

Example 3.8(i)

Take the program **length**. [ ] is replaced by the value 0, internal nodes by the binary operation **plus** and leaves by the constant 1. Diagrammatically we have, for example:

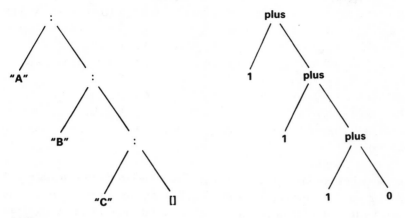

Fig. 3.8(ii)

Now consider the program **reverse**. Internal nodes are replaced by the function $S*$ (where $l_1 \; S* \; l_2 = l_2 * l_1$), each leaf, a, by the value $[a]$ and [ ] by the value [ ]. Thus, pictorially we have for example:

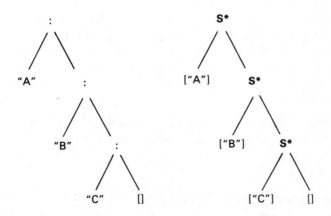

Fig. 3.8(iii)

Let us turn to programs on sexpressions. **mirror**, for example, replaces leaves by themselves and internal nodes by a reversing construction, $S:$, so that $s_1 \; S: \; s_2 = s_2 : s_1$. Diagrammatically this is just, for example:

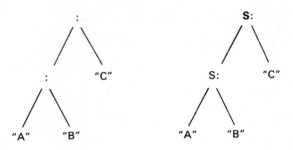

Fig. 3.8(iv)

Even searches conform to this scheme. Take the program **smember** which looks for a certain atom in an sexpression. This replaces atoms by truth values [given by (**eq** "*A*") for target atom "*A*"] and internal nodes by the logical connective **or**. Thus, for example:

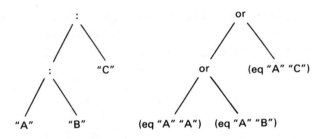

Fig. 3.8(v)

■

Given all this evidence it should not be too difficult to define a program which, given the appropriate operators, will effect the replacements.

Example 3.8(vi)

We now define such a function for list programs. It will take three arguments to replace leaves, **cons** nodes, and [ ], respectively, and return a program requiring a list input. We call the program $\mathbf{h_L}$.

$$\mathbf{h_L}\, f\, g\, j\, [\,] \quad = j$$
$$\mathbf{h_L}\, f\, g\, j\, (a{:}l) = f\,(g\,a)\,(\mathbf{h_L}\, f\, g\, j\, l)$$

It should be easy to see how f replaces **cons**, $(g\,a)$ replaces each leaf, a, and j replaces [ ].

We can provide the polymorphic type of $\mathbf{h_L}$:

$$(\forall \alpha, \beta, \delta)((\delta \to \beta \to \beta) \to (\alpha \to \delta) \to \beta \to \mathrm{List}(\alpha) \to \beta)$$

If we insist on dealing with lists of atoms then this specializes to:

$$(\forall \alpha, \beta)((\alpha \to \beta \to \beta) \to (A \to \alpha) \to \beta \to L \to \beta)$$

Given the evidence of example 3.8(i) we can set:

length $= \mathbf{h_L}$ **plus one** 0

where **one** is a program of type: $(\forall \alpha)(\alpha \to N)$ which is defined by:

one $a = 1$.

We also have: **reverse** $= \mathbf{h_L}\ S*$ **list** [ ]
where **list** $a = [a]$ as described in example 3.4.1(vi).
■

Example 3.8(vii)

A similar program can be defined for sexpression programs:

$$\mathbf{h_S}\,f\,g\,a \qquad = g\,a$$
$$\mathbf{h_S}\,f\,g\,(s_1 : s_2) = f\,(\mathbf{h_S}\,f\,g\,s_1)(\mathbf{h_S}\,f\,g\,s_2)$$

This function has the type:

$$(\forall \alpha, \beta)((\beta \to \beta \to \beta) \to (\alpha \to \beta) \to \mathrm{Sexp}(\alpha) \to \beta)$$

If we insist on sexpressions of atoms then this specializes to:

$$(\forall \alpha)((\alpha \to \alpha \to \alpha) \to (A \to \alpha) \to S \to \alpha)$$

Our examples pictured above can now be defined by $\mathbf{h_S}$.

mirror $= \mathbf{h_S}\ S$: **id**

where id is the identity function on leaves.

smember $a = \mathbf{h_S}$ **(or) (eq** a**)**

We bracket the function **or** because it is usually used as an infix operation.
■

The programs $\mathbf{h_L}$ and $\mathbf{h_S}$ are called *homomorphisms* because this is an algebraic description of their behaviour. There is great interest in programming with algebraic and even category theoretic notions at present (Rydeheard, 1981). Some guidance to this is given in the bibliographic notes.

These homomorphisms specialize into other useful higher-order constructs.

Example 3.8(viii)

Suppose we have a program, **def inc** = **plus** 1, defined over simple data (in this
case numbers). Often it is useful to extend such programs so that they work
over more complex data structures which are composed of this simple data.
Appropriate homomorphisms can be used for this purpose.
(a) Suppose, for example, that we wish to generalize **inc** so that it works over
lists of numbers. That is we need a program **inclist** which given [2 4 7] yields
[3 5 8] as a result. Naturally, this can be done by an explicit definition but the
homomorphism for lists gives us a pleasing way of achieving this. Note that,
pictorially, we want:

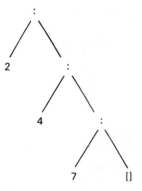
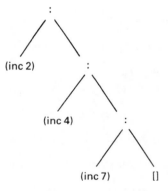

Fig. 3.8(ix)

To this end we first define:

$$\textbf{maplist } f = \textbf{h}_L \textbf{cons } f \, [\ ]$$

This operator has the type:

$$(\forall \alpha, \beta) \, ((\alpha \to \beta) \to \text{List}(\alpha) \to \text{List}(\beta))$$

Now we set: **inclist** = **maplist inc**.
(b) (**eq** "*A*") is a predicate over atoms. We can extend this to lists of atoms
easily by the program: **maplist (eq** "*A*").
(c) A similar technique can be employed for sexpressions. We might wish to
extend **inc** to sexpressions of numbers.

To do this we set:

mapsexp $f = \mathbf{h_S}$ **cons** f

and the type of this is:

$$(\forall\, \alpha, \beta)((\alpha \to \beta) \to \mathrm{Sexp}(\alpha) \to \mathrm{Sexp}(\beta))$$

Now we can define: **incsexp = mapsexp inc**.

For convenience we will often just write **map** for **maplist** and, indeed without confusion, for **mapsexp**.

■

Example 3.8(x)

Another typical requirement is the extension of some operator taking a small number of arguments to one which takes an arbitrary number of arguments. Take for example **plus** which expects two arguments. Often we require **sumlist**, which is simply the function **plus** extended to a list of arguments. Thus **sumlist** [2 3 4] = 9. Again, rather than defining this explicitly we utilize another specialization of the homomorphism for lists:

reduce $f\, l = \mathbf{h_L}\, f$ **id** 1

Here 1 is the *right identity* of f.

reduce has the type:

$$(\forall \alpha, \beta)((\alpha \to \beta \to \beta) \to \beta \to \mathrm{List}(\alpha) \to \beta)$$

Given this new function it is easy to define:

sumlist = reduce plus 0

Note the action of this in Fig. 3.8(xi).

Suppose we extend the binary operation **or** in the same way. We obtain

therexists = reduce (or) "False"

Now, t **or** "False" $= t$ so "False" is a right identity for **or**. Again, the bracketing of **or** in the definition above is a reminder that we are not using this function as an infix operator in this instance.

The same can be done for sexpressions by setting:

reduce $f = \mathbf{h_S}\, f$ **id**

and this has the type:

$$(\forall \alpha)((\alpha \to \alpha \to \alpha) \to \mathrm{Sexp}(\alpha) \to \alpha)$$

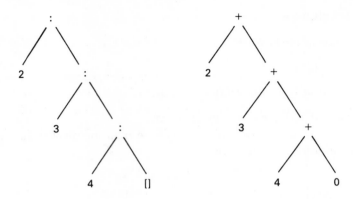

Fig. 3.8(xi)

This technique works even if f has no right identity.

The program **sumsexp = reduce plus**, for example, adds up all the numbers in an sexpression of numbers.

Finally note the following interesting definition of **member**:

> **member** a l = (**reduce** (**or**) "False") (**map** (**eq** a) l)

We will see a very similar program in Chapter 5 when we investigate a programming language which has a passion for higher-order constructs of this kind. ■

It is also possible to apply the accumulation technique to the homomorphism programs. This leads to:

$$\mathbf{h}'_L\, f\, g\, j\, [\,] \; = j$$
$$\mathbf{h}'_L\, f\, g\, j\, a : l = \mathbf{h}'_L\, f\, g\, (f\, (g\, a)\, j)\, l$$

and

$$h'_S\, f\, g\, j\, a \quad = f\, (g\, a)\, j$$
$$h'_S\, f\, g\, j\, s_1 : s_2 = \mathbf{h}'_S\, f\, g\, (\mathbf{h}'_S\, f\, g\, j\, s_2)\, s_1$$

Note that, in the former, the terminating value, j, which stays constant in $\mathbf{h}_L$, is used as the accumulator. New versions of **map** and **reduce** arise from these alternatives in the obvious way. It is not necessarily the case that $\mathbf{h}_L$ and $\mathbf{h}'_L$ are equivalent for all choices of f (in particular). This will be analysed more fully in the next chapter. It is interesting to note, however, that the versions of **reverse**, for example, which are obtained from $\mathbf{h}_L$ and $\mathbf{h}'_L$ are the expected ones which have been given earlier in this chapter.

Example 3.8(xii)

Both the **map** and **reduce** specializations of the list homomorphism h_L are useful in the following program.

Let us take lists containing no duplicate entries to represent *sets*. We wish to form the *cartesian product*, that is the set of ordered pairs from two sets. Essentially this amounts to mapping (**list2** a) over each element of the second set for every leaf a of the first set. This is, in itself, a mapping operation and suggests:

$$\textbf{cart } l \ l' = \textbf{map } (\lambda a \cdot \textbf{map (list2 } a) \ l') \ l$$

Now, given $[2, 3]$ and $[\text{“}A\text{”}, \text{“}B\text{”}, \text{“}C\text{”}]$, for example, we obtain: $[[[2, \text{“}A\text{”}], [2, \text{“}B\text{”}], [2, \text{“}C\text{”}]], [[3, \text{“}A\text{”}], [3, \text{“}B\text{”}], [3, \text{“}C\text{”}]]]$ as the result. This is not quite correct. In this example all we need to do is to **append** the two internal lists together. In general, we will end up with an arbitrary number of internal lists. Thus we need to extend **append** to arbitrary numbers of arguments. In view of the advice of this section we should use the **reduce** operator to do this:

$$\textbf{smooth} = \textbf{reduce append } [\ ]$$

which has type:

$$(\forall \alpha)(\text{List}(\text{List}(\alpha)) \rightarrow \text{List}(\alpha))$$

This allows us to define **cart** correctly by means of:

$$\textbf{cart } l \ l' = \textbf{smooth (map } (\lambda a \cdot \textbf{map (list2 } a) \ l') \ l)$$

Exercise 3.8(xiii)

(a) Extend the program **cart** to the program **cross** which forms the cartesian product of an arbitrary list of sets.
(b) Establish the types of **cart** and **cross**.
∎
∎

We will also write $(l \ \& \ l')$ for (**cart** $l \ l'$). The use of a sign commonly denoting *conjunction* is not a coincidence as we will see in Section 3.13.

3.9 Generalized parameters

In Section 3.6 we tried to apply the accumulation technique to the program **fringe**. This produced a program with improved space complexity but we commented that it does not yield an iterative system of equations and so does not execute in constant space with respect to its recursive structure under applicative evaluation.

In this section we introduce another programming technique which can yield iterative forms for some programs that the accumulation method does not. This is the technique of *generalized parameters*. It is not a particularly useful programming technique for languages with our canonical semantics but can be very important when the semantics is applicative. Indeed we will see that the program for **fringe** that we obtain is *worse* than that of Section 3.6 when executed under the canonical semantics.

Given a function f over some data type D we attempt to define a function **f'** over a more complex data type D'. The key is to choose D' so that elements of D can be embedded within D' in a unique and systematic fashion.

Example 3.9(i)

We will continue to work with one of our favourite example programs: **fringe**.

The generalization we will take is to move from single sexpressions to lists of sexpressions. Our original program is then a special case in which the list is a singleton. More exactly, recall that the type of **fringe** is:

$$(\forall\alpha)(\text{Sexp}(\alpha)\rightarrow\text{List}(\alpha))$$

Our new program, **fr**, is to have type:

$$(\forall\alpha)(\text{List}(\text{Sexp}(\alpha))\rightarrow\text{List}(\alpha))$$

Scrutiny of these types should enable the reader to see that the new program does operate over an extension of the input type of the original and that there is an obvious way to embed $\text{Sexp}(\alpha)$ in $\text{List}(\text{Sexp}(\alpha))$ (by the mapping which takes $s \in \text{Sexp}(\alpha)$ to $[s] \in \text{List}(\text{Sexp}(\alpha))$).

If we follow the advice we developed in Sections 3.6 and 3.7 we should look for some *invariant property* and use this to guide the program construction.

The fact that we are moving from a form of data (sexpressions) to lists of this data suggests that the higher-order operators of the previous section can and should be employed to capture our required property.

Suppose **fr** is applied to the list l. We expect this to be the same value as if we had applied **fringe** to each element of l and then used **append** to join all the results. Now the function **fringe** can be applied to each item in a list by extending it using the function **map** to the function (**map fringe**). The list of lists which result can be joined together by extending **append** to the function (**reduce**

append). Finally, we can write this as an equation we wish **fr** to satisfy:

fr l = (**reduce append**) (**map fringe** l)

Suppose that **fr** is given a singleton list $[s]$. This leads to the equation:

fringe s = **fr** $[s]$

Presumably if the list is empty there is nothing to flatten. The following equation seems justified because $[\ ]$ is an identity for **append**:

fr $[\ ]$ = $[\ ]$

If on the other hand the list is not empty we have two cases to consider. Firstly, the list has the form $a{:}l$ where a is a leaf. If we assume (by induction on the *structural complexity of the list argument*) that we can form the value (**fr** l) then, since the fringe of a leaf is a singleton list, we can simply place this leaf on the front of (**fr** l) and this suggests the equation:

fr $a{:}l$ = $a:$(**fr** l)

Secondly, the head of the list may be a compound sexpression and the list will then have the form $(s_1{:}s_2){:}l$. By an appeal to the *structural complexity of the head of the list* let us assume that we can compute (**fr** $s_2{:}l$). But by the same token we can further assume that we can compute **fr** $s_1{:}(s_2{:}l)$. This *seems* to be both well defined and to satisfy the required invariant (but we will not leave either to chance!) because the components will always be smaller than the compound sexpression and because the fringes of sexpressions which are rotations of one another are equal. We introduce the equation:

fr $(s_1{:}s_2){:}l$ = **fr** $s_1{:}(s_2{:}l)$

This discussion has covered all the cases and we can summarize as follows:

$$
\begin{aligned}
\textbf{fringe } s \quad &= \textbf{fr } [s] \\
\textbf{fr } [\ ] \quad &= [\ ] \\
\textbf{fr } (s_1{:}s_2){:}l \ &= \textbf{fr } s_1{:}(s_2{:}l) \\
\textbf{fr } a{:}l \quad &= a{:}(\textbf{fr } l)
\end{aligned}
$$

Exercise 3.9(ii)

Show that this version of **fringe** terminates for all sexpressions.
■

This is, as required, an iterative program and can be executed in space $O(1)$ with respect to its recursive structure under applicative evaluation with a non-strict **cons**. The space complexity due to data construction is rather curious for we fare less well. Indeed, on this score, this program is worse than that of example 3.6(vi). The space required is not dependent on the shape of the sexpression. The equations clearly show that we require one construction for every leaf, two for every internal node and one for the initialization. Since there are $n-1$ internal nodes for n leaves we have in total $1+n+2(n-1)$ which is $3n-1$ constructions in total. What we gained from one component of space we seem to lose to another. Which program we use depends largely on the relative amounts of space needed for a data cell and that required to maintain the integrity of a function call. It is, as we have mentioned before, very difficult to make precise statements about this form of space complexity without, in particular, being very precise about the operational semantics.

There is another reason why, under applicative semantics, a generalized argument version of a function might be considered and this is closely connected to the issues raised in example 3.4.2(iv) regarding unnecessary computations. If programs are evaluated applicatively we should need to find a solution to the problem of pointless computation which often occurs in the evaluation of programs like:

cequal s s' = **lequal** (**fringe** s) (**fringe** s')

One solution to this involves the generalization (of the parameters) of the functions **cequal**, **lequal** and **fringe**. **cequal** is just a special case of the new system of functions in much the same way that **fringe** is a special case of **fr**. The interesting consequence is that the (applicative) evaluation of the new system avoids the unnecessary computation. The bibliography contains references to places where this example and its implications are discussed in detail.
∎

Exercises 3.9(iii)

(a) Develop an iterative system of equations for counting the number of leaves in a sexpression. Estimate the space complexity and compare it with other programs which compute the same result.
(b) Generalize the programs **cequal** and **lequal** and convince yourself that they avoid unnecessary computation under applicative evaluation.
∎

Now we must show that this new program for computing the fringe of an sexpression is equivalent to the original program given in example 3.4.2(i).
For convenience we will write **fringe'** for the program defined above and

just **fringe** for the original program. We wish to show that **fringe'** = **fringe**. In other words: for all sexpressions s; (**fringe'** s) = (**fringe** s).

By now we are rather wary of rushing straight into a proof attempt. This caution, for this example, is well taken. There are two distinct issues which need to be addressed.

The first of these concerns the generality of the hypothesis above which is (**fringe'** s) = (**fr** [s]) and this is a rather special case of **fr**. We might predict (and we would be correct) that this specialization could cause problems in an inductive proof of the hypothesis above. We might recall from Section 3.7 that an invariant property which is used to guide a program construction leads straight to an inductive hypothesis that specializes to the required statement of correctness. Moreover, such a proof guarantees that the program construction correctly maintains the invariant and that the resulting program is well defined.

What we must show is: for all lists of sexpressions, l:

reduce append [ ] (**map fringe** l) = (**fr** l)

The second issue we have to address is the appropriate well-ordering (over lists of sexpressions) which is required for our proof to proceed.

The obvious sublist ordering which is common for list processing programs is inappropriate because of the equation:

fr $(s:s'):l =$ **fr** $s:(s':l)$

in which the list becomes **longer**. In this clause we argued that progress is being made because the structure of the head sexpression is being simplified. On the other hand, in the clause:

fr $a:l = a:($**fr** $l)$

progress is being made in a more conventional, list structural, manner.

This can be made precise by defining the ordering on arguments over which we do the inductive proof as follows:

$l \leq l'$ iff (l is a sublist of l') or
(l is not a sublist of l' but (**h** l) is a subsexpression of (**h** l')).

Proposition 3.9(iv)

For all lists of sexpressions l;

reduce append [ ] (**map fringe** l) = (**fr** l)

Proof.   By induction on the relation defined above.

Base step

> **reduce append [ ] (map fringe[ ])** =
> **reduce append [ ] [ ]** =
> **[ ]** =
> **fr [ ]**

Induction step 1

> **reduce append [ ] (map fringe** $a:l$**)** =
> **reduce append [ ] ((fringe** a**):(map fringe** l**))** =
> **(fringe** a**)** ∗ **(reduce append [ ] (map fringe** 1**))** = (hypothesis)
> **(fringe** a**)** ∗ **(fr** l**)** =
> **[**a**]** ∗ **(fr** l**)** =
> a**:(fr** l**)** =
> **fr** $a:l$

Induction step 2

> **reduce append [ ] (map fringe** $(s:s'):l$**)** =
> **reduce append [ ] ((fringe** $s:s'$**):(map fringe** l**))** =
> **(fringe** $s:s'$**)** ∗ **(reduce append [ ](map fringe** l**))** =
> **(fringe** s**)** ∗ **(fringe** s'**)** ∗ **(reduce append [ ] (map fringe** l**))** =
> **(fringe** s**)** ∗ **(reduce append [ ] (fringe** s'**):(map fringe** l**))** =
> **reduce append [ ] (fringe** s**):(fringe** s'**):(map fringe** l**)** =
> **reduce append [ ] (fringe** s**):(map fringe** $s':l$**)** =
> **reduce append [ ] (map fringe** $s:(s':l)$**)** = (hypothesis)
> **fr** $s:(s':l)$

■

Note that the ordering we needed to do this proof is suitable for the solution to exercise 3.9(ii). Indeed our example demonstrates yet again how a structural induction proof establishes both the correctness (the invariant property always holds) and the well-definedness (the variant property is well founded and is respected by the recursive structure of the program) in a single proof.

3.10 Sorting

3.10.1 Homomorphic sorts

Having introduced the notion of a homomorphism in Section 3.8 we can explore various methods of sorting elements with respect to some ordering.

Example 3.10.1(i)

Several well-known sorting algorithms are actually just *homomorphic extensions* of elementary functions. Take for example the following program:

$$
\begin{array}{lll}
\textbf{merge } l \ [\ ] & = l & \\
\textbf{merge } [\ ] \ l & = l & \\
\textbf{merge } (a{:}l) \ (b{:}l') = a{:}b{:}(\textbf{merge } l \ l') & \textbf{when } a = b \\
\textbf{merge } (a{:}l) \ (b{:}l') = a{:}(\textbf{merge } l \ (b{:}l')) & \textbf{when } a \leq b \\
\textbf{merge } (a{:}l) \ (b{:}l') = b{:}(\textbf{merge } (a{:}l) \ l') & \textbf{otherwise}
\end{array}
$$

We should like to say that **merge** has type:

$$(\forall \alpha)(\text{List}(\alpha) \to \text{List}(\alpha) \to \text{List}(\alpha))$$

but, in fact, the elements of the lists are *not* arbitrary for they must be ordered by some relation $\leq$ of type $\alpha \to \alpha \to B$ and presumably not all substitutions for α yield such a relation. In particular, there is no relation of this type on C, the type of symbolic atoms. For the rest of the discussion we assume that the lists we are considering are composed of elements which do possess such an ordering. It is easy to see that **merge** takes two lists and merges them with respect to an ordering $\leq$. The following exercise confirms this conjecture.

Exercise 3.10.1(ii)

Consider:

$$
\begin{array}{ll}
\textbf{ordered } [\ ] & = \text{``True''} \\
\textbf{ordered } [a] & = \text{``True''} \\
\textbf{ordered } (a{:}b{:}l) = \textbf{ordered } b{:}l \ \textbf{when } a \leq b \\
\textbf{ordered } l & = \text{``False''} \quad \textbf{otherwise}
\end{array}
$$

Show that, for all lists l_1, l_2;

$$((\textbf{ordered } l_1) \textbf{ and } (\textbf{ordered } l_2)) \Rightarrow \textbf{ordered } (\textbf{merge } l_1 \ l_2)$$

■

Now suppose we have an sexpression and we replace each leaf, *a*, by [*a*] and each **cons** node by **merge**. Then we have the following picture:

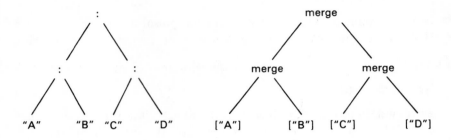

Fig. 3.10.1(iii)

If we assume, for example, that "*C*" < "*D*" < "*B*" < "*A*", then the above reduces to:

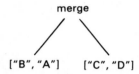

Fig. 3.10.1(iv)

and this, in turn, yields the result ["*C*", "*D*", "*B*", "*A*"].

The program that corresponds is just **mergesort = h_S merge list**.

Exercise 3.10.1(v)

Show that **merge** is associative and has left and right identities.
∎

A similar **mergesort** program which works over lists of leaves can, of course, be defined in a corresponding way:

mergesort = h_L merge list [ ]
∎

Example 3.10.1(vi)

As a second example let us consider the insertion sort algorithm. This is based on the function **insert** which, given a leaf and a list (not necessarily in order) will place the leaf to the left of the first element of the list which is equal to or greater than it.

> **insert** a [ ] $=[a]$
> **insert** a $(b{:}l)=a{:}b{:}l$ **when** $a\le b$
> **insert** a $(b{:}l)=b{:}(\textbf{insert } a\, l)$ **otherwise**

insert preserves the property of a list being in order. This is the content of:

Exercise 3.10.1(vii)

Show that:
(for all $a\in A$, $l\in L$) ((**ordered** l) $\Rightarrow$ **ordered** (**insert** $a\,l$))
∎

insertsort is just the homomorphic extension of **insert**. Thus we define:

> **insertsort** $=\textbf{h}_L$ **insert id** [ ]

and this is just: **insertsort** $=$ **reduce insert** [ ].
∎

We are really duty bound to ensure that the programs we have obtained by these extensions really are sorting programs. In order to show this we have to show that the output is an *ordered permutation* of the input. Clearly we can establish this directly, but the structuring of the homomorphism helps in the structuring of the proof. This is developed in the next theorem.

Theorem 3.10.1(viii)

Let P be a property of lists.

Suppose to begin with that $P(j)$ holds for some list j. Secondly, given a function $\textbf{g}$, from leaves to lists, suppose that $P(\textbf{g}\,a)$ holds for all leaves a. Finally suppose that $\textbf{f}$ is a binary function over lists which *preserves the property P*. We claim that, given all these suppositions, we may conclude that $P(\textbf{h}_L\ \textbf{f}\ \textbf{g}\ j\ l)$ holds for all lists l.
∎

Exercise 3.10.1(ix)

(a) Provide a proof of theorem 3.10.1(viii). It is an easy induction.
(b) State, and prove, a similar theorem for the homomorphic extension $\textbf{h}_S$.
∎

Corollary 3.10.1(x)

insertsort = $\mathbf{h_L}$ **insert id** [ ] generates ordered results [by theorem 3.10.1(viii) and a little manipulation].
mergesort = $\mathbf{h_S}$ **merge list** generates ordered results [by exercise 3.10.1(ix)].
∎

Now a sorting function not only has to generate an ordered output but also a permutation of its input. A useful theorem in this regard is a generalization of theorem 3.10.1(viii).

Theorem 3.10.1(xi)

Let P be a property over $L \times L$ so that $(P j_1 \, j_2)$ holds for some pair of lists j_1 and j_2. Given functions $\mathbf{g_1}$ and $\mathbf{g_2}$ from leaves to lists suppose that $P(\mathbf{g_1} \, a) \, (\mathbf{g_2} \, a)$ holds for all a. Finally, suppose that two binary list functions $\mathbf{f_1}$ and $\mathbf{f_2}$ preserve property P. We claim that: for all l;

$$(P \, (\mathbf{h_L} \, \mathbf{f_1} \, \mathbf{g_1} \, j_1 \, l) \, (\mathbf{h_L} \, \mathbf{f_2} \, \mathbf{g_2} \, j_2 \, l)) \text{ holds.}$$
∎

Corollary 3.10.1(xii)

(**mergesort** l) = ($\mathbf{h_L}$ **merge list** [ ] l) yields a permutation of l for all lists $l \in L$.

Proof (sketch). Define a program **isperm** $l_1 \, l_2$ which checks that l_1 is a permutation of l_2. Define a property $(P \, l_1 \, l_2)$ iff (**isperm** $l_1 \, l_2$). Check that $\mathbf{h_L}$ **append list** [ ] is the identity function on lists.

Let $f_1 =$ **merge**, $f_2 =$ **append**, $g_1 = g_2 =$ **list**, $j_1 = j_2 = [$]. By theorem 3.10.1(viii) we obtain: $P((\mathbf{h_L}$ **merge list** [ ] $l) \, (\mathbf{h_L}$ **append list** [ ] $l))$ for all l but this simply says that, for all l, (**isperm** (**mergesort** l) l) holds.
∎

The moral of this is that very often *program structuring can be of use in proof structuring*. Theorem 3.10.1(xi) is very general [we can obtain theorem 3.10.1(viii) from it, for example] and so we can determine program properties very easily by reference to the properties of their significant subprograms.

Exercise 3.10.1(xiii)

Extend theorem 3.10.1(xi) to cover the homomorphism $\mathbf{h_S}$. Use the result to prove that: **mergesort** = $\mathbf{h_S}$ **merge list**, is indeed a sorting function.
∎

3.10.2 Non-homomorphic sorting

In this section we will mention two sorting programs which are not homomorphic extensions. The first is the well-known *bubble sort*. This version is due to Meira (1982).

bubble l = **bub** (**cswap** l) l
bub l l' = l **when** (**lequal** l l')
bub l l' = **bub** (**cswap** l) l **otherwise**

cswap [ ] = [ ]
cswap $[a]$ = $[a]$
cswap $(a{:}b{:}l)$ = $a{:}$(**cswap** $(b{:}l)$) **when** $(a \leq b)$
cswap $(a{:}b{:}l)$ = $b{:}$(**cswap** $(a{:}l)$) **otherwise**

This is not a homomorphic extension in any obvious sense but **cswap** can be homomorphically extended to a sort, as the reader may like to investigate.

Exercise 3.10.2(i)

(a) Show how **cswap** can be h_S (and h_L) extended to a sort. Prove the resulting program (**swapsort**) really is a sort.
(b) If **cswap** is replaced by the program **swap** (which *always* swaps) what program is generated homomorphically by h_L?

■

Our second example is the famous algorithm *quicksort* due to Hoare.

Example 3.10.2(ii)

Quicksort is based on the selection of a *pivot* element from the set to be sorted and the partitioning of the set into two. This is done in such a way that one set contains all elements lower in order than the pivot and the other set all elements higher in order.

First we provide a function **split** which takes the pivot and the set as parameters and builds the partitioned sets in a pair of accumulators.

split a [ ] l l' = $[l, l']$
split a $(b{:}l)$ l' l'' = **split** a l $(b{:}l')$ l'' **when** $b \leq a$
split a $(b{:}l)$ l' l'' = **split** a l l' $(b{:}l'')$ **otherwise**

The sorting program is then defined by:

> **quicksort** [ ] = [ ]
> **quicksort** (*a:l*) = (**quicksort** *l'*) ∗ (**quicksort** *l''*)
>   **where** [*l'*, *l''*] = (**split** *a l* [ ] [ ])

∎

3.11 Lazy data and induction

We observed earlier that the pairing operation used in the lambda calculus **pair** = $\lambda xyz \cdot zxy$ is not strict in its first two arguments. This means that if we apply **pair** to the canonical undefined symbol W it is not the case that the expression collapses to W. Moreover we also saw that, on the contrary, the selection operations are indeed strict.

Early programming languages based on the lambda calculus, like LISP (Winston & Horn, 1981), originally took design decisions which, in certain respects, made them rather unlike the lambda calculus. For example, free variable binding was originally *dynamic*. This means that the substitution mechanism chosen was essentially that of definition 2.2.3(viii) although the so-called (upward and downward) FUNARG problems of early LISPs (that is their ability to manipulate higher-order values) make this correspondence less clear. A second major decision taken was that evaluation be applicative rather than normal order. This is a consequence of adopting a strict, *frame-based* virtual machine to execute programs (see Chapter 6 for further details of this). Finally the data constructor *CONS* which, in the lambda calculus, is just $\lambda xyz \cdot zxy$ was made strict in both its arguments. Thus (*CONS W M*) and (*CONS M W*) are necessarily equivalent to W in LISP for all expressions M.

Slowly, but surely, these differences have been noted and eventually rejected. Functional programming languages of today are essentially reconciled with the lambda calculus. The LISPKIT version of LISP (Henderson, 1980) and the influential language SCHEME (Steele & Sussman, 1975; Abelson & Sussman, 1985), which is also based on LISP, both implement substitution correctly by using static binding of free variables. They also maintain closures (see Section 2.4) for function values. Henderson & Morris (1976) and Friedman & Wise (1976) in the aptly named paper "*CONS* should not evaluate its arguments" suggested that there were excellent reasons for making *CONS* behave like $\lambda xyz \cdot zxy$. Turner's work (1979), which we will elaborate in Chapter 6, suggested that programs be evaluated in normal order, or more exactly, what we have called the canonical semantics.

In this section we will examine some of the programming and verificational consequences of employing a non-strict **cons** and evaluating programs in this way.

An important point to bear in mind is that the issues surrounding evaluation order and the semantics of the data constructor are to a large extent independent. It is possible to include a non-strict data construction into a language which is otherwise evaluated applicatively (this is what happens in the paper of Friedman & Wise) and we mentioned some of the programming consequences in Sections 3.6 and 3.9. Even the more comprehensively non-strict LISPKIT LISP language of Henderson is implemented on an applicative architecture (an SECD variant) by explicitly delaying evaluations when required.

3.11.1 Lazy data

One surprising consequence of adopting a non-strict data constructor is the possibility of programming (at least conceptually) with lists of infinite length. To see how this happens we will start with an elementary example.

Example 3.11.1(i)

Consider the following definition:

> **ones** = 1 : **ones**
> **ones** has type List(N).

Such programs are likely to cause nightmares amongst the conventional programming fraternity! We were probably taught to ensure that recursions are set up in such a way that they eventually reach a simple termination condition. The program above seems to disobey this rule in the simplest possible way. A more sophisticated response, based on our previous observations in this chapter regarding the close correspondence between recursion and induction, might suggest that such a definition is not *inductive* in the sense we have begun to use it. Indeed the reader might like to return to the discussion preceeding exercise 3.4.1(vii) to revise this issue.

The *operationally* generated feeling of disquiet that reading a program like this generates is based on the assumption that the order of program evaluation is applicative or, simply, that operations like **cons** are strict. A more theoretical (and *declarative*) perspective on this affords greater insight. The program above, and indeed all recursive programs, are, as we remarked in the last chapter, actually *equations* and are thus in need of solution. The program

above requires a solution from the set L of lists. We shall, for the time being, assume that this set contains lists of finite and infinite length. It is not difficult to see that there are two solutions to the equation **ones** = 1:**ones**. The first is the one we expect in most programming languages, the undefined value W which indicates that the program loops. If **cons** is strict it is easy to see that this value satisfies the equation since 1:$W = W$. The other solution is the list [1 1 1 1 . . .], the *infinite list of ones*. Unfortunately the recursor, Y, which we use to solve such equations always produces the *least-defined* solution which, in this case, is W. (Note, in passing, that any lambda expression is a fixpoint of $\lambda x{\cdot}x$ but $(Y\,\lambda x{\cdot}x)$ is $(\lambda x{\cdot}xx)\lambda x{\cdot}xx = W$. In a certain sense (which can be made precise) W is less defined then any lambda expression, so this is consistent with the previous remark.) Clearly it would be *desirable* to have [1 1 1 . . .] as the solution to the equation **ones** = 1:**ones** but to do this we have to *prevent W from being a fixpoint*. Under such a circumstance [1 1 1 . . .] would become the weakest fixpoint and Y will compute it. This is achieved by ensuring that **cons** is not strict in its arguments. In order to obtain a full understanding of this theoretical development the reader will have to wait until Chapter 7. For example, questions regarding partially or totally undefined (W) lists in L have been discussed but not explained or justified. For the time being we shall simply take it that **cons** is non-strict and that equations like **ones** = 1 :**ones** are well defined.
■

The ability to manipulate infinite lists of data opens up new and very interesting programming possibilities.

Example 3.11.1(ii)

The Fibonacci sequence is indeed a *sequence* of integers but the conventional method of programming it is to define a *function* which computes, from an index n, the nth term in the sequence. A more natural solution would be to represent it as a sequence (list) and then the nth term is just the nth element of the sequence. The following program is based on the observation that if one adds the Fibonacci sequence, element by element, to the tail of the Fibonacci sequence one obtains the tail of the tail of the same sequence. The entire Fibonacci sequence is formed by placing the first two terms onto this list.

> **fib** = 1 : 1 :(**sumlist fib (t fib)**)

Notice that **sumlist** is the extension of **plus** which we discussed in Section 3.8.
■

Example 3.11.1(iii)

The sequence of natural numbers can be represented by the following programs:

> **nats**   = **intsfrom** 0
> **intsfrom** n = n : (**intsfrom** (**plus** n 1))

Other sequences of numbers can be generated by filtering **nats**. Thus:

> **evens** = **filter even nats**
> **odds** = **filter odd nats**

Alternatively we could write:

> **evens**   = **map double nats**
> **double** n = **mult** n 2

nats itself can be redefined by:

> **nats** = 0 : (**map inc nats**) or even by
> **nats** = 0 : (**sumlist ones nats**)

We can generalize **evens** and **odds** to obtain sequences of elements which are not multiples of any given number:

> **multiple** m n = **eq** (**mod** n m) 0

This holds when n is a multiple of m.

A sequence without multiples of m can be defined for arbitrary m by:

> **nomultsof** m l = **filter** ((**not** $\circ$ (**multiple** m))) l

where the infix, $\circ$, is *functional composition*: $f \circ g = \lambda x \cdot f(g\ x)$.

It is easy to generalize this again to generate the sequence of prime numbers. This is based on the observation that the sequence of natural numbers with all multiples of the first n primes removed begins with the $(n+1)$th prime number. This leads to the well-known *sieve of Eratosthenes*.

Note that (**intsfrom** 2) is a sequence beginning with a prime and containing no multiples of primes less than 2 (there are none).

> **sieve** $n:l$ = n : (**sieve** (**nomultsof** n l))
> **primes**   = **sieve** (**intsfrom** 2)

■

3.11.2 Lazy induction

It is now quite clear that the sets of data elements which programs such as those in the previous section manipulate contain infinite expressions. This might be troubling the attentive reader who is concerned with program verification.

Our main technique for proving properties of programs has been induction and this rests ultimately on our ability to define a well-founded ordering over which to base the inductive argument. In many cases this has been the obvious subexpression ordering on our data objects, but occasionally (as in Section 3.4.3) we have needed to be a little more devious.

In the presence of infinite elements the prospect of attempting an inductive proof looks rather bleak. This is because such sets are not well-ordered by the subexpression relation. It is quite easy to select an element [say the element **ones** $= 1 :$ **ones** from List(N)] so that it is possible to find an infinite sequence of strictly decreasing values.

We know that at any moment we may investigate only a finite portion of such infinite structures. We can think of such investigations as revealing partial versions or approximations to the infinite structure.

For the purposes of verification we introduce a symbol W which is to represent a state of ignorance in our verificational investigations. W can be thought of as a gap in our knowledge or more concretely as a mysterious hole in a data structure about which we know nothing. The notation we choose is no coincidence. This symbol represents the prototypical undefined expression of the lambda calculus. Recall that W fails to terminate (under any evaluation scheme) and is therefore like a program which silently loops forever. This connection with the canonical non-head normal form of Chapter 2 immediately gives us many elementary properties. If **f** is strict then (**f** W) $= W$. Thus: **h** W $= W$, **t** $W = W$, **eq** W $x = W$ (**eq** x $W = W$) and **if** W x $y = W$ (but not necessarily: **if** x W $y = W$ and so on).

We think of an infinite data structure as being a *summary of its finite partial unfoldings*. Thus, for the purposes of verification, (**intsfrom** 3) for example, can be thought of as the summary of all the information we can glean from its partial, and consequently finite, versions. In this case the summary of the partial objects W, $3:W$, $3:4:W$, $3:4:5:W$ and so on.

There are two points to note. Firstly, if **cons** were strict then each of these partial objects would reduce to W and the summary of all this information would again be just W. If we think about this operationally this makes absolute sense: in LISP (where **cons** is strict) this program would enter an infinite loop immediately. We cannot glean any information from such a program however long we wait. This corresponds to the view that W represents a lack of information. Secondly, in each of the expressions above, the appearance of the sign W signals the portion of the data structure which has not yet been investigated and, therefore, about which we know nothing. Each of these is a *finite structure*.

It stands to reason that all our investigations are limited to that which can be garnered in a finite time (and so from a finite structure). In our example all investigations make use of some partial object ending in W. This is because at any moment we are always faced with a portion of the data structure which is, as yet, unexplored.

Now if we restrict ourselves to the partial objects then these are all finite and can be ordered in a very natural way. We will say that a data structure d is lower in the order than a structure d' if and only if d and d' are equal except that d contains 'holes' (W) which are filled (more exactly partially filled) in d'. This makes $W < 3: W < 3:4: W$ and so on. This ordering is made precise in Chapter 7.

Principle of partial list induction

Let P be a property of lists. $P(l)$ holds, for all *infinite* lists in L, providing that:
(a) $P(W)$ holds
(b) $P(a:l)$ holds, for all leaves a, on the assumption that $P(l)$ holds.

Furthermore, $P(l)$ holds for *all* lists if, in addition:
(c) $P([\ ])$ holds.
■

Likewise we have:

Principle of partial sexpression induction

Let P be a property of sexpressions. $P(s)$ holds, for all infinite sexpressions in S, providing that:
(a) $P(W)$ holds
(b) $P(s:s')$ holds assuming that both $P(s)$ and $P(s')$ hold.
Furthermore, $P(s)$ holds, for all sexpressions s if, in addition:
(c) $P(a)$ holds, for all leaves a.
■

What we are doing when we apply these principles is showing that P holds for all finite investigations of an infinite structure. What we need to know in order that the principles are sound is that this evidence is sufficient to ensure that P holds for summaries of finite information. In other words P holds for infinite elements. This raises some important questions. Do infinite elements really correspond to summaries of finite partial objects? Does P behave nicely in the passage from sets of finite partial objects (all the finite information corresponding to an infinite object) to actual infinite elements? To address these we require some sophisticated theory which we will develop in Chapter 7. In that chapter we will formally justify these principles.

Before we give an example we need to make an important observation. Suppose ($f\ x_1 \ldots x_n$) is defined by a series of patterned-directed clauses. f is strict in argument x_i ($1 \leq i \leq n$) if x_i is *active* in the patterned clauses. That is, the matching is effected by means of (but not necessarily exclusively by) the ith argument.

Example 3.11.2(i)

> **append** [ ] l $= l$
> **append** (a:l) l' $= a$: (**append** $l\ l'$)

The first argument is active and the second is passive. **append** is strict in its first argument. It is rather easier to see this strictness if we look at the definition in conditional form:

> **append** $l\ l'$ = if (**null** l) l' (**cons** (**h** l) (**append** (**t** l) l'))

Note that **null** is strict and the first argument of the conditional is strict. Therefore **append** is strict in its first argument.
∎

We can reason about properties of infinite lists using partial object induction.

Lemma 3.11.2(ii) (Turner, 1982b)

For all infinite lists l, l'; $l * l' = l$.

Proof

Base step

> $W * l' = W$ since the first argument of **append** is active.

Induction step

$(a:l) * l' =$
$a:(l * l') =$ (by induction)
$a:l$

∎

Proposition 3.11.2(iii)

for all infinite lists l; **reverse (reverse** l) = W.

Proof

Base step

reverse (reverse W) =
reverse W =
W since the first argument of **reverse** is active.

Induction step

reverse (reverse $(a:l)$) =
reverse ((reverse l) $* [a]$) = [by lemma 3.11.2(ii)]
reverse (reverse l) = (by hypothesis)
W

∎

These results are computationally intuitive and reinforce the idea that infinite lists are to be regarded as being characterized by the information we can learn from them by finite investigations. Lemma 3.11.2(ii) tells us that if we append a list to the right of an infinite list then no amount of finite investigation of the result can distinguish it from the original list. These results do, however, contrast quite dramatically with the corresponding results for finite lists.

Proposition 3.11.2(iv)

For all lists l (finite and infinite);

map f (map g l) = **map (f ∘ g)** l.

Proof

Base step 1

> **map f** (**map** *g W*) =
> **map f** *W* =
> *W* =
> **map** (**f** ∘ **g**) *W*

since the second argument of **map** is active.

Base step 2

> **map** *f* (**map g** [ ]) =
> **map f** [ ] =
> [ ] =
> **map** (**f** ∘ **g**) [ ]

Induction step

> **map f**(**map g** (*a*:*l*)) =
> **map** *f* ((**g** *a*):(**map g** *l*)) =
> (**f** (**g** *a*)):(**map f** (**map g** *l*)) = (by hypothesis)
> ((**f** ∘ **g**) *a*):(**map** ((**f** ∘ **g**) *l*)) =
> **map** (**f** ∘ **g**) (*a*:*l*)

■

This result is an example of a property enjoyed by all data structures whether finite or infinite. Moreover, it is an interesting relationship between two higher-order operators (composition and **map**). We will see many more examples of such relationships in Chapter 5.

In fact lemma 3.11.2(ii) suggests that **append** is *not* a useful way of combining the information in two infinite lists. For example, if *l* and *l'* are two infinite lists then if (**member** *a l*) holds (the leaf *a* appears in a finite prefix of *l*) we might expect that (**member** *a* (*l'* ∗ *l*)) holds. Clearly, by appealing to lemma 3.11.2(ii), this is just (**member** *a l'*); and this does not necessarily hold.

We should like a way of combining lists in a way which ensures that information accessible in a finite time in each list is still accessible in the result. This leads us to define a function **interlace** (but we use the infix ★ more often):

> **def** (*a*:*l*) ★ *l'* = *a*:(*l'* ★ *l*)

Notice how similar this is to **append**. This function can be extended to all lists, if required, by the extra clause:

def [ ] $\star l = l$

interlace has the type:

$(\forall \alpha)\, (\text{List}\ (\alpha) \to \text{List}\ (\alpha) \to \text{List}\ (\alpha))$

Exercise 3.11.2(v)

Show that if (**member** $a\ l$) then (**member** $a\ (l' \star l)$), for *all* lists l and l'.
■

Exercise 3.11.2(vi)

(a) Define a program which merges two, ordered, infinite lists of numbers.
(b) Define a program which, given an infinite list of leaves, removes any duplicate entries.
(c) What properties does **interlace** possess?
■

3.11.3 List comprehension

Exercise 3.11.2(v) contains a very important observation. After all the joining of lists by **append** is a very common part of many programs. The problem of accessing certain elements of infinite lists can percolate through and destroy many properties of more sophisticated programs. A good example of this is the cartesian product program of example 3.8(xii). If l' is infinite (say $[1, 2, 3, \dots]$) and l is finite (say ["A", "B"]) the program ($l\ \&\ l'$) generates the output: [["A", "1"], ["A", 2], ["A", 3], \dots] and no pair beginning with a "B" can ever be accessed in a finite number of steps. This not really satisfactory and we can do better by using the **interlace** connective instead of **append** in the definition of **smooth**. Thus:

def smooth = **reduce interlace** [ ]

Now *all* pairs can be accessed in a finite number of steps. Predicting the order in which the pairs appear is quite entertaining!

We do seem to be losing the ordering information which one usually associates with lists. For this reason some authors prefer to treat these data structures more like *sets* or at least *bags* (unordered collections which may have duplicate entries) but we will continue to refer to them as lists.

A large number of programs can be written by generating a stream of pairs (or triples and so on) by a cartesian product operation and then filtering the result for certain properties.

Example 3.11.3(i) (Turner)

The task is to generate *Pythagorean triples*. To do this we generate all possible triples and then filter them for the appropriate property.

> **ptrips = filter istriple (cross ints ints ints)**
> **istriple** $[x\ y\ z]$ = "True" **when** $(x * x) + (y * y) = z * z$
> **istriple** 1 = "False"

■

In the language KRC, Turner (1982a), having recognized the ubiquity of this programming device, introduced a notation for *list comprehension* which simplifies the presentation of many programs.

A *list abstract* will be written $[e | g_1, \ldots, g_n; p]$ where each of the g_i $(1 \le i \le n)$ is a *generator*, p is a *predicate* and e is an *expression* (involving variables introduced by the generators). A generator has the form $x \leftarrow e$ where x is a variable (this is a binding occurrence of the variable x) and e is an expression which yields a list.

Example 3.11.3(ii)

The Pythagorean triples can be generated by the following list abstract:
ptrips $= [[x\ y\ z] | x \leftarrow$ **ints**, $y \leftarrow$ **ints**, $z \leftarrow$ **ints**; $(x * x) + (y * y) = z * z]$
■

The use of square brackets to surround a list abstract is no coincidence (with its use around lists of elements). It reinforces the idea that such objects are simply lists themselves.

It seems pretty clear that these list abstracts are in a sense syntactic sugar. It was, however, a very important discovery to isolate this as a powerful programming concept and introduce a special syntax for it.

Desugaring these expressions is for the most part quite straightforward. Given $[e | g_1, \ldots, g_n; p]$ the fragment following the vertical bar is just: (**filter** p (**cross** $e_1 \ldots e_n$)) when each of the g_i has the form: $x_i \leftarrow e_i (1 \le i \le n)$. The result of this expression is a stream of *n-tuples* of the form $[v_1 \ldots v_n]$. Each of these has to be processed according to the expression e.

Exercise 3.11.3(iii)

Suppose that e is given by the following grammar of expressions:

exp : : = c (constants, including function names)
    : : = x_i (variables introduced by the generators)
    : : = (exp exp) (applications)

Show how the filtered lists should be processed for arbitrary e.
■

In practice it is useful to extend the definition of a generator to: $p \leftarrow e$, where p is a pattern. This would allow:

Example 3.11.3(iv)

Let l and l' be lists of pairs of integers. These should be regarded as relations over integers. The *composition* of l and l' can be defined as an infix operator, $\circ$, as follows:

$$\mathbf{def}\ l \circ l' = [[x\ y] | [x\ z] \leftarrow l, [z'\ y] \leftarrow l'; (\mathbf{eq}\ z\ z')]$$

■

Desugaring these more complex list abstractions is not a lot more difficult than the simple ones. The reader might like to save the next exercise until after Chapter 6 in which patterns are discussed again from an implementational point of view.

Exercise 3.11.3(v)

Show how list abstracts of the form:

$$[e\ |\ p_1 \leftarrow l_1, \ldots, p_n \leftarrow l_n; q]$$

can be programmed in terms of cartesian products and filtering.
■

3.12 Exceptions and escapes

When exceptional situations occur during program execution some action has to be taken. In some situations an indication of the problem can be passed back through the calling sequence of functions and in others (often when programming in an imperative language) an abrupt change in control can be effected.

Example 3.12(i)

As a very simple example consider the following program, defined over sexpressions, S:

> **value** $a = a$ **when (numeric** a)
> **value** $a =$ "FAIL" **otherwise**
>
> **sumints** $= \mathbf{h}_S$ **add value**; that is:
> **sumints** $(s_1 : s_2) = ($**sumints** $s_1) + ($**sumints** $s_2)$
> **sumints** a $=$ **value** a

Since the error indicator ("FAIL") percolates back through the calling sequence we need to extend addition (which we write as $+$ or as **plus**) so that:

> "FAIL" $+ n$ $=$ "FAIL"
> $n +$ "FAIL" $=$ "FAIL"
> "FAIL" $+$ "FAIL" $=$ "FAIL"

If we define a new type, $NFL = N + \{$"FAIL"$\}$ we can provide the types of these functions:

> **sumints** has type: $S \rightarrow NFL$
> **plus** has type: $NFL \rightarrow NFL \rightarrow NFL$

Thus operations on arguments which can raise an exception need to be extended so that they can cope with exceptional values. In this example we arrange for the failure to be *preserved* by the addition operator although other alternatives (such as treating all "FAIL" values as if they were zero) are possible.

■

Example 3.12(ii)

In this example we just look for a numeric atom in an sexpression.

> **findnum** $(s_1 : s_2) = $ **if** (**eq** x "FAIL") (**findnum** s_2) x **where** $x = ($**findnum** $s_1)$
> **findnum** a $= a$ **when (numeric** a)
> **findnum** a $=$ "FAIL"   **when (not (numeric** a))

Now we can encapsulate this behaviour over failure by introducing:

> $e_1 ? e_2 = $ **if** (**eq** x "FAIL") e_2 x **where** $x = e_1$

This only works when the evaluation is lazy, that is for our purposes, by the canonical operational semantics. If evaluation were applicative the new program, ?, would evaluate its arguments (whereas the explicit conditional expression appearing on the right-hand side of the equation will not).

Assuming that programs are evaluated by the canonical evaluation we can rewrite the definition above:

findnum $(s_1 : s_2) =$ (**findnum** s_1) ? (**findnum** s_2)
findnum a $\quad = a$ $\quad$ **when (numeric** a)
findnum a $\quad =$ "FAIL" **when (not (numeric** a))

This contrasts with example 3.12(i) because here we obtain a result provided at least one number is found.

■

The two examples serve to outline two different ways of combining programs which may give rise to exceptional values. The first, described in example 3.12(i) is a kind of *conjunction* which yields results when all arguments are defined. The second, in example 3.12(ii), is defined when at least one argument yields a non-"FAIL" result. This is a kind of *disjunction*.

We shall see in the next section how this observation generalizes to more sophisticated programming.

We mentioned that there is an alternative approach to the handling of exceptions which forces an abrupt change in control. In an imperative language this is the most likely context in which a *global jump* is considered. This can be undertaken because, in an imperative language, a global context (the state of accessible variables) is always present (although not explicitly so). In a functional language such a global context is not available and it may seem as if an analogous form of exception handling is not available. This is not the case, for even if a large implicit state is not available, some explicit context is often represented by the argument values a program can manipulate. The following example shows how example 3.12(i) can be reworked in this way.

Example 3.12(iii)

The program **sumints** can be written using an accumulating parameter.

sumints s $\quad =$ **sints** s 0
sints $(s_1 : s_2)$ $n =$ **sints** s_1 (**sints** s_2 n)
sints a n $\quad = a + n$ **when (numeric** a)
sints a n $\quad =$ "FAIL" **when (not (numeric** a))

sints has type: $S \rightarrow NFL \rightarrow NFL$

If we consider the program operationally we might think that the accumulator holds an integer, but this is to assume applicative evaluation. In general the accumulator holds an unevaluated expression which, *if reduced*, yields an element of *NFL*. The reader who does not immediately grasp this point is encouraged to revise Section 3.6 and, in particular, to attempt exercise 3.6(ix) (d) and exercise 3.12(iv) below. The fourth equation actually *ignores* the accumulator when the exceptional circumstance is encountered. Under canonical evaluation we save the computational cost of evaluating the expression which forms the accumulator. We can think of the accumulator as a *context* which can be accessed (as it is during a successful call to **sumints**), or indeed ignored (when an exceptional situation is encountered). It is important to note that under applicative evaluation the benefit of avoiding unnecessary computation is not felt. In an applicative regime it might be necessary to try to find a new program with improved operational characteristics by using techniques which we have introduced earlier [see, for example, example 3.4.2(iv), exercise 3.9(iii) and the paragraphs preceeding it].

Exercise 3.12(iv)

To gain a deeper operational insight into these issues it may be useful to run through the (normal and applicative) evaluation of: (**sumints** [3, "*B*", 5, 6, 7, 9, 1, 6]).
∎
∎

In Chapter 4 we will see how certain programs can be *transformed* into this style by means of special context functions called *continuations*. These are functional arguments which as the name suggests, are the place where partial results should be delivered so that computation can continue. In fact we have seen an example of continuation programming before: recall that in the lambda calculus pairing was defined as:

> **pair** $= \lambda xy \cdot \lambda z \cdot zxy$

The third argument z here is a continuation. This third argument is a function to which the two parts of the pair are supplied. In particular this continuation will be a selector function. **sumints** can be written in this style too:

Example 3.12(v)

> **sumints** n $\quad =$ **sints** n **id**
> **sints** $s_1 : s_2\, f =$ **sints** s_1 $(\lambda n \cdot (\textbf{sints}\ s_2\ (f \circ (\textbf{plus}\ n))))$
> **sints** $a\, f$ $\quad = (f\, a)$ **when** (**numeric** a)
> **sints** $a\, f$ $\quad = (f\, \text{"FAIL"})$

sints has the type: $S \rightarrow (NFL \rightarrow NFL) \rightarrow NFL$

But given our knowledge of the way that **plus** treats the value "FAIL" it is easy [we do it formally in example 4.8(i)] to see that $(f\text{"FAIL"} = \text{"FAIL"})$ for all continuations f *that* **sints** *can take as a result of the definition.* Thus we may rewrite this program:

sumints n = **sints** n **id**
sints $(s_1:s_2) f$ = **sints** s_1 $(\lambda n \cdot (\textbf{sints}\ s_2.(f \circ (\textbf{plus}\ n))))$
sints $a f$ = $(f\ a)$ **when** (**numeric** a)
sints $a f$ = "FAIL" **when** (**not** (**numeric** a))

Note that the natural control context, f, can be bypassed on encountering an error by virtue of the fourth clause above. It is also interesting to see that **plus** is never expected to accept "FAIL" as an argument in this program and so need not be extended, as it was above, to cope with these exceptional circumstances.
∎

Exercise 3.12(vi)

Check that all these definitions of **sumints** are equivalent.
∎

Quite complicated exception handling can be undertaken with continuations; although the extra machinery can be rather cumbersome as the next example shows.

Example 3.12(vii)

In this example we would like to be able to define places in a computation which should be returned to if an exception is encountered. Since there may be several different exceptional circumstances to consider, in general we might require several different (named) target points to be set up at any time. The targets for these exceptions are called *catch points* and the points at which exceptions are raised are called *throw points*. The terminology is clear: catch points are able to intercept exceptional values thrown to them from the sites of exceptions. To set this up we need to extend every function (let us say f of type $X \to Y$) with two further arguments. Firstly a *catch table* and secondly a current continuation. If we assume two types CT and $CONT$ for these we see that f becomes a function of type:

$$X \to CT \to CONT \to Y$$

The extension is actually not immediate for we really need to develop a related program f' (from f) which uses the continuation systematically. A method for doing this is discussed in Section 4.9. For the present we will not concern ourselves with the details. Thus we write $(f x\ p\ \theta)$ instead of $(f x)$ where p is the catch table and θ the continuation. Let us now turn to the question of the types CT and $CONT$.

To begin with let us introduce a type CP (catch pairs) by:

$$CP = C \times CONT \times \{\text{``Nil''}\}$$

Continuations are given by:

$$CONT = X \rightarrow Y$$

Then we can define the catch tables as follows:

$$CT = \text{List}(CP)$$

Exercise 3.12(viii)

Let p be a catch table of the form:

$$[[\text{``}A_1\text{''}, f_1], \ldots, [\text{``}A_n\text{''}, f_n]]$$

Write a function (**lookup** $a\ p$) whose type is: $C \rightarrow CT \rightarrow CONT$ and which returns the continuation associated with the first pair whose atom is a. Write a program (**extend** $a\ f\ p$) of type $C \rightarrow CONT \rightarrow CT \rightarrow CT$ and which adds a new pair to p.
∎

Given this we may introduce a program called **catch** which sets up a named catch point.

      catch $a\ f\ x\ p\ \theta = f x$ (**extend** $a\ \theta\ p$) θ
      catch has type: $C \rightarrow (X \rightarrow CT \rightarrow CONT \rightarrow Y) \rightarrow X \rightarrow CT \rightarrow CONT \rightarrow Y$

This function evaluates f at argument x in the presence of an extended catch table (recording the details of the new catch point named a).

We can also set up a function **throw** which casts its value to a named catch.

      throw $a\ f\ x\ p\ \theta = f x\ p$ (**lookup** $a\ p$)

throw has the type:

$$C \rightarrow (X \rightarrow CT \rightarrow CONT \rightarrow Y) \rightarrow X \rightarrow CT \rightarrow CONT \rightarrow Y$$

This is actually rather more difficult to understand. (**lookup** $a\ p$) clearly provides us with the appropriate continuation to which we wish to throw the value $f x$ (Note in particular how θ does not appear on the right-hand side).

However we might have expected something like:

throw $a f x p \theta = ((\textbf{lookup } a p) (f x \theta))$

However it is perfectly possible that f itself contains a throw expression and the ultimate result of this ought to bypass the throw we (thought) we were setting up. Should f contain such a subexpression then the continuation (**lookup** $a p$) (in the correct definition of **throw**) can be ignored in the same manner.

■

This example goes some way toward showing how what look like highly imperative programming features can be described in a functional language. Although we rarely have to resort to such exotic programming in practice these styles are useful for specifying the semantics of arbitrary programming languages (which we explore indirectly in Chapter 8). Moreover, these programs can often serve as the basis for further program development by transformation (which will be demonstrated in the next chapter).

3.13 Backtracking

It has recently been observed by Wadler (1985) that there is a close connection between the *conjunctive* and *disjunctive* operations of the last section, which were then aspects of exception handling, and similar operations which are required to program backtracking behaviour.

In this section we shall follow Wadler and think of a program as producing not "FAIL" or a single value but a list of values. This may be empty (a kind of failure situation) or it may possess any number of results. As a first example we will recast the **findnum** program of example 3.12(ii) in this fashion.

Example 3.13(i)

> **findnum** $(s_1 : s_2) = (\textbf{findnum } s_1) ? (\textbf{findnum } s_2)$
> **findnum** $a \qquad = [a]$ **when** (**numeric** a)
> **findnum** $a \qquad = [\ ]$ **when** (**not** (**numeric** a))

Here we will redefine the disjunctive operation as follows:

$e_1 ? e_2 = e_1 * e_2$

This is, perhaps, a surprising result. The point is that under lazy evaluation this program will generate all the solutions *on demand*. That is the appended list is not generated in extension until it is completely investigated by some enclosing process.

Note that, now, the type of **findnum** is $S \rightarrow L$.

■

Now suppose that we would like to add together the numbers generated by **findnum** from two sexpressions. In the last section we had to cope with two circumstances: either both generate a result or else one (or both) fail. In the context of backtracking we may get any number of results. Clearly, if we get no results from one or other (or both) we get no sum. On the other hand if we obtain several results from each we will generate a lot of different sums. Indeed for each value generated by one we get a sum formed by combining this value with all values generated by the other. Thus if we write:

$$\textbf{(findnum } (3:4)) + \textbf{(findnum } (1:(2:3)))$$

we require the result: [4, 5, 6, 5, 6, 7]

This suggests that the appropriate generalization of conjunction is the *cartesian product*.

Thus a binary operator like **plus** is to be extended to:

$$e_1 \blacksquare e_2 = \textbf{map (plus) } (e_1 \ \& \ e_2)$$

The extended addition operator, $\blacksquare$, has type:

$$\text{List}(N) \rightarrow \text{List}(N) \rightarrow \text{List}(N)$$

The order in which solutions are generated depends on the mechanism that **cart** (the operator, &, of Section 3.8) uses to generate the pairs.

These techniques can be used to write programs which require general backtracking behaviour.

Example 3.13(ii)

We will consider paths in a directed acylic graph:

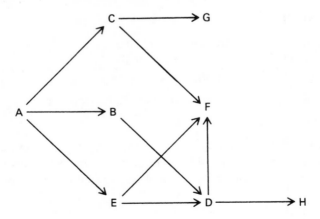

Fig. 3.13(iii)

We will represent Fig. 3.13(iii) by the following structure:

[["*A*", ["*B*", "*C*", "*E*"]], ["*B*", ["*D*"]], ["*C*", ["*F*", "*G*"]], ["*D*", ["*F*",
"*H*"]], ["*E*", ["*D*", "*F*"]], ["*F*", [ ]], ["*G*", [ ]], ["*H*", [ ]]]

More exactly we define a type, *DAG*, as follows:

DAG = List(*FP*)

where, *FP*, the type of *frontier pairs* is:

FP = *Node* × *Frontier* × {"Nil"}

where, *Frontier*, the type of *frontiers*, and, *Node*, the type of *graph node* are:

Frontier = List (*Node*)
Node   = *C*

First we define a simple function **frontier** which, given a node in the graph,
produces the nodes accessible in one arc.

frontier *a* [ ]   = [ ]
frontier *a* ([*b*, *l*]:*l*′) = *l* **when (eq** *a* *b*)
frontier *a* ([*b*, *l*]:*l*′) = (**frontier** *a* *l*′) **otherwise**

this clearly has type: *Node* × *DAG* → *Frontier*.

We are going to define a program (**route** *g* *y* *x*) whose value is *the routes in
graph g from x to y* (the ordering of these arguments will become clearer given
the definition!). This involves elements of disjunction and conjunction in the
sense described above. Consider the routes from "*A*" to "*F*". Given that the
frontier of "*A*" is ["*B*", "*C*", "*D*"] we see that a route from "*A*" to "*F*" is a route
from "*A*" to "*B*" and one from "*B*" to "*F*", or a route from "*A*" to "*C*" and one
from "*C*" to "*F*", or one from "*A*" to "*E*" and one from "*E*" to "*F*". In fact the
first route in all these alternatives is a single arc so the cartesian product
reduces to the **cons** of this single arc to all the solutions generated for the
second route in the alternative. Thus, a route in the graph is a list of nodes and
we can make this plain by: *Route* = List (*Node*). The program may be written
as follows:

route *g* *y* *x* = [[*x*]] **when (eq** *x* *y*)
route *g* *y* *x* = [ ] **when (frontier** *g* *x*) = [ ]
route *g* *y* *x* = **map** (**cons** *x*) (**smooth** (**map** (**route** *g* *y*) (**frontier** *g* *x*)))

The type of **route** is *DAG* → *Node* → *Node* → *Route*.

In this example the number of alternatives, at each stage, depends on the size of the frontier so the alternative construct (**append**) is generalized (by **reduce** to the program **smooth**) to an arbitrary number of arguments.

Suppose we want the number of routes in g from x to y which pass through a node z. This requires the full power of the conjunction operation. If (**route** g z x) gives all routes **from** x to z and (**route** g y z) gives all routes from z to y then (**routethrough** g z y x) will need to construct all possible combinations of the solutions to the two expressions above. Thus

routethrough g z y x = **map zappend** ((**route** g z x) & (**route** g y z))

Partial routes are spliced using **append** and we remarked above that if f is a combining operation then its generalization for backtracking is: (**map** f) ∘ **cart**. **zappend** is roughly the program **append**. Its definition is left as an easy exercise which can be solved by careful consideration of the types involved.

■

Example 3.13(iv)

These backtracking operations can be useful for generating relations, as this example shows. Consider the following family tree:

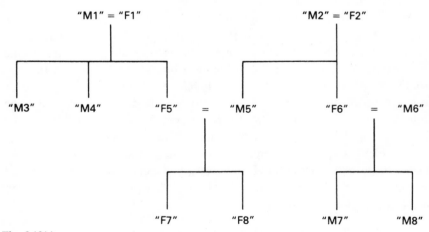

Fig. 3.13(v)

This can be described by providing a few relations (in extension)

> **male**   = ["$M1$", "$M2$", ..., "$M8$"]
> **female** = ["$F1$", "$F2$", ..., "$F8$"]

wife $= [[``F1", ``M1"], \ldots, [``F6", ``M6"]]$
father $= [[``M1", ``M3"], [``M1", ``M4"], \ldots, [``M6", ``M8"]]$

Other relations may now be derived from these. An elementary example might be **husband** = (**map swap wife**) where **swap** $[x, y] = [y, x]$ as usual. More complicated relations can be built using the disjunctive and conjunctive operations ? and &. Being a parent consists in being a father or a mother. Being a mother consists in being the wife of a father. We can write this easily:

> **parent** = **father**? **mother** and
> **mother** = **con1** (**wife** & **father**)

where **con1** is a consistency filter on **wife** & **father** and can be defined by

> **con1** [ ] $= [\ ]$
> **con1** ([[x, y] [w, z]]: l) $= [x, z]:($**con1** l) **when** $(y = w)$
> **con1**(v: l) $=$ **con1** l **otherwise**

The form of **con1** is very common and we can introduce a useful generalized consistency filter for this form:

> **con** $p \ q$ [ ] $= [\ ]$
> **con** $p \ q$ $(v: l) = (q \ v):($**con** $p \ q \ l)$ **when** $(p \ v)$
> **con** $p \ q$ $(v: l) =$ **con** $p \ q \ l$ **otherwise**

Thus we define: **mother** = **con pm qm** (**wife** & **father**) where:

> **pm** [$[x, y], [w, z]] =$ "True" **when** $(y = w)$
> **pm** v $=$ "False" **otherwise**
> **qm** $[[x, y], [w, z]] = [x \ z]$

Exercise 3.13(vi)

Define relations for **grandfather** and **brother**.
∎

A more complicated example is:

> **brotherinlaw** = (**con pb qb** (**brother** & **spouse**))?
> (**con pb qb** (**husband** & **sister**))

where **pb** = **pm** and **qb** = **qm**.

Note how this kind of programming is based on disjunctive and conjunctive searching and pattern matching (in the consistency filtering).

The use of set expressions can considerably simplify this style of programming:

$$\begin{aligned}
\textbf{mother} \quad &= \{[x\ z] \mid [x\ y] \leftarrow \textbf{wife}, [y, z] \leftarrow \textbf{father}\} \\
\textbf{brotherinlaw} \quad &= \{[x\ z] \mid [x\ y] \leftarrow \textbf{brother}, [y\ z] \leftarrow \textbf{spouse}\}\ ? \\
&\quad \{[x\ z] \mid [x\ y] \leftarrow \textbf{husband}, [y\ z] \leftarrow \textbf{sister}\} \\
\textbf{childrenof } x \quad &= \{y \mid [x\ y] \leftarrow \textbf{parent}\} \\
\textbf{aunt} \quad &= \{[x\ z] \mid [x\ y] \leftarrow \textbf{sibling}, [y, z] \leftarrow \textbf{parent}\}
\end{aligned}$$

■

Exercise 3.13(vii)

Define as many relationships as you can based on the following primitives: **all** (the *universal relation* containing everyone); **male** (as before); **spouse** and **parent**.
■

Example 3.13(viii)

An obvious application for these programming techniques is in syntax analysis. This example is based on techniques described in Wadler (1985) applied to problems described in Henderson (1980). The reader is encouraged to follow up these references to see further examples and alternative solutions.

The following is a toy syntax for English syllables in BNF notation.

$$\begin{aligned}
\langle\text{consseq}\rangle &::= \text{``}C\text{''} \mid \text{``}C\text{''}\ \langle\text{consseq}\rangle &&\text{(consonant sequences)} \\
\langle\text{vowlseq}\rangle &::= \text{``}V\text{''} \mid \text{``}V\text{''}\ \langle\text{vowlseq}\rangle &&\text{(vowel sequences)} \\
\langle\text{syllable}\rangle &::= \langle\text{consseq}\rangle\ \langle\text{vowlseq}\rangle \mid \langle\text{vowlseq}\rangle\ \langle\text{consseq}\rangle \mid \\
&\qquad \langle\text{consseq}\rangle\ \langle\text{vowlseq}\rangle\ \langle\text{consseq}\rangle
\end{aligned}$$

We wish to write a syntax analyser for this grammar. That is, a program which not only recognizes that certain patterns of Cs and Vs are syllables but also yields a data structure which makes the syntactical structure explicit. In other words a *parse tree*.

The program will take a list of the atoms "C" and "V" as input and return either [ ] (for failure) or else a pair consisting of a parse tree and the remaining unparsed part of the input list. Thus given input ["V", "C", "V"] the program should yield [[[["V"]], [["C"]]], ["V"]] where [[[["V"]], [["C"]]] is the structural description of the sequence ["V", "C"] (which is a syllable according to the grammar) and ["*V*"] is the rest of the input. Other examples are:

> **parse** ["*V*"]   =[ ] (which is a failure)
> **parse** ["*C*", "*C*", "*V*", "*C*", "*C*", "*C*"] =
>   [[[["*C*"], ["*C*"]], [["*V*"]], [["*C*"], ["*C*"], ["*C*"]]], [ ]]

(which is a completely successful parse).

We start to develop this program from some simple "parsers" for individual consonants and vowels:

> **consonant** [ ]   =[ ]
> **consonant** ("*C*":*l*) =[[[["*C*"]], *l*]
> **consonant** ("*V*":*l*) =[ ]
> **vowel** [ ]   =[ ]
> **vowel** ("*C*":*l*)   =[ ]
> **vowel** ("*V*":*l*)   =[[[["*V*"]], *l*]

These are the basic recognizers and have to be combined to recognize more complex patterns. A glance at the syntax is enough to convince us that we sometimes need to recognize one pattern *and* another (for example in ⟨consseq⟩ ::= "*C*" ⟨consseq⟩) and, at other times, one pattern *or* another (for example ⟨vowlseq⟩ ::= "*V*" | "*V*" ⟨vowlseq⟩).

It seems then that the basic structuring devices of the notation for grammars correspond to our disjunction and conjunction operations.

Let us start with the new operator | which clearly is related to our ? operation. If we had a syntactic clause with right-hand side ("*C*" | "*V*") we should want the program that corresponds to it to succeed whatever the head of the input list. Thus, we would expect the following two equations to hold:

bar consonant vowel ["*C*", "*V*", "*V*"]=[[[["*C*"]], ["*V*", "*V*"]] and also:
bar consonant vowel ["*V*", "*C*", "*C*"]=[[[["*V*"]], ["*C*", "*C*"]]

we can thus define:

> **bar** $f_1 f_2\, l = (f_1\, l)\,?\,(f_2\, l)$

Juxtaposition in the grammar is clearly related to our & operation. Given a syntax rule right-hand side starting ("*C*" "*V*") we need to ensure that the program, which corresponds to juxtaposition, should succeed only when the input list starts ["*C*", "*V*" . . . . Thus: **jux consonant vowel** ["*C*", "*V*", "*V*", "*C*"] should be equal to [[[["*C*"] ["*V*"]] ["*V*" "*C*"]] whilst, for example, we would expect: **jux consonant vowel** ["*C*", "*C*", "*V*", "*V*"]=[ ].

However this is not quite right. We need to explain how the successful matches are to be combined to give the final result. We will actually write: (**jux append consonant vowel**). That is, we take an *action* as an argument too. All this suggests we set:

jux $g\, f_1 f_2\, l =$
$[[(g\, r_1\, r_2)\; \text{rest}] \,|\, [r_1\; \text{rest}'] \leftarrow (f_1\, l),\, [r_2\; \text{rest}] \leftarrow (f_2\; \text{rest}')]$

Exercise 3.13(ix)

To see how convenient programming becomes when we have list comprehension rewrite **jux** explicitly in terms of cartesian products and filtering.
■

The program can now be given in full.

> **syllable** = **bar** (**jux list consseq vowlseq**)
> (**bar** (**jux list vowlseq consseq**) (**jux cons consseq** (**jux list vowlseq consseq**)))
>
> **consseq** = **bar consonant** (**jux append consonant consseq**)
> **vowlseq** = **bar vowel** (**jux append vowel vowlseq**)

Exercise 3.13(x)

The program above exemplifies a common situation, namely the need to extend operators like **bar** and **jux** to arbitrary numbers of arguments. Define programs **barlist** and **juxlist** that do this. The following programs should help:

> **empty** $v\, l = [v,\, l]$

This program succeeds with value v against no portion of l.

> **fail** $l = [\;\;]$

This program simply fails against any input.
■

Exercise 3.13(xi)

Write a program (in terms of ones we have developed) which repeatedly matches a pattern against the input until it fails. This program (call it **repeat**) should yield all matches, including (always) the empty match.
■

Finally, the results of a parse can be *interfaced* to a program which requires structured input by means of:

interface $f\,l = f\,v$ **where** $[v,\ [\ \ ]] = ($**parse** $l)$

This fails if (**parse** l) does not produce a complete parse.

Project 3.13(xii)

Define a grammar of arithmetic expressions. Write a parser using the techniques developed in this section. Write an evaluator which expects its input to be a parsed expression. Link the programs using the function **interface**.
■

3.14 Bibliographic notes

Other texts dealing with functional programming include Henderson (1980), Glaser *et al.* (1984) and Curien (1986), although this latter book is rather technical.

Abelson & Sussman (1985) develop a good deal of material from a purely functional perspective but also include a good deal of work with imperative features too. Darlington *et al.* (1982) is a collection of papers on the theme of functional programming and languages and their implementation.

Program verification techniques for conventional programming languages are given excellent presentations in Gries (1981), Backhouse (1986) and Manna & Waldinger (1985). Manna *et al.* (1973) is a good tutorial for inductive techniques and program verification. Loeckx & Sieber (1984) is well worth studying. It is very comprehensive and technically complete.

Readers who would like to learn more about the complexity of programs can do no better than start with Aho *et al.* (1974) a deservedly famous text on the subject.

In Section 3.8 we stressed the algebraic flavour of functional programming in an elementary way. This perspective is currently the subject of great research interest. Rydeheard's thesis (1981) develops connections between programing and category theory. Category theory is somewhat beyond the scope of this book but an interested reader could look at Arbib & Manes (1975) to begin with.

Lazy evaluation is discussed in Henderson (1980) and lazy program verification in Turner's papers (1982b) and (1984). Henderson & Morris (1976) describe an evaluator for lazy execution as do Friedman & Wise (1976). Both of these proceed by explaining how lazy evaluation can be effected on an otherwise applicative architecture. This will be taken up again in Chapter 6 when we describe Turner's approach to functional language implementation. Goldberg & Paige (1984) develop some techniques for programming with lazy data structures.

Data abstraction and modular structure are discussed in Milner (1984) and in particular in MacQueen (1984). The background and theory of types which we described in this chapter are to be found in Strachey (1967), Hindley (1969) and Milner (1978).

Abelson, H. & Sussman, G. J. (1985) *Structure and Interpretation of Computer Programs.* MIT Press, Cambridge, Mass.

Aho, A. V., Hopcroft, J. E. & Ullman, J. D. (1974) *The Design and Analysis of Computer Algorithms.* Addison-Wesley, Reading, Mass.

Arbib, M. & Manes, E. (1975) *Arrows, Structures and Functors: The Categorical Imperative.* Academic Press, New York.

Backhouse, R. C. (1986) *Program Construction and Verification.* Prentice-Hall, Englewood Cliffs, NJ.

Clocksin, W. F. & Mellish C. S. (1981) *Programming in PROLOG.* Springer, Berlin.

Curien, P. (1986) *Categorial Combinators, Sequential Algorithms and Functional Programming.* Pitman, London.

Darlington, J., Henderson, P. & Turner, D. (eds) (1982) *Functional Programming and its Applications.* Cambridge University Press, Cambridge.

Friedman, D. P. & Wise, D. S. (1976) CONS should not evaluate its arguments. In *Automata, Languages and Programming.* S. Michaelson & R. Milner (eds), pp. 257–84. Edinburgh University Press, Edinburgh.

Glaser, H., Hankin, C. & Till, D. (1984) *Principles of Functional Programming.* Prentice-Hall, Englewood Cliffs, NJ.

Goldberg, A. & Paige, R. (1984) Stream processing. *Proc. 3rd ACM Conference on LISP and Functional Programming,* Austin, Texas.

Gries, D. (1981) *The Science of Programming.* Springer, Berlin.

Haynes, C. T. *et al.* (1984) Continuations and coroutines. *Proc. 3rd ACM Conference on LISP and Functional Programming,* Austin, Texas.

Hindley, R. (1969) The principal type scheme of an object in combinatory logic. *Trans. American. Mathematical Society,* **146**, 29–60.

Henderson, P. (1980) *Functional Programming – Application and Implementation.* Prentice-Hall, Englewood Cliffs, NJ.

Henderson, P. & Morris, J. H. (1976) A lazy evaluator. *Proc. 3rd ACM Symposium on Principles of Programming Languages,* Atlanta, Georgia.

Hughes, J. (1985) Lazy memo functions. *Proc. Conference on Functional Programming and Computer Architecture, LNCS,* Vol. 201. Springer, Berlin.

Loeckx, J. & Sieber, K. (1984) *The Foundations of Program Verification.* Wiley–Teubner series in computer science, Stuttgart.

MacQueen, D. (1984) Modules for standard ML. *Proc. 3rd ACM Conference on LISP and Functional Programming.* Austin, Texas.

Manna, Z. & Waldinger, R. (1985) *The Logical Basis for Computer Programming, Vol. 1: Deductive Reasoning.* Addison-Wesley, Reading, Mass.

Manna, Z., Ness, S. & Vuillemin, J. (1973) Inductive methods for proving properties of programs. *Commun. ACM*, **16**, 491–502.

Meira, S. L. (1982) Sorting algorithms in KRC. *UKC Computing laboratory report no. 14*, University of Kent.

Michie, D. (1968) 'Memo' functions and machine learning. *Nature*, **218**, 19–22.

Milner, R. (1978) A theory of type polymorphism in programming. *J. Computing System Science*, **17**, 348–75.

Milner, R. (1984) A proposal for standard ML. *Proc. 3rd ACM Conference on LISP and Functional Programming*, Austin, Texas.

Robinson, J. A. (1979) *Logic: Form and Function*. North-Holland, New York.

Rydeheard, D. E. (1981) *Applications of category theory to programming and specification*. Ph.D. thesis, University of Edinburgh.

Steele, G. L. & Sussman, G. J. (1975) SCHEME: an interpreter for extended lambda calculus. *AI memo 349*, Massachusetts Institute of Technology, AI Lab.

Strachey, C. (1967) Fundamental concepts in programming languages. Unpublished notes.

Tillotson, M. (1985) Introduction to the functional programming language PONDER. *Tech. report no. 65*, Computer Laboratory, University of Cambridge.

Turner, D. A. (1979) A new implementation technique for applicative languages. *Software, Practice and Experience*, **9**, 31–49.

Turner, D. A. (1981) The semantic elegance of applicative languages. *Proc. ACM Conference on Functional Programming Languages and Computer Architecture*.

Turner, D. A. (1982a) Recursion equations as a programming language. In *Functional Programming and its Applications*. J. Darlington *et al.* (eds), pp. 1–27. Cambridge University Press, Cambridge.

Turner, D. A. (1982b) Functional programming and proofs of program correctness. In *Tools and Notions for Program Construction*. D. Neel (ed.), pp. 187–209. Cambridge University Press.

Turner, D. A. (1984) Functional programs as executable specifications. In *Mathematical Logic and Programming Languages*. C. A. R. Hoare & J. C. Shepherdson (eds), pp. 29–54. Prentice-Hall, Englewood Cliffs, NJ.

Turner, D. A. (1985) MIRANDA: a non strict functional language with polymorphic types. *Proc. Conference on Functional Programming and Computer Architecture, LNCS*, Vol. 201. Springer, Berlin.

Wadler, P. (1984) *Listlessness is better than laziness*. Ph.D. thesis, Carnegie Mellon University.

Wadler, P. (1985) How to replace failure by a list of successes. *Proc. Conference on Functional Programming and Computer Architecture. LNCS*, Vol. 201. Springer, Berlin.

Winston, P. H. & Horn, B. K. P. (1981) *LISP*. Addison-Wesley, Reading, Mass.

Chapter 4

Program transformation

4.1 Introduction

In proposition 3.4(iv) we proved the following result:

$$(\text{for all } l_1, l_2) \text{ \textbf{length} } (l_1 * l_2) = (\textbf{length } l_1) + (\textbf{length } l_2)$$

This asserts that the two programs are equal, that is, they give equal results for equal arguments. This, we know, is more properly termed *extensional equality*. We made this idea precise in Chapter 2 by means of:

Definition 4.1(i)

Let $f_1, f_2 \in A \to B$; $f_1 = f_2$ iff $(\forall a \in A) ((f_1 \ a) = (f_2 \ a))$
∎

However, extensional equality is not sufficient in computer science as any practising programmer will testify. We need to concern ourselves with certain *intensional* properties of programs. For example, we are always concerned with how much space a program needs and how much time it requires to execute.

This was covered in Section 3.5 and, indeed, we spent some time in the previous chapter discussing alternative programming techniques which, whilst providing extensionally equivalent results (we usually proved as much), had significantly different *intensional* properties; in particular time and space characteristics. For example, we introduced several different ways to generate the fringe of an sexpression.

It has often been claimed that program clarity and program efficiency are rather incompatible. This observation suggests that we might establish a programming methodology in which clear but inefficient programs (that are easy to verify and possess desirable properties) may be systematically transformed (by correctness-preserving methods) into efficient although probably rather opaque final programs. In particular it may be possible to transform clear, but inefficient, program schemata into other, more efficient, schemata and therefore general techniques might be made available for a wide class of programs.

172

In languages which include assignment it is very much more difficult to exploit algebraic properties in order to improve efficiency. This is, of course, because assignment imposes a sequentiality and history dependence on the computation (which is not even textually evident) which casts some doubt on the most innocent transformations. Thus in the language C, for example, none of the following are necessarily true:

$$f(\ ) = = f(\ )$$
$$f(\ ) + g(\ ) = = g(\ ) + f(\ )$$
$$f(\ ) * (g(\ ) + h(\ )) = = f(\ ) * g(\ ) + f(\ ) * h(\ )$$

Of course, by constraining assignments to the locality of a procedure definition the above rules become valid. However, since procedural abstraction is just about the most important structuring tool in such languages such an imposition would be doing more than simply paying lip-service to functional programming styles! In fact, some PASCAL descendents, like the language EUCLID, have indeed banned non-local assignment.

At the level of source-to-source program transformation the majority of the research work has been done with functional languages and notations. It may be as well to let that testimony speak for itself.

In this chapter we will describe a methodology along the lines of that developed by Burstall & Darlington (1975) and which has been extended since by many authors, notably Bird (1984), Wand (1980) and Pettorossi (1984a).

4.2 Folding and unfolding

Let us turn to our example from the previous section which exhibited expressions for determining the length of two lists. Two (extensionally) equal expressions were given, namely:

length $(l_1 * l_2)$ and
(**length** l_1) + (**length** l_2)

which have very different intensional properties regarding evaluation and efficiency. For example, the first expression requires space in which to form the composite list whilst the second requires no space for data construction.

If we found ourselves in a programming context where we often need to compute the total **length** of two lists we might be inclined to write a special function for the job. Let us call this new function **length2** and it is to have type: $(\forall \alpha)(\text{List}(\alpha) \rightarrow \text{List}(\alpha) \rightarrow N)$. We are then duty bound to ensure that the following simple proposition holds:

(for all l_1, l_2); **length2** $l_1 \, l_2 = ($**length** $l_1) + ($**length** $l_2)$

Of course, a simple way of ensuring the truth of this is to *take this as the definition of* **length2**. Of course, this does nothing to improve the efficiency of the calculation and, indeed, by introducing another level of function definition might, for some evaluation strategies, make matters slightly worse. However, we might proceed from the simple proposition above rather differently. Suppose that we use this property as an *invariant* in the sense of Section 3.7. That is, we should find a program, **length2**, for which this property always holds. Providing this program is total we would have a correct solution because the property above amounts to a correctness criterion. Totality can be established in the ordinary way by finding a variant criterion which is well founded and by ensuring that it is reduced by recursive calls. Indeed many of the programs in the last chapter were derived from properties in the manner we are now proposing, although rather less formally. We now wish to place this kind of derivation on a more formal footing. As a start on this let us try to derive a program for **length2** from the property above.

Example 4.2(i)

If we set $l_1 = [\ \ ]$ in the above we obtain:

length2 $[\ \ ] \, l = ($**length** $[\ \ ]) + ($**length** $l)$

Now, by definition **length** $[\ \ ] = 0$ and so this is just:

$0 + ($**length** $l)$

or given an easy law of addition just:

length l

Now let us set $l_1 = a:l$ to obtain:

length2 $(a:l) \, l' = ($**length** $(a:l)) + ($**length** $l')$

which, by the definition of **length**, is:

$(1 + ($**length** $l)) + ($**length** $l')$

Now addition is associative so this is:

$1 + (($**length** $l) + ($**length** $l'))$

Now the bracketed expression is the right-hand side of the invariant; thus we may write:

$$1 + (\textbf{length2}\ l\ l')$$

If we summarize this argument we find that we have achieved the equations:

$$\textbf{length2}\ [\ \ ]\ l\ = \textbf{length}\ l$$
$$\textbf{length2}\ (a\!:\!l)\ l' = 1 + (\textbf{length2}\ l\ l')$$

which, presumably, is the program we might originally have independently conceived for the job and whose correctness we would now require. If however we assume that all the manipulations we undertook preserve correctness then the final program for **length2** is extensionally equivalent to the original definition.
∎

Exercise 4.2(ii)

At this point, the reader is invited to attempt to produce a version of **length2** from the alternative specification:

$$\textbf{length2}\ l_1\ l_2 = \textbf{length}\ (l_1 * l_2)$$

Use the previous example as a guide. The program you obtain should be the same as that we achieved in the previous example.
∎

Let us now be a little more precise and reflect carefully on the example we have undertaken so as to classify the steps we have used.

Invariant (INV)

We began by postulating an invariant:

$$\textbf{length2}\ l_1\ l_2 = (\textbf{length}\ l_1) + (\textbf{length}\ l_2)$$

In general, we will allow ourselves to do this whenever necessary marking such stages (INV). Thus we can write:

$$\textbf{length2}\ l_1\ l_2 = (\textbf{length}\ l_1) + (\textbf{length}\ l_2) \qquad\qquad 1\ (\text{INV})$$

In many cases the invariant property looks rather like a definition because, as in this example, the function we are developing occurs alone on the left-hand side. There is no harm in treating these as definitions; indeed it is beneficial to think of these definitions or invariants as *specifications*. These will be marked (SPEC).

Some equations we utilize are certainly definitions and such clauses are marked (DEF).

Sometimes the invariant property is rather hard to find; we will see that these steps get the special annotation (EUREKA).

In conclusion the reader is encouraged to see that the clauses we introduce can be considered from various viewpoints. We shall utilize the annotations (DEF), (INV), (SPEC) or (EUREKA) in order to emphasize particular perspectives.

Instantiation (INS)

At two points in the transformation we selected an equation and *instantiated a variable* to a particular value. In the example above we instantiated $l_1 = [\ ]$ at first and later $l_1 = a:l$. Such steps in the transformation we shall label (INS) and we may decorate this with an indication of the definition which has been instantiated. Thus we might write:

$$\textbf{length2 } [\ ]\ l_2 = (\textbf{length } [\ ]) + (\textbf{length } l_2) \qquad\qquad 2\ (\text{INS } 1)$$

Unfolding (UNF)

At several points we ran an equation from left to right; that is we replaced occurrences of a left-hand side of an equation by its right-hand side. This process is called *unfolding* and will be marked (UNF). Again we will decorate this with some indication of the equation being unfolded. Thus:

$$(\textbf{length } (a:l)) + (\textbf{length } l_2) = (1 + (\textbf{length } l)) + (\textbf{length } l_2)$$
$$3\ (\text{UNF } \textbf{length})$$

This transformation can be described in general terms as follows:

Let E_1, E_2, F_1 and F_2 be expressions then the notation $E_1[F_1 \leftarrow F_2]$ reads *replace instances of F_1 in E_1 by F_2* (cf. lambda calculus substitution in Chapter 2). Suppose we have equations $E_1 = E_2$ and $F_1 = F_2$ then unfolding the former in the latter means introducing the equation $F_1 = F_2[E_1 \leftarrow E_2]$.

Laws (LAW)

Once or twice we used known results, or laws, to simplify or rearrange our equations. The reader thinking us pedantic in stressing that $0 + (\textbf{length } l)$ is equal to $(\textbf{length } l)$ should now see that this was merely to indicate that in general we may deploy any law or property that we possess. We indicate these steps (LAW) and the decoration, if necessary, can refer to the law in question.

Thus:

$$(1 + (\textbf{length } l)) + (\textbf{length } l') = 1 + ((\textbf{length } l) + (\textbf{length } l'))$$

4 (ASSOC +)

Folding (FLD)

This transformation we used just once in our example, and as the name suggests, is related to unfolding. To fold an equation in an expression we replace instances of the right-hand side of the equation in the expression with the left-hand side. Instances of this transformation are marked (FLD) and can be decorated if necessary. Thus:

$$1 + ((\textbf{length } l) + (\textbf{length } l')) = 1 + (\textbf{length2 } l \ l') \qquad\qquad 5 \ (\text{FLD } l)$$

The general situation may be described as follows. Given $E_1 = E_2$ and $F_1 = F_2$ we fold the former in the latter by introducing the equation $F_1 = F_2[E_2 \leftarrow E_1]$.

Abstraction (ABS)

For completeness we describe a transformational step which we did not use in an example but which we will find useful later. Suppose we have an equation $E_1 = E_2$ then we may introduce the new equation $E_1 = \textbf{let } x = F \textbf{ in } E_2[F \leftarrow x]$. Recall that:

$$\textbf{let } x = e \textbf{ in } e'$$

is just syntactic sugar for $(\lambda x \cdot e')e$.

In practice our definitions have used patterns rather than simple variables so we will extend this abstraction transformation so that we may use patterns in place of x. Thus given the equation:

$$\textbf{f } x = \textbf{g } x \, (\textbf{h } x)$$

we might write:

$$\textbf{f } x = \textbf{let } u:v = x:(\textbf{h } x) \textbf{ in } (\textbf{g } u \, v)$$

instead of:

$$\textbf{f } x = (\lambda(u:v) \cdot \textbf{g } u \, v)(x:(\textbf{h } x))$$

As we remarked in the previous chapter, the operational semantics of lambda abstraction with respect to patterns will be covered in Chapter 6. If we follow the advice above carefully and annotate the steps the resulting transformation is easy to follow and indeed easy to produce. Here is example 4.2(i) in this style:

Example 4.2(iii)

length [ ]	$= 0$	1 (DEF)
length $(a\!:\!l)$	$= 1 + ($**length** $l)$	2 (DEF)
length2 $l\;l'$	$= ($**length** $l) + ($**length** $l')$	3 (SPEC)
length2 [ ] l'	$= ($**length** [ ] $) + ($**length** $l')$	4 (INS 3)
	$= 0 + ($**length** $l')$	5 (UNF 1)
	$= $ **length** l'	6 (LAW ID $+$)
length2 $(a\!:\!l)\;l'$	$= ($**length** $(a\!:\!l)) + ($**length** $l')$	7 (INS 3)
	$= (1 + ($**length** $l)) + ($**length** $l')$	8 (UNF 2)
	$= 1 + (($**length** $l) + ($**length** $l'))$	9 (LAW ASSOC $+$)
	$= 1 + $**length2** $l\;l'$	10 (FLD 3)

We take as our definition of **length2** lines 6 and 10.
■

Exercise 4.2(iv)

Rewrite exercise 4.2(ii) in this style.
■

Our example is a variation of one due to Burstall and Darlington. The exercises are their example. Solutions to the exercises can be found in Burstall & Darlington (1977).

Example 4.2(v)

The following program has been used in the literature to demonstrate simple program transformations:

> **f** n $= $ **f**$'$ 1 n
> **f**$'$ $m\;n = ($**reduce plus** 0) (**map square** (**upto** $m\;n$))

where:

> **upto** $m\;n = m\!:\!($**upto** $(m+1)\;n)$ **when** $m \leq n$
> **upto** $m\;n = [\ ]$ **when** $m > n$

> **upto** has type: $N \to N \to \text{List}(N)$
> **f**   has type: $N \to N$
> **f**$'$ has type: $N \to N \to N$

f produces the sum of the squares of the integers from 1 to n. The three parts of the program are connected together by means of intermediate data structures. These form the *glue* which holds the parts of the program together. Interestingly, in this example, the glue is formed of *intermediate lists* but the program actually processes integers.

Exercise 4.2(vi)

Write a program in PASCAL to achieve **f** specified above. Notice how all the actions of summing, squaring and iterating through the integers are combined. Moreover there are no immediate data structures; just the variables necessary to hold the result and a count.

■

Let $m > n$ then:

$$\mathbf{f'}\ m\,n = \mathbf{(reduce\ plus\ 0)\ (map\ square\ (upto\ } m\ n))$$
$$= \mathbf{(reduce\ plus\ 0)\ (map\ square\ [\ ])}$$
$$= \mathbf{(reduce\ plus\ 0)\ [\ ]}$$
$$= 0$$

Now let $m \leq n$ then:

$$\mathbf{f'}\ m\ n = \mathbf{(reduce\ plus\ 0)\ (map\ square\ (upto\ } m\ n))$$
$$= \mathbf{(reduce\ plus\ 0)\ (map\ square\ (} m: \mathbf{(upto\ (} m+1)\ n)))$$
$$= \mathbf{(reduce\ plus\ 0)\ (square\ } m): \mathbf{((map\ square\ (upto\ (} m+1)\ n)))$$
$$= \mathbf{plus\ (square\ } m)\ \mathbf{((reduce\ plus\ 0)\ (map\ square\ (upto\ (} m+1)\ n)))$$
$$= \mathbf{plus\ (square\ } m)\ \mathbf{(f'\ (} m+1)\ n) \qquad\qquad \text{(FLD)}$$

The transformed program is simply:

$$\mathbf{f}\ n\quad = \mathbf{f'}\ 1\ n$$
$$\mathbf{f'}\ m\,n = 0 \qquad\qquad\qquad\qquad\qquad \textbf{when } m > n$$
$$\mathbf{f'}\ m\,n = \mathbf{plus\ (square\ } m)\ \mathbf{(f'\ (} m+1)\ n) \quad \textbf{when } m \leq n$$

■

We now see that the role of the intermediate lists has been removed. This program can be improved further by other techniques we will describe later in the chapter. This style of program forms the basis for the ingenious transformations yielding *listless* evaluations due to Wadler (1984). See the bibliographic notes for further details.

In this example we used a definition (that of **f′**) as an invariant and a basis for transformation. In such a circumstance the program transformation can be viewed as a process of static optimization based on symbolic execution.

It is *not* the case however that all such transformations improve matters as the next example shows.

Example 4.2(vii)

Suppose we decide to represent sets as lists (in which atoms only occur once). We can specify the program to produce the *union* of two sets (we use infix $\oplus$ for this) as follows:

$$l_1 \oplus l_2 = l_1 * (\textbf{remove } l_1 \, l_2) \tag{SPEC}$$
$$\textbf{remove } l_1 \, l_2 = \textbf{reduce delete } l_2 \, l_1 \tag{DEF}$$

remove and $\oplus$ have type: $(\forall \alpha) \, (\text{List}(\alpha) \rightarrow \text{List}(\alpha) \rightarrow \text{List}(\alpha))$

$$
\begin{aligned}
[\ ] \oplus l &= [\ ] * (\textbf{remove } [\ ] l) & 1 \quad &(\text{INS}) \\
&= \textbf{remove } [\ ] \, l & 2 \quad &(\text{UNF}) \\
&= \textbf{reduce delete } l \, [\ ] & 3 \quad &(\text{UNF}) \\
&= l & 4 \quad &(\text{UNF}) \\
a{:}l_1 + l_2 &= a{:}l_1 * (\textbf{remove } (a{:}l_1) \, l_2) & 5 \quad &(\text{INS}) \\
&= a{:}(l_1 * (\textbf{remove } (a{:}l_1) \, l_2)) & 6 \quad &(\text{UNF}) \\
&= a{:}(l_1 * (\textbf{reduce delete } l_2 (a{:}l_1))) & 7 \quad &(\text{UNF}) \\
&= a{:}(l_1 * (\textbf{delete } a \, (\textbf{reduce delete } l_2 \, l_1))) & 8 \quad &(\text{UNF}) \\
&= a{:}(\textbf{delete } a \, (l_1 * (\textbf{reduce delete } l_2 \, l_1))) & 9 \quad &(\text{LEMMA}) \\
&= a{:}(\textbf{delete } a \, (l_1 * (\textbf{remove } l_1 \, l_2))) & 10 \quad &(\text{FLD}) \\
&= a{:}(\textbf{delete } a \, (l_1 \oplus l_2)) & 11 \quad &(\text{FLD})
\end{aligned}
$$

In summary we have:

$$
\begin{aligned}
[\ ] \oplus l &= l \\
a{:}l_1 \oplus l_2 &= a{:}(\textbf{delete } a \, (l_1 \oplus l_2))
\end{aligned}
$$

Lemma 4.2(viii)

$(\textbf{not} \, (\textbf{member } a \, l)) \Rightarrow l * (\textbf{delete } a \, l') = \textbf{delete } a \, (l * l')$

■

This lemma can be applied in the transformation because the antecedent (**not** (**member** a l)) holds by virtue of the fact that atoms are not repeated in those lists which represent sets. The problem is that the expression $(l * (\textbf{delete } a \, l'))$ is a

little more efficient (why?) than the expression (**delete** a $(l * l')$). The upshot of this is that the transformed program is inferior to the original.
∎

4.3 Duplicate computations

Rather more difficult and challenging is the task of taking the direct definition of some function and then finding some way of forcing a program transformation to improve efficiency. In previous examples the specification of the desired function was sufficient to force an improvement.

Consider the rather famous (but infamous from the efficiency standpoint!) program:

fib $0 = 1$	1 (DEF)
fib $1 = 1$	2 (DEF)
fib $n = (\textbf{fib}\,(n-1)) + (\textbf{fib}\,(n-2))$	3 (DEF)

We remarked in the previous chapter that the calculation of (**fib** n) requires (**fib** $(n+1)$) function calls. This algorithm is exponential in time with respect to the argument since the series itself produces an exponential growth.

Any attempt to transform this directly is nothing more than manual execution. We *could* introduce equations like (**fib** 2) = 2 and (**fib** 3) = 5 but little is being gained, unless we know the arguments we are likely to give to **fib** will lie in a very restricted range. In that case, however, we should probably have represented the function as a small *look-up table* anyhow.

What we need is an insight into the *structure of the inefficiency* and, from this, a suggestion for improving matters.

The insight we require needs to be formalized as a definition which can be used to obtain a new form of **fib** which is genuinely more efficient. Burstall & Darlington have termed the generation of this insightful definition the EUREKA step, an apt terminology which we will copy. The extent to which program transformation might be successfully automated seems to turn on the frequency with which EUREKA steps are required.

Example 4.3(i)

In the case of the function **fib** the reason for the horrendous inefficiency is that the definition does not capture the fact that duplicated computations always yield the same result.

What we do (in fact this transformation is due to Burstall & Darlington) is introduce a function which computes the two values needed in equation 3 and transform *this* into a form which does not duplicate the evaluations.

$$\mathbf{g}\,n = (\mathbf{fib}\,(n+1)):(\mathbf{fib}\,n) \qquad \text{EUREKA!} \qquad\qquad 4\,(\text{DEF})$$

Now we can start to transform . . .

$$
\begin{aligned}
\mathbf{g}\,0 \quad &= (\mathbf{fib}\,1):(\mathbf{fib}\,0) & 5\,(\text{INS }4)\\
&= 1:1 & 6\,(\text{UNF }1,2)\\
\mathbf{g}\,(n+1) \quad &= (\mathbf{fib}\,(n+2)):(\mathbf{fib}\,(n+1)) & 7\,(\text{INS }4)\\
&= ((\mathbf{fib}\,(n+1))+(\mathbf{fib}\,n)):(\mathbf{fib}\,(n+1)) & 8\,(\text{UNF }3)\\
&= \mathbf{let}\ u\!:\!v = (\mathbf{fib}\,(n+1)):(\mathbf{fib}\,n)\ \mathbf{in}\ (u+v)\!:\!v & 9\,(\text{ABS})\\
&= \mathbf{let}\ u\!:\!v = (\mathbf{g}\,n)\ \mathbf{in}\ (u+v)\!:\!v & 10\,(\text{FLD }4)
\end{aligned}
$$

Now returning to the original definition . . .

$$
\begin{aligned}
\mathbf{fib}\,(n+2) \quad &= \mathbf{let}\ u\!:\!v = (\mathbf{fib}\,(n+1)):(\mathbf{fib}\,n)\ \mathbf{in}\ u+v & 11\,(\text{ABS }3)\\
\mathbf{fib}\,(n+2) \quad &= \mathbf{let}\ u\!:\!v = (\mathbf{g}\,n)\ \mathbf{in}\ u+v & 12\ \,(\text{FLD }4)
\end{aligned}
$$

To summarize we have:

$$
\begin{aligned}
\mathbf{fib}\ 0 &= 1\\
\mathbf{fib}\ 1 &= 1\\
\mathbf{fib}\ n &= \mathbf{let}\ u\!:\!v = (\mathbf{g}\,(n-2))\ \mathbf{in}\ u+v\\
\mathbf{g}\ 0 \ &= 1:1\\
\mathbf{g}\,n \ &= \mathbf{let}\ u\!:\!v = (\mathbf{g}\,(n-1))\ \mathbf{in}\ (u+v)\!:\!v
\end{aligned}
$$

which is linear in n.

■

It is interesting and instructive to compare and contrast this with a program to achieve the same end in a conventional imperative language and indeed to the other program computing this series which we looked at in the previous chapter. We will return to this program again later.

4.4 The correctness of program transformation

We have so far said nothing regarding the correctness of the various transformation steps that we have introduced and utilized. For the enterprise to be successful we must have confidence that they all preserve meaning. This much is quite clear for some of the steps we used, like for example, unfolding, abstraction, instantiation and the use of laws. These are of course justified by their own definitions or proofs of correctness. The process which deserves closer attention is folding.

A rigorous analysis would require much of the material of Chapter 7 so we will concentrate on providing the details informally. Folding is, in general, only a *partially* correct operation. This means that the fixpoints of recursion equations may be *weakened* by folding. By this we mean that if the original and the folded expressions both terminate they will yield equivalent results but, in general, the folded version may fail to terminate when the original expression is perfectly well defined. This informal notion of weakening is made quite precise in Chapter 7.

The upshot of this is that program transformations are bound to respect the invariant property but may not yield solutions which are as well defined. Essentially this is because *unrestricted folding does not respect variant properties*. As usual, the variant property is the one which we use to ensure termination.

To see this forcefully consider the following definition:

$$\mathbf{f}\,x = 3 \qquad\qquad\qquad 1\,\text{(DEF)}$$

Now suppose we fold this expression into itself. This means replacing 3 everywhere it occurs on the right-hand side of the expression above with ($\mathbf{f}\,x$). This yields:

$$\mathbf{f}\,x = \mathbf{f}\,x. \qquad\qquad\qquad 2\,\text{(FLD)}$$

Now we can see, by an informal operational argument, that equation 1 is everywhere defined to be 3 whilst equation 2 is everywhere undefined; that is, it terminates for no value of x. Less operationally, we note that *any* function satisfies equation 2.

This is not a pathological example although it is symptomatic of a pathological use of folding. This is to say that under certain well-defined circumstances folding is a totally correct operation; it leaves the fixpoint unchanged.

It is not difficult to see just when folding is a reasonable step in the transformation. Indeed the circumstances are very similar to the circumstances in which the induction hypothesis in a inductive proof may be applied. We need to restrict ourselves to *folding only when the argument of the equation used in the substitution is lower in the well ordering than the argument of the equation being transformed*. It is easy to see that the example above disobeys this rule. It is also instructive to check that the folding used in the program transformations of this chapter do conform to this restriction. Usually the well ordering we are alluding to here will be the familiar, structural ordering. Notice also that using the fold step with an argument structurally *similar* to the equation being transformed is rather like applying the induction hypothesis in an equally powerful way (from which one could conclude anything because any result we wish to establish could be obtained in a single step by appealing to the induction hypothesis!).

4.5 Accumulating parameters

Adding accumulating parameters to improve the efficiency of a functional program is a very well-known technique and we introduced some aspects of this process in Section 3.6. In this section we shall begin to see how programs of this kind can be systematically derived by transformation given suitable eureka definitions. Later on we shall see that it is a special case of an even more general and powerful eureka definition; but the details of this we postpone until Section 4.7.

Quite often the insight one needs to form a eureka definition rests on the observation that a given definition is, in a certain sense, a special case of a more general and applicable definition. This should be compared and contrasted with the task of finding suitably general induction hypotheses in verification proofs which we dealt with in the previous chapter. This close connection between eureka definitions and inductive hypotheses has also been observed by Bird; details of his work are given in the bibliographic notes.

Example 4.5(i)

To see this idea of the generalization of definitions forcefully we will turn to a well-known program from Chapter 3.

$$\textbf{reverse } [\ ] \ = [\ ] \qquad\qquad\qquad\qquad 1\,(\text{DEF})$$
$$\textbf{reverse } (a:l) = (\textbf{reverse } l) * [a] \qquad\qquad 2\,(\text{DEF})$$

What we should note is that, in general, a call of **reverse** is embedded in a *computational context*. In fact this context is quite specific, for it is an expression which *appends a list on the right*. In fact it is only the original call which is not embedded in a larger expression. The eureka step is to define a new function **rev**, of type: $(\forall\alpha)\,(\text{List}(\alpha)\rightarrow\text{List}(\alpha)\rightarrow\text{List}(\alpha))$ which not only reverses a list but also appends another to the right. Thus:

$$\textbf{rev } l \ z = (\textbf{reverse } l) * z \qquad\qquad\qquad 3\ (\text{INV})$$

We can now go through a process of transformations for various instantiations.

$$\textbf{rev } [\ ] z \quad = (\textbf{reverse } [\ ]) * z \qquad\qquad 4\ (\text{INS } 3)$$
$$\qquad\qquad = [\ ] * z \qquad\qquad\qquad\quad 5\ (\text{UNF } l)$$
$$\qquad\qquad = z \qquad\qquad\qquad\qquad\quad 6\ (\text{UNF } *)$$

rev $(a:l)z$	$=$(**reverse** $(a:l)$) $* z$	7 (INS 3)
	$=$((**reverse** l) $* [a]$) $* z$	8 (UNF 2)
	$=$(**reverse** l) $* ([a] * z)$	9 (LAW ASSOC $*$)
	$=$(**reverse** l) $* a:([$ $] * z)$	10 (UNF $*$)
	$=$(**reverse** l) $* a:z$	11 (UNF $*$)
	$=$**rev** l $(a:z)$	12 (FLD 3)
reverse l	$=$(**reverse** l) $* [$ $]$	13 (LAW $*$)
	$=$**rev** $l[$ $]$	14 (FLD 3)

If we summarize we see that we can replace lines 1, 2 and 3 by lines 6, 12 and 14.

reverse l $=$ **rev** l $[$ $]$
rev $[$ $]$ z $=z$
rev $(a:l)$ $z =$ **rev** l $(a:z)$

This is the program we developed in a rather less formal fashion, although with the same intension, in Section 3.6. Interesting points to note from the transformation are that we needed to exploit the fact that the operator, $*$, is associative and has a right unit (which is $[$ $]$). Furthermore, it is instructive to compare the eureka definition with the induction hypothesis we required in proposition 3.7(i).
■

Exercise 4.5(ii)

Consider the function:

factorial 0	$= 1$	1 (DEF)
factorial $(n+1)$	$=(n+1) * ($**factorial** $n)$	2 (DEF)

By providing a suitable eureka definition generate an accumulating parameter version of factorial. Notice again that the transformation turns on the associativity (and the existence of a unit) of a binary operator.
■

Example 4.5(iii)

Let us take the program schema defined over lists given in Section 3.4.1:

f $[$ $]$ $=$ **G**		1 (DEF)
f $(a:l)=$ **H** $(a:l)($ **f** $l)$		2 (DEF)

where **G** and **H** are program variables. We take the following eureka definition:

$$\mathbf{f}' \, l \, z \; = \mathbf{H} \, z \, (\mathbf{f} \, l) \qquad\qquad 3 \, (\text{EUREKA})$$

and then start to transform as follows:

$$
\begin{aligned}
\mathbf{f}' \, [\;\;] z &= \mathbf{H} \, z \, (\mathbf{f} \, [\;\;]) && 4 \quad (\text{INS } 3) \\
&= \mathbf{H} \, z \, \mathbf{G} && 5 \quad (\text{UNF } l) \\
\mathbf{f}' \, (a{:}l) z &= \mathbf{H} \, z \, (\mathbf{f}(a{:}l)) && 6 \quad (\text{INS } 3) \\
&= \mathbf{H} \, z \, (\mathbf{H}(a{:}l)(\mathbf{f} \, l)) && 7 \quad (\text{UNF } 2)
\end{aligned}
$$

At this stage we reach an impasse. If, however, we assume that **H** is associative we can obtain:

$$
\begin{aligned}
&= \mathbf{H} \, (\mathbf{H} \, z \,(a{:}l)) \, (\mathbf{f} \, l) && 8 \; (\text{LAW}) \\
&= \mathbf{f} \, l \, (\mathbf{H} \, z \, (a{:}l)) && 9 \; (\text{FLD } 3)
\end{aligned}
$$

Finally, let us suppose that **H** has a left identity l.

$$
\begin{aligned}
\mathbf{f} \, l &= \mathbf{f}' \, l \, l \\
\mathbf{f}'[\;\;] z &= \mathbf{H} \, z \, \mathbf{G} \\
\mathbf{f}'(a{:}l) z &= \mathbf{f}' \, l \, (\mathbf{H} \, z(a{:}l))
\end{aligned}
$$

This is a program transformation for a whole class of programs which match the schema for **f** and the conditions for **H**.
∎

Certainly the program of the previous exercise matches this schema. More interesting is that **reverse** also matches if we take **H** = **swappend** (where **swappend** swaps its arguments before appending). Thus it seems that in order to really take advantage of program schema transformation we need to involve not only a *matching* procedure but a procedure capable of showing *equivalences in some theory of functions*. In this example we would need to exploit the equation (**swappend** $l_1 \, l_2$) = (**append** $l_2 \, l_1$). For a development of automated program transformation via schema matching in the presence of an equational theory the reader is referred to Givler & Kieburtz (1984). Although in many cases this transformation is able to improve the space utilization of programs we must not allow ourselves to be seduced by the wide applicability of schema transformations. For example, the program **member** fits this schema but we showed in Section 3.6 that the program which results is inferior to the original.

The technique of adding a single accumulating parameter is not guaranteed to produce an iterative form as the next example which we dealt with in the previous chapter shows:

Example 4.5(iv)

We take the function **fringe**.

$$\textbf{fringe}(s_1:s_2) = (\textbf{fringe } s_1) * (\textbf{fringe } s_2) \qquad \text{1 (DEF)}$$
$$\textbf{fringe } a \quad = [a] \qquad\qquad\qquad\qquad\qquad \text{2 (DEF)}$$

A fairly obvious eureka definition is based on the observation that (**fringe** s) is often embedded in an expression which appends a list to its right.

This suggests:

$$\textbf{f } s\, l = (\textbf{fringe } s) * l \qquad\qquad\qquad\qquad \text{3 (EUREKA)}$$
of type: $(\forall\alpha)(\text{Sexp}(\alpha) \to \text{List}(\alpha) \to \text{List}(\alpha))$

Then we obtain:

$$
\begin{aligned}
\textbf{f } a\, l &= (\textbf{fringe } a) * l & \text{(INS 3)}\\
&= [a] * l & \text{(UNF 1)}\\
&= a{:}l & \text{(LAWS)}\\
\textbf{f}(s_1{:}s_2)l &= (\textbf{fringe}(s_1{:}s_2)) * l & \text{(INS 3)}\\
&= ((\textbf{fringe } s_1) * (\textbf{fringe } s_2)) * l & \text{(UNF 2)}\\
&= (\textbf{fringe } s_1) * ((\textbf{fringe } s_2) * l) & \text{(ASSOC }*)\\
&= (\textbf{fringe } s_1) * (\textbf{f } s_2\, l) & \text{(FLD 3)}\\
&= \textbf{f } s_1(\textbf{f } s_2\, l) & \text{(FLD 3)}\\
\textbf{fringe } s &= (\textbf{fringe } s) * [\ ] & \text{(LAW)}\\
&= \textbf{f } s[\ ] & \text{(FLD 3)}
\end{aligned}
$$

yielding:

$$
\begin{aligned}
\textbf{fringe } s &= \textbf{f } s[\ ]\\
\textbf{f }(s_1{:}s_2)l &= \textbf{f } s_1(\textbf{f } s_2\, l)\\
\textbf{f } a\, l &= a{:}l
\end{aligned}
$$

Again, this is the program we obtained directly in example 3.6(vi). In this context the program is *derived* from the original (which we can call the specification) by correctness-preserving transformations. No further verification is necessary. Note in particular that the new program (as we argued before) is a genuine improvement over the original.
∎

Exercise 4.5(v)

Take the original definition of **fib** given earlier. Using a suitable eureka step (hint: use the previous example as a guide) show that the definitions may be transformed into the following system of equations:

$$
\begin{aligned}
\textbf{fib } n &= \textbf{f } n\, 0 \\
\textbf{f } 0\, m &= m \\
\textbf{f } 1\, m &= m+1 \\
\textbf{f } n\, m &= \textbf{f}(n-1)\,(\textbf{f}(n-2)\, m)
\end{aligned}
$$

Notice that this transformation does *not* remove the duplicate evaluations and so must be considered a failure.

■

Exercise 4.5(vi)

Consider the following program schema with program variables G, $\blacktriangle$, J_1 and J_2:

$$
\begin{aligned}
\textbf{f}(s_1:s_2)\, x &= (\textbf{f } s_1\,(J_1\, s_1\, s_2\, x))\,\blacktriangle\,(\textbf{f } s_2\,(J_2\, s_1\, s_2\, x)) \\
\textbf{f } a\, x &= G\, a\, x
\end{aligned}
$$

Formulate a suitable eureka definition and transform **f** using it. State any assumptions you make.

■

It is noticeable how important associativity laws and the existence of identities are for this style of program transformation. It remains to be seen later whether, and how, we can deal with functions such as **mirror** which involve operators which are neither associative nor have identities. In the case of **mirror**:

$$
\begin{aligned}
\textbf{mirror}(s_1:s_2) &= (\textbf{mirror } s_2):(\textbf{mirror } s_1) \\
\textbf{mirror } a &= a
\end{aligned}
$$

the operator in question is of course **cons**.

4.6 Generalized parameters

Another technique that we have seen adopted in functional programming is that of 'generalizing arguments'. This was discussed in some detail in Section 3.9. There are two reasons why this is a useful policy. Firstly, it is another way of establishing a definition in iterative form, which is in itself often beneficial, and secondly, it can be used to remove redundant evaluation from some programs under applicative evaluation.

Example 4.6(i)

Let us begin by considering the result of adding an accumulator to **fringe**.

fringe $s = \mathbf{f}\,s[\ ]$		1 (DEF)
$\mathbf{f}\,(s_1:s_2)\,l = \mathbf{f}\,s_1(\mathbf{f}\,s_2\,l)$		2 (DEF)
$\mathbf{f}\,a\,l \quad = a{:}l$		3 (DEF)

If we are asked to evaluate $(\mathbf{fringe}((s_1{:}s_2){:}(s_3{:}s_4)))$ we will utilize equation 2 above three times to get:

$$\mathbf{f}\,s_1\,(\mathbf{f}\,s_2\,(\mathbf{f}\,s_3\,(\mathbf{f}\,s_4[\ ])))$$

There seems to be a good deal of regularity in this form of expression and we can use this to formulate a eureka definition. Naturally all evaluations of **fringe** will be of this form and the sequence of objects $s_1 \ldots s_n$ determines the expression exactly. This leads us to define for all lists of sexpressions a function **g** of type: $(\forall\alpha)(\mathrm{List}(\mathrm{Sexp}(\alpha)) \to \mathrm{List}(\alpha))$.

$\mathbf{g}[\ ] \quad = [\ ]$		4 (EUREKA 1)
$\mathbf{g}(s{:}l) \quad = \mathbf{f}\,s\,(\mathbf{g}\,l)$		5 (EUREKA 2)
$\mathbf{fringe}\,s \quad = \mathbf{f}\,s\,[\ ]$		6 (UNF)
$= \mathbf{f}\,s(\mathbf{g}[\ ])$		7 (FLD 4)
$= \mathbf{g}[s]$		8 (FLD 5)
$\mathbf{g}(a{:}l) \quad = \mathbf{f}\,a(\mathbf{g}\,l)$		9 (INS 5)
$= a{:}(\mathbf{g}\,l)$		10 (UNF 2)
$\mathbf{g}((s_1{:}s_2){:}l) = \mathbf{f}(s_1{:}s_2)\,(\mathbf{g}\,l)$		11 (INS 5)
$= \mathbf{f}\,s_1\,(\mathbf{f}\,s_2\,(\mathbf{g}\,l))$		12 (UNF 3)
$= \mathbf{f}\,s_1(\mathbf{g}(s_2{:}l))$		13 (FLD 5)
$= \mathbf{g}\,(s_1{:}(s_2{:}l))$		14 (FLD 5)

In summary we have:

fringe s	$= \mathbf{g}[s]$
$\mathbf{g}[\ ]$	$= [\ ]$
$\mathbf{g}(a{:}l)$	$= a{:}(\mathbf{g}\,l)$
$\mathbf{g}((s_1{:}s_2){:}l)$	$= \mathbf{g}(s_1{:}(s_2{:}l))$

■

This is the program we defined in the previous chapter. This definition is correct because it was derived from a program which itself was derived from the original specification of **fringe**. The astute reader will observe that **g** is nothing more than the function **rotate** which we introduced in example 3.4.3(ii). Proposition 3.4.3(iv) contains the information which is necessary to show that our use of folding in the transformation above is justified.

4.7 Continuation-based program transformation

It should be becoming clear that the key to successful program transformation lies in the selection of a suitable eureka step and that this is a creative and presumably, in general, non-trivial step. Some general principles have begun to emerge from the previous sections and they suggest techniques for designing suitable eureka definitions. In particular we have seen a tupling strategy for avoiding duplicate computations, adding an accumulator to establish an iterative form and generalized arguments which can avoid unnecessary evaluation under applicative reduction and which can produce an iterative form when the accumulator strategy fails.

In this section we discuss an even more general strategy for forming eureka definitions based on *continuations* and we shall see that many forms of the accumulation, generalized parameter and, indeed, tupling strategies are just special cases of this one. The seminal reference for the use of continuations in program transformation is Wand (1980).

Example 4.7(i)

It will be most instructive if we return to an earlier example:

$$\textbf{reverse} \; [\;] \; = [\;] \qquad\qquad\qquad\qquad 1 \; (\text{DEF})$$
$$\textbf{reverse} \; (a{:}l) = (\textbf{reverse} \; l) * [a] \qquad\quad 2 \; (\text{DEF})$$

Let us consider the recursive clause more closely. In order to see exactly what is happening we can apply β-conversion to obtain:

$$\textbf{reverse} \; (a{:}l) = (\lambda z \cdot z * [a])(\textbf{reverse} \; l)$$

which is (by introducing functional composition):

$$\textbf{reverse} \, (a{:}l) = ((\lambda z \cdot z * [a]) \circ \textbf{reverse})l$$

This has separated the recursion from everything else and we can see that the right-hand side consists of exactly two parts. Firstly, the recursion itself and, secondly, a function which describes what to do with the result of the recursion. In the clause above it is the function $(\lambda z \cdot z * [a])$ which tells us what to do with the value (**reverse** l). This function is what we generally call the *continuation function*.

Now we remarked earlier that successful verification and transformation can turn on finding the appropriate generalization of a hypothesis or definition. In this example we see that in general a call to **reverse** does not happen in isolation but in the presence of a continuation. This observation can form the basis of a eureka step which generalizes a function to account for a continuation. We introduce a new function, **r**, of type:

$$(\forall \alpha)(\text{List}(\alpha) \rightarrow (\text{List}(\alpha) \rightarrow \text{List}(\alpha)) \rightarrow \text{List}(\alpha))$$

$$\mathbf{r}\, l\, \theta = (\theta \circ \mathbf{reverse})\, l \qquad\qquad \text{EUREKA} \quad 3 \; (\text{INV})$$

Armed with this we can try out a transformation.

reverse $l = (\mathbf{id} \circ \mathbf{reverse})\, l$	4 (LAW)
$= \mathbf{r}\, l\, \mathbf{id}$	5 (FLD 3)
$\mathbf{r}[\;\;]\theta \;\;= (\theta \circ \mathbf{reverse})[\;\;]$	6 (INS 3)
$= \theta[\;\;]$	7 (UNF 1)
$\mathbf{r}(a{:}l)\theta = (\theta \circ \mathbf{reverse})(a{:}l)$	8 (INS 3)
$= \theta((\lambda z \cdot z * [a]) \circ \mathbf{reverse})\, l$	9 (UNF 2)
$= (\theta \circ ((\lambda z \cdot z * [a]) \circ \mathbf{reverse}))\, l$	10 (FLD $\circ$)
$= ((\theta \circ (\lambda z \cdot z * [a])) \circ \mathbf{reverse})\, l$	11 (ASSOC $\circ$)
$= \mathbf{r}\, l\, (\theta \circ (\lambda z \cdot z * [a]))$	12 (FLD 3)

Summarizing lines 5, 7 and 12 we have:

$$\mathbf{reverse}\, l = \mathbf{r}\, l\, \mathbf{id}$$
$$\mathbf{r}[\;\;]\theta \;\;= \theta[\;\;]$$
$$\mathbf{r}(a{:}l)\theta = \mathbf{r}\, l\, (\theta \circ (\lambda z \cdot z * [a]))$$

■

We note again that the success of this transformation lies in the existence of associativity and identity properties (but this time at the higher-order level of the function composition operator).

Hopefully though this is not the full power of eureka definitions like definition 3 above, for the program we have obtained is more complex and probably more inefficient than the iterative version we obtained earlier! In a moment we will see how these higher-order programs are to be thought of as first stages in a more elaborate transformation.

Before we move on to this let us note that the transformation above did not utilize any properties of the operator * and so this transformation technique is more general. Indeed it is possible to repeat example 4.5(iii) without the assumption that the operator **H** is associative and has a left unit.

Example 4.7(ii)

$\mathbf{f}[\;\;] \;\;= \mathbf{G}$	1 (DEF)
$\mathbf{f}(a{:}l) = \mathbf{H}(a{:}l)(\mathbf{f}\, l)$	2 (DEF)

where **G** and **H** are program variables.

$$\mathbf{f}' \, l \, \theta = (\theta \circ \mathbf{f}) \, l \qquad\qquad 3 \text{ (EUREKA)}$$
$$\mathbf{f} \, l \; = (\mathbf{id} \circ \mathbf{f}) \, l \qquad\qquad 4 \text{ (LAW)}$$
$$= \mathbf{f}' \, l \, \mathbf{id} \qquad\qquad 5 \text{ (FLD 3)}$$
$$\mathbf{f}'[\;] \theta = (\theta \circ \mathbf{f})[\;] \qquad\qquad 6 \text{ (INS)}$$
$$= \theta \, \mathbf{G} \qquad\qquad 7 \text{ (UNF 1)}$$
$$\mathbf{f}'(a:l) \, \theta = (\theta \circ \mathbf{f})(a:l) \qquad\qquad 8 \text{ (INS)}$$
$$= \theta \, (\mathbf{H}\,(a:l)\,(\mathbf{f}\,l)) \qquad\qquad 9 \text{ (UNF 2)}$$
$$= (\theta \circ ((\lambda z \cdot \mathbf{H}\,(a:l)\, z) \circ \mathbf{f})) \, l \qquad\qquad 10 \text{ (FLD } \circ)$$
$$= ((\theta \circ (\lambda z \cdot \mathbf{H}\,(a:l)\, z)) \circ \mathbf{f}) \, l \qquad\qquad 11 \text{ (ASSOC } \circ)$$
$$= \mathbf{f} \, l \, (\theta \circ (\lambda z \cdot \mathbf{H}\,(a:l)\, z)) \qquad\qquad 12 \text{ (FLD 3)}$$

That is:

$$\mathbf{f} \, l \qquad = \mathbf{f}' \, l \, \mathbf{id}$$
$$\mathbf{f}'[\;] \theta \; = \theta \, \mathbf{G}$$
$$\mathbf{f}'(a:l)\theta = \mathbf{f}' \, l \, (\theta \circ (\lambda z \cdot \mathbf{H}\,(a:l)\, z))$$

∎

The next stage in the development is the derivation of program transformations by means of *continuation representation*. A continuation representation is a data-structure which captures the *essential features* of the continuations which occur in a given program.

Example 4.7(iii)

In example 4.7(i) it is possible to find a simple representation for the continuations because a little manipulation shows that they always have the form:

$$\mathbf{id} \circ (\lambda z \cdot z * [a_n]) \circ (\lambda z \cdot z * [a_{n-1}]) \circ \, \ldots \, \circ (\lambda z \cdot z * [a_1])$$

for some n and atoms a_1 to a_n.

Now this is just:

$$(\lambda z \cdot z * a_1 : a_2 : a_3 : \ldots : a_n : [\;])$$

or:

$$(\lambda z \cdot z * [a_1 \, a_2 \, a_3 \, \ldots \, a_n])$$

by the definitions of composition and some facts about **append**. Thus continuations have the form $(\lambda z \cdot z * z')$ for some list z'. *This function can be represented by list z' itself.* This suggests that we adopt a eureka definition to capture this fact:

$$\mathbf{g} \, l \, z = \mathbf{r} \, l \, (\lambda z' \cdot z' * z) \qquad \text{(EUREKA!)}$$

Now this function, of type: $(\forall\alpha)(\text{List}(\alpha)\to\text{List}(\alpha)\to\text{List}(\alpha))$ can form the basis of a transformation:

$$\begin{aligned}
\textbf{reverse } l &= \textbf{r } l \textbf{ id}\\
&= \textbf{r } l\ (\lambda z \cdot z)\\
&= \textbf{r } l\ (\lambda z \cdot z * [\ ])\\
&= \textbf{g } l\ [\ ] \qquad\qquad\qquad\qquad\qquad\text{(FLD)}
\end{aligned}$$

$$\begin{aligned}
\textbf{g } [\ ]\ z &= \textbf{r } [\ ]\ (\lambda z' \cdot z' * z)\\
&= (\lambda z' \cdot z' * z)\ [\ ]\\
&= [\ ] * z\\
&= z
\end{aligned}$$

$$\begin{aligned}
\textbf{g } (a{:}l)\ z &= \textbf{r } (a{:}l)\ (\lambda z' \cdot z' * z)\\
&= \textbf{r } l\ (\lambda z' \cdot z' * z) \circ (\lambda z' \cdot z' * [a])\\
&= \textbf{r } l\ (\lambda z' \cdot (z' * [a]) * z)\\
&= \textbf{r } l\ (\lambda z' \cdot z' * [a] * z)\\
&= \textbf{r } l\ (\lambda z' \cdot z' * ([a] * z))\\
&= \textbf{r } l\ (\lambda z' \cdot z' * (a{:}z))\\
&= \textbf{g } l\ (a{:}z) \qquad\qquad\qquad\qquad\qquad\text{(FLD)}
\end{aligned}$$

In this we have just indicated the occasions on which we fold the eureka definition.

The definition we have achieved is precisely the one we obtained by the direct eureka definition:

$$\textbf{r } l\ z = (\textbf{reverse } l) * z$$

earlier.

∎

Exercise 4.7(iv)

Form a suitable eureka definition to transform the solution of example 4.7(ii) into the solution of example 4.5(iii). You will not be surprised that you *do now need to assume that* **H** *is associative and has a left unit.*

∎

Example 4.7(v)

As a second example in continuation representation we shall return to the Fibonacci program which we developed earlier.

If we start with the traditional recursive definition and apply a continuation-based transformation we simply achieve:

$$\mathbf{f}\,n \quad = \mathbf{f}'\,n\ \mathbf{id}$$
$$\mathbf{f}'\,0\,\theta \quad = \theta\ 1$$
$$\mathbf{f}'\,1\,\theta \quad = \theta\ 1$$
$$\mathbf{f}'\,n\,\theta \quad = \mathbf{f}\,(n-1)\ (\theta \circ (\lambda n'\cdot n' + (\mathbf{f}\,(n-2))))$$

■

Exercise 4.7(vi)

Show that this can be transformed into the program given in exercise 4.5(vi) by means of a suitable representation for the continuation. In other words the continuation-based strategy does not make much direct impact on this program.
■

However, we *can* apply these methods to the program that we produced by deleting the duplicate computations.

The key function is:

$$\mathbf{g}\,0 = 1{:}1$$
$$\mathbf{g}\,n = \mathbf{let}\ u{:}v = (\mathbf{g}\,(n-1))\ \mathbf{in}\ (u+v){:}u$$

Now if we remove the syntactic sugar this is:

$$\mathbf{g}\,0 = 1{:}1 \qquad\qquad\qquad\qquad\qquad 1\ \text{(DEF)}$$
$$\mathbf{g}\,n = ((\lambda u{:}v\cdot(u+v){:}u) \circ \mathbf{g})\,(n-1) \qquad\quad 2\ \text{(DEF)}$$

which already shows us the structure of the continuation. Again, the meaning of lambda abstracts with patterns should be reasonably clear.

Now, it is not very instructive or useful to actually transform this function into one in which the continuation occurs as a parameter. More useful is the following lemma.

Lemma 4.7(vii)

We begin by defining a function, **h**:

$$\mathbf{h} = \lambda(u{:}v)\cdot(u+v){:}u$$

and then we claim, for all $n > 0$:

$$\mathbf{g}\,n = \mathbf{h}^n\,(1{:}1)$$

Exercise 4.7(viii)

Proof

■

■

This example is interesting because the continuation processes a composite value consisting of two components. This suggests that we should introduce not one but two accumulators to hold the composite value.

Now the continuations have the form $\mathbf{h}^n$ where $\mathbf{h}$ is given in the preamble to lemma 4.7(vii). By taking the very simple expedient of representing this continuation by the exponent n (and paying regard to the previous paragraph) we can form a eureka definition:

$$\mathbf{f}\, n\, u\, v = \mathbf{h}^n\, (u:v) \qquad\qquad \text{EUREKA 3 (DEF)}$$

Where $\mathbf{f}$ has type:

$$N \rightarrow N \rightarrow N \rightarrow N$$

Now the transformation can be attempted:

$\mathbf{g}\, n$	$= \mathbf{h}^n\, (1:1)$	4 (INS 3)
	$= \mathbf{f}\, n\, 1\, 1$	5 (LEMMA)
$\mathbf{f}\, 0\, u\, v$	$= \mathbf{h}^0\, (u:v)$	6 (INS 3)
	$= (u:v)$	7 (LAW)
$\mathbf{f}\, n\, u\, v$	$= \mathbf{h}^n\, (u:v)$	8 (INS 3)
	$= (\mathbf{h}^{n-1} \circ \mathbf{h})(u:v)$	9 (LAW)
	$= \mathbf{h}^{n-1}\, ((u+v):u)$	10 (UNF)
	$= \mathbf{f}\, (n-1)(u+v)\, u$	11 (FLD 3)

In this example, then, the continuation representation is actually the first argument n rather than either (or both) accumulations. This is an iterative program.

■

We now turn to another program which we have dealt with before in this chapter: the function **fringe**. What we established in example 4.5(iv) was that adding an accumulator does not, in this case, produce an iterative form. Later, in example 4.6(i), we saw that this can be achieved by means of generalized parameters.

We shall now explore the ramifications of a continuation-based program transformation.

Example 4.7(ix)

Recall that:

$$\textbf{fringe } (s_1 : s_2) = (\textbf{fringe } s_1) * (\textbf{fringe } s_2) \qquad \text{1 (DEF)}$$
$$\textbf{fringe } a \qquad = [a] \qquad\qquad\qquad\qquad\qquad \text{2 (DEF)}$$

We shall use our (by now) familiar eureka definition:

$$\textbf{f } s \ \theta = (\theta \circ \textbf{fringe}) \ s \qquad\qquad\qquad\qquad\qquad \text{3 (DEF)}$$

which gives us a function of type:

$$(\forall \alpha)(\text{Sexp}(\alpha) \rightarrow (\text{List}(\alpha) \rightarrow \text{List}(\alpha)) \rightarrow \text{List}(\alpha))$$

and which we can transform as follows:

$$\textbf{fringe } s = (\textbf{id} \circ \textbf{fringe}) \ s$$
$$= \textbf{f } s \ \textbf{id}$$
$$\textbf{f } a \ \theta = (\theta \circ \textbf{fringe}) \ a$$
$$= \theta \ [a]$$
$$\textbf{f } (s_1 : s_2) \ \theta = (\theta \circ \textbf{fringe}) \ (s_1 : s_2)$$
$$= \theta \ ((\textbf{fringe } s_1) * (\textbf{fringe } s_2))$$
$$= (\theta \circ (\lambda z \cdot z * (\textbf{fringe } s_2))) \circ \textbf{fringe}) \ s_1$$
$$= \textbf{f } s_1 \ (\theta \circ (\lambda z \cdot z * (\textbf{fringe } s_2)))$$
$$= \textbf{f } s_1 \ (\theta \circ \lambda z \cdot ((\lambda z' \cdot z * z') \ (\textbf{fringe } s_2)))$$
$$= \textbf{f } s_1 \ (\theta \circ \lambda z \cdot (((\lambda z' \cdot z * z') \circ \textbf{fringe}) \ s_2))$$
$$= \textbf{f } s_1 \ (\theta \circ \lambda z \cdot (\textbf{f } s_2 \ \lambda z' \cdot z * z'))$$

Lemma 4.7(x)

Let θ_1 and θ_2 be continuations. For all s:
$$\theta_1 \ (\textbf{f } s \ \theta_2) = \textbf{f } s \ (\theta_1 \circ \theta_2)$$

Proof

$$\theta_1 \ (\textbf{f } s \ \theta_2) =$$
$$\theta_1 \ (\theta_2 \ (\textbf{fringe } s)) =$$
$$((\theta_1 \circ \theta_2) \circ \textbf{fringe}) \ s =$$
$$\textbf{f } s \ \theta_1 \circ \theta_2$$

as required.

∎

Combining this with the derivation we obtain the program:

fringe s $\quad=$ **f** s **id**
f $(s_1:s_2)$ θ $=$ **f** s_1 $\lambda z \cdot ($**f** s_2 $\theta \circ \lambda z' \cdot z * z')$
f a θ $\quad=\theta$ $[a]$

Lemma 4.7(x) is actually very strong. Very few functions, taking continuations, satisfy such a lemma. We will see one or two of these later in this chapter and many in Chapter 8.

The shape of the continuation is certainly more complex than any we have encountered so far. Let us just compose two to investigate what happens:

$$\lambda z_1 \cdot (\mathbf{f}\ s_1\ (\lambda z_2 \cdot (\mathbf{f}\ s_2\ \theta \circ (\lambda z_3 \cdot z_2 * z_3)))) \circ \lambda z_4 \cdot z_1 * z_4)$$

This reduces to:

$$\lambda z_1 \cdot (\mathbf{f}\ s_1\ (\lambda z_2 \cdot (\mathbf{f}\ s_2\ \theta \circ \lambda z_3 \cdot z_1 * z_2 * z_3)))$$

It is easy to see that, in general, continuations have the form:

$$\lambda z \cdot (\mathbf{f}\ s_1(\lambda z_1 \cdot \mathbf{f} \dots (\lambda z_{n-1} \cdot \mathbf{f}\ s_n\ (\lambda z_n \cdot z * z_1 * \dots * z_n)) \dots))$$

(The prefix "$\theta \circ$" disappears by virtue of the original continuation **id**.)

This form of function can be characterized by the sexpressions s_1 to s_n which it contains.

Definition 4.7(xi)

We define a representation function for these continuations:

$\mathbf{R}$ $[\ ]$ $\quad=$ **id**
$\mathbf{R}$ $(s:l)=\lambda z \cdot ($**f** s $(\mathbf{R}\ l) \circ \lambda z' \cdot z * z')$

■

Now we introduce a eureka definition of a function, **h**, of type:

$$(\forall \alpha)(\mathrm{List}(\mathrm{Sexp}(\alpha)) \to \mathrm{List}(\alpha))$$

$\mathbf{h}$ $[\ ]$ $\quad=[\ ]$
$\mathbf{h}$ $(s:l)=$ **f** s $(\mathbf{R}\ l)$

Now we may begin a transformation:

fringe s $=$ **f** s **id**
$\qquad\quad=$ **f** s $(\mathbf{R}\ [\ ])$
$\qquad\quad=\mathbf{h}$ $[s]$

$$\mathbf{h}\,(a{:}l) = \mathbf{f}\ a\,(\mathbf{R}\ l)$$
$$= \mathbf{R}\ l\ [a]$$
$$= [a] * (\mathbf{h}\ l) \qquad \text{(see exercise below)}$$
$$= a : (\mathbf{h}\ l)$$

$$\mathbf{h}\,((s_1{:}s_2){:}l) = \mathbf{f}(s_1{:}\ s_2)\,(\mathbf{R}\ l)$$
$$= \mathbf{f}\ s_1(\lambda z{\cdot}\mathbf{f}\ s_2\,(\mathbf{R}\ l) \circ \lambda z'{\cdot}z * z')$$
$$= \mathbf{f}\ s_1(\mathbf{R}\,(s_2{:}l))$$
$$= \mathbf{h}\,(s_1{:}s_2{:}l)$$

Thus we obtain the program:

$$\begin{aligned}
&\textbf{fringe}\ s && = \mathbf{h}\ [s]\\
&\mathbf{h}\ [\ ] && = [\ ]\\
&\mathbf{h}\ (a{:}l) && = a{:}(\mathbf{h}\ l)\\
&\mathbf{h}\,((s_1{:}s_2){:}l) && = \mathbf{h}\,(s_1{:}(s_2{:}l))
\end{aligned}$$

which, by now, we should recognize.

Exercise 4.7(xii)

Show that for all z: $(\mathbf{R}\ l\ z) = z * (\mathbf{h}\ l)$

∎

The interesting feature of all these examples is that we see both accumulation and generalization are special cases of continuation-based program transformation. Next we shall describe a simple continuation representation for the lambda calculus pairing operation described in Chapter 2.

Example 4.7(xiii)

Recall that the idea of pairing can be introduced into the lambda calculus by means of the function $\textbf{pair} = \lambda xyz{\cdot}zxy$. Looked at from the perspective of this chapter we see that **pair** takes two arguments x and y, which we wish to pair up as a single structure, and finally a third argument z which is a continuation. This continuation then processes, in some fashion, the arguments of the pair x and y. Clearly the processing we are thinking about here consists of the selection processes **h** and **t**. These selection operators, which we now think of as continuations, are defined as follows:

$$\mathbf{h} = \lambda p{\cdot}p(\lambda xy{\cdot}x) \quad \text{and} \quad \mathbf{t} = \lambda p{\cdot}p(\lambda xy{\cdot}y)$$

Suppose that we can ensure (by a typechecking process perhaps) that **pair** $x\,y$ may only be provided with continuations of the form $\lambda xy{\cdot}x$ or $\lambda xy{\cdot}y$ as shown above. Any pair of distinct atoms can be used to represent these continuations, say "*H*" and "*T*" (respectively).

Thus we define:

$$\mathbf{h} = (\lambda p \cdot p \ \text{"}H\text{"}) \quad \text{and} \quad \mathbf{t} = (\lambda p \cdot p \ \text{"}T\text{"})$$

and set the following eureka definition:

$$\mathbf{pair}' \ x \ y \ t = \mathbf{pair} \ x \ y \ (\mathbf{R} \ t)$$

where **R** is given as follows:

$$\mathbf{R}\text{"}H\text{"} = \lambda xy \cdot x \quad \text{and} \quad \mathbf{R}\text{"}T\text{"} = \lambda xy \cdot y$$

This transforms simply:

$$
\begin{aligned}
\mathbf{pair}' \ x \ y \ \text{"}H\text{"} &= \mathbf{pair} \ x \ y \ (\mathbf{R}\text{"}H\text{"}) \\
&= \mathbf{pair} \ x \ y \ (\lambda xy.x) \\
&= x
\end{aligned}
$$

and

$$
\begin{aligned}
\mathbf{pair}' \ x \ y \ \text{"}T\text{"} &= \mathbf{pair} \ x \ y \ (\mathbf{R} \ \text{"}T\text{"}) \\
&= \mathbf{pair} \ x \ y \ (\lambda xy.y) \\
&= (\lambda xy.y)x \ y \\
&= y
\end{aligned}
$$

Data structures, such as this example, are discussed in detail in Abelson & Sussman (1985) and optimizations like this are used in the implementation of functional languages built directly from the lambda calculus (PONDER, Tillotson, 1985, for example).
■

Our final example in this section demonstrates how continuation-based transformations can be used to simplify certain *non-linear recursions*.

Example 4.7(xiv)

The Ackermann function is often used in texts on computability as an example of a function which is not primitive recursive.

$$
\begin{aligned}
\mathbf{f} \ 0 \ y &= y + 1 \\
\mathbf{f} \ x \ 0 &= \mathbf{f} \ (x - 1)l \\
\mathbf{f} \ x \ y &= \mathbf{f} \ (x - 1)(\mathbf{f} \ x \ (y - 1))
\end{aligned}
$$

Our continuation-based transformation is based on earlier eureka steps.

$$\mathbf{f}' \ x \ y \ \theta = (\theta \circ (\mathbf{f} \ x)) \ y$$

Armed with this function, of type: $N \to N \to (N \to N) \to N$, we proceed as follows:

$$\mathbf{f}\,x\,y = (\mathbf{id} \circ (\mathbf{f}\,x))\,y$$
$$= \mathbf{f}'\,x\,y\,\mathbf{id} \qquad\qquad \text{(FLD)}$$

$$\mathbf{f}'\,0\,y\,\theta = (\theta \circ (\mathbf{f}\,0))\,y$$
$$= \theta\,(y+1)$$

$$\mathbf{f}'(x+1)\,0\,\theta = (\theta \circ (\mathbf{f}(x+1)))\,0$$
$$= \theta\,(\mathbf{f}\,x\,l)$$
$$= (\theta \circ (\mathbf{f}\,x))\,l$$
$$= \mathbf{f}'\,x\,l\,\theta \qquad\qquad \text{(FLD)}$$

$$\mathbf{f}'\,(x+1)\,(y+1)\,\theta = (\theta \circ (\mathbf{f}(x+1)))\,(y+1)$$
$$= \theta\,(\mathbf{f}\,(x+1)\,(y+1))$$
$$= \theta\,(\mathbf{f}\,x\,(\mathbf{f}(x+1)\,y))$$
$$= (\theta \circ (\mathbf{f}\,x) \circ (\mathbf{f}(x+1)))\,y$$
$$= \mathbf{f}'(x+1)\,y\,(\theta \circ \mathbf{f}\,x) \qquad\qquad \text{(FLD)}$$

The continuations in this example have a very simple form:

$$(\mathbf{f}\,x_1) \circ (\mathbf{f}\,x_2) \circ \; \ldots \; \circ (\mathbf{f}\,x_n)$$

This can be represented by a list of the embedded values. It is most convenient to place these in reverse order. This leads to the definition of a representation function:

$$\mathbf{R}[\;] \;= \mathbf{id}$$
$$\mathbf{R}(x{:}l) = (\mathbf{R}\,l) \circ (\mathbf{f}\,x)$$

and then to a suitable eureka step for a new transformation based on this new function, $\mathbf{g}$ of type: $N \to N \to \text{List}(N) \to N$:

$$\mathbf{g}\,x\,y\,l = \mathbf{f}'\,x\,y\,(\mathbf{R}\,l)$$

$$\mathbf{f}\,x\,y =$$
$$\mathbf{f}'\,x\,y\,\mathbf{id} =$$
$$\mathbf{g}\,x\,y\,[\;] \qquad\qquad \text{(FLD)}$$
$$\mathbf{g}\,0\,y\,[\;] =$$
$$\mathbf{f}'\,0\,y\,\mathbf{id} =$$
$$\mathbf{id}\,(y+1) =$$
$$y+1$$

$$\mathbf{g}\,0\,y\,(x{:}l) =$$
$$\mathbf{f}'\,0\,y\,(\mathbf{R}(x{:}l)) =$$
$$\mathbf{f}'\,0\,y\,(\mathbf{R}\,l) \circ (\mathbf{f}\,x) =$$
$$((\mathbf{R}\,l) \circ (\mathbf{f}\,x))\,(y+1) =$$
$$\mathbf{f}'\,n\,(y+1)\,(\mathbf{R}\,l) = \qquad\qquad \text{(FLD)}$$

$$\mathbf{g}\,n(y+1)l \qquad\qquad\qquad\text{(FLD)}$$
$$\mathbf{g}(x+1)0\,l=$$
$$\mathbf{f}'(x+1)0(\mathbf{R}\,l)=$$
$$\mathbf{f}'\,x\,1(\mathbf{R}\,l)=$$
$$\mathbf{g}\,x\,1\,l \qquad\qquad\qquad\text{(FLD)}$$

$$\mathbf{g}(x+1)(y+1)l=$$
$$\mathbf{f}'(x+1)(y+1)(\mathbf{R}\,l)=$$
$$\mathbf{f}'(x+1)\,y(\mathbf{R}\,l)\circ(\mathbf{f}\,x)=$$
$$\mathbf{f}'(x+1)\,y(\mathbf{R}(x{:}l))=$$
$$\mathbf{g}(x+1)(x{:}l) \qquad\qquad\qquad\text{(FLD)}$$

In summary:

$$\mathbf{g}\,0\,y[\ ] \quad =y+1$$
$$\mathbf{g}\,0\,y(x{:}l) \ =\mathbf{g}\,x(y+1)l$$
$$\mathbf{g}\,x\,0\,l \quad\ \ =\mathbf{g}(x-1)\,1\,l$$
$$\mathbf{g}\,x\,y\,l \quad\ \ =\mathbf{g}\,x(y-1)((x-1){:}l)$$

Note that this is a linear recursion.

The continuation transform is very general. Every lambda term, for example, corresponds to another term which processes a continuation. Specifically, to each term M we associate a term M' as follows:

(i) v' $\quad\quad =(\lambda\theta\cdot\theta v)$ $\qquad\qquad\qquad$ when $v\in VAR$

(ii) $(\lambda v\cdot M\,)'$ $\ =(\lambda\theta\cdot\theta(\lambda v\cdot M'))$ $\qquad\qquad$ when $v\in VAR$,

$\qquad\qquad\qquad\qquad\qquad\qquad\qquad\qquad$ $M\in EXP$

(iii) $(M_1\,M_2)'\ =\lambda\theta\cdot M'_1(\lambda m_1\cdot M'_2(\lambda m_2\cdot(m_1\,m_2\,\theta)))$ $\quad$ when $M_1,M_2\in EXP$

The interesting and crucial point is that M' is an iterative form. In this context this means that no operand is an applicative expression. This tells us something quite striking about the lambda calculus and sequentiality. The continuation transform is described by Meyer & Wand (1985) and sequentiality is covered by Curien (1986).

4.8 Ignoring continuations

There is a sense in which the most powerful act one can perform with a continuation is to ignore it! We shall see later that this is central to a description of that programming horror known as **GOTO**, in functional terms. For the moment we are concerned with the problem of exception handling which we discussed in Section 3.12.

Suppose we are engaged in a complicated computational process when we detect an error situation. In a conventional imperative language it is probably in this circumstance more than any other that we might be tempted to use a sudden **GOTO** some global label at which recovery can begin. The reason for the abrupt change of control is to avoid having to let the control percolate the error back through the probably quite complicated calling sequence of procedures and functions which led us to the point at which the error was detected. This abrupt change of control allows us to avoid having to ensure that all procedures and functions know how to react to unexpected error values. In modern languages structured escapes (sometimes called *escapers*) are available. For example, the word **exit** in ALGOL 68 wrests control to the statement following the serial clause enclosing the exit. In BCPL writing **resultis** E where E is any expression jolts control to the surrounding statement **valof** G where G is the command which includes the **resultis.** In C, when the final result of a function can be computed, we can terminate the function body prematurely with the incantation **return** E where E is to be the result. In some LISP systems (CATCH I E) and (THROW I E) behave rather like the **valof** and **resultis** constructs described above, except they work with named targets. These constructs were explained in more detail in Section 3.12. These are all more or less general forms of the idea captured in the problem above: how to exit on error.

The next example reviews one or two ideas from Section 3.12 and shows how continuation transformations can make an impact.

Example 4.8(i)

Suppose that we have an expression in which the leaves are (probably) numbers. The following program forms the sum of the fringe of such an expression yielding the atom "FAIL" if the fringe is not entirely numeric.

$$\textbf{sumints } (s_1 : s_2) = (\textbf{sumints } s_1) + (\textbf{sumints } s_2)$$
$$\textbf{sumints } a \quad = a \qquad\qquad \textbf{when (numeric } a)$$
$$\textbf{sumints } a \quad = \text{"FAIL"} \quad \textbf{when (not (numeric } a))$$

In this example we are assuming that the function + has been extended as follows:

$$n + \text{"FAIL"} \qquad = \text{"FAIL"}$$
$$\text{"FAIL"} + n \qquad = \text{"FAIL"}$$
$$\text{"FAIL"} + \text{"FAIL"} = \text{"FAIL"}$$

The type of the extended addition operator is: $NFL \to NFL \to NFL$ as we saw in the previous chapter, where $NFL = N + \{\text{"FAIL"}\}$. **sumints** has type:

$$S \to NFL$$

Since we have no explicit or even implicit sense of context built into the definition above there is no chance of terminating the main call to:

sumints $((3:4):(“B”:6))$

when the atom "B" is encountered. What actually happens depends of course on the precise details of the evaluation but certainly in this case the error eventually percolates back to the main call, which is a rather inefficient way of proceeding.

It is clear from the previous paragraph that it is the lack of availability of a context which causes the problem. In a conventional language global labels might well be available and these form a control context which can be exploited. In the spirit of this chapter we seem to be looking again at an opportunity to utilize continuation-based transformations.

If we adopt our, by now, standard eureka definition we can transform the above into the following set of equations based on a function, **sints**, of type:

$$S \to (NFL \to NFL) \to NFL$$

sumints s	$=$ **sints** s **id**	
sints $(s_1:s_2)\, \theta$	$=$ **sints** $s_1 (\theta \circ \lambda n \cdot ($**sints** $s_2 \lambda n' \cdot n + n'))$	
sints $a\, \theta$	$= \theta\, a$	**when (numeric** a**)**
sints $a\, \theta$	$= \theta\, “FAIL”$	**when (not (numeric** a**))**

So far so bad: the error still percolates back through the continuation.

However, continuations have the form:

$$[\lambda n \cdot (\textbf{sints}\ s_i\ \lambda n' \cdot n + n')]^m \quad m \geq 0; \quad m \geq i \geq 0$$

and it is *not* difficult to prove by induction on m that:

$$[\lambda n \cdot (\textbf{sints}\ s_i\ \lambda n' \cdot n + n')]^m (“FAIL”) = “FAIL”$$

If we apply this law to the new definition we get:

sumints s	$=$ **sints** s **id**	
sints $(s_1:s_2)\theta$	$=$ **sints** $s_1 (\theta \circ \lambda n \cdot ($**sints** $s_2 \lambda n' \cdot n + n'))$	
sints $a\, \theta$	$= \theta\, a$	**when (numeric** a**)**
sints $a\, \theta$	$= “FAIL”$	**when (not(numeric** a**))**

It is the clause **sints** $a\, \theta = “FAIL”$ which causes most interest for the continuation θ has been ignored possibly saving a lot of irrelevant computation.

In order to derive a reasonable first order function from this definition we need to be a little more devious than we have been up to now. We wish to make use of the following observation about the continuations which **sints** makes use of:

$$(\forall\ \theta)\,(\exists\ n)\,(\forall\ m)\,((\theta\ m) = n + m)$$

Exercise 4.8(ii)

Prove this fact.
∎

This suggests that we can model continuations by numbers. Naturally, there are many continuations which are characterized by a given number which implies that we need to define not a function but a relation between continuations and their representations:

Let $\approx\ \subseteq NFL \times (NFL \rightarrow NFL)$. We define:

$$n \approx f \text{ iff } (\forall\ m \in NFL)\,((f\,m) = n + m))$$

Note for example that: $n \approx (\lambda n' \cdot n + n')$ whence $0 \approx \mathbf{id}$.

Instead of *defining* a new function **ssnts** of type $S \rightarrow NFL \rightarrow NFL$ in terms of **sints** we specify a *constraint*:

$$(\forall\ z)\,(\forall\ \theta)\,((z \approx \theta) \Rightarrow ((\forall\ s)\,(\mathbf{ssnts}\ s\ z) = (\mathbf{sints}\ s\ \theta)))$$

We use this to obtain a definition of **ssnts** as follows:

> **sumints** $s =$
> **sints** $s\ \mathbf{id} =$
> **ssnts** $s\ 0$
> since $0 \approx \mathbf{id}$

Let $z \approx \theta$ and (**numeric** a).

> **ssnts** $a\ z =$
> **sints** $a\ \theta =$
> $\theta\ a =$
> $a + z$

Let $z \approx \theta$ and **not** (**numeric** a).

> **ssnts** $a\ z =$
> **sints** $a\ \theta =$
> $\theta\ a =$
> "FAIL"

Let $z \approx \theta$.

$$\textbf{ssnts}\,(s_1 : s_2)\,z =$$
$$\textbf{sints}\,(s_1 : s_2)\,\theta =$$
$$\textbf{sints}\;s_1\,(\theta \circ (\lambda n \cdot \textbf{sints}\;s_2\,(n' \cdot n + n'))) =$$
$$\textbf{sints}\;s_1\,(\lambda n \cdot \theta(\textbf{sints}\;s_2\,(\lambda n' \cdot n + n'))) =$$
$$\textbf{sints}\;s_1\,(\lambda n \cdot \textbf{sints}\;s_2\,(\theta \circ (\lambda n' \cdot n + n'))) =$$
$$\textbf{sints}\;s_1\,(\lambda n \cdot \textbf{sints}\;s_2\,(\lambda n' \cdot \theta(n + n'))) =$$
$$\textbf{sints}\;s_1\,(\lambda n \cdot \textbf{sints}\;s_2\,(\lambda n' \cdot n + n' + z)) =$$
$$\textbf{sints}\;s_1\,(\lambda n \cdot n + (\textbf{sints}\;s_2\,(\lambda n' \cdot n' + z))) =$$
$$\textbf{sints}\;s_1\,(\lambda n \cdot n + (\textbf{ssnts}\;s_2\,z)) =$$
$$\textbf{ssnts}\;s_1\,(\textbf{ssnts}\;s_2\,z)$$

Note how lemma 4.7(x) (stated in terms of **sints**), and some simple corollaries of it, are used in the last case. We will return to transformations guided by relations in Chapter 8 where the relations will be very much more complex than the one used here.

In summary, we have:

$$\textbf{sumints}\;s \quad\ = \textbf{ssnts}\;s\;0$$
$$\textbf{ssnts}\,(s_1 : s_2)z = \textbf{ssnts}\;s_1\,(\textbf{ssnts}\;s_2\;z)$$
$$\textbf{ssnts}\;a\;z \quad\ = z + a \qquad \textbf{when (numeric}\;a)$$
$$\textbf{sints}\;a\;z \quad\ = \text{``FAIL''} \quad \textbf{when (not(numeric}\;a))$$

■

Note that programs like this, when evaluated applicatively, do not avoid unnecessary computation nor do they avoid passing the error back through an (extended) addition operation. Under a normal order operational semantics addition does not need to be extended and an arbitrary amount of irrelevant computation can be avoided (in the accumulator). It turns out that all the control devices outlined above which are used in conventional languages can be given precise description functionally by means of continuations. We shall discuss this further in Chapter 8.

4.9 Continuations and sequencing

In the following discussion let us take it that any function name decorated with a prime (for example $\textbf{f}'$) is related to the 'unprimed' function name ($\textbf{f}$) by the following definition:

$$\textbf{f}'\,\theta\,s = (\theta \circ \textbf{f})\,s$$

Notice that for later convenience we have permuted the continuation and the main argument in this definition [cf. the eureka definition of example 4.7(i) for example]. Thus if $\mathbf{f}$ has the type $S \to S$ then $\mathbf{f}'$ will have type: $S \to (S \to S) \to S$.

Suppose we have a composite program given by $\mathbf{h} = \mathbf{f} \circ \mathbf{g}$. We might expect the functions $\mathbf{f}'$, $\mathbf{g}'$ and $\mathbf{h}'$ to be related by some modified composition operator. We can derive the appropriate generalization by the following short program transformation:

$$
\begin{aligned}
\circ' \mathbf{f} \mathbf{g}\, \theta\, s &= (\theta \circ (\mathbf{f} \circ \mathbf{g}))\, s && \text{(EUREKA)} \\
&= ((\theta \circ \mathbf{f}) \circ \mathbf{g})\, s \\
&= \mathbf{g}' (\theta \circ \mathbf{f})\, s && \text{(FLD)} \\
&= \mathbf{g}' (\mathbf{f}'\, \theta)\, s && \text{(FLD)}
\end{aligned}
$$

There are two important points here.

Firstly notice the change in the order of application: it is $\mathbf{g}'$ which takes $\mathbf{f}'$ as an argument. This should be compared with the ordinary composition operator $\mathbf{f} \circ \mathbf{g}\, s = \mathbf{f} (\mathbf{g}\, s)$ in which $\mathbf{f}$ takes $(\mathbf{g}\, s)$ as an argument. Operationally this is rather obvious because we wish the data structure s to be processed by $\mathbf{g}$ before passing control on to $\mathbf{f}$ for further processing.

Secondly, a more subtle point. It should be observed that the *glue* which combines functions together is no longer the data structure (as it is in: $\mathbf{f} \circ \mathbf{g}\, s = \mathbf{f} (\mathbf{g}\, s)$), but rather the control structure of the program. That is, the sequence of actions specified by the programs is made manifest in the continuation. The data structure has, so to speak, been *factored out*.

All this is rather reminiscent of an important concept in imperative languages. This is the sequencing operator which is often written with a semicolon (cf. the ALGOL family of languages). Such an operator joins programs by control rather than by data and the data structure becomes an almost independent quantity to which primitive actions make reference.

To mark this similarity let us define a binary connective as follows:

$$\mathbf{f} ; \mathbf{g} = \mathbf{g} \circ' \mathbf{f}$$

This leads by a one-line transformation to $(\mathbf{f} ; \mathbf{g})\, \theta = \mathbf{f}' (\mathbf{g}'\, \theta)$

Exercise 4.9(i)

Prove that ; is associative and has left and right units.

■

Example 4.9(ii)

To find the square of the length of the fringe of a sexpression s we would usually write **square (length (fringe** s**))** whereas we may now write:

(fringe ; length ; square) id s

Notice that this is more than just writing the functions in sequential order (which we could have done easily by setting $\mathbf{f} ; \mathbf{g} = \mathbf{g} \circ \mathbf{f}$) for it is the control rather than the data structure which is responsible for gluing together the three component functions.

■

The ability to *pull* a datum out like this from a program can be very useful for it makes it clear when a data structure may be *destructively updated* with equanimity. Naturally our programming language does not support the articulation of destructive updating but this issue can be addressed by an implementation. Suppose for example we consider the program (**update** $a\ s\ l$) which updates the atom a to have value s in the substitution list l (cf. Section 3.4.4). We might ask: under what circumstances can we destructively alter l and under what circumstances can we not? Clearly, if other expressions share the substitution list l, a destructive change will destroy referential transparency and all will be lost. Some research has gone into determining when these circumstances pertain and some of this is referenced in the bibliographic notes at the end of the chapter since the details are beyond the scope of this book. In particular it has been shown that if arguments can be cancelled out of equations altogether (by the rule of extensionality) then this is a sufficient condition for maintaining a single data structure and effecting changes destructively. Notice that in a conventional language this is almost exactly the situation we are presented with. There is but one global state which is destructively updated and, moreover, the state never appears explicitly in a program; it has essentially been cancelled everywhere. The point to bear in mind is that we can exploit the destructive updating phenomenon *explicitly* in a conventional language but we cannot in a functional language even if the implementation is clever enough to see when such a policy is reasonable (and indeed desirable) on efficiency grounds.

To finish the section and to pursue the relationship between continuations and sequencing still further let us return to the idea of ignoring a continuation. From now on we assume that all functions expect continuations before their main arguments and we will on occasions use the same function name to stand for the original programs (which do not take continuations). This suggests we redefine the sequencing operator as follows:

$$(\mathbf{f} ; \mathbf{g})\,\theta = \mathbf{f}(\mathbf{g}\,\theta)$$

Notice that this is now nothing more than higher-order functional composition (composition at a higher functional level). Previously we had $(\mathbf{f} \circ \mathbf{g})\,s = \mathbf{f}(\mathbf{g}\,s)$ where $\mathbf{f}$ and $\mathbf{g}$ have type: $S \rightarrow S$.

In the definition above we have $\theta \in S \to S$ and thus **f** and **g** have type: $((S \to S) \to (S \to S))$. Let us define a new type:

$$C = S \to S$$

of *continuation values*. We see that **f** and **g** have type: $C \to C$; that is, they are *continuation transformers*. The operator ; is just *functional composition of continuation transformers*. In summary we have

$$\circ \in ((S \to S) \to (S \to S) \to (S \to S))$$
$$\text{and} \quad ; \ \in ((C \to C) \to (C \to C) \to (C \to C))$$

Now **f** and **g** may simply be continuation versions of standard programs. These are exactly the programs for which lemma 4.7(x) holds. This shows that we can embed the set of all continuation-free programs into the set of continuation programs by means of an embedding, I, given by: $I\mathbf{f} = \lambda\theta \cdot \theta \circ \mathbf{f}$ This is just our eureka definition from Section 4.7.

However, it is clear that elements of $C \to C$, the continuation transformers, are not restricted to such programs as we indicated after lemma 4.7(x).

Example 4.9(iii)

Consider the program $\mathbf{f}_1 ; \mathbf{f}_2 ; \ldots ; \mathbf{f}_n$. If this were a program in an imperative language we might be able to *label* any of the constituents $\mathbf{f}_i$. What would the label signify? Presumably, based on the idea that a label establishes *the meaning of the program from $\mathbf{f}_i$ onward*, we should set the label at $\mathbf{f}_i$ equal to the value of: $(\mathbf{f}_i ; \mathbf{f}_{i+1} ; \ldots ; \mathbf{f}_n)$. Let us refer to the label at $\mathbf{f}_i$ as l_i and the value of this as $\theta_i (= \mathbf{f}_i ; \mathbf{f}_{i+1} ; \ldots ; \mathbf{f}_n)$.

Consider the program $\mathbf{gotol}_i = \lambda\theta \cdot \theta_i$. Notice how the continuation this program is given (θ) is promptly ignored and θ_i substituted. This seems to capture the idea of a jump to l_i exactly. For example the program

$$(\mathbf{fringe} ; \mathbf{length} ; \mathbf{gotol}_5 ; \mathbf{cube} ; \mathbf{square} ; \mathbf{inc})\,\mathbf{id}\ s$$

provides us with the value $\mathbf{inc}\,(\mathbf{square}\,(\mathbf{length}\,(\mathbf{fringe}\ s)))$.
■

Exercise 4.9(iv)

Define the program $\mathbf{gotol}_5$ with respect to the program above and then evaluate the program with respect to input $(("A":"B"):("C":"D"))$.
■

Things become a lot more complicated if backward jumps are entertained for the simple reason that the label values themselves contain the jump function which contains the same label value. The values in these cases are given by suitable fixpoint solutions of the recursive descriptions. We shall elaborate this further in Section 8.2.2.

We are not necessarily advocating that continuations be utilized in such a fashion in a functional program. It should however be clear by now that continuations are extremely powerful and even the most unconstrained of imperative programming features can be described by them. We will return to this topic again in Chapter 8.

4.10 Bibliographic notes

Some of the earliest work on program transformation was concerned with the task of translating recursive specifications of tasks into flowcharts. The work of Strong (1971) and Walker & Strong (1973) are good examples of this approach.

The ideas of unfolding, folding and eureka definitions were introduced by Burstall & Darlington (1975, 1976, 1977). Darlington went on to develop the work more comprehensively (1977). In particular Darlington (1978) contains some excellent examples of the transformation of a specification for sorting into various well-known strategies.

Wegbreit (1976) considers goal-directed program transformation. In particular, by associating time and space costs to the underlying programming language he shows how programs with improved characteristics can be derived.

Richard Bird, more recently, has introduced some new and interesting techniques, including: recursion introduction (1977a, 1977b), promotion strategies (1984) and tabulation techniques (1980). He has also made a number of suggestions for a programming notation suitable for program development based on transformation techniques (1981). Colussi (1984) also advocates that programming should proceed by transformation, although he works with the stepwise refinement of imperative programs.

The problem of matching programs to schema for the purpose of invoking general transformations is covered in Givler & Kieburtz (1984). They use a dialect of FP, a language we will introduce in the next chapter. Huet & Lang (1978) use second-order patterns to express program transformations. Their work establishes the correctness of proposed methods by appealing to the denotational semantics of an imperative language. We will discuss denotational semantics in Chapter 7. Pettorossi (1984a, 1984b) has more recently developed the tupling strategies of Burstall & Darlington and some of the earlier work of Walker & Strong to more powerful transformational techniques.

Continuation-based methods are introduced by Wand (1980) and discussed most recently by Meyer & Wand (1985). Adding continuations to denotational semantics (which are expressed in a functional notation) has been tackled by Sethi & Tang (1980). Other interesting recent work on finite differencing has been undertaken by Paige & Koenig (1982).

Optimizations of applicative programs which utilize intermediate lists is the subject of Wadler (1984). The detection of circumstances under which data may be destructively updated is addressed in Raoult & Sethi (1983) and Schmidt (1985).

Abelson, H. & Sussman, G. J. (1985) *The Structure and Design of Computer Programs*. MIT Press, Cambridge, Mass.

Bird, R. S. (1977a) Notes on recursion elimination. *Commun. ACM*, **20**, 434–9.

Bird, R. S. (1977b) Improving programs by the introduction of recursion. *Commun. ACM*, **20**, 856–63.

Bird, R. S. (1980) Tabulation techniques for recursive programs. *Computing Surveys*, **12**, 403–17.

Bird, R. S. (1981) Notational suggestions for transformational programming, *Tech. report. RCS 144*. Department of Computer Science, University of Reading.

Bird, R. S. (1984) The promotion and accumulation strategies in transformational programming. *ACM Trans. Programming Languages and Systems*, **6**, 487–504.

Burstall, R. M. & Darlington, J. (1975) Some transformations for developing recursive programs. *Proc. International Conference on reliable software*, Los Angeles.

Burstall, R. M. & Darlington, J. (1977) A transformation system for developing recursive programs. *J. ACM*, **24**, 44–67.

Colussi, L. (1984) Recursion as an effective step in program development. *ACM Trans. Programming Languages and Systems*, **6**, 55–67.

Curien P. J. (1986) *Categorial Combinators, Sequential Algorithms and Functional Programming, Research Notes in Computer Science*. Pitman, London.

Darlington, J. (1977) Program transformation and synthesis: present capabilities, *Tech. report 77/43*, Department of Computer Science, Imperial College, London.

Darlington, J. (1978) A synthesis of several sorting algorithms. *Acta Informatica*, **11**, 1–30.

Darlington, J. & Burstall, R. M. (1976) A system which automatically improves programs. *Acta Informatica*, **6**, 41–60.

Givler, J. S. & Kieburtz, R. B. (1984) Schema recognition for program transformations. *Proc. ACM. Symposium on LISP and Functional Programming*, pp. 74–84, Austin, Texas.

Huet, G. & Lang, B. (1978) Proving and applying program transformations expressed with second order patterns. *Acta Informatica*, **11**, 31–55.

Meyer, A. R. & Wand, M. (1985) *Continuation semantics in typed lambda calculi, LNCS*, Vol. 217, Springer, Berlin.

Paige, R. & Koenig, S. (1982) Finite differencing of computable expressions. *ACM Trans. Programming Languages and Systems*, **4**, 402–54.

Pettorossi, A. (1984a) *Methodologies for transformations and memoing in applicative languages*. Ph.D. thesis, University of Edinburgh, Computer science memo CST-29-84.

Pettorossi, A. (1984b) A powerful strategy for deriving efficient programs by transformation. *ACM Symposium on LISP and Functional Programming*, Austin, Texas.

Raoult, J.-C. & Sethi, R. (1983) The global storage needs of a subcomputation. *Proc. ACM Symposium on Principles of Programming Languages*, pp. 148–57.

Schmidt, D. A. (1985) Detecting global variables in denotational specifications. *ACM Trans. Programming Languages and Systems*, **7**, 299–310.

Sethi R. & Tang, A. (1980) Constructing call-by-value continuation semantics, *J. ACM*, **27**, 580–97.

Strong, H. R. (1971) Translating recursion equations into flow charts. *Journal of Computing and System Science*, **5**, 254–85.

Tillotson, M. (1985) Introduction to the functional language "PONDER", *Tech. report no. 65.* Computer Laboratory, University of Cambridge.

Wadler, P. L. (1984) *Listlessness is better than laziness.* Ph.D. thesis, Department of Computer Science, Carnegie Mellon University.

Walker, S. A. & Strong, H. R. (1973) Characterisations of flowchartable recursions. *Journal of Computing and System Science*, **7**, 404–47.

Wand, M. (1980) Continuation based program transformation strategies, *J. ACM*, **27**, 164–80.

Wegbreit, B. (1976) Goal directed program transformation. *IEEE Trans. Software Engineering*, **SE2**, 69–80.

Chapter 5

FP systems

5.1 Introduction

In this chapter we examine the proposal for a novel functional programming style which has been advocated by John Backus. The seminal reference is Backus's *Turing Award Lecture for the ACM* (1978), the first sections of which should be compulsory reading for any serious computing scientist.

As we have remarked before, conventional programming may be thought of as operating at three levels: firstly, at the level of values (data structures); secondly, the level of *functions* or operations on values; and thirdly, at the level of *combining forms*; that is, those programming language features which are usually fixed and which form the "backbone" of all programs. In conventional languages it is usual to find that values may be combined in a variety of ways. Typically they can be bound to variables, passed into functions as arguments and returned from functions as results. The emphasis of programming in these languages rests on the manipulation of these values. This emphasis is reinforced by the observation that, in many languages, functions may not be manipulated so freely. Often, in particular, they may not be returned as results from other functions. Furthermore, this emphasis on the values is compounded by the rigidity of the combining forms. Ultimately, in these languages, all programs, no matter how sophisticated, are structured by a backbone of these fixed forms. Examples of these are the various looping constructs such as **while-do** and **for-next** together with sequencing and assignment. Conversely, it turns out that the combining forms of many languages possess properties which are not enjoyed by either data structures or functions. One example of this might be a degree of type polymorphism. PASCAL data and procedures cannot express polymorphism but the assignment combining form, := , may be used in a context of any type, providing the right-hand expression has a type which agrees with the left-hand variable. Furthermore, the operator **new**, which obtains new objects, can be used to generate objects of arbitrary specified type.

When we view programming languages in this way, that is, as a hierarchy of functional levels, it is natural to ask why the various levels are treated rather differently from one another. In general, this has to do with the structure of machines (virtual or actual). For example, the reason why functions cannot be returned as results of other functions, in certain languages, is because the virtual machine of the language is *stack based* (we shall see this in Chapter 6). The reason why the combining forms are fixed, as Backus has observed, is even more insidious for it is connected with the *actual* machine architecture which is typically Von Neumann. It is, in the final analysis, necessary to be able to break up any operation into small data transactions (at the level of the machine word) and, to every complex data structure (an array for example), provide a control-combining form (a **for-next** loop for example) appropriate for fitting the computation to the machine architecture.

One important feature of FP systems is the de-emphasis of the underlying data structures of the language. Instead, these systems concentrate on functions over data together with combining forms, which in FP are *functionals* (functions over functions). This de-emphasis is immediately apparent notationally since the stark fact is that FP systems are *variable free*. Programming consists of constructing functions from others by means of functionals (which Backus calls functional forms).

There are, as one might expect, a large number of consequences of this style of programming and we will spend much time in this chapter elaborating and discussing them.

Backus argues that the traditional Von Neumann machine imposes two bottlenecks on computing. The first is the physical bottleneck of the connection between the store and processor of such a machine. Transactions take place at a grain size determined by the word size of the machine. An example of such a transaction might be the updating of the store given some specified address. Since the problem of programming is to map the task onto machine state changes he suggests that there must be "a less primitive way of making big changes to the store than by pushing vast numbers of words back and forth along the Von-Neumann bottleneck" (Backus, 1978).

The second bottleneck he identifies is the intellectual bottleneck imposed by the physical one which keeps us constrained to word-by-word habits of thought. This manifests itself in the design of the programming languages which we use. If these variables are closely allied to the word, assignment becomes the major operation denoting traffic from processor to store and sequencing of statements (often denoted by a semicolon) imposes the rigid scheduling order on which the assignments crucially depend. The reader may object that variables in, say, ALGOL 68 can denote more ambitious values which require arbitrary storage requirements but, even given ALGOL 68's claim of orthogonality, the full manipulative power of simple values like integers (which are essentially just words) is not enjoyed by arbitrary data structures or, more specifically, by function values. Indeed, it was necessary in

such languages to make manifest the concept of the word by means of *ref*
values (pointers) to provide even the degree of flexibility they possess. Thus
rather than de-emphasizing the machine there is still a tendency to stress a
comprehensive view of the store as a mass of fixed length cells with their
addresses.

Backus has argued then that conventional languages have tended to
contain a core which accurately reflects the architecture of the Von Neumann
paradigm and that, ultimately, programming comes down to fitting in with
this sequence of updating transactions.

Advocates of ALGOL 68 and other more modern structural languages,
will still have many points to raise on this topic and it is fair to say that
Backus's paper is a polemic which continues to be hotly debated. Two things
are clear: the debate is genuine and purposeful and the consequences of
Backus's arguments have led him to develop a novel class of functional
programming systems.

5.2 Objects, functions and functionals

In this section we will elaborate an FP system which is very similar to the one
given by Backus in his original paper.

It is possible to treat our FP as a special collection of functions and
functionals defined in our KRC-like notation over a data type (defined below)
of *objects* (rather than over lists or sexpressions) and for which the operational
semantics is *applicative*. Indeed this is how the semantics of the various FP
constituents are described below. However, in order that our FP examples
conform to the notation used in the literature we shall take some lexical
liberties with the notation we have used up to now.

The first of these is rather simple: we allow ourselves the liberty of using
Greek letters for the names of some of the functions we introduce. The second
is more interesting (and is becoming more widely available in real programming languages); this is the provision of *mix-fix* operators. Up to now we
have allowed ourselves the luxury of permitting *infix* operators along with the
conventional *prefix* notation. Mix-fix operators allow us to define operators
whose argument positions may be distributed arbitrarily around the operator
sign. An example of a mix-fix operator that we use is the *conditional functional*:

$$\_ \xrightarrow{} \_ , \_$$

The underscoring indicates the position of the three arguments. A second example might be a more perspicuous version of the substitution function we introduced in example 3.4.4(i). Instead of writing:

substitute *s a s'*

we might introduce a mix-fix operator: $\_[\_ \leftarrow \_]$, taking three arguments as indicated by the underscores. We could then write:

$s[a \leftarrow s']$

rather as we do in the lambda calculus.

Finally, we will use patterns like $\langle x_1, \ldots, x_n \rangle$ to stand for an arbitrary tuple object (for $n \geq 0$) which is a slight generalization of the patterns we have used up to now.

Perhaps the most interesting corollary of expounding FP semantics in our earlier notation is that we can view this chapter as an investigation into the consequences of defining a collection of special functions and higher-order operators in (applicative) KRC or MIRANDA, and restricting ourselves to programming with these. In other words, *everything which we demonstrate in this chapter for FP follows in any applicative, functional language which can articulate the FP sets of functions and functionals*. The reader is, therefore, encouraged not to view the material of this chapter as in any sense *orthogonal* to that of the previous two but as an investigation into those same topics of program construction, verification and transformation in a somewhat different direction.

5.2.1 Objects

We shall begin by describing the set of values which are to be manipulated by FP programs. These are called *objects* and are just sequences (including the empty sequence) of objects or atoms. Objects, then, are rather like sexpressions except that compound objects are *tuples* of arbitrary length rather than just pairs, which is the case for sexpressions.

If we let A, as usual, stand for the set of *atoms* the description above suggests that the set O of *objects* is given by the data type definition:

$$O = A + O*$$

where:

$$X* = \{\langle \ \rangle\} + X + (X \times X) + (X \times X \times X) + \ldots$$

Further details of solutions to such equations can be found in Chapter 7 and Appendix A.

We will not employ a special data constructor for the summand $O*$ of O. We shall use angled brackets to denote tuple objects as Backus does. Recall that the data types N, B and C are summands of A, thus $\langle 3, \langle$ "True", "Hymnen" $\rangle, 4 \rangle$ is an object.

Finally, among the atoms is a distinguished atom $\perp$ pronounced *undefined* or *bottom* (this rather odd pronunciation will be explained in Chapter 7). This atom plays a very important role because it has the ability to collapse sequences in which it occurs in the following sense: if there exists an i such that $x_i = \perp$ then $\langle x_1, \ldots, x_n \rangle = \perp$. Note that the appearance of $\perp$ at any depth in a complicated object is sufficient to collapse that object to $\perp$. For example $\langle a, \langle \perp, b \rangle, c \rangle = \perp$ and so on. The best way to think of this is to view the equality relation on O as an extension of the natural equality on O (which is just the pointwise extension of equality on A) which equates all such elements to $\perp$.

The sign, $\perp$, which Backus uses is, perhaps, rather unfortunate as $\perp$ is usually reserved as a notation for *non-termination* in the semantic meta-theory of programs. This will be made more clear in Chapter 7. In this text we have reserved the sign, W, for a *program* (fragment) which fails to terminate [and, therefore, has $\perp$ (a *semantic value*) as its meaning]. Following Backus we use $\perp$ rather than W in this chapter but the reader ought to be aware of the notational confusion this might introduce for the unwary.

5.2.2 Functions

Let us now turn to functions over objects. It is interesting and important to note that all FP functions whether primitive or user-defined have the same type: they are *unary* mappings from O to O. Of course since O is closed under arbitrary products of O this hardly matters since operators like **plus**, which are usually thought of as binary operations, just expect an argument object which is a pair of objects. Note that in FP, functions like **plus** are *not* treated in curried form; they are unary simply because the cartesian products of O are subspaces of O. The advantage of treating all functions as unary is that it simplifies the interface between one function and another when they are combined in functional expressions.

Every FP system possesses a set of primitive functions and we shall be selecting a number, but not all, of those given by Backus and subsequently used by other authors in more recent work. A central feature of all FP functions (primitive and user-defined) is that they preserve $\perp$. This means that for all FP functions f; $f \perp = \perp$. Another terminology for this, which we have seen before, is to say that all FP functions are *strict*.

We shall now give a set of primitive functions for the FP system which we shall be studying in the rest of this chapter.

Selector functions

These generalize the **h** and **t** selectors we have seen in earlier chapters. For all natural numbers, s, we define:

$$\mathbf{s} \langle x_1, \ldots, x_n \rangle = x_s \qquad \text{when } 1 \leqslant s \leqslant n$$
$$\mathbf{s}\, x = \bot \qquad \text{otherwise}$$

For example: $\mathbf{2} \langle a, b, c \rangle = b$ and $\mathbf{3} \langle a, b \rangle = \bot$.

$$\mathbf{tl} \langle x_1, \ldots, x_n \rangle = \langle x_2, \ldots, x_n \rangle \qquad \text{when } n \geqslant 1$$
$$\mathbf{tl}\, x = \bot \qquad \text{otherwise}$$

Predicates

$$\mathbf{at}\, \bot = \bot$$
$$\mathbf{at}\, x = \mathbf{atom}\, x$$

This is just the strict extension of the primitive predicate **atom**. Although we have named this function **at** here to remove ambiguity we will write it as **atom** as usual hereafter.

$$\mathbf{eqq}\, \bot = \bot$$
$$\mathbf{eqq} \langle x, y \rangle = \mathbf{eq}\, x\, y$$

Again this is just the strict extension of a primitive predicate. We will write **eqq** as **eq** for convenience in the sequel.

Arithmetic and logical operators

$$\mathbf{plus} \langle n, n' \rangle = n + n'$$
$$\mathbf{plus}\, x = \bot$$

and in a similar fashion for other arithmetic operators. Sometimes we use $+$ for **plus** and so on.

$$\mathbf{\&} \langle t, t' \rangle = t \text{ and } t'$$
$$\mathbf{\&}\, x = \bot$$

Constructors

There are two primitive constructors which place objects in sequences to the left and to the right.

$$\textbf{apndl} \, \langle \, x, \langle \, z_1, \ldots, z_n \, \rangle \, \rangle = \langle \, x, z_1, \ldots, z_n \, \rangle \qquad (n \geq 0)$$
$$\textbf{apndl} \, x \qquad\qquad\qquad = \bot$$

$$\textbf{apndr} \, \langle \, \langle \, z_1, \ldots, z_n \, \rangle, x \, \rangle = \langle \, z_1, \ldots, z_n, x \, \rangle \qquad (n \geq 0)$$
$$\textbf{apndr} \, x \qquad\qquad\qquad = \bot$$

Constant functions

These effectively name objects at the function level. For every FP object x we have a function $\bar{\textbf{x}}$ which yields a constant result x for all arguments. Actually, strictness forces this to fail when $\bar{\textbf{x}}$ is given $\bot$ as an argument. More formally, we have:

$$\bar{\textbf{x}} \, \bot = \bot$$
$$\bar{\textbf{x}} \, z \ = x$$

Finally, we include the identity function on objects. It is written **id** and is defined in the obvious way:

$$\textbf{id} \, x = x$$

Note that, like all the other primitives, it is strict.

This concludes our small set of FP primitive functions. Before we can show how user-defined functions are introduced it will be necessary for us to explain how primitives can be put together into larger functional expressions. This is achieved by the FP *combining forms* or *functionals* which we shall now turn to.

5.2.3 Functionals

Unlike FP functions, FP combining forms have various arities. That is, they may take more than one argument. We start with the most obvious way to put functions together.

Composition

If **f** and **g** are FP functions then so is **f** ∘ g. ∘, pronounced *composition*, is as usual, a binary combining form. As expected it is defined as an infix operator:

$$(\textbf{f} \circ \textbf{g}) \, x = \textbf{f}(\textbf{g} \, x)$$

It is very tempting to define composition, as many mathematicians now do, as $(\mathbf{f} \circ \mathbf{g}) \, x = \mathbf{g}(\mathbf{f} \, x)$ for this enables expressions in FP to be read naturally from left to right. We have not given in to temptation in this book in order to allow the interested reader to pursue the topic in the literature with ease. However, it might soon be time to adopt the more perspicuous notation, and indeed to place the argument to the left of the function instead. We would then write: $(x \, (\mathbf{f} \circ \mathbf{g})) = (x \, \mathbf{f}) \mathbf{g}$. Composition clearly preserves strictness.

Construction

Since objects can be tupled to form a single object it is sensible to provide a way to tuple functions into a single function. This is the *construction functional* which is also known as *target tupling*. This is our first example of a *mix-fix* operator.

Let $\mathbf{f}_i$ be FP functions for $1 \le i \le n$:

$$[\mathbf{f}_1, \ldots, \mathbf{f}_n] \, x = \langle \mathbf{f}_1 \, x, \ldots, \mathbf{f}_n \, x \rangle$$

There are two things to note. Firstly, we shall not distinguish between constructions of different arity. Secondly, it is important to notice that since object formation is strict the function $[\mathbf{f}_1, \ldots, \mathbf{f}_n]$ is strict if any of the $\mathbf{f}_i$ are. Thus the construction functional also preserves strictness.

Product functional

Related to construction is the *product functional*. This is another way of tupling functions together. We use an infix, $\times$, to denote this functional:

Let $\mathbf{f}_1$ and $\mathbf{f}_2$ be FP functions then:

$$(\mathbf{f}_1 \times \mathbf{f}_2) \, \langle x_1, x_2 \rangle = \langle \mathbf{f}_1 \, x_1, \mathbf{f}_2 \, x_2 \rangle$$
$$(\mathbf{f}_1 \times \mathbf{f}_2) x \qquad = \perp$$

Conditional

The conditional functional is a ternary operator, as usual. We are used to conditional commands and indeed to conditional expressions (which yield value results) but here we are dealing with a conditional which yields a *function* as a result of the conditional test. It is written and defined as a mix-fix operator:

$$\_ \rightarrow \_ , \_$$

Let **p**, $\mathbf{f}_1$ and $\mathbf{f}_2$ be FP functions.

$$(\mathbf{p}\rightarrow\mathbf{f}_1;\mathbf{f}_2)x=\mathbf{f}_1\,x \qquad \textbf{when p } x=\text{``True''}$$
$$(\mathbf{p}\rightarrow\mathbf{f}_1;\mathbf{f}_2)x=\mathbf{f}_2\,x \qquad \textbf{when p } x=\text{``False''}$$
$$(\mathbf{p}\rightarrow\mathbf{f}_1;\mathbf{f}_2)x=\perp \qquad \textbf{otherwise.}$$

It is quite clear that $\mathbf{p}\rightarrow\mathbf{f}_1;\mathbf{f}_2$ is a strict function if **p**, $\mathbf{f}_1$ and $\mathbf{f}_2$ are strict. This observation may cause some alarm or confusion because the conditional operator in known programming languages is non-strict, and necessarily so. For example we often write:

if $n=0$ **then** 0 **else** x/n

in order that the division is protected. If the conditional were strict then the fact that the value x/n is undefined at $n=0$ would make the whole expression undefined and the ruse of protecting the division with a conditional *will just not work!*

This is a delicate issue that needs careful thought. Although $\mathbf{p}\rightarrow\mathbf{f}_1;\mathbf{f}_2$ is a strict function, for all strict functions **p**, $\mathbf{f}_1$ and $\mathbf{f}_2$, it is not the case that $\rightarrow$ is a *strict functional*. To see this more precisely we had better be more explicit about strict functionals. Just as a strict function preserves the undefined value a strict functional preserves the undefined function. The undefined function is of course $\bar{\perp}$ the 'constantly undefined' function. Now composition and tupling not only produce strict functions when given strict arguments they are also strict as functionals. That is, in these cases: $\bar{\perp}\circ\mathbf{g}=\bar{\perp}$; $\mathbf{f}\circ\bar{\perp}=\bar{\perp}$ and $[\mathbf{f}_1,\ldots,\bar{\perp},\ldots,\mathbf{f}_n]=\bar{\perp}$. The conditional functional is not a strict functional because it is *not* the case that $(\mathbf{p}\rightarrow\bar{\perp};\mathbf{g})$ or $(\mathbf{p}\rightarrow\mathbf{f};\bar{\perp})$ are necessarily equivalent to $\bar{\perp}$ (although $(\bar{\perp}\rightarrow\mathbf{f};\mathbf{g})=\bar{\perp}$) whereas $(\mathbf{p}\rightarrow\mathbf{f}_1;\mathbf{f}_2)\perp=\perp$ for all strict **p**, $\mathbf{f}_1$ and $\mathbf{f}_2$.

Apply-to-all

The construction functional steers an object into a tuple of functions, whereas the functional we turn to now steers a function into a tuple of objects:

$$(\alpha\mathbf{f})\langle x_1,\ldots,x_n\rangle=\langle\mathbf{f}x_1,\ldots,\mathbf{f}x_n\rangle \qquad \textbf{when } n\geq0$$
$$(\alpha\mathbf{f})x=\perp \qquad \textbf{otherwise}$$

This then is a straightforward function definition in our notation. We allow it to be named by a Greek letter in order to stay close to Backus's own style. Furthermore we adopt his convention that α binds tighter than application. This will allow us to write $(\alpha\mathbf{f}\,x)$ for $((\alpha\mathbf{f})\,x)$.

Deep apply

The functional α only distributes its function argument along the outermost sequence of objects. The deep apply functional β applies a function to all components of an arbitrary object. Since a component may be an atom or a sequence object β has two arguments to cover these cases:

$$(\beta\ \mathbf{f}\ \mathbf{g})\ \langle x_1, \ldots, x_n \rangle = \mathbf{g}\ (\alpha\ (\beta\ \mathbf{f}\ \mathbf{g})\ \langle x_1, \ldots, x_n \rangle)$$
$$(\beta\ \mathbf{f}\ \mathbf{g})\ x \qquad\qquad = \mathbf{f}\ x \qquad \textbf{when atom}\ x$$

Insert functionals

FP contains three insert functionals or *reduction operators* as they are sometimes called. They are unary functionals and have the effect, roughly, of extending a function from an operation over objects (of some kind) to sequences of such objects.

We describe first the *right-insert* functional:

$$(/_\mathbf{R}\,\mathbf{f})\ \langle x \rangle \qquad\qquad = x$$
$$(/_\mathbf{R}\,\mathbf{f})\ \langle x_1, \ldots, x_n \rangle \quad = \mathbf{f}\langle x_1, (/_\mathbf{R}\,\mathbf{f})\ \langle x_2, \ldots, x_n \rangle \rangle\ (n \geq 2)$$
$$(/_\mathbf{R}\,\mathbf{f})\langle\ \rangle \qquad\qquad = 1_\mathbf{R} \qquad \text{(the right unit of } \mathbf{f} \text{ if it exists)}$$

Left insert follows a similar pattern:

$$(/_\mathbf{L}\,\mathbf{f})\ \langle x \rangle \qquad\qquad = x$$
$$(/_\mathbf{L}\,\mathbf{f})\ \langle x_1, \ldots, x_n \rangle = \mathbf{f}\langle (/_\mathbf{L}\,\mathbf{f})\ \langle x_1, \ldots, x_{n-1} \rangle, x_n \rangle\ (n \geq 2)$$
$$(/_\mathbf{L}\,\mathbf{f})\langle\ \rangle \qquad\qquad = 1_\mathbf{L} \qquad \text{(the left unit of } \mathbf{f} \text{ if it exists)}$$

Finally the *concurrent insert* which is essentially non-deterministic in its evaluation. Since it may only be sensibly used with associative $\mathbf{f}$ this does not make any serious impact:

$$(/_\mathbf{c}\,\mathbf{f})\ \langle x \rangle \qquad\qquad = x$$
$$(/_\mathbf{c}\,\mathbf{f})\ \langle x_1, \ldots, x_n \rangle \quad = \mathbf{f}\langle (/_\mathbf{c}\,\mathbf{f})\ \langle x_1, \ldots, x_i \rangle, (/_\mathbf{c}\,\mathbf{f})\ \langle x_{i+1}, \ldots, x_n \rangle \rangle$$
$$(n \geq 2)\ (1 \leq i \leq n)$$
$$(/_\mathbf{c}\,\mathbf{f})\langle\ \rangle \qquad\qquad = 1 \qquad \text{(the unit of } \mathbf{f} \text{ if it exists)}$$

We shall assume that application of these insert functionals to a function $\mathbf{f}$ binds tighter than application of functions to objects. This allows us to write $(/\mathbf{f}\,x)$ instead of $((/\mathbf{f})\,x)$.

This concludes our description of the FP system.

It is very important that we should note that since all primitive functions are strict and since all the functionals preserve strictness we have the result (by induction) that *any expression built up by functionals from primitive operators denotes a strict object function.*

This presentation differs from Backus's own in one important respect. He writes functional application with an infix colon. Thus our (**f** x) he would write as **f**: x. We could define the colon as an infix operator with this semantics by writing:

$$\mathbf{f}: x = \mathbf{f}\ x$$

but in view of our use for the colon (as a data constructor) almost everywhere else in the book we refrain from doing this.

Exercise 5.2.3(i)

Many of the functional forms described above are reminiscent of the higher-order operations described towards the end of Chapter 3. Identify these.
∎

5.3 Definitions in FP

Now we can turn to programming in such a language.

A definition in FP is written:

def f = e

where **f** is the function name and e is a function expression built up from primitive functions and other user-defined functions (including **f** so as to allow direct recursion) by means of combining forms or functionals. Thus a definition in FP is just a definition in our earlier notation which utilizes the functionals and functions which we have introduced in the previous sections. Note in particular that such functions are combinatorial, that is, they are variable free.

5.3.1 Simple definitions

We shall start with some elementary examples and then move on to more adventurous programming later.

Example 5.3.1(i)

def eq0 = **eq** ∘ [**id**, $\bar{\mathbf{0}}$]

This new function, **eq0**, is built from the primitives **eq**, **id** and $\bar{\mathbf{0}}$ by two functionals: composition and construction.

The idea is that **eq0** is a unary predicate yielding "True" just when its argument is zero. Using the definitions of the previous section we can show that **eq0** has expected properties:

$$\begin{aligned}
\textbf{eq0 } 0 &= \\
(\textbf{eq} \circ [\textbf{id}, \overline{\textbf{0}}]) \, 0 &= \\
\textbf{eq}([\textbf{id}, \overline{\textbf{0}}] \, 0) &= \\
\textbf{eq} \langle \textbf{id } 0, \overline{\textbf{0}} \, 0 \rangle &= \\
\textbf{eq} \langle 0, 0 \rangle &= \\
\text{"True"}
\end{aligned}$$

also:

$$\begin{aligned}
\textbf{eq0 } 3 &= \text{"False"} \\
\textbf{eq0 } \langle x_1, \ldots, x_n \rangle &= \text{"False" and of course} \\
\textbf{eq0 } \bot &= \bot
\end{aligned}$$

■

Exercise 5.3.1(ii)

(a) Check these last three statements.
(b) Write definitions in FP for the following:
    (i) **inc** which increments its numeric argument.
    (ii) **square** which squares its numeric argument.
    (iii) **cube** which cubes its numeric argument.
    (iv) **null** which yields "True" for $\langle \ \rangle$.

■

Example 5.3.1(iii)

As a second example we shall show that the product functional is really just syntactic sugar because we can program it by other means.

Consider the expression $[\textbf{f}_1 \circ \textbf{1}, \textbf{f}_2 \circ \textbf{2}]$.

If we evaluate this at argument $\langle x_1, x_2 \rangle$ we obtain:

$$\begin{aligned}
&[\textbf{f}_1 \circ \textbf{1}, \textbf{f}_2 \circ \textbf{2}] \, \langle x_1, x_2 \rangle = \\
&\langle \textbf{f}_1 \circ \textbf{1} \, \langle x_1, x_2 \rangle, \textbf{f}_2 \circ \textbf{2} \, \langle x_1, x_2 \rangle \rangle = \\
&\langle \textbf{f}_1(\textbf{1} \, \langle x_1, x_2 \rangle), \textbf{f}_2(\textbf{2} \, \langle x_1, x_2 \rangle) \rangle = \\
&\langle \textbf{f}_1 \, x_1, \textbf{f}_2 \, x_2 \rangle
\end{aligned}$$

This is just $(\textbf{f}_1 \times \textbf{f}_2) \, \langle x_1, x_2 \rangle$.

■

Two things emerge here which we will take up in later sections. Firstly, we seem to be establishing the equivalence of two programs. How do we show that programs are equivalent in general? Secondly, this is only a partial or conditional equivalence for $(\mathbf{f}_1 \times \mathbf{f}_2)\langle x_1, x_2, x_3 \rangle = \perp$ whereas $[\mathbf{f}_1 \circ 1, \mathbf{f}_2 \circ 2]\langle x_1, x_2, x_3 \rangle = \langle \mathbf{f}_1 x_1, \mathbf{f}_2 x_2 \rangle = (\mathbf{f}_1 \times \mathbf{f}_2)\langle x_1, x_2 \rangle$. How do we capture this conditional equivalence?

5.3.2 Recursive definitions

Let us move on to some more adventurous examples.

Example 5.3.2(i)

Suppose we wish to take an object z and sequence $\langle x_1, \ldots, x_n \rangle$ and produce a result $\langle \langle z, x_1 \rangle, \ldots, \langle z, x_n \rangle \rangle$. We will call this, as Backus does, **distl** (distribute left). This suggests a recursive solution:

$$\textbf{def distl} = \textbf{null} \circ 2 \rightarrow [\ ]; \quad \textbf{apndl} \circ [(\textbf{id} \times 1), \quad \textbf{distl} \circ (\textbf{id} \times \textbf{tl})]$$

Taking $\langle x \langle \ \rangle \rangle$ as input we see that $(\textbf{null} \circ 2)\langle x \langle \ \rangle \rangle = \textbf{null}\,(2\langle x \langle \ \rangle \rangle) = \textbf{null}$ $\langle \ \rangle = $ "True" so the first arm of the conditional is selected: $[\ ] \langle x, \langle \ \rangle \rangle = \langle \ \rangle$ (we could equally well replace the empty tuple $[\ ]$ by $\mathbf{2}$ in this context). If the argument is $\langle z, \langle x_1, \ldots, x_n \rangle \rangle$ then $\textbf{null} \circ 2\ \langle z_1 \langle x_1, \ldots, x_n \rangle \rangle = \textbf{null}$ $\langle x_1, \ldots, x_n \rangle = $ "False" so the second arm is selected: $\textbf{apndl} \circ [(\textbf{id} \times 1), \textbf{distl}$ $\circ (\textbf{id} \times \textbf{tl})]\ \langle z, \langle x_1, \ldots, x_n \rangle \rangle = \textbf{apndl}\ (\langle \textbf{id}\ z, 1\ \langle x_1, \ldots, x_n \rangle \rangle, \textbf{distl}\ \langle \textbf{id}\ z, \textbf{tl}$ $\langle x_1, \ldots, x_n \rangle \rangle = \textbf{apndl}\ (\langle z, x_1 \rangle, \textbf{distl}\ \langle z, \langle x_2, \ldots, x_n \rangle \rangle$. Assuming by induction that the recursive **distl** provides us with $\langle \langle z, x_2 \rangle, \ldots, \langle z, x_n \rangle \rangle$ we have $\textbf{apndl}\ \langle \langle z, x_1 \rangle, \langle \langle z, x_2 \rangle, \ldots, \langle z, x_n \rangle \rangle \rangle = \langle \langle z, x_1 \rangle, \ldots, \langle z, x_n \rangle \rangle$ as required.
∎

Exercise 5.3.2(ii)

Write a function **distr** which given $\langle \langle x_1, \ldots, x_n \rangle, z \rangle$ yields
$\langle \langle x_1, z \rangle, \ldots, \langle x_n, z \rangle \rangle$.
∎

The previous example was guided by imagining how we would program in a *first-order* language of functions and values. It is not all that difficult to translate such programs into *second-order* programs of functionals and functions. For example we could define functions:

> **def length** $=$ **null** $\rightarrow \bar{0}$; **inc** $\circ$ **length** $\circ$ **tl**
> **def reverse** $=$ **null** $\rightarrow$ [ ]; **append** $\circ$ [**reverse** $\circ$ **tl**, [**1**]]
> **def append** $=$ **null** $\circ$ **1** $\rightarrow$ **2**; **apndl** $\circ$ [**1** $\circ$ **1**, **append** $\circ$ (**tl** $\times$ **id**)]

Exercise 5.3.2(iii)

Transliterate the definitions of other programs from Chapter 3, for example **factorial**, **reverse** (with accumulator) in the same way. In fact there is an exact correspondence between the programs: application is converted to composition; references to arguments are converted to selector functions and so on. This suggests . . .
■

Project 5.3.2(iv)

Write an algorithm which given a first-order program definition in conditional form (let us say as a parse tree) produces its FP equivalent.
■

5.3.3 Using recursive functionals

To a great extent we have been missing the point. FP provides a large number of functional forms which encode recursive strategies. For example α, β and the insert operators $/_L$, $/_R$, $/_C$ are all of this type.

FP programming 'style' suggests we learn to use these powerful operators to produce compact and possibly non-recursive solutions to problems. We will call such programs *closed forms*. Of course, as we mentioned at the beginning of the chapter, such a 'style' can be developed in any higher-order functional language by packaging recursion in suitable higher-order operators (like **lrec**, **srec**, $\mathbf{h}_L$, **map**, . . . of Chapter 3) and then using them non-recursively.

As an example let us take the function **length** again, and start from first principles.

Example 5.3.3(i)

We wish to compute the length of a sequence, say, $\langle x_1, \ldots, x_n \rangle$. Each item counts for 1. Suppose we actually replace all the objects x_i by 1. We then have

$\langle 1, \ldots, 1 \rangle$ which is an n-tuple consisting entirely of the atom 1. The length of the sequence is just the sum of these numbers. Addition, we know, is a primitive operator and acts to add *pairs*; but the insert functional we learned, in the last section, is designed to extend such functions to sequences of arguments. Now in order to convert any of the x_i to 1 we simply have to arrange for x_i to be an argument to $\bar{1}$ (the "constantly 1" function). In order to give this function to all the x_i we can use the α operation. Since addition is associative it does not actually matter which insert operation we use. Putting these ideas together we are led to define length as follows:

$$\textbf{def } \text{length} = /_c + \, \circ \, \alpha \bar{1}$$

We can reduce this expression on a typical argument:

$$(/_c + \circ \alpha \bar{1}) \langle "A", "B", "C", "D" \rangle =$$
$$/_c + (\alpha \bar{1} \langle "A", "B", "C", "D" \rangle) =$$
$$/_c + \langle \bar{1} "A", \bar{1} "B", \bar{1} "C", \bar{1} "D" \rangle =$$
$$/_c + \langle 1, 1, 1, 1 \rangle =$$
$$+ \langle /_c + \langle 1, 1 \rangle, /_c + \langle 1, 1 \rangle \rangle =$$
$$+ \langle + \langle /_c + \langle 1 \rangle, /_c + \langle 1 \rangle \rangle, + \langle /_c + \langle 1 \rangle, /_c + \langle 1 \rangle \rangle \rangle =$$
$$+ \langle + \langle 1, 1 \rangle + \langle 1, 1 \rangle \rangle =$$
$$+ \langle 2, 2 \rangle =$$
$$4$$

Notice how various parts of this evaluation could be done concurrently. This explicit concurrency in the use of the α and / forms, for example, makes FP and related languages exciting from an implementation viewpoint.
■

Example 5.3.3(ii)

As a second example let us take, as a task, a program called **last**, which given an argument $\langle x_1, \ldots, x_n \rangle$ will yield x_n. It is easy to see how to do this using explicit recursion but of course, we should like to find a simple closed form. Actually this is rather easy because selecting x_n from $\langle x_1, \ldots, x_n \rangle$ is just a generalization of picking x_2 from $\langle x_1, x_2 \rangle$. This second task can be directly solved using the selector **2**. Again, it is the insert operation which generalizes a function to arbitrary sequences so this seems to be the way forward. In this case do we need to worry about which of the insert forms to use? This just depends on algebraic properties of the function to be inserted. In this case we observe that the function **2** is associative since:

$$\textbf{2} \langle x_1, \textbf{2} \langle x_2, x_3 \rangle \rangle = \textbf{2} \langle \textbf{2} \langle x_1, x_2 \rangle, x_3 \rangle$$

so we may utilize whichever insert operator we please. Therefore we can define:

def last $=/_c 2$

It should be becoming clear that the functional forms of FP are quite powerful and code up general recursive strategies, thus allowing compact non-recursive solutions to a number of problems.
■

Exercise 5.3.3(iii)

Other functions like **member, reverse, delete** and so on have pleasing non-recursive solutions which the reader may like to try to find. Several of these will appear in a later section when we show how a powerful expansion theorem can be employed to transform some recursive definitions into closed forms.
■

To finish this section we will develop an FP program which forms finite cartesian products of sets of atoms.

Example 5.3.3(iv)

Let us take a sequence of atoms to represent a set. We will begin by trying to solve the simpler problem of finding the cartesian product of just two sets. Thus given an argument:

$$\langle \langle "A", "B", "C" \rangle, \langle 1, 2 \rangle \rangle$$

for example, we wish our function (call it **cross**) to yield:

$$\langle \langle "A", 1 \rangle, \langle "A", 2 \rangle, \langle "B", 1 \rangle, \langle "B", 2 \rangle, \langle "C", 1 \rangle, \langle "C", 2 \rangle \rangle$$

This seems like a generalization of either the **distl** or **distr** operations which we described earlier. If, for example, we apply **distr** to the input above we obtain:

$$\langle \langle "A", \langle 1, 2 \rangle \rangle, \langle "B", \langle 1, 2 \rangle \rangle, \langle "C", \langle 1, 2 \rangle \rangle \rangle$$

At this point we need to take each triple like $\langle "A", \langle 1, 2 \rangle \rangle$ and distribute the first atom over the second and third. This is achieved by **distl**. However we will need to do this to all triples in the sequence above. This is done by using the apply-to-all functional α:

$$\alpha \, (\textbf{distl}) \, \langle \langle "A", \langle 1, 2 \rangle \rangle, \langle "B", \langle 1, 2 \rangle \rangle, \langle "C", \langle 1, 2 \rangle \rangle \rangle =$$
$$\langle \langle \langle "A", 1 \rangle, \langle "A", 2 \rangle \rangle, \langle \langle "B", 1 \rangle, \langle "B", 2 \rangle \rangle, \langle \langle "C", 1 \rangle, \langle "C", 2 \rangle \rangle \rangle$$

This is almost what we require. At least we have created all the elements using the composite α **distl** $\circ$ **distr**.

All we now need to do is to append the three sequences of pairs into a simple sequence of pairs.

We do possess a function for appending a pair of sequences but it is just a transliteration of the familiar recursive definition we introduced in Chapter 3. First we should look to see if **append** can be defined using functional forms and secondly see if there is a natural way of extending it to cope with an arbitrary number of sequences. It is clear that the number of sequences we will need to append in our present example depends on the size of the first argument set; this has size three for the input we have been considering.

Example 5.3.3(v)

append needs to take an input:

$$\langle\langle\text{``}A\text{''}, \text{``}B\text{''}, \text{``}C\text{''}\rangle, \langle 1, 2, 3\rangle\rangle$$

and yield:

$$\langle\text{``}A\text{''}, \text{``}B\text{''}, \text{``}C\text{''}, 1, 2, 3\rangle$$

as a result. Appending, as we know, is like a generalized form of **apndl**. More exactly, if we take the input above and obtain:

$$\langle\text{``}A\text{''}, \text{``}B\text{''}, \text{``}C\text{''}, \langle 1, 2, 3\rangle\rangle$$

by means of an **apndr** operation, the rest is simply a successive **apndl** cascade placing each of "C", "B" and "A" onto the right-hand list. Again this can be achieved by extending **apndl** by means of the insert operator. It is vital here that we select the correct functional because **apndl** is not associative. Clearly the correct order of evaluation places "C" onto $\langle 1, 2, 3\rangle$ before "B" and before "A". The correct functional is therefore $/_R$. Thus we define:

> **def append** $= /_R$ **apndl** $\circ$ **apndr**

Exercise 5.3.3(vi)

There is a very similar definition for **append** which uses $/_L$. Find it.
■

Extending our functions to several sequences is simplicity itself; we just use the insert functional to extend it to a sequence of arguments. This suggests:

> **def concat** $= /(/_R$ **apndl** $\circ$ **apndr**$)$

Notice that the expression $/_R$ **apndl** $\circ$ **apndr** is, as is by now well known, an

associative operation. This means that we may use whichever insert functional we choose to generalize **append**.
∎

Turning out attention back to the cartesian product we can complete our definition of products of pairs now:

$$\textbf{def cross} = \textbf{concat} \circ \alpha\textbf{distl} \circ \textbf{distr}$$

Generalizing this to arbitrary cross-products is a little more than simply extending **cross** by using an insert functional. What we have to do, essentially, is to see that **cross** as defined above can be made a little more regular. At present the argument we give **cross** is a pair of sequences of set elements. The clue to producing a general cross-product function is contained in rewriting the binary cross-product function above so that it will work when the argument is a pair of sequences (as before) but where the elements are singleton sequences. If we do this then the regularity this provides (*everything* is a sequence of some sort) allows us to generalize the function easily. In this case we would be given:

$$\langle\langle\langle 1\rangle, \langle 2\rangle, \langle 3\rangle\rangle, \langle\langle \text{“}A\text{”}\rangle, \langle \text{“}B\text{”}\rangle\rangle\rangle$$

as an argument instead of:

$$\langle\langle 1, 2, 3\rangle, \langle \text{“}A\text{”}, \text{“}B\text{”}\rangle\rangle$$

After applying this to α **distl** $\circ$ **distr** we would have the sequence:

$$\langle\langle\langle\langle 1\rangle, \langle \text{“}A\text{”}\rangle\rangle, \langle\langle 1\rangle, \langle \text{“}B\text{”}\rangle\rangle\rangle, \langle\langle\langle 2\rangle, \langle \text{“}A\text{”}\rangle\rangle, \langle\langle 2\rangle, \langle \text{“}B'\rangle\rangle\rangle,$$
$$\langle\langle\langle 3\rangle, \langle \text{“}A\text{”}\rangle\rangle, \langle\langle 3\rangle, \langle \text{“}B\text{”}\rangle\rangle\rangle\rangle$$

If we now apply **concat** the answer will be:

$$\langle\langle\langle 1\rangle, \langle \text{“}A\text{”}\rangle\rangle, \langle\langle 1\rangle, \langle \text{“}B\text{”}\rangle\rangle, \langle\langle 2\rangle, \langle \text{“}A\text{”}\rangle\rangle, \langle\langle 2\rangle, \langle \text{“}B'\rangle\rangle,$$
$$\langle\langle 3\rangle, \langle \text{“}A\text{”}\rangle\rangle, \langle\langle 3\rangle, \langle \text{“}B\text{”}\rangle\rangle\rangle$$

We would rather not have to deal with elements as singleton sequences so would like to collapse these brackets before output. This is easily effected by processing the last result by α **append** which yields the expected result:

$$\langle\langle 1, \text{“}A\text{”}\rangle, \langle 1, \text{“}B\text{”}\rangle, \langle 2, \text{“}A\text{”}\rangle, \langle 2, \text{“}B\text{”}\rangle, \langle 3, \text{“}A\text{”}\rangle, \langle 3, \text{“}B\text{”}\rangle\rangle$$

Likewise, we do not wish to enter elements of our sets as singleton sequences. Preprocessing with the function $\alpha \alpha$ [**id**] puts the ordinary notation:

$$\langle\langle \text{“}A\text{”}, \text{“}B\text{”}, \text{“}C\text{”}\rangle, \langle 1, 2\rangle\rangle$$

into the form:

$$\langle\langle\langle \text{“}A\text{”}\rangle, \langle \text{“}B\text{”}\rangle, \langle \text{“}C\text{”}\rangle\rangle, \langle\langle 1\rangle, \langle 2\rangle\rangle\rangle$$

It is necessary to use two α functionals to 'drive' the [**id**] function through to the atoms. Note that [**id**] $x = \langle x \rangle$ when x is not $\perp$. Our final new version for **cross** is:

$$\textbf{def cross} = \alpha \textbf{ append} \circ \textbf{concat} \circ \alpha \textbf{distl} \circ \textbf{distr}$$

when we provide it with arguments preprocessed by $\alpha\alpha$ [**id**].

Now this generalizes to arbitrary sequences of sets by means of the insert functional rather easily:

$$\textbf{def cart} = /\textbf{cross} \circ \alpha\alpha \,[\textbf{id}]$$

■

We will now leave programming examples in FP and turn to some of the formal properties of the language. In the next section we turn to the task of verification in FP systems.

5.4 The algebra of programs

We have seen forcefully how the emphasis of FP programming rests at the level of functionals and functions. It switches attention from how data (objects in FP) are to be manipulated (by functions) to consider how programs (functions) can be combined to form others (by the functionals).

One major theme of Backus's development is to study the relationship between programs built using the various functionals. These relationships are expressed by a number of *algebraic laws*, which capture various properties of the functionals. Once established, they can be used to prove correctness and equivalence of programs and even to effect optimizations and compilations by a process of program transformation.

5.4.1 Assertions about programs

We introduce three *meta-language symbols* for the description of these laws:

Definition 5.4.1(i)

For all $\mathbf{f}, \mathbf{g} \in F$; $\mathbf{f} \leq \mathbf{g}$ iff for all $x \in O$; $((\mathbf{f}\,x) = \perp) \vee ((\mathbf{f}\,x) = (\mathbf{g}\,x))$
■

Definition 5.4.1(ii)

For all $\mathbf{f}, \mathbf{g} \in F$; $\mathbf{f} = \mathbf{g}$ iff $\mathbf{f} \leq \mathbf{g} \wedge \mathbf{g} \leq f$
■

Definition 5.4.1(iii)

For all $\mathbf{p}, \mathbf{f}, \mathbf{g} \in F$; $\mathbf{p} \twoheadrightarrow \mathbf{f} = \mathbf{g}$ iff for all $x \in O$; $((\mathbf{p}\, x) = \text{"True"}) \Rightarrow (\mathbf{f}\, x) = (\mathbf{g}\, x)$
∎

These notions allow us to express the *partial equivalence, equivalence* and *conditional equivalence* of programs.

Before we move onto the laws let us look at a simple example. Consider the function: $\overline{\text{"True"}}$. This is the *constantly "True" function*. Note that it is strict like all FP functions. Thus it only gives the answer "True" if its argument is properly defined. This motivates the following definition:

def defined $= \overline{\text{"True"}}$

For convenience we will, in future, often write **T** for "True" and **F** for "False". Thus, the function above might be defined:

def defined $= \overline{\mathbf{T}}$

Now consider the following assertion

defined $\circ \mathbf{f} \twoheadrightarrow \mathbf{f} = \mathbf{g}$

This asserts that $\mathbf{f}$ and $\mathbf{g}$ yield equivalent results providing $\mathbf{f}$ is defined. This statement appears to be equivalent to $\mathbf{f} \leq \mathbf{g}$.

We can capture this with the assertion (**defined** $\circ \mathbf{f} \twoheadrightarrow \mathbf{f} = \mathbf{g}$) iff $\mathbf{f} \leq \mathbf{g}$. There are other occasions when we will wish to embed FP assertions into predicate logic like this, for example, laws L11 and L13 below. These laws serve to underline that reasoning essentially takes place in a first-order theory with FP programs as the terms and with just one predicate symbol: $\_ \twoheadrightarrow \_ = \_$. (In view of the example above, and the definition of $=$, we can do with just the conditional equivalence predicate.)

The relation $\twoheadrightarrow$ introduced above is particularly important and can be used to formulate precise conditions under which two programs are equivalent, as we shall see.

We shall be inclined to state relationships which are inherent properties of the functionals and which do not depend on the constituent functions appearing as arguments. As a convention we shall take it that, unless stated, all the functions appearing in the laws are *universally quantified*. Thus L1 below should be read:

$$(\forall \mathbf{f}_1) \ldots (\forall \mathbf{f}_n)(\forall \mathbf{g})([\mathbf{f}_1, \ldots, \mathbf{f}_n] \circ \mathbf{g} = [\mathbf{f}_1 \circ \mathbf{g}, \ldots, \mathbf{f}_n \circ \mathbf{g}])$$

5.4.2 Laws

In this section we present, without much in the way of discussion, some of the many relationships which hold for the FP system we have defined. The reader who wishes to consult a more comprehensive list of laws can find one in Backus's original paper and in the papers of Williams referenced at the end of the chapter. Here we have selected a set of laws all of which play a role in future sections of the chapter.

(L1) $[\mathbf{f}_1, \ldots, \mathbf{f}_n] \circ \mathbf{g} = [\mathbf{f}_1 \circ \mathbf{g}, \ldots, \mathbf{f}_n \circ \mathbf{g}]$

(L2) $\alpha \mathbf{f} \circ [\mathbf{g}_1, \ldots, \mathbf{g}_n] = [\mathbf{f} \circ \mathbf{g}_1, \ldots, \mathbf{f} \circ \mathbf{g}_n]$

(L3) $(\mathbf{p} \to \mathbf{f}_1; \mathbf{f}_2) \circ \mathbf{g} = \mathbf{p} \circ \mathbf{g} \to \mathbf{f}_1 \circ \mathbf{g}; \mathbf{f}_2 \circ \mathbf{g}$

(L4) $\mathbf{f} \circ (\mathbf{p} \to \mathbf{g}_1; \mathbf{g}_2) = \mathbf{p} \to \mathbf{f} \circ \mathbf{g}_1; \mathbf{f} \circ \mathbf{g}_2$

(L5) $\mathbf{apndl} \circ [\mathbf{f}, [\mathbf{g}_1, \ldots, \mathbf{g}_n]] = [\mathbf{f}, \mathbf{g}_1, \ldots, \mathbf{g}_n]$
      (similarly for **apndr**)

(L6) $\mathbf{distl} \circ [\mathbf{f}, [\mathbf{g}_1, \ldots, \mathbf{g}_n]] = [[\mathbf{f}, \mathbf{g}_1], \ldots, [\mathbf{f}, \mathbf{g}_n]]$
      (similarly for **distr**)

(L7) $/_R\mathbf{f} \circ [\mathbf{g}_1, \ldots, \mathbf{g}_n] = \mathbf{f} \circ [\mathbf{g}_1, /_R\mathbf{f} \circ [\mathbf{g}_2, \ldots, \mathbf{g}_n]]$

(L8) $/_R\mathbf{f} \circ [\mathbf{g}] = \mathbf{g}$ (similarly for $/_L$)

(L9) $\mathbf{defined} \circ \mathbf{f}_2 \twoheadrightarrow 1 \circ [\mathbf{f}_1, \mathbf{f}_2] = \mathbf{f}_1$ (and so on for more complex constructions)

(L10) $\mathbf{defined} \circ \mathbf{f} \twoheadrightarrow \bar{\mathbf{x}} \circ \mathbf{f} = \bar{\mathbf{x}}$

(L11) $(\mathbf{p} \twoheadrightarrow \mathbf{f} = \mathbf{g}) \Rightarrow (\mathbf{p} \to \mathbf{f}; \mathbf{h}) = (\mathbf{p} \to \mathbf{g}; \mathbf{h})$

(L12) $(\mathbf{p} \to \mathbf{f}_1; \mathbf{f}_2) = \mathbf{not} \circ \mathbf{p} \to \mathbf{f}_2; \mathbf{f}_1$

(L13) $((\mathbf{defined} \circ \mathbf{p} \wedge \mathbf{p}) \twoheadrightarrow \mathbf{f} = \mathbf{g}) \Rightarrow (\mathbf{p} \to \mathbf{f}; \mathbf{g}) = \mathbf{g}$

(L14) $(\mathbf{p} \to \mathbf{f}; \mathbf{q} \to \mathbf{f}; \mathbf{g}) = \mathbf{or} \circ [\mathbf{p}, \mathbf{q}] \to \mathbf{f}; \mathbf{g}$

(L15) $\mathbf{p} \twoheadrightarrow ((\mathbf{p} \to \mathbf{f}; \mathbf{g}) = \mathbf{f})$

(L16) $\mathbf{id} \circ \mathbf{f} = \mathbf{f} \circ \mathbf{id} = \mathbf{f}$

5.4.3 The correctness of algebraic laws

We are bound to require proof that these algebraic relationships hold. This means that we need to establish their correctness with respect to the semantics of the functionals we gave earlier.

Proposition 5.4.3(i)

Law (L2) is sound with respect to the semantics of FP given earlier.

Proof

$$(\alpha \mathbf{f} \circ [\mathbf{g}_1, \ldots, \mathbf{g}_n])x \quad = $$
$$\alpha \mathbf{f}([\mathbf{g}_1, \ldots, \mathbf{g}_n]x) \quad = $$

$$\alpha f\langle g_1 x, \ldots, g_n x\rangle$$
$$\langle f(g_1 x), \ldots, f(g_n x)\rangle \quad =$$
$$\langle (f \circ g_1)x, \ldots, (f \circ g_n)x\rangle \quad =$$
$$[f \circ g_1, \ldots, f \circ g_n]x$$

■

Exercise 5.4.3(ii)

Show that (L1), (L3) and (L4) are correct with respect to the semantics of Section 5.2.

■

Proposition 5.4.3(iii)

Law (L8) is sound.

Proof

$$(/_R f \circ [g_1, \ldots, g_n])x \quad =$$
$$/_R f([g_1, \ldots, g_n]x) \quad =$$
$$/_R f\langle g_1 x, \ldots, g_n x\rangle \quad =$$
$$f\langle g_1 x, /_R f\langle g_2 x, \ldots, g_n\rangle\rangle \quad =$$
$$f\langle g_1 x, (/_R f \circ [g_2, \ldots, g_n])x\rangle \quad =$$
$$(f \circ [g_1, /_R f \circ [g_2, \ldots, g_n]])x$$

■

Exercise 5.4.3(iv)

Prove (L5) and (L6) correct.

■

More interesting are the conditional equivalences (L9)–(L13). Actually, these are very easy to check but are very important results that we will use often in a later section on program transformation.

Proposition 5.4.3(v)

Laws (L11) and (L13) are sound. Essentially these results tell us how the FP conditional relates to the conditional predicate in the meta-theory.

Proof

(L11)
Assume $p \rightarrowtail f = g$

$$(\mathbf{p} \to \mathbf{f}; \mathbf{h})x = \mathbf{f}\, x \text{ if } \mathbf{p}\, x = \text{"True"}$$
$$= \mathbf{g}\, x \text{ by assumption}$$
$$= (\mathbf{p} \to \mathbf{g}; \mathbf{h})x \text{ since } \mathbf{p}\, x = \text{"True"}$$

Alternatively:

$$(\mathbf{p} \to \mathbf{f}; \mathbf{h})x = \mathbf{h}\, x \text{ if } \mathbf{p}\, x = \text{"False"}$$
$$= (\mathbf{p} \to \mathbf{g}; \mathbf{h})x \text{ since } \mathbf{p}\, x = \text{"False"}$$

Finally:

$$(\mathbf{p} \to \mathbf{f}; \mathbf{h})x = \perp \text{ if } (\mathbf{p}\, x) = \perp$$
$$= (\mathbf{p} \to \mathbf{g}; \mathbf{h})x$$

(L13)
Assume $(\mathbf{p} \twoheadrightarrow \mathbf{f} = \mathbf{g})$
$$(\mathbf{p} \to \mathbf{f}; \mathbf{g})x = \mathbf{f}\, x \text{ if } \mathbf{p}\, x \text{ is "True"}$$
$$= \mathbf{g}\, x \text{ by assumption}$$

Alternatively:

$$(\mathbf{p} \to \mathbf{f}; \mathbf{g})x = \mathbf{g}\, x \text{ if } \mathbf{p}\, x = \text{"False"}$$

and these are sufficient if $\mathbf{p}$ is defined at x.
∎

5.4.4 Using the algebra

It is possible to use the algebra to prove properties of programs. In this section we will look at just a few examples of this.

Proposition 5.4.4(i)

Our first example concerns the relationship between the apply-to-all functional α and the concatenate program of the last section. Recall that we defined: **def concat** $= /_C (/_R \mathbf{apndl} \circ \mathbf{apndr})$. We will show that the following holds:

$$\alpha\, \mathbf{f} \circ \mathbf{concat} = \mathbf{concat} \circ \alpha(\alpha \mathbf{f})$$

Proof. This is a kind of commutative condition and we will exploit it in example 5.4.4(iii). Recall that $\mathbf{f} = \mathbf{g}$ is a shorthand for $\mathbf{f} \le \mathbf{g}$ and $\mathbf{g} \le \mathbf{f}$. This in turn is shorthand for: **defined** $\circ\, \mathbf{f} \twoheadrightarrow \mathbf{f} = \mathbf{g}$ and **defined** $\circ\, \mathbf{g} \twoheadrightarrow \mathbf{f} = \mathbf{g}$. To show equivalence then we establish firstly that they are equivalent when $\mathbf{f}$ is defined and also that they are equivalent over the domain of definition of $\mathbf{g}$.

In this particular example a quick inspection reveals that the domain of definition of $\alpha(\alpha f)$ and **concat** are the same: they are well-defined over the subset of objects consisting of sequences of sequence of objects. Another way of putting this is to say the domain of definition is the range of the function.

$$[[f_{11} \ldots f_{1n_1}][f_{21} \ldots f_{2n_2}] \ldots [f_{m1} \ldots f_{mn_m}]] \text{ for } m \geq 0,\ n_m \geq 0$$

We shall exploit this in the following:

$\alpha f \circ \textbf{concat} \circ [[f_{11} \ldots] \ldots [\ldots f_{mn_m}]] =$
(by the definition of **concat**)
$\alpha f \circ [f_{11} \ldots f_{mn_m}] =$
(by L2)
$[f \circ f_{11} \ldots f \circ f_{n_m}] =$
(by **concat** again)
$\textbf{concat} \circ [[f \circ f_{11} \ldots] \ldots [\ldots f \circ f_{mn_m}]] =$
(by L2)
$\textbf{concat} \circ [\alpha f \circ [f_{11} \ldots] \ldots \alpha f \circ [\ldots f_{mn_m}]] =$
(by L2)
$\textbf{concat} \circ \alpha(\alpha f) \circ [[f_{11} \ldots] \ldots [\ldots f_{mn_m}]]$

and the proof is complete.

∎

Proposition 5.4.4(ii)

Our second example again concerns the concatenate program. In a language whose data objects are essentially sequences it should come as no surprise that many results, concerning the relationship of **concat** with other functional forms, are very important. This result shows us how **concat** and the insert functional $/_c$ are related.

We shall show that:

$$/_c f \circ \textbf{concat} = /_c f \circ \alpha(/_c f)$$

Proof. Again, a cursory glance shows that the domains of definition of both sides of this equivalence are the same. Like the previous example it is the set of sequences of sequences of objects. We utilize the same trick as we did above.

$/_c f \circ \textbf{concat} \circ [[f_{11} \ldots] \ldots [\ldots f_{mn_m}]] =$
(by **concat**)
$/_c f \circ [f_{11} \ldots f_{mn_m}] =$
(by $/_c$ rules several times)

$$/_c \mathbf{f} \circ [/_c \mathbf{f} \circ [\mathbf{f}_{11} \ldots] \ldots /_c \mathbf{f} \circ [\ldots \mathbf{f}_{mn_m}]] =$$
(by L2)
$$/_c \mathbf{f} \circ \alpha(/_c \mathbf{f}) \circ [[\mathbf{f}_{11} \ldots] \ldots [\ldots \mathbf{f}_{mn_m}]]$$

and the proof is complete.

■

Proposition 5.4.4(iii)

We now turn to a generalization of proposition 3.4.1(iv) which claimed that the length of a concatenated sequence of sequences is equal to the sum of the lengths of the sequences in the sequence. More formally, this is stated as follows:

$$/_c + \circ \alpha(\mathbf{length}) = \mathbf{length} \circ \mathbf{concat}$$

Proof. Notice that the domain of definition (sequences of sequences of objects) is the same for both expressions. Now:

length ∘ concat =
(definition of **length**)
$/_c + \circ \alpha \, \bar{\mathbf{1}} \circ \mathbf{concat} =$
[example 5.4.4(i)]
$/_c + \circ \mathbf{concat} \circ \alpha(\alpha\bar{\mathbf{1}}) =$
[example 5.4.4(ii)]
$/_c + \circ \alpha(/_c +) \circ \alpha(\alpha\bar{\mathbf{1}}) =$
[exercise 5.4.4(iv) below]
$/_c + \circ \alpha(/_c + \circ \alpha\bar{\mathbf{1}}) =$
(definition of **length**)
$/_c + \circ \alpha(\mathbf{length})$
as required.

■

Probably the most important thing we should realize is that this proof is purely *equational*. The corresponding proof in Chapter 3 is obtained by structural induction on data structures. This simplification is, at the most obvious level, due to the fact that the definitions and programs are not directly recursive; they are merely algebraic formulae and are manipulated (by algebraic properties) as such. However, this is almost begging the question. A more enlightening explanation is that the induction, like the recursion, is *localized* in the functional forms. To be explicit consider the definition of $/_R$:

$$/_R \mathbf{f} \langle x \rangle \qquad\qquad = x$$
$$/_R \mathbf{f} \langle x_1, \ldots, x_n \rangle = \mathbf{f} \langle x_1, /_R \mathbf{f} \langle x_2, \ldots, x_n \rangle \rangle$$

This is a recursive definition. To show that:

$$/_R f\langle x_1, \ldots, x_n \rangle = f\langle x_1, f\langle x_2, \ldots, f\langle x_{n-1}, x_n \rangle \ldots \rangle \rangle$$

we use induction (on the length of the sequence).

Exercise 5.4.4(iv)

Show that the following holds:

$$\alpha \mathbf{f} \circ \alpha \mathbf{g} = \alpha(\mathbf{f} \circ \mathbf{g})$$

■

5.4.5 Further program properties

We shall see in Sections 5.5 and 5.6 occasions when we have to deal with *n-ary iterates* of functions. We define $\mathbf{f}^n$, the *n*-ary iterate of $\mathbf{f}$, to be $\mathbf{f} \circ \ldots n$-times $\ldots \circ \mathbf{f}$. That is, more formally:

$$\mathbf{f}^0 \quad = \mathbf{id}$$
$$\mathbf{f}^{n+1} = \mathbf{f} \circ \mathbf{f}^n$$

A useful result in this context is:

Lemma 5.4.5(i)

$$\mathbf{pair} \rightarrowtail (\mathbf{f}_1 \times \mathbf{f}_2)^n = \mathbf{f}_1^n \times \mathbf{f}_2^n$$

where:

$$\mathbf{def\ pair} = \mathbf{eq} \circ [\mathbf{length}, \bar{\mathbf{2}}]$$

Proof. We can prove this by induction. First, though, we notice that:

$$\mathbf{pair} \rightarrowtail \mathbf{id} \times \mathbf{id} = \mathbf{id}$$

and, of course, that:

$$\mathbf{id}^n = \mathbf{id}$$

Base step

$$(\mathbf{f}_1 \times \mathbf{f}_2)^0 = \mathbf{id}$$
$$= \mathbf{id} \times \mathbf{id}$$
$$= \mathbf{f}_1^0 \times \mathbf{f}_2^0$$

Induction step

$$(f_1 \times f_2)^{n+1} =$$
$$(f_1 \times f_2) \circ (f_1 \times f_2)^n = \qquad \text{(by induction)}$$
$$(f_1 \times f_2) \circ (f_1^n \times f_2^n) = \qquad \text{[example 5.3.1(iii)]}$$
$$[f_1 \circ 1, f_2 \circ 2] \circ (f_1^n \times f_2^n) =$$
$$[f_1 \circ 1 \circ (f_1^n \times f_2^n), f_2 \circ 2 \circ (f_1^n \times f_2^n)] = \text{[lemma 5.4.5(ii)]}$$
$$[f_1 \circ f_1^n \circ 1, f_2 \circ f_2^n \circ 2] =$$
$$f_1^{n+1} \times f_2^{n+1} \qquad \text{as required.}$$

∎

Another useful result concerns the relationship between the cross-product functional and the selectors.

Lemma 5.4.5(ii)

(a) $\& \circ [\textbf{pair}, \textbf{defined} \circ f_2] \twoheadrightarrow 1 \circ (f_1 \times f_2) = f_1 \circ 1$
(b) $\& \circ [\textbf{pair}, \textbf{defined} \circ f_1] \twoheadrightarrow 2 \circ (f_1 \times f_2) = f_2 \circ 2$

Proof. Given the protection afforded by **pair** we may rewrite $1 \circ (f_1 \times f_2)$ as $1 \circ [f_1 \circ 1, f_2 \circ 2]$. Since **defined** $\circ f_2$ holds, we have it that this is equivalent to $f_1 \circ 1$ by L9. Part (b) follows in a similar fashion.
∎

5.5 Linear recursion and expansion

In Section 5.3 we gave a definition in FP of a program to compute the length of a sequence:

$$\textbf{def length} = \textbf{null} \to \bar{0}; \textbf{inc} \circ \textbf{length} \circ \textbf{tl}$$

This, we commented, is a trivial transliteration of the recursive program we introduced in Chapter 3. Example 5.3.3(i) was dedicated, however, to finding a closed form for **length**; that is, a non-recursive program which exploits the functional forms which FP puts at our disposal. We were eventually led to the program:

$$\textbf{def length} = /_C + \circ \alpha \bar{1}$$

Whilst we contrasted the sequentiality of the former definition with the concurrency of the latter we avoided asking an obvious question: are these programs equivalent?

It is this question, and others like it, which we wish to address here.

Now the first program is, of course, not so much a definition as an equation (in the variable **length**) although we know how to solve such things using a fixpoint operator. It is evident that simple algebraic manipulation like that of the previous section is not going to be enough for this kind of task because of the explicit recursion. What we need is a technique for manipulating recursive definitions. We can then deploy it to show that programs, like the two above, are equivalent.

Backus has described a result which defines circumstances under which a recursive definition may be *unwound* into an *infinite* non-recursive (therefore closed) form. The technique applies only to a restricted class of recursive definitions called *linear recursions*. It is still an open problem to find techniques for the manipulation of other more general *non-linear* recursions.

The definition we provide is that of Backus (1978). A more permissive definition is given in Backus (1981a) and we shall refer to this later.

Definition 5.5(i) Linear expansion (Backus)

Let $Q(k)$ be an FP expression in free function variable k. $Q(k)$ is a *linear form* providing
(a) $Q(\bot) = \bot$
(b) $Q(\mathbf{a} \to \mathbf{b}; \mathbf{c}) = Q_1(\mathbf{a}) \to Q(\mathbf{b}); Q(\mathbf{c})$
for some FP expression $Q_1(k)$ in free function variable k. Q_1 is called the *predicate transformer*.
■

Theorem 5.5(ii) (Backus)

Consider the following definition:

$$\mathbf{def\ f} = \mathbf{p} \to \mathbf{g}; Q(\mathbf{f})$$

If $Q(k)$ is a linear form with predicate transformer $Q_1(k)$ then **f** may be expressed:

$$\mathbf{f} = \mathbf{p} \to \mathbf{g}; Q_1(\mathbf{p}) \to Q(\mathbf{g}); \dots; Q_1^n(\mathbf{p}) \to Q^n(\mathbf{g}); \dots$$
■

We start with an immediate application of this result.

Theorem 5.5(iii) (Backus)

The function:

$$\mathbf{def\ f} = \mathbf{p} \to \mathbf{g}; \mathbf{h} \circ [\mathbf{i}, \mathbf{f} \circ \mathbf{j}]$$

may be written:

$$\mathbf{f} = \mathbf{p} \to \mathbf{g}; \ \mathbf{p}_1 \to \mathbf{g}_1; \ \ldots; \ \mathbf{p}_n \to \mathbf{g}_n; \ \ldots$$

where:

$$\mathbf{p}_n = \mathbf{p} \circ \mathbf{j}^n \ \text{and} \ \mathbf{g}_n = /\mathbf{h} \circ [\mathbf{i}, \mathbf{i} \circ \mathbf{j}, \ldots, \mathbf{i} \circ \mathbf{j}^{n-1}, \mathbf{g} \circ \mathbf{j}^n]$$

Proof. We first determine that $Q(k) = \mathbf{h} \circ [\mathbf{i}, \ k \circ \mathbf{j}]$ is a linear form. Once we have done this we can apply theorem 5.5(ii).

$$
\begin{aligned}
Q(\bar{\bot}) &= \mathbf{h} \circ [\mathbf{i}, \ \bar{\bot} \circ \mathbf{j}] && \text{(by definition } Q) \\
&= \mathbf{h} \circ [\mathbf{i}, \ \bar{\bot}] && \text{(by definition } \circ) \\
&= \mathbf{h} \circ \bar{\bot} && \text{(by definition } [\ ]) \\
&= \bar{\bot} && \text{(by definition } \circ) \\[6pt]
Q(\mathbf{a} \to \mathbf{b}; \mathbf{c}) &= \mathbf{h} \circ [\mathbf{i}, (\mathbf{a} \to \mathbf{b}; \mathbf{c}) \circ \mathbf{j}] && \text{(by definition } Q) \\
&= \mathbf{h} \circ [\mathbf{i}, \mathbf{a} \circ \mathbf{j} \to \mathbf{b} \circ \mathbf{j}; \mathbf{c} \circ \mathbf{j}] && \text{(L3)} \\
&= \mathbf{h} \circ (\mathbf{a} \circ \mathbf{j} \to [\mathbf{i}, \mathbf{b} \circ \mathbf{j}]; [\mathbf{i}, \mathbf{c} \circ \mathbf{j}] && \text{(lemma)} \\
&= \mathbf{a} \circ \mathbf{j} \to \mathbf{h} \circ [\mathbf{i}, \mathbf{b} \circ \mathbf{j}]; \mathbf{h} \circ [\mathbf{i}, \mathbf{c} \circ \mathbf{j}] && \text{(L4)} \\
&= Q_1(\mathbf{a}) \to Q(\mathbf{b}); Q(\mathbf{c}) && \text{(definition } Q)
\end{aligned}
$$

as required, by setting $Q_1(k) = k \circ \mathbf{j}$.

Applying theorem 5.5(ii) we obtain expression for the terms in the linear expansion:

$$
\begin{aligned}
\mathbf{p}_n &= Q_1^n(\mathbf{g}) = \mathbf{g} \circ \mathbf{j}^n \\
\mathbf{g}_n &= Q^n(\mathbf{g}) = \mathbf{h} \circ [\mathbf{i}, Q^{n-1}(\mathbf{g}) \circ \mathbf{j}] \\
&= \mathbf{h} \circ [\mathbf{i}, \mathbf{h} \circ [\mathbf{i} \circ \mathbf{j}, \ldots, \mathbf{h} \circ [\mathbf{i} \circ \mathbf{j}^{n-1}, \mathbf{g} \circ \mathbf{j}^n] \ldots]] \\
&\qquad \text{(by continued expansion and L1 repeatedly)} \\
&= /\mathbf{h} \circ [\mathbf{i}, \mathbf{i} \circ \mathbf{j}, \ldots, \mathbf{i} \circ \mathbf{j}^{n-1}, \mathbf{g} \circ \mathbf{j}^n] \\
&\qquad \text{(by L7)}
\end{aligned}
$$

∎

We can now show an application of this theorem. It is apparent in this development how degrees of speciality can be accommodated naturally: the linear expansion theorem applies to all linear $Q(k)$. If we settle on $Q(k) = \mathbf{h} \circ [\mathbf{i}, \mathbf{f} \circ \mathbf{j}]$ we obtain theorem 5.5(iii) in which the extra information can be used to simplify the expression $Q^n(k)$ and $Q_1^n(k)$. In the example below we finally introduce particular functions for $\mathbf{p}, \mathbf{g}, \mathbf{h}, \mathbf{i}, \mathbf{j}$. This then, of course, allows even more simplification to take place.

Theorem 5.5(iv)

The function:

$$\mathbf{def \ length} = \mathbf{null} \to \bar{\mathbf{0}}; \ \mathbf{inc} \circ \mathbf{length} \circ \mathbf{tl}$$

may be transformed into the equivalent program:

def length $= / + \, \circ \, \alpha \bar{\mathbf{1}}$

Proof. This may either be viewed as the equivalence proof we discussed earlier or, alternatively, if we had no idea in advance of the final closed form of the function, we could view this proof as a program transformation.

The intended domain of definition for these programs consists of the non-atomic objects, that is, sequence objects. For the time being we will take it that the definitions are guarded by the following predicate:

def seq $= $ **not** $\circ$ **atom**

Given the definition of **inc** [incidentally the solution to exercise 5.3.1(ii), part(i)] we can write the original definition as:

def length $= $ **null** $\to \bar{\mathbf{0}}; \; + \circ [\bar{\mathbf{1}}, $ **length** $\circ$ **tl**]

Now this is the form of program described by the previous theorem 5.5(iii) where:

$\mathbf{p} = $ **null**; $\mathbf{g} = \bar{\mathbf{0}}; \mathbf{h} = +; \mathbf{i} = \bar{\mathbf{1}}; \mathbf{j} = $ **tl**

Using this result immediately we can write our function as:

$$
\begin{aligned}
\textbf{length} = \textbf{null} \quad &\to \bar{\mathbf{0}}; \\
\textbf{null} \circ \textbf{tl} \quad &\to / + \circ [\bar{\mathbf{1}}, \bar{\mathbf{0}} \circ \textbf{tl}]; \\
\textbf{null} \circ \textbf{tl}^2 \quad &\to / + \circ [\bar{\mathbf{1}}, \bar{\mathbf{1}} \circ \textbf{tl}, \bar{\mathbf{0}} \circ \textbf{tl}^2]; \\
&\vdots \\
\textbf{null} \circ \textbf{tl}^n \quad &\to / + \circ [\bar{\mathbf{1}}, \bar{\mathbf{1}} \circ \textbf{tl}, \ldots, \bar{\mathbf{1}} \circ \textbf{tl}^{n-1}, \bar{\mathbf{0}} \circ \textbf{tl}^n]; \\
&\vdots
\end{aligned}
$$

Now this can be massaged further using algebraic laws and a little creativity.

Lemma 5.5(v)

Let $\mathbf{f}_i$ be constant functions, $1 \leq i \leq n$:

$$
\begin{aligned}
\textbf{null} \circ \textbf{tl}^n \to\to [\mathbf{f}_1, \mathbf{f}_2 \circ \textbf{tl}, \ldots, \mathbf{f}_n \circ \textbf{tl}^n] = \\
[\mathbf{f}_1, \mathbf{f}_2, \ldots, \mathbf{f}_n]
\end{aligned}
$$

Proof. Just notice that **null** $\circ$ **tl**^{n} is true just in the case that its argument has length n, for if it is less the function is undefined and if more it yields "False". For all other cases it is undefined. Given this information we may use (L10), *n* times, to obtain the right-hand side from the left.

■

Getting back to the main proof we can apply this result to each arm of the infinite conditional since each is protected by a guarding predicate that ensures the guard of the lemma above will be true. This gives us (by L11):

$$\begin{aligned}
\textbf{length} = \textbf{null} &\quad \rightarrow \bar{\textbf{0}}; \\
\textbf{null} \circ \textbf{tl} &\quad \rightarrow / + \circ [\bar{\textbf{1}}, \bar{\textbf{0}}]; \\
\textbf{null} \circ \textbf{tl}^2 &\quad \rightarrow / + \circ [\bar{\textbf{1}}, \bar{\textbf{1}}, \bar{\textbf{0}}]; \\
&\quad \vdots \\
\textbf{null} \circ \textbf{tl}^n &\quad \rightarrow / + \circ [\underbrace{\bar{\textbf{1}}, \bar{\textbf{1}}, \ldots, \bar{\textbf{1}}}_{n\text{ times}}, \bar{\textbf{0}}]; \\
&\quad \vdots
\end{aligned}$$

We shall proceed from here in two ways. Firstly, we utilize a rather obvious result which the reader may verify as an exercise in pedantry:

Exercise 5.5(vi)

$$/ + \circ [\underbrace{\bar{\textbf{1}}, \bar{\textbf{1}}, \ldots, \bar{\textbf{1}}}_{n\text{ times}}, \bar{\textbf{0}}] = \bar{\textbf{n}}$$

■

Applying this we get:

$$\begin{aligned}
\textbf{length} = \textbf{null} &\quad \rightarrow \bar{\textbf{0}}; \\
\textbf{null} \circ \textbf{tl} &\quad \rightarrow \bar{\textbf{1}}; \\
\textbf{null} \circ \textbf{tl}^2 &\quad \rightarrow \bar{\textbf{2}}; \\
&\quad \vdots \\
\textbf{null} \circ \textbf{tl}^n &\quad \rightarrow \bar{\textbf{n}}; \\
&\quad \vdots
\end{aligned}$$

which read informally says "the length of an empty sequence is zero; the length of a sequence of one element is one; the length of a sequence of two elements is two . . .". This establishes the correctness of the recursive definition.

A second, more interesting line of reasoning, is based on the following lemma:

Lemma 5.5(vii)

$$\textbf{null} \circ \textbf{tl}^n \rightarrow\!\!\!\rightarrow \underbrace{(f \times \ldots \times f)}_{n\text{ times}} = \alpha f$$

Proof. Again this rests on the observation that the guard is true just in case its argument is a sequence of length n.

■

The very interesting and powerful aspect of this lemma is that the right-hand side of the equivalence is independent of n. This form of lemma is of great importance.

Exercise 5.5(viii)

■
$$/_c + \circ [\mathbf{f}_1, \ldots, \mathbf{f}_n, \bar{\mathbf{0}}] = /_c + \circ [\mathbf{f}_1, \ldots, \mathbf{f}_n]$$

As a rule these very "obvious" relationships turn up very frequently in FP programming. It is always worthwhile establishing them with care for, although they are often obvious for certain well-defined arguments and functions, occasionally they do not have the same domain of definition and form only a partial equivalence.

Applying this second lemma, then the first and by virtue of L11 we obtain:

$$\begin{aligned}
\mathbf{length} = \mathbf{null} \quad &\to \bar{\mathbf{0}}; \\
\mathbf{null} \circ \mathbf{tl} \quad &\to /_c + \circ \alpha \bar{\mathbf{1}}; \\
\mathbf{null} \circ \mathbf{tl}^2 &\to /_c + \circ \alpha \bar{\mathbf{1}}; \\
&\;\;\vdots \\
\mathbf{null} \circ \mathbf{tl}^n &\to /_c + \circ \alpha \bar{\mathbf{1}}; \\
&\;\;\vdots
\end{aligned}$$

Note that:

$$\mathbf{null} \twoheadrightarrow \bar{\mathbf{0}} = /_c + \circ \alpha \bar{\mathbf{1}}$$

This means we can replace $\mathbf{0}$ in the above by $/_c + \circ \alpha \bar{\mathbf{1}}$ by virtue of (L11). Notice how the various arms are now all the same. We now perform an "infinite number of applications" of (L14) and one of (L15):

$$\mathbf{seq} \twoheadrightarrow \mathbf{length} = /_c + \circ \alpha \bar{\mathbf{1}}$$

The appearance of **seq** here is due to the infinite disjunction of predicates **null** $\circ$ **tl**^{n} which results from the application of (L14).

Finally we relax the initial guarding predicate **seq** which has kept us, up to now, within our intended domain of definition.

A little thought will convince us that if either the original recursive program or the new closed form are given an atomic argument the result will be $\perp$. Thus we may finally claim that the two programs are equivalent.

■

Example 5.5(ix)

In Section 5.3 we introduced a recursive definition for **append** given by:

$$\textbf{def append} = \textbf{null} \circ 1 \rightarrow 2; \quad \textbf{apndl} \circ [1 \circ 1, \textbf{append} \circ (\textbf{tl} \times \textbf{id})]$$

We will take it that this program is protected by the guard **pairseq** given as follows:

$$\textbf{pairseq} = \& \circ [\textbf{seq, seq}]$$

and we shall exploit this during the transformation. When the transformation is complete we can check that the resulting program has the same domain of definition as the original to establish complete equivalence. This technique of transforming under the assumption that the arguments are in some sense reasonable, seems to be the appropriate strategy to adopt and was a technique we utilized in the previous example. Annexing the question of checking out pathological arguments to the end localizes the trouble. Note that the guard need not exactly characterize the expected domain of definition, although in this example it does. All we need are appropriate assumptions for the transformation to proceed smoothly.

This FP definition has the form described by theorem 5.5(iii). In this example we have:

$$\textbf{p} = \textbf{null} \circ 1; \quad \textbf{g} = 2; \ \textbf{h} = \textbf{apndl}; \quad \textbf{i} = 1 \circ 1; \quad \textbf{j} = \textbf{tl} \times \textbf{id}$$

Applying theorem 5.5(iii) we can rewrite our definition as follows:

$$\textbf{append} = \textbf{p} \rightarrow \textbf{g}; \ \textbf{p}_1 \rightarrow \textbf{g}_1; \ldots; \ \textbf{p}_n \rightarrow \textbf{g}_n; \ldots \text{ where}$$
$$\textbf{p}_n = \textbf{p} \circ \textbf{j}^n = \textbf{null} \circ 1 \circ (\textbf{tl} \times \textbf{id})^n$$
$$= \textbf{null} \circ 1 \circ \textbf{tl}^n \times \textbf{id}^n$$
$$= \textbf{null} \circ \textbf{tl}^n \circ 1$$

and:

$$\textbf{g}_n = /\textbf{h} \circ [\textbf{i}, \ \textbf{i} \circ \textbf{j}, \ldots, \textbf{i} \circ \textbf{j}^{n-1}, \ \textbf{g} \circ \textbf{j}^n] =$$
$$/\textbf{apndl} \circ [1 \circ 1, \ 1 \circ 1 \circ (\textbf{tl} \times \textbf{id}), \ldots, 1 \circ 1 \circ (\textbf{tl} \times \textbf{id})^{n-1}, \ 2 \circ (\textbf{tl} \times \textbf{id})^n$$
$$/\textbf{apndl} \circ [1 \circ 1, \ 1 \circ \textbf{tl} \circ 1, \ldots, 1 \circ \textbf{tl}^{n-1} \circ 1, \ \textbf{id}^n \circ 2] =$$
$$/\textbf{apndl} \circ \textbf{apndr} \circ [[1 \circ 1, \ 1 \circ \textbf{tl} \circ 1, \ldots, 1 \circ \textbf{tl}^{n-1} \circ 1], \ \textbf{id}^n \circ 2] =$$
$$/\textbf{apndl} \circ \textbf{apndr} \circ [[1, \ 1 \circ \textbf{tl}, \ldots, 1 \circ \textbf{tl}^{n-1}] \circ 1, \ \textbf{id} \circ 2] =$$
$$/\textbf{apndl} \circ \textbf{apndr} \circ ([1, \ 1 \circ \textbf{tl}, \ldots, 1 \circ \textbf{tl}^{n-1}] \times \textbf{id})$$

We now need:

Exercise 5.5(x)

$$\textbf{null} \circ \textbf{tl}^n \rightarrowtail [1, \ 1 \circ \textbf{tl}, \ldots, 1 \circ \textbf{tl}^{n-1}] = \textbf{id}$$

∎

Returning to our main argument we have that:

$$\mathbf{g}_n = /\mathbf{apndl} \circ \mathbf{apndr} \circ (\mathbf{id} \times \mathbf{id})$$

but under the original protection of the predicate **pairseq** we can simplify this to:

$\mathbf{g}_n = /\mathbf{apndl} \circ \mathbf{apndr} \circ \mathbf{id}$ and then:
$\mathbf{g}_n = /\mathbf{apndl} \circ \mathbf{apndr}$ by (L16).

Note that $\mathbf{g}_n$ is independent of n so every $\mathbf{g}_n$ is now the same. The program for **append** now looks like this:

$$
\begin{aligned}
\mathbf{append} = \mathbf{null} \circ \mathbf{1} &\quad \rightarrow \mathbf{2} \\
\mathbf{null} \circ \mathbf{tl} \circ \mathbf{1} &\quad \rightarrow /\mathbf{apndl} \circ \mathbf{apndr}; \\
\mathbf{null} \circ \mathbf{tl}^2 \circ \mathbf{1} &\quad \rightarrow /\mathbf{apndl} \circ \mathbf{apndr}; \\
\vdots &\qquad \vdots \\
\mathbf{null} \circ \mathbf{tl}^n \circ \mathbf{1} &\quad \rightarrow /\mathbf{apndl} \circ \mathbf{apndr}; \\
\vdots &\qquad \vdots
\end{aligned}
$$

Note that (under the global protective assumption of **pairseq**):

$$\mathbf{null} \circ \mathbf{1} \rightarrowtail \mathbf{2} = /\mathbf{apndl} \circ \mathbf{apndr}$$

So, by (L11), we obtain a situation in which every conditional arm is the same. It is now a simple matter to obtain the final result by (L14) and (L15):

$$\mathbf{pairseq} \rightarrowtail \mathbf{append} = /\mathbf{apndl} \circ \mathbf{apndr}$$

and the transformation is complete.

We finally need to relax the guard **pairseq** and check the programs outside this protecting predicate. Certainly by the definition of **apndr** and $\times$ (in the original expression) both programs are undefined if the argument is not a pair. By **apndr** and $\mathbf{1} \circ \mathbf{1}$ (in the original program) we conclude that the programs are both undefined if the first argument is not a sequence. By **apndl** (in both programs) we see that both programs are undefined if the second argument is not a sequence. Thus we may remove the guard **pairseq** and claim that the two programs are equivalent.

■

5.6 BLFs and the composition theorem

So far we have worked with two recursive definitions which conform to the form specified by theorem 5.5(iii). Clearly there are many functions of interest which will not conform. As a simple example consider:

$$\textbf{reverse} = \textbf{null} \to [\ \ ];\ \textbf{append} \circ [\textbf{reverse} \circ \textbf{tl}, [\textbf{1}]]$$

Now there is a simple way to transform this into a form which does match by utilizing a function:

$$\textbf{def swap} = [\textbf{2, 1}]$$

and then rewriting the function:

$$\textbf{reverse} = \textbf{null} \to [\ \ ];\ (\textbf{append} \circ \textbf{swap}) \circ [[\textbf{1}], \textbf{reverse} \circ \textbf{tl}]$$

The reason for bracketing the compositions as indicated is to show exactly how this is to match the form specified by theorem 5.5(iii). The reader is invited to try:

Exercise 5.6(i)

Show that **reverse** above can be transferred into the expression:

$$/(\textbf{append} \circ \textbf{swap}) \circ \alpha[\textbf{id}]$$

You will need a lemma to obtain the term $\alpha[\textbf{id}]$.
∎

Naturally in general such a simple fix will not be available. So in spite of the trick employed above we will return, and study, the original definition of **reverse**.

A second possibility might be to prove that **reverse** may be linearly expanded directly, or prove a theorem similar to 5.5(iii) which describes a program form of which reverse is an instantiation. Both these are plausible but it is clear that this exercise may be the thin end of the wedge: we may end up proving a very large number of general schemes linearly expansive, each with relatively slight applicability. The solution advocated by Backus (1981a) is to provide a small class of simple and highly applicable forms (called *basic linear forms or BLFs*) which are linearly expansive and to provide a *composition theorem* which preserves the linear expansion properties. In fact the primitive forms he describes are essentially single function forms, as we will see shortly. The solution to our problem with **reverse** (or a more general scheme which covers it) is reduced to showing how the function (scheme) can be constructed from the BLFs by means of the composition theorem.

Theorem 5.6(ii)

Basic linear forms (Backus)

(a) Let $Q(f) = \mathbf{r}$ for some function $\mathbf{r}$ then $Q(f)$ is linearly expansive with
$Q_1(f) = \mathbf{r}$
(b) Let $Q(f) = \mathbf{r} \circ f$ for some function $\mathbf{r}$ then $Q(f)$ is linearly expansive with
$Q_1(f) = f$
(c) Let $Q(f) = f \circ \mathbf{r}$ for some function $\mathbf{r}$ then $Q(f)$ is linearly expansive with
$Q_1(f) = Q(f)$
(d) Let $Q(f) = [\mathbf{g}, f]$ for some $\mathbf{g}$ then $Q(f)$ is linearly expansive with
$Q_1(f) = f$
(e) Let $Q(f) = \mathbf{p} \rightarrow \mathbf{q};\ f$ then $Q(f)$ is linearly expansive with $Q_1(f)$
$= \mathbf{p} \rightarrow \text{``True''};\ f$
∎

Exercise 5.6(iii)

Prove (b), (c) and (d) above.
∎

Exercise 5.6(iv)

Generalize (d) above to show that if $Q(f) = [\mathbf{g}_1, \ldots, \mathbf{g}_{i-1}, f, \mathbf{g}_{i+1}, \ldots, \mathbf{g}_n]$ then $Q(f)$ is linearly expansive for all n and when f appears in any position $1 \leq i \leq n$.
∎

It is important to note that Backus discovered that the definition of a linear form may be made more permissive and indeed the more relaxed definition is required for proving (a) and (e) above. For reference we give the revised definition here. The interested reader should consult Backus (1981a) for full justification and could then usefully prove (a) and (e) above as exercises.

Definition 5.6(v) Linear forms (Backus)

Let $Q(f)$ be a functional form in one free function variable f.
$\quad Q(f)$ is a *linear form* (LF) providing:
(a) $Q(\mathbf{a} \rightarrow \mathbf{b};\ \mathbf{c}) = Q_1(\mathbf{a}) \rightarrow Q(\mathbf{b});\ Q(\mathbf{c})$
for some functional form $Q_1(k)$ in one free variable k.
(b) If $Q(\bar{\perp})(x) \neq \perp$ for some object x then for all functions, $\mathbf{g}$, we have: $Q_1(\mathbf{g})(x)$
$= \text{``True''}$.
∎

It can be seen that the original condition that $Q(\bar{1})=\bar{1}$ has been weakened providing the predicate transformer behaves appropriately. The point is that theorem 5.5(ii) still holds under this, new, definition of LF.

Theorem 5.6(vi) The composition theorem (Backus)

If $G(k)$ and $H(k)$ are linear forms, with predicate transformers $G_1(k)$, $H_1(k)$, then $G(H(k))$ is a linear form with predicate transformer $G_1(H_1(k))$.

Half proof (revised LF definition required)

$$G(H(\mathbf{a} \to \mathbf{b}; \mathbf{c})) =$$
$$G(H_1(\mathbf{a}) \to H(\mathbf{b}); H(\mathbf{c})) \text{ since } H \text{ is a LF}$$
$$G_1(H_1(\mathbf{a})) \to G(H(\mathbf{b})); G(H(\mathbf{c})) \text{ since } G \text{ is a LF}$$

The rest of the proof is beyond the scope of this book.
∎

We can now form a great number of LFs. For example here is a simpler proof of theorem 5.5(iii).

Theorem 5.6(vii)

$$\mathbf{f} = \mathbf{p} \to \mathbf{g}; \mathbf{h} \circ [\mathbf{i}, \mathbf{f} \circ \mathbf{j}]$$

may be rewritten as:

$$\mathbf{f} = \mathbf{p} \to \mathbf{g}; \mathbf{p}_1 \to \mathbf{g}_1; \ldots; \mathbf{p}_n \to \mathbf{g}_n; \ldots$$

where:

$$\mathbf{p}_n = \mathbf{p} \circ \mathbf{j}^n$$
$$\mathbf{g}_n = /\mathbf{h} \circ [\mathbf{i}, \mathbf{i} \circ \mathbf{j}, \ldots, \mathbf{i} \circ \mathbf{j}^{n-1}, \mathbf{g} \circ \mathbf{j}^n]$$

Proof. By theorem 5.5(ii) and laws it is sufficient to show that

$$Q(k) = \mathbf{h} \circ [\mathbf{i}, k \circ \mathbf{j}] \text{ is a LF.}$$

Let $H(f) = f \circ \mathbf{j}$
$G(f) = [\mathbf{i}, f]$
$F(f) = \mathbf{h} \circ f$

These are all BLFs by theorem 5.6(vii).

Using the composition theorem for LFs we see that:

$$Q(k) = \mathbf{h} \circ [\mathbf{i}, k \circ \mathbf{j}] = F(G(H(k)))$$
$$\text{and } Q_1(k) = F_1(G_1(H_1(k))) = k \circ \mathbf{j}$$

∎

Exercise 5.6(viii)

Let $f = p \to g$; $Q(f)$ where: $Q(k) = h \circ [k \circ i, j]$. Show that f may be rewritten equivalently as

$$f = p \to g; \, p_1 \to g_1; \, p_2 \to g_2; \, \ldots$$

where:

■ $p_n = k \circ i^n$ and $g_n = /_L h \circ [k \circ i^n, j \circ i^{n-1}, \ldots, j \circ i, j]$

Exercise 5.6(ix)

Consider the following definition:

$$\textbf{fac} = \textbf{eq0} \circ 1 \to 2; \, \textbf{fac} \circ [\textbf{dec} \circ 1, \textbf{mult}]$$

which is an accumulating parameter definition of the factorial function. Describe a more general class of function of which **fac** is an example and prove that it is LE.
■

The linear expansion theorem gives us an unusual and novel way of reasoning about or transforming recursive programs. Since programs are infinitely unwound we are faced quite often with the prospect of applying FP laws to infinite programs and occasionally to applying conventional laws infinitely often. It is wise, and indeed interesting, to consider this style of reasoning and to make sure that it is a sound method. We shall, in Chapter 7, spend some time elaborating the theory which can be used to show these processes are acceptable. Once the reader has mastered Chapter 7 the papers by Williams (see bibliographic notes) can be consulted for a precise explanation. For the moment, we shall content ourselves with an elaboration of a couple of the laws that are often necessary. Most often, these are just infinite counterparts to laws with which we are familiar, for example, the laws:

$$(p \to f; \, g) \circ h = p \circ h \to f \circ h; \, g \circ h \text{ and}$$
$$h \circ (p \to f; \, g) = p \to h \circ f; \, h \circ g$$

can both be generalized to:

$$(p_0 \to f_0; \, p_1 \to f_1; \, \ldots) \circ h = p_0 \circ h \to f_0 \circ h; \, p_1 \circ h \to f_1 \circ h;$$
$$h \circ (p_0 \to f_0; \, p_1 \to f_1; \, \ldots) = p_0 \to h \circ f_0; \, p_1 \to h \circ f_1; \, \ldots$$

We shall finish the section with a more ambitious example in which we shall see a need for reasoning of the second kind; that is, the application of algebraic laws infinitely often to an infinite program.

    We shall transform a recursive definition of the predicate **member** into a closed form.

Example 5.6(x)

Consider the following recursive definition of the predicate **member** in FP.

$$\textbf{member} = \textbf{null} \circ 2 \to \bar{F}; \; \textbf{eq} \circ (\textbf{id} \times 1) \to \bar{T}; \; \textbf{member} \circ (\textbf{id} \times \textbf{tl})$$

For convenience we have again shortened "True" to T and "False" to F for this example.

Our aim is to transform this into a non-recursive closed form which exploits the functionals of FP. We will assume that this definition is guarded by the predicate: $\& \circ [\textbf{atom}, \textbf{seq}]$.

To begin let us simply investigate the essential structure of this program by studying the following program schema:

$$\textbf{f} = \textbf{p} \to \textbf{g}; \; \textbf{h} \to \textbf{i}; \; \textbf{f} \circ \textbf{j}$$

We may write this as:

$$\textbf{f} = \textbf{p} \to \textbf{g}; \; Q(\textbf{f}) \text{ where } Q(k) = \textbf{h} \to \textbf{i}; \; k \circ \textbf{j}$$

Now we would like to unwind this schema using linear expansion but we need first to check that the definition is linearly expansive. We can do this by exploiting theorem 5.6(ii) and the composition theorem.

$$\begin{aligned} \text{Set } F(k) &= \textbf{h} \to \textbf{i}; \; k & \text{and} \\ H(k) &= k \circ \textbf{j} & \text{then} \\ Q(k) &= F(H(k)) \end{aligned}$$

Thus $Q(k)$ is linearly expansive by theorem 5.6(ii) (c) and (e) and theorem 5.6(vi).

These propositions also tell us what the predicate transformer is:

$$\begin{aligned} Q_1(k) &= F_1(H_1(k)) & \text{where} \\ F_1(k) &= \textbf{h} \to \bar{T}; \; k \\ H_1(k) &= k \circ \textbf{j} & \text{hence} \\ Q_1(k) &= \textbf{h} \to \bar{T}; \; k \circ \textbf{j} \end{aligned}$$

Now by simple inductive arguments it is easy to see that:

$$Q^n(k) = \textbf{h} \to \textbf{i}; \; \textbf{h} \circ \textbf{j} \to \textbf{i} \circ \textbf{j}; \; \ldots; \; \textbf{h} \circ \textbf{j}^{n-1} \to \textbf{i} \circ \textbf{j}^{n-1}; \; k \circ \textbf{j}^n$$

and that:

$$Q_1^n(k) = \textbf{h} \to \bar{T}; \; \textbf{h} \circ \textbf{j} \to \bar{T} \circ \textbf{j}; \; \ldots; \; \textbf{h} \circ \textbf{j}^{n-1} \to \bar{T} \circ \textbf{j}^{n-1}; \; k \circ \textbf{j}^n$$

and we may write **f** as:

$$\textbf{f} = \textbf{p} \to \textbf{g}; \; Q_1(\textbf{p}) \to Q(\textbf{g}); \; Q_1^2(\textbf{p}) \to Q^2(\textbf{g}); \; \ldots$$

by the linear expansion theorem.

Exercise 5.6(xi)

Now it is possible to simplify these expressions further and the reader may like to show that **f** may be written as:

$$\mathbf{f} = \mathbf{p} \rightarrow \mathbf{g};$$
$$\mathbf{h} \rightarrow \mathbf{i}; \; \mathbf{p} \circ \mathbf{j} \rightarrow \mathbf{g} \circ \mathbf{j}$$
$$\mathbf{h} \circ \mathbf{j} \rightarrow \mathbf{i} \circ \mathbf{j};$$
$$\mathbf{p} \circ \mathbf{j}^2 \rightarrow \mathbf{g} \circ \mathbf{j}^2;$$
$$\mathbf{h} \circ \mathbf{j}^2 \rightarrow \mathbf{i} \circ \mathbf{j}^2; \ldots$$

∎

But as we saw earlier during the proof of theorem 5.5(iv) there are often good reasons for not cancelling out information as far as possible.

If we now return to the function **member** we see that it is an instantiation of the program scheme in which:

$$\mathbf{p} = \mathbf{null} \circ \mathbf{2}; \; \mathbf{g} = \bar{F}; \; \mathbf{h} = \mathbf{eq} \circ (\mathbf{id} \times \mathbf{1}); \; \mathbf{i} = \bar{T} \text{ and } \mathbf{j} = \mathbf{id} \times \mathbf{tl}$$

Exercise 5.6(xii)

Again, as an exercise, the reader may like to substitute into the equation for **f** provided in exercise 5.6(xi) and check that this establishes the correctness of **member**.
∎

If we substitute in $Q^n(k)$ we obtain:

$$Q^n(\mathbf{g}) = \mathbf{eq} \circ (\mathbf{id} \times \mathbf{1}) \rightarrow \bar{T};$$
$$\mathbf{eq} \circ (\mathbf{id} \times \mathbf{1}) \circ (\mathbf{id} \times \mathbf{tl}) \rightarrow \bar{T} \circ (\mathbf{id} \times \mathbf{tl});$$
$$\mathbf{eq} \circ (\mathbf{id} \times \mathbf{1}) \circ (\mathbf{id} \times \mathbf{tl})^{n-1} \rightarrow \bar{T} \circ (\mathbf{id} \times \mathbf{tl})^{n-1}; \; \bar{F} \circ (\mathbf{id} \times \mathbf{tl})^n$$

Exercise 5.6(xiii)

Check that the terms following $\bar{T}$ and $\bar{F}$ in this expression may be deleted.
∎

This then yields:

$$Q^n(\mathbf{g}) = \mathbf{eq} \circ (\mathbf{id} \times \mathbf{1}) \rightarrow \bar{T};$$
$$\mathbf{eq} \circ (\mathbf{id} \times \mathbf{1} \circ \mathbf{tl}) \rightarrow \bar{T};$$
$$\mathbf{eq} \circ (\mathbf{id} \times \mathbf{1} \circ \mathbf{tl}^2) \rightarrow \bar{T};$$
$$\mathbf{eq} \circ (\mathbf{id} \times \mathbf{1} \circ \mathbf{tl}^{n-1}) \rightarrow \bar{T}; \; \bar{F}$$

and we can write this:

$$Q^n(\mathbf{g}) = \mathbf{or} \circ [\mathbf{eq} \circ (\mathbf{id} \times 1), \mathbf{or} \circ [\mathbf{eq} \circ (\mathbf{id} \times 1 \circ \mathbf{tl}),$$
$$\mathbf{or} \circ [\, \ldots, \mathbf{or} \circ [\mathbf{eq} \circ \ (\mathbf{id} \times 1 \circ \mathbf{tl}^{n-1}), \bar{F}] \ldots]]]$$

Now, clearly, we can delete the $\bar{F}$ to get:

$$Q^n(\mathbf{g}) = \mathbf{or} \circ [\mathbf{eq} \circ (\mathbf{id} \times 1), \mathbf{or} \circ [\mathbf{eq} \circ (\mathbf{id} \times 1 \circ \mathbf{tl}),$$
$$\mathbf{or} \circ [\, \ldots, \mathbf{eq} \circ (\mathbf{id} \times 1 \circ \mathbf{tl}^{n-1}) \ldots]]]$$

(L7) then provides:

$$Q^n(\mathbf{g}) = /\mathbf{or} \circ [\mathbf{eq} \circ (\mathbf{id} \times 1), \mathbf{eq} \circ (\mathbf{id} \times 1 \circ \mathbf{tl}), \ldots,$$
$$\mathbf{eq} \circ (\mathbf{id} \times 1 \circ \mathbf{tl}^{n-1})]$$

and by (L12):

$$Q^n(\mathbf{g}) = /\mathbf{or} \circ \alpha(\mathbf{eq}) \circ [\mathbf{id} \times 1, \mathbf{id} \times 1 \circ \mathbf{tl}, \ldots, \mathbf{id} \times 1 \circ \mathbf{tl}^{n-1}]$$

Writing the cross-product as a tuple gives:

$$Q^n(\mathbf{g}) = /\mathbf{or} \circ \alpha(\mathbf{eq}) \circ [[\mathbf{id} \circ 1, 1 \circ 2], \ldots, [\mathbf{id} \circ 1, 1 \circ \mathbf{tl}^{n-1} \circ 2]]$$

Now we see that (L6) can be applied.

$$Q^n(\mathbf{g}) = /\mathbf{or} \circ \alpha(\mathbf{eq}) \circ \mathbf{distl} \circ [\mathbf{id} \circ 1, [1 \circ 2, \ldots, 1 \circ \mathbf{tl}^{n-1} \circ 2]]$$

Now using (L1) and replacing the cross-product:

$$Q^n(\mathbf{g}) = /\mathbf{or} \circ \alpha(\mathbf{eq}) \circ \mathbf{distl} \circ [\mathbf{id} \times [1, 1 \circ \mathbf{tl}, \ldots, 1 \circ \mathbf{tl}^{n-1}]]$$

Assuming $Q^n(k)$ is guarded appropriately [we shall see that it is by $Q_1^n(k)$] and given that the entire definition is guarded by the protective assumption we see that:

$$(\mathbf{id} \times [1, 1 \circ \mathbf{tl}, \ldots, 1 \circ \mathbf{tl}^{n-1}]) =$$
$$(\mathbf{id} \times \mathbf{id}) =$$
$$\mathbf{id}$$

which gives us by (L16):

$$Q^n(\mathbf{g}) = /\mathbf{or} \circ \alpha(\mathbf{eq}) \circ \mathbf{distl}$$

which we are pleased to see is independent of the iterate n.

Let us now turn our attention to the predicate parts of the expansion. Recall that:
$$Q_1^n(\mathbf{p}) = \mathbf{h} \rightarrow \bar{T}; \ \mathbf{h} \circ \mathbf{j} \rightarrow \bar{T} \circ \mathbf{j}; \ \ldots; \ \mathbf{h} \circ \mathbf{j}^{n-1} \rightarrow \bar{T} \circ \mathbf{j}^{n-1}; \ \mathbf{p} \circ \mathbf{j}^n$$

We should like to delete the terms $\mathbf{j}^i$ for $1 \leq i \leq n-1$ which post compose the function $\bar{T}$ in this expression. We notice that the term $Q_1^n(\mathbf{p})$ is guarded by the previous predicate $Q_1^{n-1}(\mathbf{p})$. In fact, $Q_1^n(\mathbf{p})(x)$ can only be evaluated when $Q_1^{n-1}(\mathbf{p})(x) = F$. So we can justifiably write:

$$Q_1^n(\mathbf{p}) = \mathbf{h} \to \bar{T}; \ \mathbf{h} \circ \mathbf{j} \to \bar{T}; \ \ldots; \ \mathbf{h} \circ \mathbf{j}^{n-1} \to \bar{T}; \ \mathbf{p} \circ \mathbf{j}_n$$

Now by the same guarding expression $Q_1^{n-1}(\mathbf{p})$ it follows that we may delete all terms $\mathbf{h} \circ \mathbf{j}^i \to \bar{T}$ for $0 \le i \le n-2$ as these occur in this expression too, hence:

$$Q_1^n(\mathbf{p}) = \mathbf{h} \circ \mathbf{j}^{n-1} \to \bar{T}; \ \mathbf{p} \circ \mathbf{j}^n$$

Under the assumption that $\mathbf{p} \circ \mathbf{j}^n$ is defined we can re-express this as

$$Q_1^n(\mathbf{p}) = \mathbf{or} \circ [\mathbf{h} \circ \mathbf{j}^{n-1}, \mathbf{p} \circ \mathbf{j}^n]$$

Now let us substitute for $\mathbf{h}$, $\mathbf{j}$ and $\mathbf{p}$ using our definition of **member**

$$Q_1^n(\mathbf{null} \circ 2) = \mathbf{or} \circ [\mathbf{eq} \circ (\mathbf{id} \times 1) \circ (\mathbf{id} \times \mathbf{tl})^{n-1}, \ \mathbf{null} \circ 2 \circ (\mathbf{id} \times \mathbf{tl})^n]$$

which by proposition 5.4.5(ii) can eventually be written:

$$Q_1^n(\mathbf{null} \circ 2) = \mathbf{or} \circ [\mathbf{eq} \circ (\mathbf{id} \times 1 \circ \mathbf{tl}^{n-1}), \ \mathbf{null} \circ \mathbf{tl}^n \circ 2]$$

Now we can use the following observations. Firstly, we have assumed that the second part of the argument is a sequence of length n, for some n. This tells us that there exists an n such that $Q_1^n(\mathbf{null} \circ 2) = \bar{T}$ since $\mathbf{null} \circ \mathbf{tl}^n$ is true just in case its argument is a sequence of exactly length n. Secondly, if $\mathbf{eq} \circ (\mathbf{id} \times 1 \circ \mathbf{tl}^{n-1})(x) = T$ then this implies that $(/\mathbf{or} \circ \alpha(\mathbf{eq}) \circ \mathbf{distl})(x) = T$. The upshot of this is that we can safely replace the predicate Q_1^n ($\mathbf{null} \circ 2$) by the predicate Q_2^n ($\mathbf{null} \circ 2$) where $Q_2^n(k) = k \circ \mathbf{j}^n$. In other words they are conditionally equivalent. Now we are in a very similar position to our earlier examples and we can quickly show that **member** $= /\mathbf{or} \circ \alpha(\mathbf{eq}) \circ \mathbf{distl}$.

■

5.7 Beyond linear expansion

Suppose we have a program defined by an equation of the form $\mathbf{f} = \mathbf{p} \to \mathbf{g}; H(\mathbf{f})$ for some term H. This we can, by repeated substitution, unwind into the infinite term:

$$\mathbf{f} = \mathbf{p} \to \mathbf{g}; H(\mathbf{p} \to \mathbf{g}; \ldots) \tag{E1}$$

In general this expression is going to be very complex and difficult to handle. We know that if H is linear we have $H(\mathbf{a} \to \mathbf{b}; \mathbf{c}) = H_1(\mathbf{a}) \to H(\mathbf{b}); H(\mathbf{c})$ and so the above equation may be simplified to:

$$\mathbf{f} = \mathbf{p} \to \mathbf{g}; H_1(\mathbf{p}) \to H(\mathbf{g}); H^2(\mathbf{p} \to \mathbf{g}; \ldots)$$

or just:

$$\mathbf{f} = \mathbf{p} \to \mathbf{g} \; ; \; H_1(\mathbf{p}) \to H(\mathbf{g}) \; ; \; H_1^2(\mathbf{p}) \to H^2(\mathbf{g}); \; \ldots$$

The last section was devoted to programs which can be described using terms like H with this linearity property.

Naturally other programs do not fit into this paradigm for they are non-linear. For example: $H(k) = \mathbf{h} \circ [k \circ \mathbf{i}, \; k \circ \mathbf{j}]$ is not linear.

Exercise 5.7(i)

Convince yourself of this fact.
∎

If we try to unwind such an H in E1 above we obtain a *tree-like* expression which is hard to manage.

Exercise 5.7(ii)

$$\text{Let } H(k) = \mathbf{h} \circ [k \circ \mathbf{i}, \; k \circ \mathbf{j}]$$

Evaluate:
(a) $H(\mathbf{p} \to \mathbf{q}; \; H(\mathbf{f}))$
(b) $H(\mathbf{p} \to \mathbf{q}; \; H(\mathbf{p} \to \mathbf{q}; \; H(\mathbf{f})))$
∎

This exercise should convince us that linear forms are very pleasant to work with and that non-linear programs look daunting.

Backus himself suggested that functions like the class given by $\mathbf{f} = \mathbf{p} \to \mathbf{q}$; $H(\mathbf{f})$ where $H(k) = \mathbf{h} \circ [k \circ \mathbf{i}, \; k \circ \mathbf{j}]$ might be thought of slightly differently. Let $Q(k_1, k_2) = \mathbf{h} \circ [k_1 \circ \mathbf{i}, \; k_2 \circ \mathbf{j}]$. Now $H(k) = Q(k, k)$. If we consider Q we can separate out the two occurrences of k. Maybe, for example, Q is *linear in each argument taken separately*. This leads us to define the so-called *bilinear forms*.

Definition 5.7(iii)

$Q(k_1, k_2)$ is *bilinear* providing there exist terms $Q_1(k)$ and $Q_2(k)$ such that for all $\mathbf{a}$, $\mathbf{b}$ and $\mathbf{c}$ we have:
(a) $Q(\mathbf{a} \to \mathbf{b}; \; \mathbf{c}, \; \mathbf{h}) = Q_1(\mathbf{a}) \to Q(\mathbf{b}, \mathbf{h}), \; Q(\mathbf{c}, \mathbf{h})$
(b) $Q(\mathbf{h}, \; \mathbf{a} \to \mathbf{b}; \; \mathbf{c}) = Q_2(\mathbf{a}) \to Q(\mathbf{h}, \mathbf{b}), \; Q(\mathbf{h}, \mathbf{c})$
(c) $Q(\mathbf{I}, \mathbf{h}) = \mathbf{I}$
(d) $Q(\mathbf{h}, \mathbf{I}) = \mathbf{I}$
∎

Exercise 5.7(iv)

Show that $Q(k_1, k_2) = \mathbf{h} \circ (k_1 \times k_2)$ is a bilinear form.
∎

Note that this definition not only requires the form Q to be linear in each argument, but also ensures that the predicate transformers are independent of **h** in both cases.

One way forward in these circumstances is described by the following example:

Example 5.7(v)

Suppose we wish to compute the sequence of atoms which form the fringe of an arbitrary binary tree of atoms where a binary tree is just an atom or a sequence of binary trees of length 2. This is the usual fringe problem we have dealt with more than once before. Recursively, in FP this might be written:

$$\mathbf{f} = \mathbf{atom} \rightarrow [\mathbf{id}]; \ \mathbf{append} \circ (\mathbf{f} \times \mathbf{f})$$

This fits the following schema:

$$\mathbf{f} = \mathbf{p} \rightarrow \mathbf{q}; \ Q(\mathbf{f}, \mathbf{f})$$

where $Q(k_1, k_2) = \mathbf{h} \circ (k_1 \times k_2)$. Now this is just $Q(k_1, k_2) = \mathbf{h} \circ [k_1 \circ \mathbf{1}, k_2 \circ \mathbf{2}]$ since we are assuming the arguments to conform to the definition of a binary tree above. We know that this is bilinear.

Exercise 5.7(vi)

Define a predicate **btree** with which we can protect the program **f** during the transformation.
∎

Setting $H(k) = Q(\mathbf{f}, k)$ we can write the function in the form $\mathbf{f} = \mathbf{p} \rightarrow \mathbf{q}; \ H(\mathbf{f})$. Given the bilinearity of $Q(k_1, k_2)$ and the results above we see that this is a linear form. In fact it is our "old faithful" $H(k) = \mathbf{h} \circ [\mathbf{m}, k \circ \mathbf{j}]$ (where $\mathbf{m} = \mathbf{f} \circ \mathbf{i}$). We know that this can be written as

$$\mathbf{f} = \mathbf{p} \rightarrow \mathbf{g}; \ \mathbf{p}_1 \rightarrow \mathbf{g}_1; \ \ldots; \ \mathbf{p}_n \rightarrow \mathbf{g}_n; \ \ldots$$

where:

$$\mathbf{p}_n = \mathbf{p} \circ \mathbf{j}^n \text{ and } \mathbf{g}_n = /\mathbf{h} \circ [\mathbf{m}, \mathbf{m} \circ \mathbf{j}, \ldots, \mathbf{m} \circ \mathbf{j}^{n-1}, \mathbf{g} \circ \mathbf{j}^n]$$

or in this case:

$$\mathbf{g}_n = /\mathbf{h} \circ [\mathbf{f} \circ \mathbf{i}, \mathbf{f} \circ \mathbf{i} \circ \mathbf{j}, \ldots, \mathbf{f} \circ \mathbf{i} \circ \mathbf{j}^{n-1}, \mathbf{g} \circ \mathbf{j}^n]$$

We can now see how this applies to the fringe program by substituting for $\mathbf{h}, \mathbf{i}, \mathbf{j}$, $\mathbf{p}$ and $\mathbf{q}$.

This gives:

$$\mathbf{p}_n = \mathbf{atom} \circ \mathbf{2}^n \text{ and}$$
$$\mathbf{g}_n = /\mathbf{append} \circ [\mathbf{f} \circ 1, \mathbf{f} \circ 1 \circ 2, \ldots, \mathbf{f} \circ 1 \circ 2^{n-1}, [\mathbf{id}] \circ 2^n]$$

Now it is easy to see from the original definition that $\mathbf{atom} \rightarrowtail \mathbf{f} = [\mathbf{id}]$ combining this with the observation that each $\mathbf{g}_n$ is guarded by $\mathbf{p}_n$ of the form $\mathbf{atom} \circ \mathbf{2}^n$ allows us to rewrite $\mathbf{g}_n$ as:

$$\mathbf{concat} \circ [\mathbf{f} \circ 1, \mathbf{f} \circ 1 \circ 2, \ldots, \mathbf{f} \circ 1 \circ 2^{n-1}, \mathbf{f} \circ 2^n]$$

and then using (L2) to extract the $\mathbf{f}$ using the α combinator we obtain:

$$\mathbf{concat} \circ \alpha\mathbf{f} \circ [1, 1 \circ 2, \ldots, 1 \circ 2^{n-1}, 2^n]$$

The tuple expression is redundant, as the reader may like to verify. Therefore the program may be written:

$$\mathbf{f} = \mathbf{atom} \rightarrow [\mathbf{id}];$$
$$\quad \mathbf{atom} \circ 2 \rightarrow \mathbf{concat} \circ \alpha\mathbf{f};$$
$$\quad \mathbf{atom} \circ 2^2 \rightarrow \mathbf{concat} \circ \alpha\mathbf{f};$$

Collapsing this as usual yields:

$$\mathbf{f} = \mathbf{atom} \rightarrow [\mathbf{id}]; \ \mathbf{concat} \circ \alpha\mathbf{f}$$

This is just $\mathbf{f} = \beta([\mathbf{id}], \mathbf{concat})$.

In fact this is a relatively simple use of bilinear forms but it at least serves to show that there is some hope of manipulating non-linear recursions. Extending these ideas must be an area of great interest for future researchers.

5.8 Conclusions

FP offers a wide variety of algebraic laws which express powerful statements about program equality. This is achieved by developing a language of functions and functionals as opposed to the more conventional languages based on what Backus calls *object-level* program descriptions. By fixing the sets of primitive functions and functionals he establishes a *second-order* programming language. Even though KRC, for example, tends to utilize data-level programming there is no restriction on the functional level of the data; consequently languages such as KRC are *higher order*. One upshot of this has been mentioned more than once: FP can be simulated in KRC rather easily, indeed, since we gave the FP semantics in "KRC" we have actually presented this simulation.

In his papers Backus often remarks that some of the theorems which can be proved in the algebra programs would be fiendishly difficult to articulate in an object-level language and may quite possibly go unnoticed for this reason. This is probably true, although the moral we should draw might simply be to spend more of programming effort in the development of higher-order combinators (and investigating their relationships) in our data-level languages.

The reasons for doing this are several. It has been commonly agreed that higher-order operators are beneficial in program construction; one piece of advice which confirms this is the suggestion that there should be, to every *type constructor* a corresponding *function constructor*. For example consider the type constructors × and →. These should be accompanied by two functionals × and → with the following semantics:

> Let $f \in A \to B$ and $g \in C \to D$ for any types A, B, C and D.
> Define: $f \times g \in A \times B \to C \times D$ as it is in FP.
> Define: $f \to g \in A \to D$ to be $\lambda h \in B \to C \cdot g \circ h \circ f$.

This advice follows the development in the mathematical world of *category theory* which we have already had occasion to mention in Chapter 3.

A second reason for developing the algebra of functionals in a data-level language turns on the readability of programs. More than one commentator has mentioned the terse nature of FP programs and wondered how large-scale programs could be written in such a style. This also brings in issues of typing. FP is an untyped (or more properly, single typed) system and such systems are now considered less attractive than they once were because of the understanding we now have about polymorphic types. Furthermore, in the more recent presentations, Backus has introduced extended function definitions which, to some extent, re-introduce object-level descriptions as a concession to readability.

Thirdly, FP fixes a set of functional connectives with which we are invited to construct our programs. Our higher-level language allows us to define these and any others (at any functional level) that we might need. Whilst this is true there is no doubt that at present the most interesting work on the algebra of higher-order operators is that developed in the work of Backus and Williams.

Finally, the mathematically sophisticated reader might feel slightly uneasy about the FP systems; an uneasiness based on elegance rather than anything else. FP systems are based on a large number of primitives and it is not clear that some are not, in a precise sense, redundant. For example, the functions **distr** and **distr** are primitives in Backus's system but as we saw in example 5.3.2(i) they can be defined from other primitives. Mathematical systems consisting of a large number of non-logical connectives give rise to a large number of axioms or laws. It is less clear, and more difficult to prove that there are sufficient axioms (and not too many) to characterize the intended system. This worry is justified for FP; the collections of laws provided in the various accounts (even when based on the same set of primitives) varies enormously, and this gives little confidence that they are in any sense necessary and sufficient. In fact there is one law (the associativity of the composition functional) which does not appear in *any* of the presentations, although it is widely employed in the proofs of theorems! A suitable basis for a higher-order combinatorial programming language are the *Cartesian closed categories* which we mention in the bibliographic notes. These are founded on a small collection of primitive functions and functionals and a correspondingly small set of axioms.

5.9 Bibliographic notes

The papers of Backus (1978, 1981a, 1981b, 1985) and Williams (1981, 1982a, 1982b) are essential reading for anyone contemplating further study. Backus (1978) is the famous Turing Award paper in which FP systems are introduced and motivated. The first few sections of this amount to a devastating and polemical attack on the Von Neumann machine and "Von Neumann languages". In the latter parts of this paper a related system called FFP (formal functional systems) is introduced. This is used to provide FP systems with an operational semantics. FFP is a first-order language but with a reflection principle which enables programs to be represented (coded) as data. In this way higher-order operators can be simulated. Williams (1981, 1982b) describes an algorithm for generating the FFP representation of an FP form $Q(f)$.

Much of the work on extending the linear expansion theorem to more general cases is developed in Backus (1981a) and Williams (1982a). Williams relaxes the requirement that $Q(k)$ be linear and considers cases when $Q(k)$ behaves linearly over those functions which are actually used in the expansion. Thus he deals with a kind of local linearity. In particular he considers the overrun tolerant forms and the p–q distributive forms. The former are a special case of the bilinear forms which we have already considered. Certain constraints on bilinearity force the expansions to behave in reasonable ways and this is sufficient to enable the manipulation of many "divide and conquer" programs. The p–q distributive programs insist on a local linearity condition. They allow distributivity (which is already relaxed in linearity to allow for a predicate transformer) to be relaxed to allow for a consequent transformer as well. Transformations of FP program schemes are developed in Kieburtz & Shultis (1981) and more recently in Backus (1985).

Backus (1981a) introduces extended definitions. These aim to exploit the readability of object-level programs and to provide useful algebraic laws. The machinery necessary for this is rather messy (although not conceptually difficult) and it is not clear whether this approach is as useful as is claimed.

FP systems seem to stand in relation to conventional functional languages as the combinatory calculus does to the lambda calculus. Category theory adopts a combinatory approach to mathematics stressing the functional level (more properly 'arrow' or 'morphism' level) rather than the object level. Many researchers have commented that FP systems are reminiscent of the categorical presentation of the (typed) lambda calculus – the Cartesian closed categories. These are higher-order systems and seem to provide the most suitable basis for further development. Bellot (1985) makes a start and Guttag (1982) introduces types into the system but by far the most comprehensive and sophisticated treatment is due to Curien (1986) whose book we have already had occasion to mention. See also Curien (1985) for an introduction. This work has ramifications in the area of programming language implementation and we will mention his work again in the bibliographic notes of the next chapter.

Backus, J. W. (1978) Can programming be liberated from the Von Neumann style? A functional style and its algebra of programs, *Commun. ACM*, **21**, 613–40.

Backus, J. W. (1981a) The algebra of functional programs: function level reasoning, linear equations and extended definitions. In *Formalisation of Programming Concepts, LNCS*, Vol. 107, pp. 1–43. Springer, Berlin.

Backus, J. W. (1981b) Function level programs as mathematical objects. *Proc. ACM Conference on Functional Programming Languages and Computer Architecture.*

Backus, J. W. (1985) From function level semantics to program transformation and optimisation. In *Proc. Int. Conference on Theory and Practice of Software Development.* H. Ehrig, C. Floyd, M. Nivat & J. Thatcher (eds), *LNCS*, Vol. 186, pp. 60–91. Springer, Berlin.

Bellot, P. (1985) High order programming in extended FP. *Proc. Conference on Functional Programming Languages and Computer Architecture, LNCS*, Vol. 201, pp. 65–80. Springer, Berlin.

Curien, P. (1985) Categorical combinatory logic. *12th Colloquium on Automata, Languages and Programming, LNCS*, Vol. 194, pp. 130–9. Springer, Berlin.

Curien, P. (1986) *Categorial Combinators, Sequential Algorithms and Functional Programming.* Pitman, London.

Guttag, J. (1982) Notes on using types and type abstraction in functional programming. In *Functional Programming and its Applications.* J. Darlington, P. Henderson & D. A. Turner (eds), pp. 103–28. Cambridge University Press, Cambridge.

Kieburtz, R. B. & Shultis, J. (1981) Transformations of FP program schemes. *Proc. ACM Conference on Functional Programming and Computer Architecture.*

Williams, J. H. (1981) Formal representations for recursively defined functional programs. In *Formalisation of Programming Concepts, LNCS*, Vol. 107, pp. 460–70. Springer, Berlin.

Williams, J. H. (1982a) On the development of the algebra of functional programs. *Trans. Programing Languages and Systems*, **4,** 733–57.

Williams, J. H. (1982b) Notes on the FP style of functional programming. In *Functional Programming and its Applications*. J. Darlington, P. Henderson & D. A. Turner (eds), pp. 73–101. Cambridge University Press, Cambridge.

Chapter 6

Implementation

New ideas regarding machine organization and program execution are being developed at an almost alarming rate. The development and great interest in functional languages is certainly a major factor in this research area. The other influences are the tremendous advances in hardware science, particularly in fabrication techniques, which have led to a situation in which one can experiment more freely with novel machine architectures. These new architectures often consist of many processing elements, but even new monoprocessor architectures are being contemplated which are a far cry from the traditional Von Neumann machine paradigm.

In the first section of this chapter we will describe an abstract machine which forms the basis for the execution of a wide class of modern programming languages. We do this not only because some functional languages are implemented this way but because it is then rather easier to see the significance of more recent execution methods. In the following sections we will look at in turn, lazy racks, combinator compilation and evaluation, supercombinator compilation, the G-machine, typechecking and memoization.

6.1 Activation record structures

To begin with we will describe a conventional virtual machine which forms the run-time structure for many conventional languages as well as some functional languages. What we shall attempt to describe is the meaning of a programming language with respect to some machine architecture. In other words we shall be describing the action the various parts or features of the programming language have on some machine state. This is often termed an operational semantics for the language. We have, in fact, already seen an example of such an operational semantics in Chapter 2. In that example the programming language was the lambda calculus, and the machine architecture was the SECD machine. The semantics were given by the transformation function **transform**.

The term *virtual machine* in the opening paragraph of this section is particularly significant. In practice, of course, the actual machine architecture will be more or less inappropriate for a language we wish to implement. To pursue the example above: we might wish to implement an applicative evaluator for the lambda calculus on some microprocessor-based computer. Naturally the architecture of this computer will be different to that of the SECD machine. The solution is to use the registers and memory of the computer to form stack, environment, control and dump structures and to write short code sequences which effect the various auxiliary operations of the SECD machine, such as **lookup** and **extend**. By doing this we make the computer look like an SECD machine. This then is the meaning of the term virtual machine. It is the virtual architecture formed by the allocation of space and registers and maintained by the structure of the machine code which is generated from the source program.

It is perhaps surprising that a great number of programming languages utilize the same virtual machine which following conventional terminology we will call the *Activation Record Machine* (ARM).

Languages such as PASCAL, the ALGOLs, SIMULA and even LISP can all be described more or less in terms of the ARM architecture. One reason why this is so is that all these languages, and indeed many others, are based predominantly around the concept of the recursive procedure or function.

Firstly, evey function and procedure is associated with a *template activation record*. This is a data structure template which is to represent the values of various items which will be necessary for the execution of a function or procedure body.

In order to appreciate fully the nature and roles of the values in a template let us take a look at a typical procedure definition written in an ALGOL-like notation:

procedure $f(w)$;
   begin
     int x, y;
     $x := 6 + z$;
     $z := 7$
   end

There are basically two pieces of information which we need to record in the template. Firstly, we shall need an entry point into the code which results from compiling the body of the procedure. Secondly, we shall need to provide a means of finding the values of variables (like z in the example) which are not declared locally. This we shall call the *global environment*. Notice how similar this is to the *closure* concept of the SECD machine which consists of the body of the lambda expression and an environment for providing the binding variables.

So much for a procedure definition but what happens when we call a procedure? The key here is to associate every invocation (call) of a procedure with an *activation record*. This is a data structure containing all the information necessary for the proper execution of a procedure. Notice that each procedure is defined just once so there is but one activation record template for each procedure. On the other hand a procedure may be called many times, possibly even recursively. It is important to see that there will be a separate activation record associated with *every* invocation. The activation record data-structure consists of five parts.

The first part is known as *work space* which is a small data area used during the execution of the body of the procedure for the storing of partial results and values. This will be used in the evaluation of $6+z$ in the example program above. This workspace is rather like the stack component in the SECD machine.

The second component of the activation record is the *local environment* and this is a place where the bindings of variables declared locally in a procedure will be stored. In our example program the local environment will consist of three slots, two for the values of the local variables x and y and a third for the single parameter w.

The third component is the *global environment*. This information is in fact available from the template of the procedure. The reason for this is that the global environment stays constant over all the invocations of a procedure. As we remarked above, this component allows us to find the values of variables defined globally. There is an analogy between the local and global environments of an activation record and the environment slot in the SECD machine. The global environment is therefore set when a procedure is defined (in the template) and not when it is called. Thus the binding of free variables is *static* in the sense of ALGOL and LISPKIT LISP.

The fourth and fifth fields are related to the dump component of the SECD machine in that they establish the link between the current activation and the activation which invoked the current one. The fourth field is a return code pointer which shows where execution should continue once the currently executing procedure is finished. The fifth field points to the activation record which is associated with the calling procedure. We can be a little more precise about the connection with the SECD machine here. Recall that the dump in an SECD state is itself an SECD state. The return code pointer is rather like the control part of the dump whilst the fifth slot is analogous to the stack, environment and dump elements of the dump.

The reader may have noticed that we have not so far made any analogy between the SECD machine control field and the AR structure. This seems like an oversight for it is this field in the SECD machine which contains the program and drives execution forward. In the ARM this control field is analogous to the program counter register which of course will point to the code we wish to execute.

To complete the picture let us return to the global environment slot in an activation record. This is to provide the values of variables declared globally. Now of course all values are declared locally to some procedure and will therefore appear in the local environment slot of some activation record. The global environment therefore is no more than a pointer to the activation record of the procedure in which the current procedure is defined. This is the textually enclosing procedure. If it should turn out that the global variable is not defined locally even in the textually surrounding procedure then we can continue the access through *its* global environment field and so on.

The concept of a virtual machine may be even clearer now: when compiling a program in (say) PASCAL we produce a sequence of instructions for the target machine which, when evaluated, gives rise to an activation record structure which the code is designed to access and maintain.

The picture we have described is quite complicated. At any moment during the execution of a program there may be many activation records in existence, although only one will be active. The others are suspended in the meantime and will be reawakened on the completion of the execution of others. This raises the interesting question of how all these activation records fit together into a single large data-structure. In languages such as LISP and PASCAL every procedure must terminate before its caller can be reactivated. This is a "last invoked first to finish" regime and in terms of activation records, would read "last record to be built is the first record to be finished with". This is clearly the last in–first out nature of a stack. Thus in such languages the activation records are at all times organized as a stack. This is not true for languages such as SIMULA in which entities rather like procedures (which are called *class objects* or *co-routines*) may become suspended temporarily and later resumed. In such a language the activation records are organized as a tree. We shall not say more about this but the interested reader may like to consult some of the material in the bibliography for further study.

In order to consolidate some of the ideas above let us take a simple example program and show the state of the activation record structure at one point in its execution. One final point which might require clarification is that it is usual to treat the main program as an anonymous and parameterless procedure which is called, automatically, in order to get the program execution going.

Example 6.1(i)

```
begin
  int x, y;
  procedure f(z);
    begin
      int a, b;
      a := 6;
      if z > 0 then f(0);
    end;
  x := 4;
  f(2)
end
```

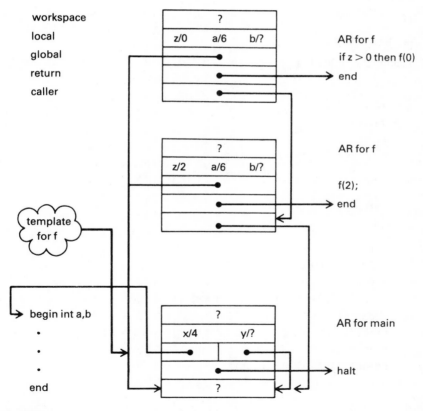

Fig. 6.1(ii)

There is a good deal of alternative terminology in the literature for that which we have introduced above. Activation records are also known as invocation records, process state descriptions and frames. The global environment slot is often termed the environment link or the static link (so called because it follows exactly the static structure of the procedure nesting in the program). The fifth component in an activation record which points to the caller's activations is sometimes called the dynamic link (because it follows exactly the dynamic calling sequence of the program execution).

In languages in which the AR structure is known to be stack-like we would of course allocate space in contiguous storage and utilize registers to identify the top and bottom of the active record.

When a procedure terminates it is easy to regain the previous activation record by moving the top register down to the current base register and then loading the base register with the dynamic link field.
∎

Example 6.1(iii)

Consider the following programs:

```
begin
    int n, r;
    input n;
    r := 1;
    while n ≠ 0 do begin r := r * n;
                          n := n - 1
                    end;
    output r
end

begin
    function f(n, r);
        begin
        if n = 0 then r else f(n - 1, r * n)
        end;
    int x;
    input x;
    output f(x, 1)
end
```

Both these programs compute the factorial of an integer. The first is an iteration and the second is a program based on the accumulating parameter version we originally developed in Section 3.6.

Since the first program contains no calls to a procedure or function we see that it is executed in the constant space allocated for the activation record associated with the main program. The second program, however, executes in space proportional to the input. This is so because the procedure f is recursive and there will be $n+2$ activation records (including the main program) created during execution, when the input is n, and at one point (when the first argument to f is zero) all $n+2$ frames will be extant. This seems to contradict our claim in Section 3.5 that programs in iterative form are executed in constant space.

We will shortly see how to alter this execution strategy so that the second program executes in constant space.

Notice that every recursive call of f after the initial invocation has an activation in its dynamic link which has no program fragment left to execute. The saving of the activation record of these calls to f seem unnecessary for on return these activations themselves immediately terminate and return in their own turn.

Clearly, this activation record machine is very conservative in its behaviour. It arranges that during the execution of nested processes all the information contained in the suspended processes is saved even though this may not be used.
∎

This example is an extreme (but not pathological) case in which no information regarding the calling procedure is required after the called procedure is complete. In general we will probably require some, but not necessarily all, of the information associated with the caller when we return from nested activations.

Example 6.1(iv)

Consider the following variation of the program for computing factorials.

```
begin
  function f(n);
    begin
      if n = 0 then 1 else n * f(n − 1)
    end;
  int x;
  input x;
  output f(x)
end
```

In this program the binding of the parameter n of the procedure f will indeed be required after the recursive call. In fact we would either need its binding in the local environment to be saved or else its value placed and saved on the workspace. Either way, after the recursive call there is still a little processing to be done in order to multiply the value of the recursive call to the parameter n. No other binding information is required however and so f need not, for example, preserve the global environment over the recursive call.

■

Attempting to determine and take advantage of information concerning the usuage of variables in some systematic way has a long and distinguished research history, particularly in the USA where the development of efficient LISP systems has been a major preoccupation.

For the rest of the section let us assume that the information required to form the activation record of the current process is stored in some set of registers. Clearly when a new process is invoked these registers will be required to store the new activation record. What we need to determine is what needs to be saved whilst the registers are being reused.

It seems improbable that a thorough dynamic analysis of arbitrary programs could be undertaken which would provide an optimal scheme for register allocation and preservation. Indeed as computer scientists we tend to develop an instinct for the uncomputable – and this problem looks to be such.

In the operational semantics developed so far, using a framed stack, the solution is particularly cautious; at every procedure invocation the current frame (now thought of as residing in a set of registers) is entirely saved in store. Presumably there is a less conservative alternative.

Two disciplines for register saving have been used which to some extent improve on the *save-all* strategy and these are named after the function or procedure whose responsibility it is to save the values. These are the *caller saves* and *callee saves* strategies. In the former the procedure which is currently operating, and about to call another, has the responsibility of saving any registers it might require later, when the function it is about to call has completed. This means it can decide to save only those values it knows it will need later. On the other hand it may, of course, save a register which is not utilized by the function it invokes.

In *callee saves* the responsibility is left to the procedure which is called from the currently operating procedure. In this case it can be arranged that only those registers the callee requires will be saved. However, conversely, it may save registers which the caller will not, in the future, require.

Under both these regimes it is easy to see that the number of slots required in an activation record will not be fixed. This presents a problem in the framed stack approach for a corollary of its simplicity is that the various values stored can always be found at fixed offsets from the base of any frame. In our description of the ARM, for example, the return link is always at an offset of one from the base of the frame and the global environment at an offset of two.

The simplest solution to this is to adopt the so-called *unframed stack* strategy. In this case we do not think of a stack of activations at all but just a stack of values which are pushed as and when required by the caller or callee. Whilst this strategy of register frame saving is an improvement it is not yet very sophisticated. As we remarked earlier both *caller saves* and *callee saves* have disadvantages. The problem is that to detect situations in which these techniques are overly cautious is essentially a *dynamic* problem. After all, the optimizations they can make on behalf of the caller or callee are based only on static properties of the function and procedure definitions.

6.2 Lazy racks

In order to improve matters some dynamic optimization which can deal with the interaction between the register needs of the calling procedure and called procedure is certainly necessary. We would hope that a register is only saved when the caller will require the contents later and the callee will actually need to overwrite it. Actually the callee may not overwrite such a register itself but may call further functions or procedures which do. This means that the interaction may extend over an arbitrary number of procedure invocations. But how can we look ahead in order to determine if both caller and some future callee actually require a register?

This is the question that led Steele & Sussman (1979) to develop a new data abstraction called a *rack*. A rack is roughly a *register–stack pair* on which four operations are defined: ASSIGN the register a value; FETCH the register contents; SAVE the register (on the internal stack); RESTORE (the top of the stack) to the register. It is possible now to use a set of racks instead of the set of registers with associated stack that we have described so far. We shall take it that there are two operations on a register called READ and STORE and two on a stack called PUSH and POP all with the obvious meanings. It is now easy to see one simple way of implementing the rack operations in terms of the register and stack which comprise it. Register READs are replaced by FETCHes; STOREs by ASSIGNs; PUSHes to the single stack are replaced by the appropriate SAVE (on a specialized stack) and POPs are just RESTOREs. The only difference is that whereas we had previously considered a single unframed stack of mixed values we have now many stacks (one for each register) on which values of a single kind are saved.

The advantage this gives is that we may allow a rack to implement its SAVEs and RESTOREs exactly how it pleases. Given the naïve translation of operations above we certainly gain no advantage. However we can now provide some answer to the question posed at the end of the last section. We do not actually look ahead for a point at which a register is actually required before saving it. We simply make the process of saving *lazy*. This means that when we need to execute a SAVE we do no more than record in the rack the fact that the contents of the register are important, but we do not actually execute the push to the stack. Now if the flow of control eventually takes us to a point where an ASSIGN or a further SAVE is required on the rack we can first save the contents on the stack before overwriting the register. Once the contents are safely stacked we can with confidence remove the warning notice we set earlier when the SAVE was encountered.

On the other hand if the register was not required after the SAVE by the callee, or any of the functions called from the callee, we will eventually return control to the caller and encounter a RESTORE. The warning would then tell us that the contents are valuable. In this case the RESTORE has nothing to do (except to turn off the warning) for the value was not placed on the stack during the execution which started with the corresponding SAVE.

To make this work we arrange for the rack to be provided with a single flag which has two states. Externally the rack behaves as if it were just a register connected to a stack in the fashion described above. Internally it can be made to implement its stack operations lazily using the flag. Sussman claims the concept of rack came to him in a dream one night. Since then Sussman & Steele have referred to the delayed push in a rack as 'dreaming' which they claim, is a suitable occupation for a lazy architecture.

This strategy is cost-effective only if the operations to test the flag and to load and read the register are cheap compared with the stack operations. This is often the case for the stack will usually be situated in store with the overhead of memory access.

We finish this section with the algorithms for the rack operations ASSIGN, FETCH, SAVE and RESTORE in terms of the register operations READ and STORE, the flag operations SET, UNSET and BUSY (with the obvious interpretations) and the stack operations PUSH and POP.

```
FETCH    = READ
ASSIGN   = PUSH;
           UNSET;
           STORE    (if BUSY)
ASSIGN   = STORE    (if not BUSY)
```

SAVE	= PUSH	(if BUSY)
SAVE	= SET	(if not BUSY)
RESTORE	= UNSET	(if BUSY)
RESTORE	= POP	(if not BUSY)

This implementation of a rack effectively contains a dynamic optimizer for the sequence SAVE; RESTORE.

Interestingly enough, empirical study led Sussman & Steele to realize that this abstraction is not all that good for the maintenance of the environment which has the habit of changing infrequently across functions calls but which is often required for evaluation of any procedure body. A careful look at the factorial program earlier will show that the global environment is the same in all recursive frames. It is often the case that the caller will require the environment after the callee completes and that the callee will require the register too. If the value the callee requires is actually the same as the caller a lot of work is still being done for nothing. Steele & Sussman have described a mechanism in which a counter is associated with a value and the counter indicates the number of times the value has effectively been replicated. If the value does change which makes the stacking vital it will be necessary to store the replication counter too. This is a considerable overhead in its own right but needs to be compared with the time saved maintaining a replication count. Further details of this and other techniques are given in the bibliographic notes.

6.3 Combinator compilers

6.3.1 Introduction

For conventional machine architectures a program of machine code instructions is essentially a sequence or list of actions to be performed. In order to compare this with the new combinator-based architectures it will be useful to view a conventional machine code program as a right linear binary tree. That is to say, every node is the sequencing of an instruction on the left branch with an instruction, or right linear binary tree of instructions, on the right branch.

In such machines it is usual for this tree of actions to remain fixed during execution. The operational semantics of the tree is a change in some machine state which probably consists of some registers and some global memory. More precisely, each instruction designates some small change of state (alter a register, store to a memory cell) and the act of sequencing instructions is to compose such state changes into more elaborate ones. In practice the program is stored in the machine state itself and may be changed in just the same way as any data. Indeed the language COBOL at one stage possessed a statement called ALTER which did just this to effect changes in the destination of GOTO instructions. It has long been regarded as poor programming practice to work in this way for such changes do not in general preserve the meaning of the program and this makes reasoning about the program (whether formal or informal) very difficult indeed, if not impossible for all practical purposes.

Combinator architectures and machines differ quite radically from this paradigm. Put starkly, combinator programs are *not* evaluated in the presence of a global state for there exists, in the machine, nothing except the program. Furthermore, evaluation of the program proceeds *only* by altering the structure of the program. Again this is very different from the conventional approach. In a moment we shall see why this is harmless in such machines.

The basis for this approach is due to Turner (1979a) who outlined the practicality of using the combinatory expressions we introduced in Chapter 2 as programs for a machine in which the basic instructions would be combinators like S, K and I. Evaluation then consists of reducing these combinator expressions.

Programs are again binary trees of instructions in such a machine but these are not necessarily right linear trees. Moreover, the nodes of the tree are not sequencing operators but are, in fact, mainly application operators. That is, a node represents the application of its left subprogram to its right subprogram. In a conventional machine it represents the sequencing of its left subprogram (an instruction) *before* its right subprogram.

This immediately suggests that there exists a large amount of exploitable parallelism in combinatory programs because, while sequencing implies a linearity and sequentiality of execution, application makes no demands on the order of reduction of its arguments; they can be reduced in any order or even simultaneously. The reason why altering the program itself is a safe procedure in such machines is quite evident: the reduction rules for the combinators preserve meaning. The newly altered program always has the same meaning as the original.

6.3.2 Combinatory compilation

In Section 6.4 we embark on a detailed description of exactly how such machines implement combinators as instructions and combinatory expressions as programs, but here we deal with the subject of compilation. For this enterprise to be successful we need to know that we can compile our programs into combinatory expressions which may be run on such a machine.

The basis of this form of program compilation is, not surprisingly, the abstraction algorithm of Chapter 2. Along with the combinators which this algorithm introduces it is necessary to introduce a variety of other combinators. Some of these arise because we will be using data structures which are introduced independently of the lambda calculus. That is, we take numbers, atoms, and so on, as primitive objects; we do not view them as distinguished lambda expressions, as we did in Chapter 2. We begin with a very simple example which exemplifies this.

Example 6.3.2(i)

We take a simple numeric program written in conditional, rather than clausal, form:

   def f $n =$ **if** $(n = 0)$ 1 $(n * (f (n - 1)))$

This can be compiled by a simple abstraction (with respect to n).

   def f $= [n]$ **if** $(n = 0)$ $1(n * (f (n - 1)))$

This yields the following combinatory code:

   f $= S(S (S (K$ **if** $) (S (S (K$ **eq**$) (K$ $0)) I))$
   $(K$ $1)) (S (S (K$ **times**$) I) (S (K$ **f**$)$
   $(S (S (K$ **minus**$) I) (K$ $1))))$

Note that this expression involves combinators called **if, eq, times** and **minus** along with the expected S, K and I. These are *not* shorthands for lambda expressions for, as we remarked above, we do not wish to use lambda representations for primitive data structures – for the sake of efficiency, we take direct representations. None the less, we do expect *agreement* between the independent representation and the lambda representation. We will have to return to this in detail later. Naturally, we can apply some of the optimizations, given in Chapter 2, to our compiled program. This yields:

   f $= S (C (B$ **if** $($**eq** $0)) 1) (S$ **times** $(B$ **f** $(C$ **minus** $1)))$
∎

Things, however, are more complicated than this for we have adopted a notation for expressing programs which is syntactically more complex than simple lambda abstraction. The two major differences we have to cope with are the introduction of definition by clauses and abstraction with respect to general patterns.

   In order to develop the compiling scheme for this form of function definition it is necessary to begin with a formal, syntactic definition. The

development of the extra combinators and the compiling algorithm we present
is due to Turner. The reader will find reference to his research in the
bibliographic notes at the end of the chapter.

Definition 6.3.2(ii)

The syntax of programs is given by the following productions in Backus Naur
Form.

> fundef $::=$ clause|clause fundef
> clause $::=$ **def** v $pl=e$
> pl $::=$ empty$|p|pl$ p
> p $::=v|c|(p)|p:p$
> v variables
> pl pattern lists
> p patterns
> c constants
> e expressions

■

With this syntax at our disposal we can give a systematic description of the
compiling process.

We shall specify a mapping **compile** which, given elements of the
programming language, yields combinatory expressions. For notational
convenience we will surround syntactic items with square brackets.

We start with whole function definitions.

compile [clause fundef] $= T$ (**compile** [clause])(**compile** [fundef])

T is a new combinator which is used to combine the code of a series of clauses.
In fact this combinator requires three arguments in order to become saturated.
The first is the code for the first clause; the second is the code for all the
subsequent clauses (gathered together by further T combinators). The third
argument of T is the actual parameter when the function is executed. The T
combinator attempts to evaluate this with the first clause. If this fails (because
the actual parameter does not match this clause) the value is passed on to the
code for the subsequent clauses.

> $T x y z = y z$ **when** $x z = F$
> $T x y z = T(x z)(y z)$ **when** $(x z)$ is an applicative expression
> $T x y z = x z$ **otherwise**

F is a *failure combinator*. $F x = F$ for all x so failure is persistent. Failures occur
when matching arguments to patterns or guards cannot be satisfied. The

second of these definitions of T is necessary because matching takes place on data structures and sometimes (in multi-argument functions) it is necessary to undertake further evaluation to discover whether or not a particular function clause matches the actual parameter.

We can now move on to individual clauses.

compile $[\textbf{def}\, v\, pl = e] = [pl]\, e$

The notation $[pl]\, e$, as before, signifies abstraction, but this time with respect to a pattern list. We now move on to this:

$$[\text{empty}]\, e = e$$
$$[pl\, p]\, e \quad = [pl]([p]\, e)$$

Thus lists of patterns are abstracted one by one starting at the right-most pattern. Patterns themselves are dealt with as follows:

$[v]e \quad = \text{as before} \quad [\text{see definition } 2.3.1(\text{i})]$
$[(p)]e \quad = [p]e \quad\quad\quad (\text{patterns in brackets only indicate}$
$\quad\quad\quad\quad\quad\quad\quad\quad\quad\quad\quad \text{grouping})$
$[p_1 : p_2]e = U[p_1]([p_2]e)$

This last clause explains how data structure patterns can be compiled. This is achieved by splitting up the subpatterns and abstracting with respect to these in sequence yielding $[p_1]\, ([p_2]\, e)$. This expression expects arguments one at a time. On the other hand the expression $[p_1 : p_2]\, e$ expects a single combined argument. The relationship between one and the other is essentially the currying relationship. Thus U is the *uncurrying combinator*. It is defined as follows:

$$U\, x\, y{:}z = x\, y\, z$$
$$U\, x\, y \quad = F \quad\quad \textbf{otherwise}$$

The other case we have to consider is abstraction with respect to a constant.

$$[c]\, e = M\, c\, e$$

M is the *matching combinator* and is the prime reason why a failure can occur. Essentially we wish to yield e only when $[c]\, e$ is given an argument c which matches. Thus we define:

$$M\, c\, e\, c = e$$
$$M\, c\, e\, x = F$$

This concludes the generalized notion of abstraction.

Generalized abstraction is not the only generalization that we entertain. Since **cons** is our basic data constructor it makes sense for conceptual and efficiency reasons to represent $e_0:e_1$ as:

          and not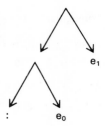

Thus we may be confronted with $[v]e_0:e_1$. What should this be?

$$[v]e_0:e_1 = S_:[v]e_0[v]e_1$$

where $S_: x\,y\,x = (x\,z):(y\,z)$.

The introduction of a new S-like combinator suggests that new, related, optimizations exist.

Proposition 6.3.2(iii)

(a) $S_:(K\,E_1)(K\,E_2) = K\,(E_1:E_2)$
(b) $S_:(K\,E_1)I \quad = \mathbf{cons}\,E_1$
(c) $S_:(K\,E_1)E_2 \quad = B_:E_1\,E_2$
(d) $S_:E_1(K\,E_2) \quad = C_:E_1\,E_2$
where $\quad B_: x\,y\,z = x:(y\,z)$

Exercise 6.3.2(iv)

Prove (a), (c) and (d) above. Define $C_:$ appropriately.
■

Proof of (b).

$$
\begin{aligned}
S_:(K\,E_1)I\,x &= \\
(K\,E_1\,x):I &= \\
E_1:x &= \\
\mathbf{cons}\,E_1\,x
\end{aligned}
$$

■

Programs can include λ-abstraction explicitly. Since we can handle abstraction with respect to arbitrary patterns we can include expressions like $\lambda pl \cdot e$ where pl is, as above, a list of patterns. In fact this is necessary because our language includes declaration forms like the following:

> **let** $p = e$ **in** e' and
> e' **where** $p = e$

These are just syntactic sugar for the expression

> $(\lambda p \cdot e') e$

Compiling such expressions is trivial:

> **compile** $[\lambda pl \cdot e] = [pl]$ (**compile** $[e]$)

The recursion takes care of abstracts in e. This means that (**compile** $[e]$) is always defined. In general this simply recurses over the subexpressions of e and has no effect. However, on lambda abstracts it is defined as above. Thus when we write (**compile** $[e]$) the effect will be to "compile away" all the explicit lambda abstracts in e. The details of this are given in full in Table 6.3.3(i).

Finally we have to deal with guarded clauses.

These have the following form:

> **def f** $pl = e$ **when** e'

We take it that this is just syntactic sugar for:

> **def f** $pl = $ **if** e' e F

In this expression F is the failure combinator which was introduced for the purposes of defining the matching combinator M and the uncurrying combinator U.

We must now amend the compiling rule for clauses to take these extensions into account.

> **compile def** v $pl = e$ **when** $e' = [pl]$ (**if**(**compile** $[e']$)(**compile** $[e]$) F)

6.3.3 Further optimizations

Even with the optimization rules we introduced in Chapter 2 and those of the last section for the combinator S, it turns out that the size of the compiled expression will still grow at least quadratically with the number of abstractions performed.

Turner (1979b) has provided an elegant and simple mechanism for handling multiple abstractions which has the effect of reducing this relationship to a linear one.

To see this clearly consider the expression $E_0 E_1$ and suppose that we wish to compute $[x\,y\,z]\,E_0\,E_1$. Using the original abstraction definition and the optimizations we obtain the following sequence of partially compiled expressions.

$$[w\,x\,y\,z]\,E_0\,E_1 =$$
$$[w\,x\,y]\,S\,[z]\,E_0\,[z]\,E_1 =$$
$$[w\,x]\,S\,(B\,S\,[y\,z]\,E_0)\,[y\,z]\,E_1 =$$
$$[w]\,S\,(B\,S\,(B\,(B\,S)\,[x\,y\,z]\,E_0))\,[x\,y\,z]\,E_1 =$$
$$S\,(B\,S\,(B\,(B\,S)\,(B\,(B\,(B\,S))\,[w\,x\,y\,z]\,E_0)))\,[w\,x\,y\,z]\,E_1$$

It is clear that large *constant only* expressions build up which have the effect of steering arguments correctly to subabstracts. Presumably there is a more straightforward way to do this; indeed this is what Turner discovered. He introduced a single new S-like combinator called S', defined by:

$$S'\,k\,x\,y\,z = k\,(x\,z)\,(y\,z)$$

Now given a combinator W and expression E we define $W_0 E$ and $W^{n+1}E = W(W^n E)$. This allows us to redefine our algorithm for multiple abstractions:

$$[x_1\ \ldots\ x_n]\,E_0\,E_1 = S'^{n-1}\,S\,[x_1\ \ldots\ x_n]\,E_0\,[x_1\ \ldots\ x_n]\,E_1$$
$$[x_1\ \ldots\ x_n]\,E = [x_1\ \ldots\ x_{n-1}]([x_n]\,E) \qquad \textbf{otherwise}$$

This when applied to our example above yields the compiled expressions:

$$[w\,x\,y\,z]\,E_0\,E_1 =$$
$$[w\,x\,y]\,S\,[z]\,E_0\,[z]\,E_1 =$$
$$[w\,x]\,S'\,S\,[y\,z]\,E_0\,[y\,z]\,E_1 =$$
$$[w]\,S'\,(S'\,S)\,[x\,y\,z]\,E_0\,[x\,y\,z]\,E_1 =$$
$$S'(S'(S'\,S))\,[w\,x\,y\,z]\,E_0\,[w\,x\,y\,z]\,E_1$$

We can now amend our compilation rules to allow these optimizations:

$$[pl\ p]\,e_0\,e_1\ = S'^n\,S\,[pl\ p]\,e_0\,[pl\ p]\,e_1$$
$$[pl\ p]\,e_0{:}e_1\ = S'^n\,S_{:}\,[pl\ p]\,e_0\,[pl\ p]\,e_1$$
$$[pl\ p]\,e\ \ \ \ \ = [pl]([p]\,e)\ \textbf{otherwise}$$

where n is the length of the complex pattern pl.

The various clauses, introduced above, can now be drawn together to form the summary shown in Table 6.3.3(i).

Table 6.3.3(i)

---

compile [clause fundef] $= (T(\textbf{compile} \text{ [clause]}) (\textbf{compile} \text{ [fundef]}))$
compile [def $v\, pl = e$] $= [pl]\, (\textbf{compile}\, [e])$
compile [def $v\, pl = e$ when e'] $= [pl]\, (\text{if}\, (\textbf{compile}\, [e'])\, (\textbf{compile}\, [e])\, F)$
compile [def $v\, pl = e$ otherwise] $= \textbf{compile}$ [def $v\, pl = e$]
compile [$e_0 e_1$] $= (\textbf{compile}\, [e_0]) (\textbf{compile}\, [e_1])$
compile [$e_0 : e_1$] $= (\textbf{compile}\, [e_0]) : (\textbf{compile}\, [e_1])$
compile [c] $= c$
compile [$\lambda pl \cdot e$] $= [pl]\, (\textbf{compile}\, [e])$
compile [let $p = e$ in e'] $= \textbf{compile}\, [(\lambda p \cdot e')\, e]$
compile [e where $p = e'$] $= \textbf{compile}\, [(\lambda p \cdot e)\, e']$
$[pl\, p]\, (e_0\, e_1) = S'''\, S\, [pl\, p]\, e_0 [pl\, p]\, e_1$
$[pl\, p]\, (e_0 : e_1) = S'''\, S_: [pl\, p]\, e_0 [pl\, p]\, e_1$
where n is the length of the pattern list pl.
$[pl\, p]\, e = [pl]\, ([p]\, e)$ otherwise.
$[v]\, v = I$
$[v]\, v' = K\, v'$
$[v]\, (e_0\, e_1) = S[v]\, e_0 [v]\, e_1$
$[v]\, (e_0 : e_1) = S_: [v]\, e_0 [v]\, e_1$
$[(p)]\, e = [p]\, e$
$[p_1 : p_2]\, e = U([p_1]\, ([p_2]\, e))$
$[c]\, e = M\, c\, e$

Exercise 6.3.3(ii)

This description does not contain references to the optimizations given in proposition 2.3.1(i) and proposition 6.3.2(iii). Reformulate the compiler to incorporate these.
∎

The compiling scheme presented in this section outlines the principles of combinatory compilation. In certain respects we have made simplifying assumptions and settled on certain interpretations when there is debate in the literature about the exact semantics of certain constructs (for example the semantics of pattern matching involving tuples or refutable patterns in guarded equations). The interested reader will need to consult the literature for further guidance on these subtleties.

6.3.4 The principle of abstraction

In Chapter 2 we showed that the expression $[x]E$ really is an abstraction of E, with respect to x, by showing that the operator $[x]$ obeys the principle of abstraction.

In the last section we have extended this considerably and we would wish to check that the generalizations introduced do indeed satisfy this requirement. Thus we are obliged to prove a generalization of the principle of abstraction.

Proposition 6.3.4(i)

For all pattern lists, pl, and expressions, E, we have:

$$([pl]E)\, pl = E$$

Proof. We set up a well-founded order as follows: $pl < pl'$ when pl is a shorter pattern list than pl' or when pl and pl' have the same length but pl is structurally simpler than pl'. $E < E'$, as usual, when E is a structurally simpler expression than E'. Next $(pl, E) < (pl', E')$ when $pl < pl'$ or $pl = pl'$ and $E < E'$. Since pl is always a finite list of finite patterns and E a finite expression it is clear that $<$ is well founded. Now we do induction on this ordering.

> *Case 1:* $pl = pl\, p$
> *Case 1a:* $E = E_0\, E_1$
>> $([pl\, p]E_0\, E_1)\, pl\, p =$
>> $S'\, S\, [pl\, p]E_0\, [pl\, p]E_1\, pl\, p =$
>> $S\, ([pl\, p]E_0\, pl)([pl\, p]E_1\, pl)\, p =$
>> $([pl\, p]E_0\, pl\, p)([pl\, p]E_1\, pl\, p) = \text{(induction)}$
>> $E_0\, E_1$
>
> *Case 1b:* $E = E_0 : E_1$
> Similarly.
> *Case 1c: otherwise*
>> $([pl\, p]E)\, pl\, p \qquad =$
>> $([pl]([p]E)\, pl)\, p \quad = \text{(induction)}$
>> $[p]E\, p \qquad\qquad = \text{(induction)}$
>> E

> *Case 2:* $pl = p$
> *Case 2a:* $p = v$
>> see proposition 2.3.1(iii) and
>> $[v](E_0 : E_1)v \qquad =$
>> $S. \, [v]E_0\, [v]E_1\, v \quad =$
>> $([v]E_0\, v):([v]E_1\, v) = \text{(induction)}$
>> $E_0 : E_1$

Case 2b: $p = c$

  $([c]E) c =$

  $M c E c =$

   E

Case 2c: $p = (p)$

  $([(p)]E)(p)$

  $([p]E) p = $ (induction)

   E

Case 2d: $p = p_1 : p_2$

  $([p_1 : p_2]E) p_1 : p_2 =$

  $U [p_1] ([p_2]E) p_1 : p_2 =$

  $[p_1] ([p_2]E) p_1 p_2 = $ (induction)

  $([p_2]E) p_2 = $ (induction)

   E

■

6.4 Evaluating combinatory expressions

In this section we describe how combinatory expressions can be represented as directed, cyclic graphs of binary nodes. We also show how such graphs can be processed according to various combinator rewrite rules.

6.4.1 Representations and rewrites

We have entertained exactly two operations in our language: functional application and the data constructor **cons**, which we write as an infix colon. These are both binary operators and so we can represent them by labelled binary nodes. The two fields of these nodes are to contain (pointers to) appropriate subexpressions. In the case of application this means the operator and the operand. In the case of data construction this means the head and tail subexpressions. Such nodes will be written

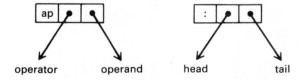

Fig. 6.4.1(i)

Chapter 6

Now functional application associates to the left so, given expressions E_0, E_1 and E_2 the composite expression $S\ E_0\ E_1\ E_2$ should be represented by the (tree):

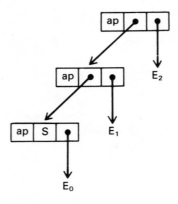

Fig. 6.4.1(ii)

On the other hand data construction associates to the right. This suggests that the list consisting of the subcomponents E_0, E_1 and E_2 [$E_0\ E_1\ E_2$] which is short for $E_0:E_1:E_2:$Nil should be represented by the (tree):

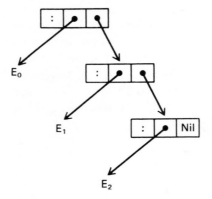

Fig. 6.4.1(iii)

The expression represented by Fig. 6.4.1(ii) is an example of a fully saturated combinatory expression. This suggests that it may be rewritten (by some evaluating process) according to the defining rule of S; that is: $S\,E_0\,E_1\,E_2 = E_0\,E_2\,(E_1\,E_2)$.

In terms of our chosen representation this might be:

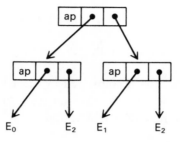

Fig. 6.4.1(iv)

This is (formally) correct but fails to take full advantage of the representation. The reader will recall from Chapter 2 that a graphical representation is ideal for making the natural sharing of subexpressions explicit. By making the lower two nodes in Fig. 6.4.1(iv) share E_2 we will avoid copying the expression (which may be arbitrarily large) but, more importantly, we need to reduce E_2 only once (if at all). To make this work we adopt the following representation for the S combinator reduction:

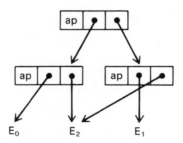

Fig. 6.4.1(v)

Having adopted this representation we see that the data structures are now directed acyclic graphs rather than just simple trees. This immediately raises a new and important consideration regarding combinator rewrites.

When we reduce an expression, like that described by Fig. 6.4.1(ii), we can no longer be sure that we are not sharing it with other expressions in the graph.

This makes the choice of the nodes themselves in the rewrite an important issue. Up to now we have not specified the identity of the three nodes which appear in Fig. 6.4.1(v). This is a crucial design decision as the following example shows.

Example 6.4.1(vi)

Assume that the three cells used in the rewrite described by Figs 6.4.1(ii) and 6.4.1(v) are all distinct.

Further assume that the topmost cell in Fig. 6.4.1(ii) is shared by two superexpressions one of which [the left-hand arrow in Fig. 6.4.1(vii) below] is actually instigating the rewrite. The situation before and after the rewrite is given as follows:

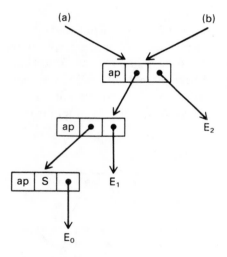

Fig. 6.4.1(vii)

■

This example shows that by assuming that all cells are distinct we can lose the sharing property which an S combinator rewrite is so careful to set up. Clearly, if at a later stage the second pointer – labelled (b) above – instigates a rewrite it will do so through the *old* expression and not the reduced one. All we achieve by this approach is a saving of some of the space costs of copying E_2 but without the saving of the re-evaluation time.

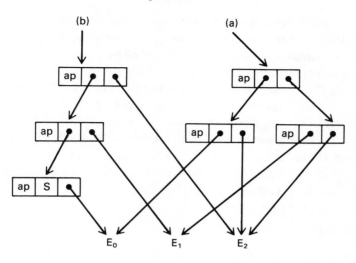

Fig. 6.4.1(viii)

The solution, however, is quite simple. We ensure that the head cells in Figs 6.4.1(ii) and 6.4.1(v) are *identical*. This means that we *overwrite* the pointer fields of the head cell of Fig. 6.4.1(ii) in order to form Fig. 6.4.1(v). After the reduction of Fig. 6.4.1(vii) we now have:

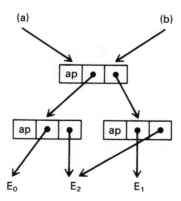

Fig. 6.4.1(ix)

Notice now that the sharing is maintained. This overwriting smacks of assignment; a programming technique we avoid in functional languages. Are we retreating on this score?

To see that we are not it is important to see that the value of the cell before and after the rewrite is exactly the same (an assignment always *changes* the value in a cell unless, of course, it is redundant).

The reader may now wonder whether the other cells in the reduction are identical to those before reduction. They are not. Notice that the value of these cells after the rewrite is in neither case equal, in general, to either cell before the rewrite. Under certain (sharing-free) circumstances, which we discuss below, however, these cells can be used in the rewrite. This is a feature of storage management and not a theoretical consequence of graph reduction.

It should now be clear how some other combinators, like C and B for example, can be rewritten in similar fashion.

Exercise 6.4.1(x)

Draw representations of saturated B and C combinators before and after reduction. Which cells need to be made identical?

■

Things are a little more complicated for the combinators K and I and we now turn to them.

A saturated K combinator will be represented, of course, by:

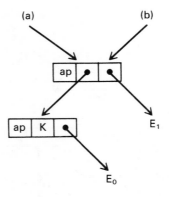

Fig. 6.4.1(xi)

The result of this is just E_0. In this expression, however, E_0 is represented as a single pointer and not a cell. How are we supposed to ensure that the sharing indicated in the figure is preserved?

If we suppose that E_0 is itself a graph (rather than say an integer or atom) we could copy its *own* head node into the head cell of Fig. 6.4.1(xi). To see that this is unsatisfactory consider the following example.

Example 6.4.1(xii)

Consider the expression $K\ (E_0\ E_1)\ E_2$ such that the entire expression and the subexpression $E_0\ E_1$ are shared by various superexpressions.

Suppose we attempt to solve the problem above by copying the head node of $E_0\ E_1$ into the head node of the entire expression. Pictorially we have:

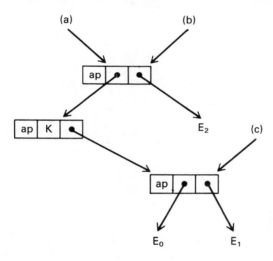

Fig. 6.4.1(xiii)

This is the situation before reductions. Notice the $E_0\ E_1$ is shared with a pointer (c). After the reduction, on the advice above, we obtain:

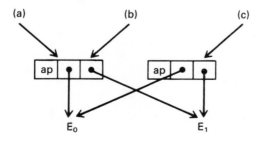

Fig. 6.4.1(xiv)

∎

Clearly if $E_0 E_1$ is reduced via the pointer (b) then (c) will not feel the benefit. Likewise, if (c) instigates reduction (b) will not benefit. Some sharing has been lost.

The solution, again, is not difficult. Recall that the I combinator is an identity operator. We utilize this here and turn the head node of Fig. 6.4.1(xi) into an *indirection node* with I in the left field and the result, E_0, in the right field. The sense of this is probably best appreciated if we take Fig. 6.4.1(xiii) as the initial graph. After reduction the graph is transformed into:

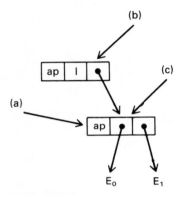

Fig. 6.4.1(xv)

Notice, now, that (b) shares with (c) the application $E_0 E_1$ (through the indirection node). It is also important to see that the indirection node is bypassed by (a) (which instigated the reduction). In this example eliding the indirection node for (a) is sensible but not crucial. However, let us turn to the I combinator itself.

A graph representing a saturated I combinator would have the form:

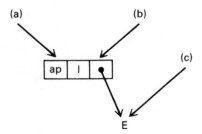

Fig. 6.4.1(xvi)

Again the single result E has to be used to overwrite the head cell. Using the technique above we form an indirection node of the form $I\ E$ to preserve the sharing properties of (b) and (c). This looks rather strange because the final graph we are suggesting is exactly the same as the original graph! This looks like an infinite regress. However there is a subtle difference because the final graph is actually:

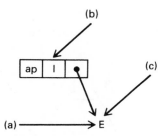

Fig. 6.4.1(xvii)

The action is simply for the pointer (a) to elide the I node and so point to its single argument. Progress is therefore being made after all.

We have said nothing so far with respect to primitive combinators such as **plus**, **h** or **t**. These are covered in the next section for, as we will now see, they make certain demands on evaluation order.

Example 6.4.1(xviii)

Consider the graph:

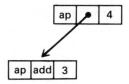

Fig. 6.4.1(xix)

Using our technique above we can certainly overwrite the head cell with an indirection node like

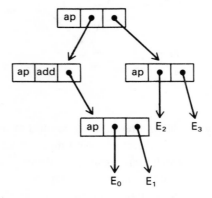

Fig. 6.4.1(xx)

Things are, in general, more complex. Suppose the expression to reduce is:

Fig. 6.4.1(xxi)

Clearly the expression $E_0 \, E_1$ cannot be added to $E_2 \, E_3$. Presumably we need to reduce these to integers first (hopefully this can be done) and then effect the addition (with the consequent introduction of an indirection node). This begins to take us into the realms of evaluation order so we will explain such reductions in the context of reduction strategies.
■

Finally we need to address techniques for handling recursion. As we know, this can be done by introducing a Y combinator with the following rewrite rule:

$$Y \, E = E \, (Y \, E)$$

Notice that since $Y \, E$ is saturated this extends to $E \, (E \, (Y \, E))$ and to $E^n(Y \, E)$ for all $n \geq 0$. $Y \, E$ could rewrite as follows:

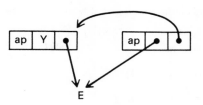

Fig. 6.4.1(xxii)

However we must be careful here. The cell on the right is the *same cell* as that on the left by virtue of our discussions earlier. Indeed *Y E* and *E*(*Y E*) have the same value. This suggests that *Y E* reduces to:

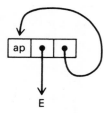

Fig. 6.4.1(xxiii)

Our data structures have become yet more general; they are now *directed cyclic graphs*.

To see exactly what is required, and indeed what transpires during evaluation, we take a simple example.

Example 6.4.1(xxiv)

Consider the definition:

    def intsfrom $n = n$: (**intsfrom** (**plus** n 1))

To compile this we know that we must form $[n](n$: (**intsfrom** (**plus** n 1))). This is the expression:

    $S_. I$ (B **intsfrom** (C **plus** 1))

Note that this still contains a variable, namely, **intsfrom**. Using the *Y*

combinator we know that to solve the recursive equation we form
Y (**[intsfrom]**(*S*: I (**B intsfrom** (*C* **plus** 1)))).

This is the expression:

$$Y (B (S_.) (C B (C \textbf{ plus } 1)))$$

This is represented by the graph:

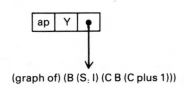

(graph of) (B (S: I) (C B (C plus 1)))

Fig. 6.4.1(xxv)

But the discussion above suggests that this is just:

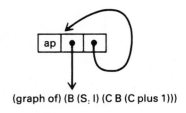

(graph of) (B (S: I) (C B (C plus 1)))

Fig. 6.4.1(xxvi)

This application saturates the abstraction which was undertaken with respect
to **intsfrom**, so this expression reduces to that shown in Fig. 6.4.1(xxvii).
Note how the circularity of the recursive definition is now directly set up.
∎

This final graph is however nothing more than the graph of [*n*] (*n*:**intsfrom**
(**plus** *n* 1)) but where the variable **intsfrom** has been replaced by a pointer to the
whole expression. In a practical system this can be obtained without recourse
to the *Y* combinator, and without the extra abstraction at all. We might say
that the description above justifies the implementation trick described below.

In a practical system the identifiers which we have placed in the graphs as
tokens would inevitably be references to some data structure (usually called a
descriptor) associated with a *symbol table*. Such descriptors contain information about variables (their type, for example, but in particular the code

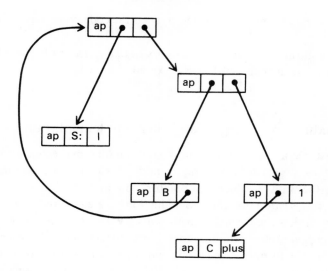

Fig. 6.4.1(xxvii)

associated with them if they are functions). Therefore, in practice, the graph of
intsfrom = [*n*] (*n*:(**intsfrom** (**plus** *n* 1))) would be

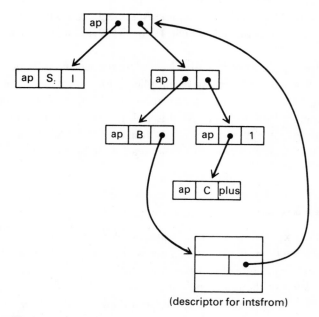

(descriptor for intsfrom)

Fig. 6.4.1(xxviii)

The pointer emanating from the descriptor is the code pointer associated with **intsfrom**.

Clearly during evaluation, *descriptors can be elided* (rather like *I* combinators are) and the effect of Fig. 6.4.1(xxvii) obtained.

6.4.2 Reduction strategies and their implementation

In the last section we showed how combinatory expressions can be represented as directed cyclic graphs and provided some specific details regarding the ways in which combinators rewrite according to their definitions. In this section we turn to reduction strategies and the associated machinery necessary to make them work. We also justify our reduction strategy by paying close attention to its power to terminate whenever possible, and, indeed, the form of expressions which result from such reductions.

Clearly in any large graph there are going to be several combinators which are saturated. We need to decide which to evaluate first. The simplest way would be to adopt some form of bottom–up evaluation by means of a simple recursive evaluator. This approach clearly reduces expressions *innermost first* and so effects an applicative evaluation strategy. For many reasons which we have discussed before we do not wish to do this. Rather, we want a *normal-order* reduction. This is a *leftmost outermost* strategy and is implemented most easily by introducing a stack which Turner (1979a) calls the *left ancestors stack*.

Given any graph the combinator we wish to reduce first is found by tracing down the left field of successive (application) nodes until we reach a combinator. The left ancestors stack is used to hold successive leftmost nodes until the combinator is found. At this point, providing the combinator is saturated, the arguments required can be found on the stack. Once the rewrite is finished the stack can be reset to the head node of the reduct.

Example 6.4.2(i)

Consider the expression *S I* (*K* 3) **plus** *4*. We trace its evaluation when controlled by a left ancestors stack. Since we have now a clear picture of how the graphs are represented we will adopt a rather more abstract notation for the graphs. We use the following convention: if a binary node is unlabelled then it is to be interpreted as an application node. A data node, on the other hand, will be written with a colon.

The original state will be:

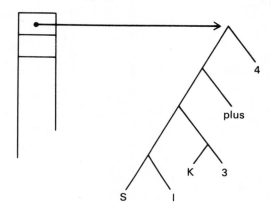

Fig. 6.4.2(ii)

After stacking the left ancestors of *S* we obtain:

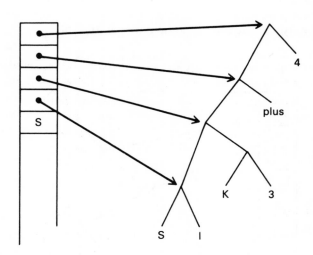

Fig. 6.4.2(iii)

The *S* reduction can now be done and the stack unwound to the head cell of the reduction. This yields:

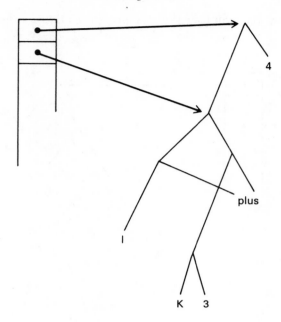

Fig. 6.4.2(iv)

Now stacking twice places the *I* combinator on the stack.

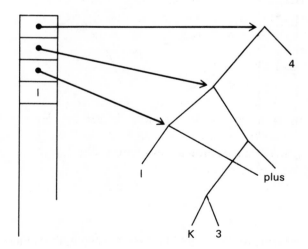

Fig. 6.4.2(v)

Now recall that the action of this is simply to elide the *I* combinator on the stack (the *I* remains in the graph as an indirection node). This gives rise to:

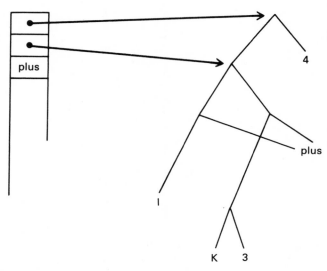

Fig. 6.4.2(vi)

It is unnecessary to stack any further for we already have a constant on the stack. Moreover it is saturated and so may be reduced.

The problem is that whilst the second argument, 4, is an integer, the first argument, which is (*K* 3 **plus**) is not. We discussed this somewhat in the last section and indicated there that somehow we need to obtain integer arguments before **plus** can reduce. In this example it is rather obvious that *K* 3 **plus** reduces to an integer but of course we have to explain how the evaluator uncovers this. The obvious solution which is indeed the correct solution is to obtain evaluated forms of the two arguments of **plus** before proceeding. Since this is nothing more than an ordinary evaluation, like the one we are currently undertaking, we can just call the evaluator *recursively* on these arguments. These recursive calls also need to use the stack of course, but this can be done by *marking* the current top of stack and supplying this to the recursive calls as if it were an empty stack. We draw a heavy line on the stack to indicate such a mark. When the first recursive call is about to begin the machine state is:

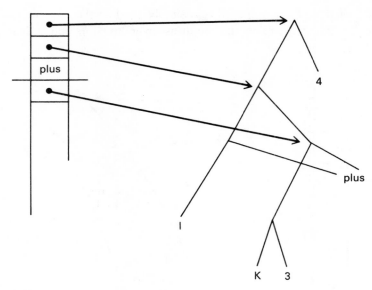

Fig. 6.4.2(vii)

After moving down the left branch of this expression and finding the *K* combinator we can effect a *K* rewrite. An indirection node appears in the graph but the stack contains the reduced form.

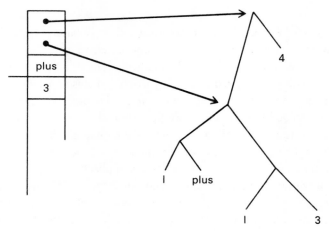

Fig. 6.4.2(viii)

This is a normal form. The recursive evaluation is complete and we can return with 3 as the result.

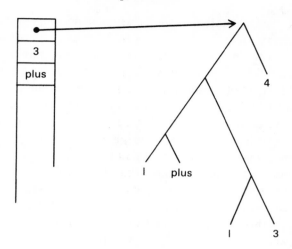

Fig. 6.4.2(ix)

Note how the argument position is used to store the result temporarily. Now the second recursive evaluation can start. This one is rather trivial and we will not go through it in detail. After its reduction is complete the addition takes place and the **plus** reduction is complete.

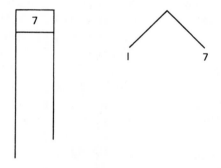

Fig. 6.4.2(x)

∎

The astute reader will have noted that the reduction order was by no means leftmost reduction at all stages. This occurs because we adopt numbers and arithmetic as fixed independent entities and we do not, at this level of description, have any internal structure for the representation of numbers and addition. This is ultimately a question of efficiency. It makes more sense to utilize the direct representation of numbers and numeric operations provided by our underlying architecture than to code these up into some lambda formulation. However by avoiding the lambda formulation we cannot process additions in normal order. It is, however, the case that the lambda formulation of addition is *strict* in both arguments (we saw this in Chapter 2). Consequently, it is immaterial which order of evaluation we employ for such expressions. Thus by moving to applicative reduction in this case we do not lose any termination properties for the machine. This is good mental hygiene; whenever we use some direct representation for a quantity with a lambda formulation we can check our evaluation decision against the lambda formulations to ensure things are as they should be. For example we run into the same difficulty with operators on data structures like **h** and **t**. These two evaluate their arguments applicatively on this architecture and this is justified because the lambda formulations $\lambda p \cdot p \lambda xy \cdot x$ and $\lambda p \cdot p \lambda xy \cdot y$ are strict. Remember however that **cons** is not strict in either of its arguments under the lambda interpretation. Therefore the similar combinator we use in the evaluation (which does not use the lambda term $\lambda xyz \cdot zxy$) must not evaluate either of its arguments.

It should be quite apparent that this form of evaluator has a large storage requirement, and indeed a large storage turnover. If we recall the S and K reductions we will notice that every S reduction requires two fresh cells and every K reduction reduces the number of cells sharing its second argument. Clearly some form of storage management is required. One novel approach to this has been developed by researchers developing a machine for combinator reduction called SKIM (Stoye *et al.*, 1984; Clarke *et al.*, 1980).

The idea is best appreciated by a simple thought experiment. Suppose we had pointers of two colours, say blue and red. Further let us use these as follows: use a red pointer if this is a *unique reference* to a cell and a blue pointer if it is a *multiple reference*. When we do an S-reduction, for example, we can, by looking at the colour of the pointers, determine whether the cells representing the redex are shared by other cells. If they are not we may safely use them in the rewrite.

In practice coloured pointers can be simulated by providing each pointer with a *one-bit reference count* (or flag). If the flag is 1 (we will write m for convenience) the pointer is blue and if 0 (we write u) the pointer is red. To see how this can be exploited in detail we will go through an example reduction.

Example 6.4.2(xi)

Consider the following redex with its pointers coloured by flags described above.

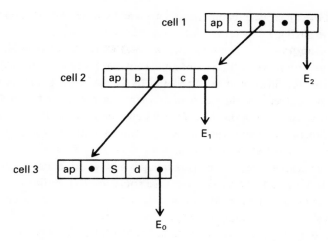

Fig. 6.4.2(xii)

In this diagram the dots in pointer flags denote 'don't care' and a, b, c and d are *variables* over flag values.

After the reduction the expression will have the following form:

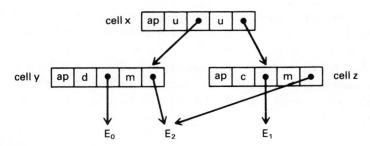

Fig. 6.4.2(xiii)

We will first explain how the relationships between cells 1, 2 and 3 and cells x, y and z are determined by the flags.

We know already that cell x and cell 1 are identical. Now suppose both flags a and b are u (that is they are unique pointers). Since cell 2 and cell 3 are not shared we can recycle them immediately and use them as cells y and z. Thus we do some garbage collection and storage allocation without troubling the garbage collector or storage allocation system. Clearly if both a and b are m we may not reuse either cell and we obtain cells y and z from the free list of cells. Suppose now that flag a is u but flag b is m. Here we may reuse cell 2 but not cell 3. Finally we have the assignment of m for flag a and u for flag b. Our first reaction (that cell 3 may be reused) is quite wrong for cell 3 has multiple references through the unique pointer (from cell 2) from cell 1. In this circumstance neither cell can be reused.

This approach is *correct* because a u flag is always an accurate reflection of the sharing of cells. It is *cautious* because sometimes an m flag is actually a unique pointer. This occurs because certain reductions can reduce sharing which the sharers cannot appreciate.

We must finally explain the assignments of flags in Fig. 6.4.2(xii). Cell x contains u pointers. This is acceptable because whether cells y and z are new cells or recycled cells there cannot be other cells sharing them. The left fields of cells y and z inherit the flags of the right fields of cells 2 and 3 as expected. Finally, since we set up an explicit sharing of the head cell of the expression E_2 it is necessary for the flags in the right fields of cells y and z to be m.
∎

Other refinements to the basic evaluator are motivated by the desire to remove the need for the left ancestors stack. For argument access during combinator reduction a *pointer reversal* strategy can be adopted which is reminiscent of the Deutch–Schorr–Waite marking algorithm developed for garbage collection. Special combinators can be defined which enable even strict combinators to be evaluated without using the stack. The interested reader should consult the bibliography for further details.

Under what circumstances does evaluation on this machine terminate? We might naïvely assume that it halts when the expression being reduced is brought to normal form. To see that this is incorrect consider the following.

Example 6.4.2(xiv)

Consider the following combinatory expression with its ancestors stack for reduction [see Fig. 6.4.2(xv)].
Unfortunately the combinator S is not saturated and a reduction cannot take place. The head cell is returned unchanged. Notice, however, that the expression as a whole does contain the redex $(K\ E_1\ E_2)$ so it is *not* in normal form.
∎

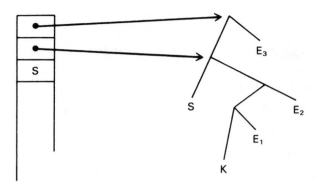

Fig. 6.4.2(xv)

The reduction strategy which this evaluator adopts is essentially *head reduction*. That is, at each stage the head redex is reduced if it has one. This strategy is guaranteed to find the *head normal form* of an expression, if it has one. Note that in example 6.4.2(xv) the expression $S(K E_1 E_2) E_3$ is a head normal form. The reader may like to reconsult Chapter 2 at this stage to revise some of these notions and properties. Further details can be found in Barendregt (1984, Chap. 8).

There are sound intuitive and theoretical reasons why we wish to view evaluation as head reduction and find results as head normal forms. We start with the intuitions.

The relationship between the evaluator and the programmer is a kind of dialogue. The programmer provides expressions, and partial expressions to the evaluator which reduces them according to the algorithm described in this section. Loosely speaking, the evaluator can never be quite sure that it has at any moment been given the entire expression, after all we curry our functions as much as possible and supply arguments to them one by one.

From the intuitive standpoint let us look at our example expression $S(K E_1 E_2) E_3$. Maybe another argument is forthcoming. If so the leftmost redex of $S(K E_1 E_2) E_3$ (which would be reduced under normal evaluation) would become an *innermost redex* as in $S(K E_1 E_2) E_3 E_4$. Clearly in this circumstance the correct redex is the head redex and the expression becomes $(K E_1 E_2) E_4(E_3 E_4)$. The moral is that *non-head redexes can become applicative*, innermost, redexes if further arguments are forthcoming. The following example shows how things could go very wrong.

Example 6.4.2(xvi)

Suppose we define the following functions:

> **def y** f = f(**y** f)
> **def h** g n = n:(g(**plus** n 1))

The program **y** compiles to the code sequence S I **y**. **h** compiles to $B(S. I)$ $(C B(C$ **plus** 1)) [see example 6.4.1(xxiv)].

Given these we then define:

> **def intsfrom** = **y h**

If we evaluate this expression we go through the following steps:

> **intsfrom** =
> **y h**   =
> $S I$ **y h** =
> I **h** (**y h**) =
> **h**(**y h**)   =
> $B(S. I) (C B (C$ **plus** 1)) **intsfrom** =
> $S. I (C B.(C$ **plus** 1) **intsfrom**)

Now this is a head normal form and the evaluator halts. If we tried to obtain a normal form we would first do the C redex and then start on **intsfrom** all over again.

If we subsequently apply another argument (say 3) to our head normal form the evaluator can continue a little:

> $S. I (C B (C$ **plus** 1) **intsfrom**) 3 =
> (I 3):($C B(C$ **plus** 1) **intsfrom** 3) =
> 3:($C B(C$ **plus** 1) **intsfrom** 3)

The evaluator again halts here, as required, even though it is not a normal form.
∎

Let us now look at this from a more theoretical perspective. If the evaluator attempts to obtain a normal form for (**y h**) it loops. Moreover, if it attempts to discover a normal form for *any* expression without normal form it loops. In other words *it would treat all expressions without normal form as undefined.* In the theory of the lambda calculus, however, it turns out that if one adds an axiom which equates all non-normal forms the theory becomes inconsistent! [see proposition 2.2.3(xxvii)]. In fact it is perfectly acceptable for a machine to act in this fashion but we do not obtain as much information as we might. That is to say there are some expressions which would put the normal-order evaluator into a loop (and which would be interpreted as undefined) when they have perfectly well-defined interpretations [like the expression (**y h**) does]. What we know from the lambda calculus is that it is quite reasonable to equate all expressions with no *head* normal form and this is what the (head normal) evaluator we have described does; it loops when given expressions like *S I I*(*S I I*), which has no head normal form. Further explanation of these observations requires the lambda calculus concept of Böhm trees; readers who have read this far in Barendregt can probably work out the details for themselves!

6.4.3 Symbolic evaluation

It is, of course, possible that the type of results obtained by reducing the arguments of strict operators will be incorrect. For example the first argument to the conditional could turn out to be a number or indeed an arbitrary combinator expression in head normal form. In such a case what can one do?

This highlights an interesting property of combinatory code: it may be *symbolically decompiled*. In fact, this is actually no more than a restatement of the principle of abstraction which states that an expression can be recovered from its abstracted form by applying an appropriate argument.

One possible strategy we can adopt in these exceptional circumstances is to make each strict combinator return an unevaluated expression when the types of its arguments are not correct. Thus if we try to evaluate (**plus** 3(**eq** 3 4)) the result will be (**plus** 3 False). If this expression is provided to some global expression which also expects a number then this too will return a symbolic result incorporating the term (**plus** 3 False). The final result of such an evaluation will be an expression in which the error is explicit.

Symbolic evaluation can also be used in some circumstances when the result of an evaluation still contains combinators. This can happen quite often because in a language which allows currying we often only partially apply the functions we define. Suppose, having defined a function **append**, we evaluate **append** [1 2 3]. Since we provide only one argument it is clear that the final form of this evaluation will contain unsaturated combinators. It would be rather unconventional to return to a user an expression which effectively includes compiled code. In such cases *symbolic arguments* can be provided (these are just variables) and reduction forced to saturate and remove all combinators. As we described above, strict operators which are given inappropriate (in this case symbolic) arguments return an unevaluated expression. Of course, if we add extra arguments to any expression we will have to pay this back, in some sense. One way of doing this is to prefix the final result with appropriate lambda bindings.

To see all this more clearly consider the following example.

Example 6.4.3(i)

Consider the program:

$$\text{def } \textbf{twice } f\, x = f(f\, x)$$

This compiles to $(S\ B\ I\ )$. If we try to evaluate the expression (**twice plus**) the result will be $(B\ \textbf{plus}(I\ \textbf{plus}))$ which still contains the combinators B and I because the function has only been partially evaluated. If we evaluate (**twice plus**) in the presence of a *symbolic argument* x we should get as a result the expression (**plus(plus** x)). This happens because of the decision we made above regarding strict combinators with inappropriate arguments. Since the x has been applied 'for free', so to speak, we can pay this back by prefixing the expression with a lambda binding. Thus the result of evaluating (**twice plus**) will be $\lambda x \cdot \textbf{plus}(\textbf{plus}\ x)$.

A further interesting point is that if we try to evaluate the expression (**twice**) we will obtain the result $\lambda f \cdot \lambda x \cdot f(f\, x)$. This provides an adequate, pretty printing facility for function definitions by utilizing the evaluation itself.
∎

It is quite easy for an implementation based on these ideas to arrange to record the formal parameters used in a definition in the symbol table along with the function being defined. This allows the same symbols (f and x in the example) to be used during symbolic evaluation.

6.5 Supercombinator-based machines and compilers

6.5.1 Introduction

The traditional combinator-based compilation strategy provides a fixed set of combinators into which programs are translated. The evaluator is also designed to reduce graphs of combinators from this fixed set. As we have seen it is possible to work with a small set of combinators because of the theoretical result which shows that any computable function can be expressed as an S–K-combinatory expression. From a practical point of view we know that in order to achieve a tolerable efficiency certain optimizations can and must be made.

A rather different approach first advocated by Hughes (1982) is the proposal that combinators should be introduced for individual programs and should be tailored exactly to the task at hand. So rather than translate a program into a fixed set of combinators a compiler should, on this advice, *reveal* a set of combinators for the purpose. For historical reasons these have become known as *supercombinators*, but in fact they are no different to any others.

There seem to be three main points which led Hughes to develop this approach. Firstly, the compiled form of source programs using conventional combinators is far removed from the source language. We have seen, however, that – using symbolic evaluation – a degree of reconnection to the source program is possible. Secondly, compilation is quite slow because a large number of optimizations have to be employed to keep the compiled code within reasonable limits of size. Thirdly, each execution step is very small. This can mean that the overhead in linking each step together (finding the leftmost combinator, accessing the arguments and so on) can dominate the execution time. Of these it is perhaps the third which is most significant. It would be far better if each reduction did somewhat more for then it would dominate the overhead rather than vice versa.

This approach clearly has implications for machines for we can hardly expect to build all possible combinators into an architecture! We will begin with the task of supercombinator generation and we will take up the problem of evaluation later.

6.5.2 Generating combinatory forms

The goal is to take a functional program and to convert it into a combinatory form (that is, a term composed – by application – entirely of constants and variables) by introducing new combinators in an optimal way.

To see very roughly at first how this can be done let us consider an arbitrary lambda expression $(\lambda x \cdot x\ y)$ and see how this can be represented as a combinatory form.

We can see instantly that the subexpression $(x\ y)$ is already a combinatory form so our attention moves to the whole expression $(\lambda x \cdot x\ y)$. This is not a combinator for it has a free variable y. By abstracting with respect to this free variable we obtain the combinator $(\lambda y \cdot \lambda x \cdot x\ y)$ which we denote $C1$. Its defining equation is $(C1\ y\ x = x\ y)$ and it is easy to see that the original lambda term is just $(C1\ y)$. The task is complete for we have reduced the term to a combinatory expression by introducing a new combinator, which in this case is $C1$. Let us analyse a more complex expression.

Example 6.5.2(i)

Consider the lambda term $(\lambda x \cdot (\lambda y \cdot y\ x)(\lambda z \cdot z\ x)\ w)$. Taking the leftmost innermost abstraction first we see it is no more than $(C1\ x)$ with $(C1\ y\ x = x\ y)$ as above. Likewise the term $(\lambda z \cdot z\ x)$ is just $(C1\ x)$. So far we have the definition of $C1$ together with the equivalent expression $(\lambda x \cdot (C1\ x)(C1\ x)\ w)$. To make this a combinator we abstract with respect to w yielding the expression $(\lambda w \cdot \lambda x \cdot (C1\ x)(C1\ x)\ w)$.

   This leads us to define a combinator $(C2\ w\ x = (C1\ x)(C1\ x)\ w)$ and to set the original expression to $(C2\ w)$. To summarize all this we have translated $(\lambda x \cdot (\lambda y \cdot y\ x)(\lambda z \cdot z\ x)\ w)$ into the following two combinator definitions and expression:

> $C1\ y\ x = x\ y$
> $C2\ w\ x = (C1\ x)(C1\ x)\ w$
> $C2\ w$.

■

Questions now almost ask themselves. If an expression has several free variables which do we abstract first? Are these combinators optimal and in what sense? Can this procedure be extended to recursive definitions?

   The answers to these will emerge from the consideration of a realistic program.

Example 6.5.2(ii)

> **append** $[\ ]\ y = y$
> **append** $(a{:}l)\ y = a{:}(\textbf{append}\ l\ y)$

If we put this into conditional form and remove the recursion by introducing the fix-point finder we obtain the expression:

> **append** $= Y(\lambda f \cdot \lambda x \cdot \lambda y \cdot \textbf{if}\ (\textbf{eq}\ x\ [\ ])\ y\ (\textbf{cons}\ (\textbf{h}\ x)(f(\textbf{t}\ x)\ y)))$

The smallest subexpression of this which is not a combinatory form is the abstract $\lambda y \cdot \textbf{if}\ (\textbf{eq}\ x\ [\ ])\ y\ (\textbf{cons}\ (\textbf{h}\ x)(f(\textbf{t}\ x)\ y))$. This has free variables x and f. For the time being we shall not worry about the order in which these should be abstracted to form a combinator. Using the advice gleaned from the simple examples above we are led to introduce a combinator $C1$ subject to the definition:

> $C1\ x f\ y = \textbf{if}\ (\textbf{eq}\ x\ [\ ])\ y\ (\textbf{cons}\ (\textbf{h}\ x)(f(\textbf{t}\ x)\ y))$

then the expression above is just $(C1 \ x f)$. If we replace the abstract above with this combinatory expression we get the following definition:

append $= Y(\lambda f \cdot \lambda x \cdot C1 \ x f)$

The smallest subexpression of this which is not combinatory is the abstract $(\lambda x \cdot C1 \ x f)$. This has free variable f so we introduce a combinator $C2$ for the expression $(\lambda f \cdot \lambda x \cdot C1 \ x f)$. Its rewrite rule is therefore $(C2 f x = C1 \ x f)$. The expression above is just $(C2 f)$ and **append** is now defined as follows: **append** $= Y(\lambda f \cdot C2 f)$. Now $\lambda f \cdot C2 f$ is already a combinator. This suggests the introduction of a combinator $C3$ given by $(C3 f = C2 f)$. The definition of **append** is now simply the combinatory form $(Y \ C3)$.

In summary we now have:

$$
\begin{aligned}
\textbf{append} \ \ &= Y \ C3 \\
C3 f \ \ &= C2 f \\
C2 f x \ \ &= C1 \ x f \\
C1 \ x f y \ \ &= \textbf{if (eq } x \ \textbf{nil)} \ y \ (\textbf{cons (h } x)(f(\textbf{t } x) \ y))
\end{aligned}
$$

This is clearly not optimal. We could easily simplify this to:

$$
\begin{aligned}
\textbf{append} \ \ &= Y \ C2 \\
C2 f x \ \ &= C1 \ x f \\
C1 \ x f y \ \ &= \textbf{if (eq } x \ \textbf{nil)} \ y \ (\textbf{cons (h } x)(f(\textbf{t } x) \ y))
\end{aligned}
$$

but this is not all. Suppose we had set:

$$C1 f x \ y = \textbf{if (eq } x \ \textbf{nil)} \ y \ (\textbf{cons (h } x)(f(\textbf{t } x) \ y))$$

then we should have subsequently generated $C2 f x = C1 f x$ and $C3 f = C2 f$. From this we see that $C3 = C2 = C1$ by extensionality. Thus we could have derived:

$$
\begin{aligned}
\textbf{append} \ \ &= Y \ C1 \\
C1 f x \ y \ \ &= \text{if (eq } x \ \textbf{nil)} \ y \ (\textbf{cons (h } x)(f(\textbf{t } x) \ y))
\end{aligned}
$$

■

There is, however, an even more serious problem which is to do with laziness. In combinator evaluators, expressions are evaluated at most once. We saw that this could be achieved using the *SKI* family of combinators by a leftmost graph reduction in which the root node of an expression is overwritten by its result and in which repeated subexpressions are shared not copied. We would certainly like to ensure that any other compilation and evaluation approach possesses this same desirable property. Unfortunately, as it stands, the translation of the function **append** given above in example 6.5.2(ii) does not have this property. This observation and its solution are due to Hughes and is the major contribution of the theory of supercombinators. To see the problem clearly let us consider the following example.

Example 6.5.2(iii)

> **def sillyid** = **append** [ ]

This is a function which appends [ ] to the argument it is given.

If we apply this to the original definition and proceed to evaluate lazily (leftmost reduction) we get the following:

> **append** [ ] =
> $\lambda y \cdot$ **if** (**eq** [ ] [ ]) y (**cons** (**h** [ ])(**append** (**t** [ ]) y))

Now on a fully lazy evaluator, after the first application of **sillyid** to an argument, the subexpression (**eq** [ ] [ ]) would evaluate to "True" and the abstract would essentially become:

> $\lambda y \cdot$ **first** y (**cons** (**h** [ ])(**append** (**t** [ ]) y))
> where **first** $x\ y = x$

We now need only supply an argument y to get y straight back again on subsequent calls to **sillyid**. This happens because a fully lazy evaluator will reduce an expression at most once.

On the other hand suppose we reduce our original combinatory represent-ation of **append**. This would yield the following sequence of expressions:

> **append** [ ] = $Y\,C3$ [ ]
> $\qquad\qquad = C3\,(Y\,C3)$ [ ]
> $\qquad\qquad = C2\,(Y\,C3)$ [ ]
> $\qquad\qquad = C1$ [ ] $(Y\,C3)$

but reduction has to stop here because the $C1$ combinator requires a third argument in order to become saturated and to allow the rewrite to occur. So if we make our definition of **sillyid** using the combinators we generated above we will obtain **sillyid** = $C1$ [ ] $(Y\,C3)$.

Each time **sillyid** is given an argument, say x, it will rewrite the combinator $C1$ to provide us with:

> **if** (**eq** [ ] [ ]) x (**cons** (**h** [ ])(($Y\,C3$)(**t** [ ]) x))

The strictness condition on **if** forces evaluation of **eq** [ ] [ ] to yield "True" giving:

> **first** x (**cons** (**h** [ ])(($Y\,C3$)(**t** [ ]) x))

and this reduces immediately to *x*. In this case notice how (**eq** [ ] [ ]) will be evaluated *every time* **sillyid** *is applied*. This clearly breaks our requirement that expressions are evaluated at most once. The combinator form of the program we obtained in the earlier example does not implement fully lazy evaluation.

■

Hughes identified expressions not involving the bound variable as being those for which repeated evaluation can occur. Such expressions are in this sense *free expressions* (by analogy with free variables). Free expressions are a generalization of free variables. In fact a free variable is a *minimal* free expression in the sense that it does not contain any subexpressions which are free. Of course it satisfies this definition degenerately since a variable can contain no proper subexpressions.

Of greater significance are the *maximal free expressions* which are not proper subexpressions of any free expression. For example the maximal free expressions of the lambda abstract $\lambda x \cdot y\,(x\,(y\,y))$ are $(y\,y)$ and (leftmost) *y*. All this is covered in detail in Chapter 2 and the reader may like to refer to this now by way of revision.

When we produced the combinatory forms from the expressions in examples 6.5.2(i) and 6.5.2(ii) we always removed the *minimal* free expressions, that is, the free variables. The solution to the non-lazy behaviour of the earlier definitions is always to remove the *maximal* free expressions from the expression under consideration.

In example 6.5.2(i) the free variables were also the maximal free expressions so their combinator versions are indeed lazy. It will come as no surprise, since we have already highlighted the problem, that our treatment of **append** does not follow the new advice.

Example 6.5.2(iv)

Let us start again with the definition:

append $= Y(\lambda f \cdot \lambda x \cdot \lambda y \cdot \mathbf{if}\,(\mathbf{eq}\,x\,[\ ])\,y\,(\mathbf{cons}\,(\mathbf{h}\,x)(f(\mathbf{t}\,x)\,y)))$

Taking the innermost non-combinatory expression which is:

$\lambda y \cdot \mathbf{if}\,(\mathbf{eq}\,x\,[\ ])\,y\,(\mathbf{cons}\,(\mathbf{h}\,x)(f(\mathbf{t}\,x)\,y))$

we see that there are three maximal free expressions. These are (**if** (**eq** x [ ])), (**cons** (**h** x)) and ($f(\mathbf{t}\,x)$). We therefore abstract with respect to these expressions which produces the following lambda expression:

$\lambda pqry \cdot p\,y\,(q\,(r\,y))$

If we call this $C1$ then we obtain the rewrite $(C1\ p\ q\ v\ y = p\ y\ (q\ (r\ y)))$ and the original expression becomes, simply:

$(C1\ (\textbf{if}\ (\textbf{eq}\ x\ [\ \ ]))(\textbf{cons}\ (\textbf{h}\ x))(f\ (\textbf{t}\ x)))$

Substituting this back into the definition of the function we obtain:

append $= Y(\lambda f \cdot \lambda x \cdot C1\ (\textbf{if}\ (\textbf{eq}\ x\ [\ \ ]))(\textbf{cons}\ (\textbf{h}\ x))(f\ (\textbf{t}\ x)))$

The innermost non-combinatory subexpression of this is:
$(\lambda x \cdot C1\ (\textbf{if}\ (\textbf{eq}\ x\ [\ \ ]))\ (\textbf{cons}\ (\textbf{h}\ x))(f\ (\textbf{t}\ x)))$ In this expression there is only one maximally free expression and this is the variable f. This suggests the introduction of a combinator $C2$ with the definition:

$C2\ f\ x = C1\ (\textbf{if}\ (\textbf{eq}\ x\ [\ \ ]))(\textbf{cons}\ (\textbf{h}\ x))(f\ (\textbf{t}\ x))$

Substituting back into the definition of append we obtain:

append $= Y(\lambda f \cdot C2\ f)$

$(\lambda f \cdot C2\ f)$ has no maximally free expressions; indeed it does not have any free variables. We immediately define $C3$ subject to $(C3\ f = C2\ f)$ and then this gives us **append** $= Y\ C3$ as the final result. In summary we now have the following definitions:

append	$= Y\ C3$
$C3\ f$	$= C2\ f$
$C2\ f\ x$	$= C1\ (\textbf{if}\ (\textbf{eq}\ x\ [\ \ ]))(\textbf{cons}\ (\textbf{h}\ x))(f\ (\textbf{t}\ x))$
$C1\ p\ q\ r\ y$	$= p\ y\ (q\ (r\ y))$

Naturally we can delete either $C3$ or $C2$ since they are extensionally equal.
■

We now see how evaluation of (**sillyid** x), defined in example 6.5.2(iii), proceeds when **append** is defined by the system of combinators derived in example 6.5.2(iv).

First we observe the evaluation when **sillyid** is defined:

$$\begin{aligned}
\textbf{sillyid} &= \textbf{append}\ [\ \ ] \\
&= Y\ C3\ [\ \ ] \\
&= C3\ (Y\ C2)\ [\ \ ] \\
&= C2\ (Y\ C3)\ [\ \ ] \\
&= C1\ (\textbf{if}\ (\textbf{eq}\ [\ \ ]\ [\ \ ]))(\textbf{cons}\ (\textbf{h}\ [\ \ ]))((Y\ C3)(\textbf{t}\ [\ \ ]))
\end{aligned}$$

Now when **sillyid** is applied to x we obtain the following:

$\textbf{sillyid}\ x =$
$C1\ (\textbf{if}\ (\textbf{eq}\ [\ \ ]\ [\ \ ]))(\textbf{cons}\ (\textbf{h}\ [\ \ ]))((Y\ C3)(\textbf{t}\ [\ \ ]))\ x =$

if (**eq** [ ] [ ]) x (**cons** (**h** [ ])((*Y* *C*3)(**t** [ ]) *y*)) =
first x (**cons** (**h** [ ])((*Y* *C*3)(**t** [ ]) *y*)) =
x

This evaluation has caused (**if** (**eq** [ ] [ ])) to be evaluated to a form we have referred to by the name **first**. Now on subsequent evaluations **sillyid** deploys this reduced form, and we avoid the duplicate computation.

We must now turn to the question of ordering arguments in supercombinator definitions.

It is apparent that often there exist several maximal free expressions in a given abstraction. This gives us some freedom because when we introduce the appropriate combinator we may order these arguments in any way we choose.

In fact, this ordering *can* make a difference to the final result and so we ought to think carefully about it. It should be stressed that the ordering of supercombinator arguments does not affect the lazy properties we have discussed above. It can, however, affect the number and size of the supercombinators we generate. To see this we will take a simple example.

Example 6.5.2(v)

Consider the expression $\lambda a \cdot \lambda b \ldots \lambda c \cdot$ (**eq** a c) **or** b .... Suppose we apply the technique developed above.

Consider the innermost abstraction:

$\lambda c \cdot$ (**eq** a c) **or** b

This has maximal free expressions (**eq** a) and b. We introduce a combinator $C1$ of three arguments. But in which order should we take the free expressions? There are two choices. One is to define $C1$ x y $z = (x z)$ **or** y and then set the abstract to $C1$ (**eq** a) b. The other is to set $C1'$ x (**eq** y) $z = (y z)$ **or** x and then set the abstract to $C1'$ b (**eq** a).

Taking the first of these options we will later attack the abstract $\lambda b \cdot \ldots C1$ (**eq** a) $b \ldots$ which has maximal free expression ($C1$ (**eq** a)). This suggests we define $C2$ in such a way that the abstract becomes ($C2 \ldots$ ($C1$ (**eq** a)) $\ldots$). Taking the other option we consider the abstract $\lambda b \cdot \ldots C1'$ b (**eq** a). This has maximal free expression a. We would then define $C2'$ so that the abstract becomes ($C2' \ldots$ (**eq** a) $\ldots$). In the former case the combinator $C1$ gets applied earlier when only one parameter has become available. This structure may thus be shared more widely, and so evaluated less frequently. The ordering is quite easy to determine. We list the parameters for maximal free expressions in order of *decreasing freeness*. This means we take free variables to be ordered by the *distance* (number of lambdas) from their binding occurrences. In this example, a is more free than b so we list a first in the definition of the combinator $C1$.

■

This ordering ensures that maximal expressions are larger and fewer in number than in an arbitrary ordering of parameters. The sooner expressions are created the more widely they become shared and the sooner they rewrite.

Exercise 6.5.2(vi)

Consider the expression

$$\lambda x\ y\ z \cdot z\ (x\ y)(z\ (x\ y))$$

Formulate a system of supercombinators for this abstract. What do you think should happen to repeated maximal free expressions in general?

■

6.5.3 Supercombinator evaluation

The compiling process described in the previous section is rather strange. Usually one thinks of a compiler as translating from a source language into a fixed machine code. The supercombinator abstractor described above seems to do two things. Firstly, it translates programs into combinatory expressions, and secondly it describes a set of combinators and provides reduction rules for them. In other words, it generates an instruction set (and a semantics for these instructions) along with the compiled code.

Even the combinatory evaluation techniques of Section 6.4 begin to look conventional against these suggestions.

It is therefore clear that a machine suitable for evaluating supercombinator expressions cannot possess a fixed set of combinator reduction rules. It cannot possibly know or store all supercombinators. Rather, we need move to a different level of description. Such a machine will be a general-purpose graph manipulation engine. Therefore its instructions will be those which allow for the manipulation, copying and building of general graph structures. In order to interface the output we have generated so far (which consists of combinator code and combinator definitions) we will have to provide some further compilation process which can take each supercombinator definition and yield a sequence of graph manipulation instructions which, when executed, will implement its rewrite rule.

The most exciting architecture for evaluating supercombinator graphs is the *G-machine* due to Johnsson (1983) and Kieburtz (1985). This is an architecture which reduces supercombinator expression graphs by means of a leftmost ancestors stack and rewrites supercombinators using sequences of G-code instructions which are generated from supercombinator definitions by a supercombinator compiler.

We will begin by showing how the graphs are manipulated by primitive instructions by considering a simple combinator definition. At this stage we will sidestep the compilation of this combinator into G-machine code. In the following section we give some details of how this compilation is achieved.

Example 6.5.3(i)

Consider the combinator **intsfrom** whose definition is given by the reduction rule:

intsfrom $n = n : ($**intsfrom** $($**inc** $n))$

Now at some stage the state of the machine might be:

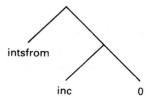

Fig. 6.5.3(ii)

Now, given the definition above we hope that this graph can be rewritten as is shown in Fig. 6.5.3(iii).

The combinator **intsfrom** must be compiled into a sequence of graph manipulation instructions which will effect this transformation. The compiler produces the sequence:

PUSH 1; PUSHFUN **inc**; MKAP; PUSHFUN **intsfrom**: MKAP; PUSH 2; CONS; UPDATE 3; RET 2

We will explain how this is generated from the definition in the next section. Now we show how this sequence of instructions forms the reduced graph.

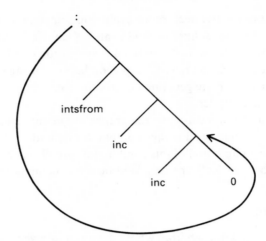

Fig. 6.5.3(iii)

When given a graph the machine pushes ancestors in a similar way to the evaluator described in Section 6.4. The major difference is that at each stage *both* left and right ancestors are stacked by this machine. This allows particularly swift access to any part of the graph, and simplifies the kind of instructions which are required.

Suppose that the machine has reached the state in which the left branch of the graph is the combinator **intsfrom**. It is at this stage that the sequence above is required for rewriting purposes.

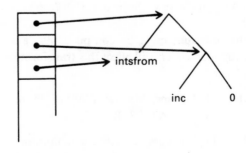

Fig. 6.5.3(iv)

The first instruction is PUSH 1 which requires us to push a copy of the 1st value on the stack (the top is considered the 0th value). This then yields:

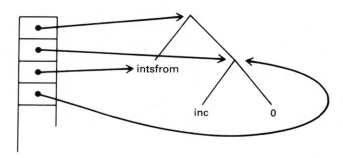

Fig. 6.5.3(v)

The next instruction PUSHFUN **inc** exhorts us to push the combinator **inc** onto the stack producing:

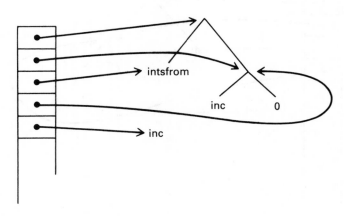

Fig. 6.5.3(vi)

Chapter 6

MKAP is an instruction which forms application nodes from the top two items of the stack. These are popped off and the new application pushed. This gives:

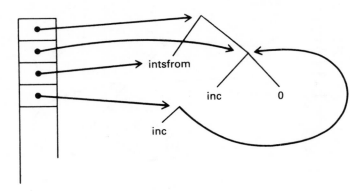

Fig. 6.5.3(vii)

PUSHFUN **intsfrom**, as above, just pushes a constant function symbol onto the stack:

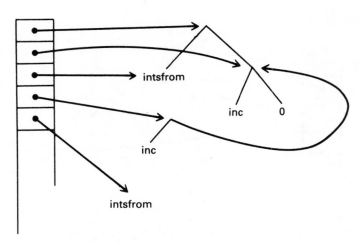

Fig. 6.5.3(viii)

and MKAP then produces:

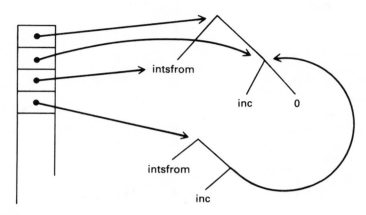

Fig. 6.5.3(ix)

PUSH 2 pushes the 2nd value onto the stack (recall the top value is the 0th). We now obtain:

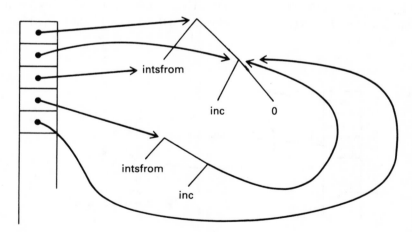

Fig. 6.5.3(x)

The CONS instruction is rather like the MKAP instruction for it takes the top two elements of the stack and forms a **cons** node. This is then pushed onto the stack after popping the two arguments. Our example has now reached the state:

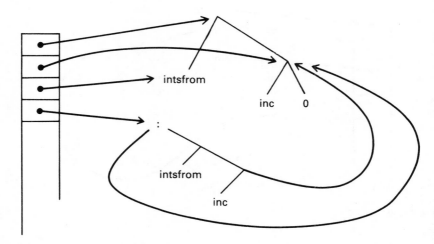

Fig. 6.5.3(xi)

At this stage we should see that the graph which is currently on the top of the stack is the one we are trying to produce. The rest of the code is housekeeping. Firstly UPDATE 3 overwrites the 3rd value on the stack with the 0th (which is the top value) giving:

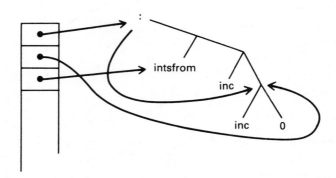

Fig. 6.5.3(xii)

Finally RET 2 pops the top two values on the stack (that is the 0th and 1st values) and returns control to the sequence of instructions which called the combinator **intsfrom** yielding:

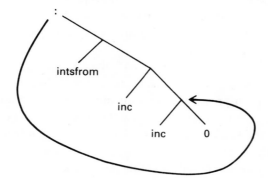

Fig. 6.5.3(xiii)

as required.
∎

Other, more general-purpose instructions we have not used here are EVAL [which instigates the evaluation of a graph on a fresh (or marked) stack] and UNWIND which, in a single instruction, pushes all ancestors down the left spine of the graph until it finds a combinator.

6.5.4 Supercombinator compilation

This all seems very neat but we have not shown how such machine code sequences can be generated by combinatory definitions.

In fact the compilation of the combinators takes place in a straightforward syntax directed fashion.

The compiler can be thought of as a function taking various arguments and returning a code sequence as result. Thus

$$C \in EXP \to ENV \to DEPTH \to CODE \to CODE$$

Here EXP is the set of combinatory expressions which we hope to compile and ENV is a set of *environments*. These are functions which relate variables used in the combinator definition (like n in the previous example) to their current positions on the stack. $DEPTH$ is actually just the set of natural numbers. This argument represents the depth the stack will have reached when evaluation reaches the current expression being compiled. $CODE$ is the set of G-code programs. The fourth argument can be thought of as a context or continuation. That is, it represents the code we execute after the current expression has been compiled. The final co-domain of the compiling function is, of course, *CODE* since we expect the result of a compilation to be a G-code program. For convenience we will surround the first argument of C with square brackets. This isolates, notationally, the program being compiled from the other auxiliary arguments.

Let **arid** be the empty environment, that is, the environment which contains no bindings of variables to stack positions. If r is an environment then let the notation $r[x|v]$ read "the environment r updated at variable x to the stack position v". Thus $r[x|v]$ is almost the same as r. It just differs in its binding for x. These stack positions are *absolute* values numbered with respect to the *base* of the stack.

We first see how to compile a combinator definition:

$$C[\![\,fx_1 \ldots x_n = e\,]\!] \text{ arid } 0 \langle\ \rangle = C[\![e]\!]\, r\, 2n + 1\ (\text{UPDATE } 2n + 1;$$
$$\text{RET } 2n)$$

where $r = \textbf{arid}\,[x_1|2n][\ \ldots\ ][x_n|2]$.

This says that when we try to build the target graph (which is the expression E) we may know that the arguments of f (which are x_1 to x_n) are on the stack at various positions (this is recorded in the environment) and that the stack depth at this point is $2n + 1$. Note that the arguments are arranged at alternate stack positions. This occurs because, as we noted above, this machine stacks *both* left and right ancestors as it unwinds down to the leftmost combinator. The final argument tells us that when we have completed building the graph for e we can update the stack and return.

Some other useful parts of the compiling function are:

$$C[\![\,f\,]\!]\, r\, n\, c = \text{PUSHFUN } f;\ c$$

This says that on encountering a combinator name we may plant a PUSHFUN instruction with the appropriate name.

$$C[\![\,e_1 : e_2\,]\!]\, r\, n\, c =$$
$$C[\![e_2]\!]\, r\, n\, (C[\![e_1]\!]\, r\, n + 1\ (\text{CONS};\ c))$$

Thus to compile a CONS expression we first compile the two subgraphs e_1 and e_2 and then we plant a CONS instruction. Notice how e_1 is compiled in the presence of a stack with depth one bigger than the first expression; this of course is to accommodate the result of e_2.

$$C[\![\,e_1 e_2\,]\!]\, r\, n\, c =$$
$$C[\![e_2]\!]\, r\, n\, (C[\![e_1]\!]\, r\, n + 1\ (\text{MKAP};\ c))$$

This is rather similar: once the operator and operand have been compiled we may plant the instruction which will form the application node.

$$C[\![x]\!]\, r\, n\, c = \text{PUSH}\ (n - r(x))$$

If we encounter a variable during compilation we can obtain the corresponding graph from the stack. We know that this is so because all the arguments x_1 to x_n are pushed onto the stack during the initial unwind phase. However, which is the correct stack position? The environment contains the bindings of variables to stack positions but these were created in a context before the construction of the target graph. At future points in the construction the stack may be arbitrarily deep. To determine the correct offset we need both the current depth of the stack and the environment binding.

Example 6.5.4(i)

We are now in a position to see how the code for **intsfrom** is generated.

$C[\![\text{intsfrom } n = n\colon \text{intsfrom(inc } n)]\!]$ **arid** $0 \langle\ \rangle =$
$C[\![n\colon \text{intsfrom(inc } n)]\!]$ (**arid** $[2|n]$) 3 (UPDATE 3; RET 2) =
(let us set $r = $ **arid** $[2|n]$)
$C[\![\text{intsfrom(inc } n)]\!]\, r\, 3\, (C[\![n]\!])\, r\, 4$(CONS; UPDATE 3; RET 2) =
$C[\![\text{intsfrom(inc } n)]\!]\, r\, 3$ (PUSH 2; CONS; UPDATE 3; RET 2)

Notice that we obtain PUSH 2 because at this point the stack depth is 4 and n is bound to 2 in the environment r. Let us set $Z = $ (PUSH 2; CONS; UPDATE 3; RET 2) for convenience. Continuing the compilation we obtain:

$C[\![\text{inc } n]\!]\, r\, 3\, (C[\![\text{intsfrom}]\!]\, r\, 4\,(\text{MKAP}; Z)) =$
$C[\![\text{inc } n]\!]\, r\, 3$ (PUSHFUN **intsfrom**; MKAP; Z) =
$C[\![n]\!]\, r\, 3\, (C[\![\text{inc}]\!]\, r\, 4\,(\text{MKAP}; \text{PUSHFUN } \textbf{intsfrom}; \text{MKAP}; Z)) =$
$C[\![n]\!]\, r\, 3$ (PUSHFUN **inc**; MKAP; PUSHFUN **intsfrom**; MKAP; Z) =
PUSH 1; PUSHFUN **inc**; MKAP; PUSHFUN **intsfrom**; MKAP; Z

We obtain the argument 1 for PUSH in $(C[\![n]\!]\, r\, 3 \ldots)$ because $3 - r(n) = 1$ since $r(n) = 2$ as above.

Now if we expand the abbreviated code sequence Z we have the final code sequence PUSH 1; PUSHFUN **inc**; MKAP; PUSHFUN **intsfrom**; MKAP; PUSH 2; CONS; UPDATE 3; RET 2 as we expect.

∎

In fact the definition of the supercombinator compiler given by Johnsson is necessarily more complex than that described here. We have simplified the presentation of the small fragment presented above for expository purposes.

Nevertheless the examples give much of the flavour of the G-machine and G-code. The example we have discussed is also treated more comprehensively in Johnsson (1983). The interested reader should be able to appreciate the extra subtlety of Johnsson's complete description with relative ease.

Exercise 6.5.4(ii)

Take the combinators generated by supercombinator abstraction in example 6.5.2(iii) and compile them to G-machine code. Check the result on a small example graph.
■

Exercise 6.5.4(iii)

Can you explain why the code for the expression e_2 *precedes* e_1 in the compilation of expressions such as $(e_1 : e_2)$ and $(e_1 e_2)$.
■

Plenty of details have been omitted in this brief description of supercombinator generation and evaluation. This particular technique of implementing functional languages has spawned immense research activity. The generation of supercombinators from pattern-directed equations and recursive **let** expressions are two topics we have left out in our development. The material presented here should be sufficient to enable the interested reader to follow up these, and other, topics in the literature.

6.6 Typechecking

6.6.1 General considerations

As we saw in Chapter 3 some functional programming languages advocate a type discipline which goes well beyond those which have been envisaged for conventional languages. It is worth recalling that the introduction of higher-order and polymorphic types into programming has largely laid to rest the somewhat sterile arguments concerning the relative merits and demerits of strongly typed and untyped languages. Naturally, though, the increased sophistication of these type structures implies that the problem of type-checking programs will be correspondingly more complicated.

Most modern typecheckers are based on, or are extensions of, an algorithm described by Milner (1978).

Polymorphic typecheckers must, of course, check type compatibility but they also have to be able to determine the types of arbitrary expressions. In determining the type of an expression the algorithm must provide the most general type that the expression can possess. That is, it must not instantiate any polymorphism unnecessarily for if it did we would lose some, or all, of the flexibility that a polymorphic object can enjoy.

For the rest of this section, we will use the notation for types we introduced in Chapter 3. In fact, for expository purposes, the types we consider will be just a simple subset of those we discussed there. In particular we will only consider one higher-order type constructor, List, which we defined in Section 3.2.1. We now give the definition of type expressions which we will utilize in this section, in order to make things quite clear.

Definition 6.6.1(i)

We construct a set $TEXP$ of types inductively from the set $PRIM$ of *primitive types* and $TVAR$ of *type variables*:

(a) $a \in PRIM$ $\Rightarrow a \in TEXP$
(b) $\alpha \in TVAR$ $\Rightarrow \alpha \in TEXP$
(c) $t_1, t_2 \in TEXP$ $\Rightarrow t_1 \to t_2 \in TEXP$
(d) $t_1, t_2 \in TEXP$ $\Rightarrow t_1 \times t_2 \in TEXP$
(e) $t \in TEXP$ $\Rightarrow \text{List}(t) \in TEXP$
(f) $t \in TEXP, \alpha \in TVAR$ $\Rightarrow \forall \alpha \cdot t \in TEXP$
(g) nothing else is in $TEXP$.
∎

We will assume that application (of the type constructor, List, to any argument type) binds more tightly than any other type constructor; consequently we omit the brackets in: "List(t)" everywhere possible.

Let us now consider how the typing of expressions might go. We will assume that $PRIM$ contains the primitive types of integers and Booleans and we will write these as i and b, respectively.

Suppose we have a function f of type $\forall \alpha \cdot \alpha \to \alpha$ and an argument x of type i. We must ask ourselves what type the expression $(f\ x)$ has. It is obvious that the domain of f must match the type of x; so α needs to be instantiated to i. This is satisfactory for f has the type $\alpha \to \alpha$ for *all* instantiations of α. Of course the co-domain of f is also bound by the polymorphism so the type of the expression $(f\ x)$ is i and f has been specialized in this instance to $i \to i$. Suppose that f now has the type $\forall \alpha \cdot \forall \beta \cdot \alpha \to \beta \to \alpha$ and x, as before, has the type i. Again α must be instantiated to i and we could then type the expression $(f\ x)$ as $i \to i$ with f specialized to $i \to i \to i$ without introducing a conflict. In this case, however, we have instantiated the polymorphism more than is actually required. The expression $(f\ x)$ is a function expecting another argument. By forcing β to be i

we prevent (**f** x) behaving as a polymorphic function and we force it to behave as a function of fixed type **i**→**i**. Of course the correct type of (**f** x) is ∀β·β→**i** with the polymorphism preserved. This might seem a contrived example but consider the combinator *K*. Its axiom is:

$$K x y = x$$

If we work with typed objects it is clear that *K* takes two arguments of arbitrary type and returns one whose type is given by the type of the first argument. It is therefore a polymorphic function of type ∀α·∀β·α→β→α as above. Now we do not wish to restrict the number of expressions which can be correctly typed in an arbitrary fashion. This would happen, however, if we failed to determine the most general (most polymorphic) type possible for every expression. For if we typed (*K* 3) as **i**→**i** (which we have seen is not as polymorphic as possible) we would have to reject the expression (*K* 3 "True") as mistyped [because "True" has type **b**, (*K* 3) has type **i**→**i** and **i** cannot be reconciled with **b**]. On the other hand, if we take the type of (**K** 3) to be ∀β·β→**i** (which is the most polymorphic type we can assign to it) then (*K* 3 "True") is well typed; indeed it has type **i**.

The constraint which plays the major role in the example above is that which insists that the type of the domain of a function must match (in some sense) the type of any argument it is given. The key to typing (*K* 3) is to be found in the process of matching the variable α (in α→β→α) with the type **i**.

In a similar fashion, consider the conditional. If we have an expression **if** e_0 e_1 e_2 we shall require the types of e_1 and e_2 to be equivalent (again, in some sense). This is a constraint called *balancing*. It is a very important constraint for without *balanced arms* the type of the whole conditional expression would not be known until the program was evaluated (for until then the *value* of e_0 would not be available).

Therefore, in this example the key to typing the expression resides in the process of matching the types of e_1 and e_2 (and indeed matching e_0 with **b** since the first argument of a conditional must be Boolean).

These examples suggest that the ability to find a common consistent type for two (or more) types is central to the process of typechecking. Furthermore this has to be done in such a way that the type provided is the most general, that is, the most polymorphic type, which is consistent. The well-known algorithm which can achieve this is, of course, the *unification algorithm* which we looked at as a programming exercise in Section 3.4.4. Not only does this provide a substitution which unifies terms but it does so in the most general way. No variable is instantiated by this algorithm if it does not have to be. This is precisely what we require since a type variable in a type expression represents a degree of polymorphism and the substitution of a type for a type variable removes this.

The polymorphic typechecking algorithm of Milner performs a bottom–up synthesis of the type of an expression by solving type constraints which are introduced by the structure of the expression. We have seen examples of such constraints above: the type of the domain of a function must be consistent with any argument it is given. Also, the first argument of the conditional must be consistent with the type **b**. The solving of the constraints is effected by the unification of type expressions.

6.6.2 Constraints

In this section we will provide comprehensive details of the constraints which are imposed by the various operations which form our functions.

The programs are founded on some primitive operations and it is necessary to equip these with appropriate types. Some of the operators, like **h, t** and the conditional, rarely make explicit occurrences in our programs because we use pattern-directed invocation of clauses. Nevertheless, we include all these in the definition.

Definition 6.6.2(i)

The types of the primitive list operations:

$$\mathbf{h} \in \forall \alpha \cdot \text{List}(\alpha) \rightarrow \alpha$$
$$\mathbf{t} \in \forall \alpha \cdot \text{List}(\alpha) \rightarrow \text{List}(\alpha)$$
$$\mathbf{cons} \in \forall \alpha \cdot \alpha \rightarrow \text{List}(\alpha) \rightarrow \text{List}(\alpha)$$
$$\mathbf{eq} \in \forall \alpha \cdot \alpha \rightarrow \alpha \rightarrow \mathbf{b}$$
$$\mathbf{if} \in \forall \alpha \cdot \mathbf{b} \rightarrow \alpha \rightarrow \alpha \rightarrow \alpha$$
$$[\ ] \in \forall \alpha \cdot \text{List}(\alpha)$$

■

What about variables which occur in programs? How should we assign types to these? In isolation, we can say very little about the type of a variable. When such a situation is encountered we assign variables the type $\forall \alpha \cdot \alpha$. This is the most general type we can express in our type language. Later, because the context in which the variable sits provides additional type information, the type associated with a variable may become more specialized.

Let us now consider the abstraction, $\lambda v \cdot E$, which could occur in one of our programs. Firstly, we deal with the new bound variable as explained above.

Now we attempt to type E in a context equipped with the type of v. If this suggests that the type of E is t, then the type of the expression is $\lambda v \cdot E$ is $\forall \alpha \cdot \alpha \rightarrow t$. This suggests that the typing process needs to be given a context along with the expression which it has to type. We will call this context the *type environment*. This is just an association of type variables to types. The constraint which every abstract $\lambda v \cdot E$ imposes is the extension of this type environment to record the type of the bound variable v.

In general, the quantity following the lambda in an abstract can be more complicated. Indeed, patterns of various kinds can occur in these contexts. Nevertheless, the constraint is essentially the same as we will see clearly in a later example.

We now consider an application like $(E_0\ E_1)$. Suppose these type individually to t_0 and t_1, respectively. What constraint do these have to satisfy? Presumably E_0 ought to be some kind of function which expects (or at least permits) an argument of type t_1. With this intuition in mind, we insist that $(E_0\ E_1)$ types correctly subject to the constraint that t_0 unifies with $\forall \alpha . t_1 \rightarrow \alpha$. This is sufficient to ensure that E_1 is a suitable argument for E_0. The type of the whole expression is given by the type (if any) to which α becomes instantiated.

This is, of course, a very common form of expression for us and is sufficiently involved to demand a small example of its own.

Example 6.6.2(ii)

Consider the application (**cons** 3). We first type **cons** and 3. Since both are elementary this succeeds with the types $\forall \alpha \cdot \alpha \rightarrow (\mathrm{List}(\alpha) \rightarrow \mathrm{List}(\alpha))$ and i, respectively. For the application to be well formed the constraint above demands that we unify $\forall \alpha \cdot \alpha \rightarrow (\mathrm{List}(\alpha) \rightarrow \mathrm{List}(\alpha))$ with $\forall \alpha \cdot i \rightarrow \alpha$. This is more clearly seen if we drop the explicit quantification and standardize the expressions apart [with respect to the (now) free variables]. $\alpha \rightarrow (\mathrm{List}(\alpha) \rightarrow \mathrm{List}(\alpha))$ has to be unified with $i \rightarrow \beta$. This succeeds with $\alpha = i$ and $\beta = \mathrm{List}(\alpha) \rightarrow \mathrm{List}(\alpha)$ which is: List $i \rightarrow$ List i. We conclude that the expression (**cons** 3) is well typed and has the type $\mathrm{List}(i) \rightarrow \mathrm{List}(i)$ (the type that β has been instantiated to).

∎

There is a constraint imposed by the structure of the definitional form: **def f** $= E$ (we will assume that the parameters are abstracted on the right-hand side). Clearly, the type of **f** has to match the type of E. This may seem at first sight to be no more than an *assignment* of the type of E to **f** but this is not so. E may itself contain **f** (as a recursive call). It is clearly necessary that its use in E be consistent with the type it obtains by the definition as a whole. To achieve this, we impose the following constraint. Firstly, we treat **f** as a new variable (assigning it the type $\forall \alpha \cdot \alpha$). We now type E in this context. Suppose this succeeds with type t. We now unify t with the type of **f** (which may have been instantiated if E contains **f**).

Even if E does not contain **f** it is still necessary to go through this process for two reasons. Firstly, the assignment of t to α (since **f** has type $\forall \alpha \cdot \alpha$) gives us the final type of the function if it is given as a single clause. Secondly, if it is not given by a single clause, we need to check that the various clauses describe a consistent type for **f**. So if we have a program given by the two clauses $\mathbf{f} = E_1$ and $\mathbf{f} = E_2$ we proceed as follows. The first clause is typed by the policy described above. When confronted with the second (or subsequent) clauses we do *not* treat **f** as a new variable (obviously). We simply type the right-hand side to obtain t_2 (the type of E_2) and then unify this with the type of **f** which has resulted so far from previous clauses.

In our representation of programs which we described in Section 6.4, we decided that it would be advantageous to treat the data construction **cons** as an infix operation. The advice above (for typing applications) is sufficient to explain how to type $(E_0 : E_1)$ if this is to be represented with **cons** as a prefix operator (like all the others). It is therefore necessary to describe how to type expressions like $(E_0 : E_1)$ when the representation is actually infix. We begin by determining the types, t_0 and t_1 of E_0 and E_1. The type of **cons** is, of course, $\forall \alpha \cdot \alpha \rightarrow \mathrm{List}(\alpha) \rightarrow \mathrm{List}(\alpha)$. We unify this with the type: $\forall \beta \cdot t_0 \rightarrow t_1 \rightarrow \beta$. If this succeeds then the expression $(E_0 : E_1)$ is well typed and has type β (or the type to which this is instantiated).

We now turn to more general forms of abstraction. In the discussion above we dealt, for simplicity, with ordinary abstraction over variables. Clearly, we need to deal with abstraction over general patterns.

Suppose we wish to type the expression $\lambda p\, cp \cdot E$ where p is a pattern and cp is a pattern sequence. This is just shorthand for $\lambda p \cdot \lambda cp . E$. Thus, we need to address ourselves to the task of typing expressions like $\lambda p \cdot E$ where p is a single pattern. We begin by typing p and E to obtain t_0 and t_1. Things are, however, a little more complex for, in determining the type of p, we need to arrange that every instance of a variable is treated as a *declaration*. This means that we introduce a new type $\forall \alpha \cdot \alpha$ whenever we encounter a variable in p. To take a simple, but commonly occurring, form as an example let us consider the abstract $\lambda a{:}l.3$. Clearly, 3 has type **i**, a and l are both treated as declarations and are associated with types $\forall \alpha \cdot \alpha$ and $\forall \beta \cdot \beta$ (say). Solving with respect to the constraint, described above, for **cons** gives us the type $\forall \alpha \cdot \mathrm{List}(\alpha)$ for the pattern as a whole. The type of the entire expression is, therefore, $\mathrm{List}(\alpha) \rightarrow \mathbf{i}$. When the pattern contains no variable, as in $\lambda [\ ] \cdot 3$, we still proceed in the same way: $[\ ]$

has type $\forall\alpha\cdot\text{List}(\alpha)$ and 3 has type **i**. This implies that the expression $\lambda[\ ]\cdot 3$ has type $\forall\alpha\cdot\text{List}(\alpha)\rightarrow\textbf{i}$, as expected.

Finally, we see how our earliest example above, the conditional expression, imposes its constraints. We noted that conditionals should be balanced and should have a Boolean first argument. This suggests that to type (**if** $E_0 E_1 E_2$) we first obtain types for E_0, E_1 and $E_2 (t_0, t_1$ and $t_2)$ and then check the conditions. This means unifying t_0 with **b** and unifying t_1 with t_2 to effect balancing. Note that t_1 and t_2 may be different but may still unify. Thus balancing is an active, not a passive, process. The type of (**if** $E_0 E_1 E_2$) is the type which results from the balancing unification.

This completes the informal description of constraints and primitive types.

6.6.3 Typechecking definitions

We begin with a word about representation. In practice, it is usual to suppress the binding of polymorphic variables. Therefore, any type expression with free type variables is assumed to be universally polymorphically quantified. This does mean, however, that type expressions must be *standardized apart* to avoid the possible conflict of similar variable names. For example, when a new program variable is introduced we associate it with a type variable α rather than $\forall\alpha\cdot\alpha$. The suppressing of the prefix means that α must be a *new* type variable. This avoids the possibility of clashes with other type variables in use at the same time. By the same token, different instances of primitive operations, like **cons**, must be standardized apart, for the same reason.

We are now in a position to type significant expressions. This is done by applying the constraints outlined above in a post-order, left to right traversal of the expression tree. As we explained above, this traversal takes with it a type environment which contains the bindings of program variables to their currently instantiated types.

We will provide two examples, giving rather more detail in the first.

Example 6.6.3(i)

We will type the program **length**. For clarity, we present the clauses of this program as trees. The integers associated with the leaves and nodes indicate the order in which the subexpressions are typed. In this example, all type variables have the form α_i for some i. We assume that new type variables are provided by increasing the index i sequentially.

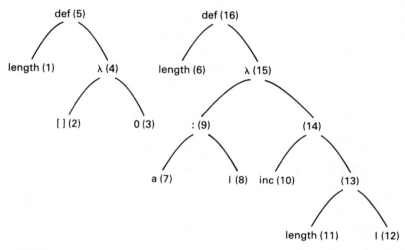

Fig. 6.6.3(ii)

(1) **length** is given a new type variable α_1 and this binding is recorded in the type environment.
(2) [ ] is a primitive operation. We standardize it apart from everything by expressing its type in terms of a new type variable α_2. Thus the type of this is just List α_2.
(3) 0 is also a primitive. It has type **i**.
(4) The type of the abstract, then, is just List $\alpha_2 \rightarrow$**i**.
(5) Finally, we unify this type with that of **length**. Since this clause is not recursive, the environment still records the type of length as α_1. The unification succeeds trivially, setting $\alpha_1 = $ List $\alpha_2 \rightarrow$**i**.
(6) Now the variable **length** is not being defined (as it is the second clause). We find that the type of **length** is now List $\alpha_2 \rightarrow$**i**.
(7) The variable a is being defined. We associate a with a new variable α_3 and record this in the environment.
(8) Now the variable l is defined. This also gets bound in the environment to a new type variable α_4.

(9) With new type variable α_5 we form $\alpha_3 \rightarrow (\alpha_4 \rightarrow \alpha_5)$ and unify this with $\alpha_6 \rightarrow (\text{List } \alpha_6 \rightarrow \text{List } \alpha_6)$. Note that the type of **cons** is standardized apart by using a new variable α_6. The result of this unification is success with the substitution $\alpha_3 = \alpha_6$; $\alpha_4 = \text{List } \alpha_6$ and $\alpha_5 = \text{List } \alpha_6$. The type of the expression is thus List α_6.

(10) **inc** is a function whose type is $i \rightarrow i$.

(11) **length** is bound to List $\alpha_2 \rightarrow i$ in the environment.

(12) l is bound to α_4 (by virtue of stage 8 above) in the environment. Stage (9) instantiated this to List α_6.

(13) To obtain the type of this application we have to unify List $\alpha_2 \rightarrow i$ with List $\alpha_6 \rightarrow \alpha_7$ (where α_7 is a new type variable). This gives i as the type of the application.

(14) Likewise, for this application we unify $i \rightarrow i$ with $i \rightarrow \alpha_8$ (where α_8 is, again, a new type variable). The type of this expression is also i.

(15) The types generated at stages (9) and (14) are List α_6 and i, respectively. This means that the type of this abstract is List $\alpha_6 \rightarrow i$. We now remove the bindings of a and l from the environment.

(16) Finally, we check the consistency of the recursive invocation – at stage (11) – with the entire clause. This amounts to unifying List $\alpha_2 \rightarrow i$ with List $\alpha_6 \rightarrow i$. This is the final result of the type analysis.

We conclude that **length** has type $\forall \alpha \cdot \text{List } \alpha \rightarrow i$.

∎

Example 6.6.3(iii)

Our second example concerns the program **append**. The analysis we provide for this is more terse than that given in the previous example. We use the following notation: unifications (say, between t_0 and t_1) will be written as an infix tilde $(t_0 \sim t_1)$. We will not record explicitly all the instantiations generated by such unifications. Most of these are quite apparent. It is, however, useful to note situations in which variables become equivalent by instantiations like $\alpha_3 = \alpha_6$, and so on. We will record these instantiations explicitly by placing equivalent variables in square brackets. The convention is that the rightmost element of these brackets is the representative used in subsequent expressions. Finally, we record entries and deletions in the type environment as follows: $+(v \, \alpha)$ read "program variable v is bound to type variable α and this is added to the environment". $-(v \, \alpha)$ is the dual notation for a deletion.

Again we provide a tree structured description of the program and label the leaves and nodes in the order in which they are processed.

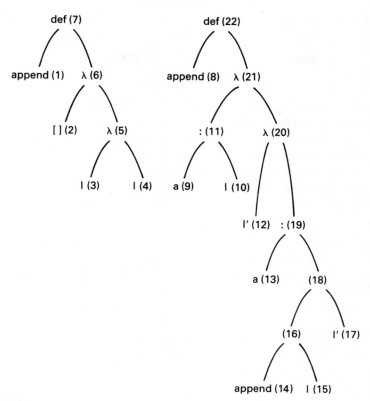

Fig. 6.6.3(iv)

(1) α_1 ; +(append α_1);

(2) List α_2 ;

(3) α_3 ; +(l α_3);

(4) α_3 ;

(5) $\alpha_3 \rightarrow \alpha_3$;

(6) List $\alpha_2 \rightarrow (\alpha_3 \rightarrow \alpha_3)$;

(7) List $\alpha_2 \rightarrow (\alpha_3 \rightarrow \alpha_3)$; $\alpha_1 \sim$ List $\alpha_2 \rightarrow (\alpha_3 \rightarrow \alpha_3)$; $-(l \ \alpha_3)$;

(8) List $\alpha_2 \rightarrow (\alpha_3 \rightarrow \alpha_3)$;

(9) α_4 ; +(a α_4);

(10) α_5 ; +(l α_5);

(11) List α_7 ; $\alpha_4 \rightarrow (\alpha_5 \rightarrow \alpha_6) \sim \alpha_7 \rightarrow$ (List $\alpha_7 \rightarrow$ List α_7); $[\alpha_4 \ \alpha_7]$;

(12) α_8 ; +(l' α_8);

(13) α_7 ;

(14) List $\alpha_2 \to (\alpha_3 \to \alpha_3)$;

(15) List α_7;

(16) $\alpha_3 \to \alpha_3$; List $\alpha_2 \to (\alpha_3 \to \alpha_3) \sim$ List $\alpha_7 \to \alpha_9$; $[\alpha_2 \alpha_4 \alpha_7]$;

(17) α_8;

(18) α_3; $\alpha_3 \to \alpha_3 \sim \alpha_8 \to \alpha_{10}$; $[\alpha_8 \alpha_{10} \alpha_3]$ $[\alpha_2 \alpha_4 \alpha_7]$;

(19) List α_{12}; $\alpha_7 \to (\alpha_3 \to \alpha_{11})$ $\alpha_{12} \to ($List $\alpha_{12} \to$ List $\alpha_{12})$;
      $[\alpha_8 \alpha_{10} \alpha_3]$ $[\alpha_2 \alpha_4 \alpha_7 \alpha_{12}]$;

(20) $\alpha_3 \to$ List α_{12}; $-(l'\ \alpha_3)$

(21) List $\alpha_{12} \to (\alpha_3 \to$ List $\alpha_{12})$; $-(l$ List $\alpha_{12})$ $-(a\ \alpha_{12})$;

(22) List $\alpha_{12} \to ($List $\alpha_{12} \to$ List $\alpha_{12})$; List $\alpha_{12} \to (\alpha_3 \to \alpha_3) \sim$ List $\alpha_{12} \to$
      $(\alpha_3 \to$ List $\alpha_{12})$; $-($**append** ... $)$

Thus the type of append, as expected, is $\forall \alpha \cdot$ List $(\alpha) \to ($List $(\alpha) \to$ List $(\alpha))$.
∎

Exercise 6.6.3(v)

Using notation as described in example 6.6.3(ii), determine the type of the following programs.

(a)

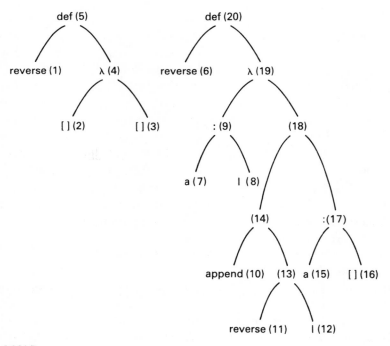

Fig. 6.6.3(vi)

(b) **member**; defined as usual.

(c) **map**; defined as usual.

∎

Project 6.6.3(vii)

Write a program to implement the typechecking process. A unification function was developed in Section 3.4.4.

∎

This section has introduced the essential ideas behind typechecking and type synthesis for polymorphically typed functional languages. There are a number of issues which we have studiously avoided in this introduction. Among these are the problems of generic versus non-generic variables in local function definitions, certain special features of recursive and non-recursive **let** expressions, mutual recursion and typing in the presence of *coercions*. These topics can be followed up in the literature once the essential ideas introduced here are understood.

6.7 Memoization

The technique of supercombinator abstraction arranges, by its manipulation of maximal free expressions, to avoid repeated evaluations whenever possible. This is the *full laziness* property. It is perhaps worth stressing again that *all* the techniques for combinator abstraction described in the Section 6.5 are *correct*. The advantages of abstracting with respect to maximal free expressions accrue from an evaluation strategy similar to that described in Section 6.4.2. If we evaluate combinatory expressions naïvely (say by avoiding all the opportunities to share common subexpressions) then the benefit of manipulating maximal free expressions is lost. Even so we might ask whether other evaluation optimizations can be undertaken which improve the time and/or space performance of program execution. To see at least one respect in which things might be improved we return to an earlier example.

Example 6.7(i)

> **def sillyid = append [ ]**

We have seen how, by careful abstraction, we can avoid repeated evaluation of constant subexpressions within this program. In particular it is the subexpression (**eq** [ ] [ ]) which is dealt with in this example. Consider, however, the following pair of definitions:

> **def sillyid1** = **append** [ ]
> **def sillyid2** = **append** [ ]

In each case the subexpression (**eq** [ ] [ ]) will be reduced the first time that each function is applied. Across definition boundaries, of course, similar expressions can be repeatedly evaluated. Can this be addressed?
∎

One proposal that has been suggested (Stoye *et al.*, 1984) is a way of exploiting the idle time for an evaluator by invoking a process which attempts to apply an equality test on various parts of the 'live' graph structure. If such a process finds two distinct, yet equal, graphs it may arrange some sharing and thus free some storage. Of course some time benefit follows later if and when the graph is reduced.

Under this regime it is (just) possible that the common expression: (**eq** [ ] [ ]) will be recognized in both programs above and so the repeated evaluation avoided. In fact this process may eventually detect that the two definitions are equal and only one copy of everything would result. **sillyid1** and **sillyid2** would become identical.

Another technique which has been advocated, particularly for avoiding repeated data structures, is the notion of a *hashing cons* (or just *hash cons*). Under this scheme the address of the **cons** cell is discovered from the arguments it is given (usually by generating a hash value from them and maintaining a hash table). By this method similar instances can be recognized and made common.

A third, and actually closely related but more general, strategy is the introduction of *memoization*. We first mentioned this as long ago as example 3.5(ii) as a way of improving recursive definitions which, like the recurrence formula for the Fibonacci sequence, involve massive amounts of recomputation. The idea is simplicity itself and superficially very attractive but is more involved than might at first be suspected.

In its original manifestation (Michie, 1968) a *memo function* is simply associated with a table (accessed by any search strategy required, in particular by hashing techniques) of previously computed results. When a memo function is applied a search of the table for the argument is undertaken. If the argument is present the result is retrieved. If it is not then the result is computed and recorded in the table before it is returned. Programs like the recurrence formula for Fibonacci suddenly become quite efficient in terms of time. The space complexity of course has to take into account the storage requirements of the table. Thus Fibonacci requires space $O(n)$ in this respect.

In languages without memo functions (almost all!) this method of computing natural but inefficient recursions can be simulated by the explicit introduction of a table of results: a technique often referred to as *dynamic programming*. In the case of Fibonacci we should also be able to take advantage of the fact that only the two largest values ever need to be remembered, which allows us to optimize the table still further to include only two entries. The memo approach then specializes to the natural iterative solution which requires two accumulators, and which we derived by continuation-based program transformation techniques in example 4.7(v).

There are, however, more serious problems than this and these are related to the issues of complex data and lazy evaluation.

In the case of programs like Fibonacci the data type over which they compute is very simple and the equality test very cheap. In general our programs have been defined over more complex types than this – typically lists and sexpressions of atoms. In order to determine whether an argument has been seen before we need to undertake an expensive (recursive) equality test with a time complexity which is dependent on the size of the argument. This is itself a major problem but there is worse to come. Our evaluation strategy is, typically, lazy. We do *not* evaluate arguments in full unless we need to access every part of them. The equality test makes full evaluation necessary for all arguments and we lose lazy function application.

A solution to both of these problems has been proposed by Hughes (1985). His suggestion amounts to relaxing the test on the similarity of arguments a little. Primitive values, as before, are tested for absolute equality but complex data structures are only tested for *equality of representation*. This is clearly weaker [consider the two expressions (**eq** [ ] [ ]) in our example above which are equal but which do not have equal representations]. This test is executed with time complexity $O(1)$ even for complex data, for we need only check to see if the root cell of the representation (an address) has been encountered before. Not only is this a cheap test but we avoid fully evaluating the argument too. Thus laziness is preserved.

It would be possible to include a predicate in the language itself which tests for equality of representations. Languages such as LISP do this by including a function EQUAL (structural equality) and EQ (equality of representations). It is easy to see that one destroys referential transparency by adopting the latter predicate. Indeed, if the idle time of the evaluator is used to seek out equal expressions as we suggested above, then an expression like (EQ x y) might return "False" at one moment and "True" somewhat later!

One surprising corollary of Hughes's proposal is that many data structures which are represented by circular lists generate similar circular results.

Example 6.7(ii)

Consider the program **def ones** = 1:**ones**. Our description of recursion in Section 6.4.1 tells us that this will be represented by the graph:

Fig. 6.7(iii)

Now let us define:

  def twos = **map inc ones**

Consider the alternative definition:

  def twos = 2:**twos**

These do not generate similar representations. The latter, as expected, produces:

Fig. 6.7(iv)

However, **(map inc ones)**, after an arbitrary amount of investigation, will expand to:

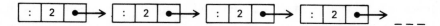

Fig. 6.7(v)

which takes up increasing amounts of storage.

If **map** is *memoized on equality of representation* then the following occurs when (**map inc ones**) is forced to evaluate:

> **map inc ones** =
> **map inc** 1:**ones** =
> $(1+1)$:(**map inc ones**) =
> 2:(**map inc ones**)

Since **ones** is a cyclic structure the arguments to **map** have equal representations. The recursive call to **map** yields the previously calculated result (2:(**map inc ones**)). This is the structure of Fig. 6.7(iv).

Similar recognition of cycles occurs in more complex cases.
■

For the remainder of this section we will indicate a memo function by replacing the symbol **def** in a definition by **memo**.

We have noted that some programs when evaluated by graph reduction tend to take up monotonically increasing quantities of store as they become more and more "unwound". The program (**map inc ones**) is a good example of this. This application of memo functions seems to have prevented this, but they introduce a similar problem of their own in this regard. The table of arguments which have already been supplied to a memo function also grows monotonically and it is not clear when such a table, if ever, can be removed as garbage. To some extent this can be overcome by introducing *local definitions* which go out of scope at certain times. Under these circumstances the associated table can also be removed. To see this consider the following example.

Example 6.7(vi)

Consider the definition:

> **def** z = 1:2:3:z

and the function:

> **def** w = map inclist z

Eventually (when the fourth element of **w** is required) the cyclic version of **w** is created and the need for the saved values of (**map inc**) is removed. However, as things stand, these saved values will persist. One solution is to arrange that **map** is not itself a memo function but introduces a memo function [for each invocation of (**map f**)] and which memoizes on the second (list) argument.

> **def** map f l = **m** l **where memo m** $a:l' = (f\,a):(\mathbf{m}\,l')$

Now an **m** will exist for each invocation of **map**. Just as soon as the cycle is set up the invocation of **map** becomes inaccessible and will be collected (along with the table of values set up for **m**) by the garbage collector.
■

Example 6.7(vii)

We return to the program **balance** which was originally discussed in Section 3.4.3 [example 3.4.3(vi)]. At that stage we were more concerned about techniques of program verification and, in particular, how to set up suitable well-founded orderings for induction proofs. We did, however, comment on an inefficiency in this program which we can now address.

> **def balance** $a = a$
> **def balance** $(s_1 : s_2) = (\textbf{balance}\ s_1) : (\textbf{balance}\ s_2)$
> $\qquad\qquad$ **when** $(\textbf{abs}\ (\textbf{unbal}\ (s_1 : s_2))) < 1$
> **def balance** $(s_1 : s_2) = \textbf{let}\ a : s_3 = (\textbf{roll}\ s_2)$
> $\qquad\qquad$ **in** $(\textbf{balance}\ ((s_1 : a) : s_3))$
> $\qquad\qquad$ **when** $(\textbf{unbal}\ (s_1 : s_2)) < 0$
> **def balance** $(s_1 : s_2) = \textbf{let}\ s_3 : a = (\textbf{unroll}\ s_1)$
> $\qquad\qquad$ **in** $(\textbf{balance}\ (s_3 : (a : s_2)))$
> $\qquad\qquad$ **when** $(\textbf{unbal}\ (s_1 : s_2)) > 0$

The auxiliary program **unbal** is given by:

> **def unbal** $(s_1 : s_2) = (\textbf{ca}\ s_1) - (\textbf{ca}\ s_2)$
> **def unbal** $a = 0$

This is used to control the invocation of the clauses of **balance**. **unbal**, in its turn, uses the program **ca (countatoms)** to determine the relative weights of the compound sexpressions.

Suppose we give **balance** the argument $(("A":"B"):("C":"D"))$ (without loss of generality). Since there are two atoms in each subexpression the second clause applies and the problem reduces to $(\textbf{balance}\ ("A":"B")):(\textbf{balance}\ ("C":"D"))$. Again the atoms in the left and right subexpressions are counted to determine the degree of imbalance. This involves the recomputation of $(\textbf{ca}\ "A")$, $(\textbf{ca}\ "B")$, $(\textbf{ca}\ "C")$ and $(\textbf{ca}\ "D")$ since these were already evaluated for the calls to $(\textbf{ca}\ ("A":"B"))$ and $(\textbf{ca}\ ("C":"D"))$ for the calculation of $(\textbf{unbal}\ (("A":"B"):("C":"D")))$. The solution is to employ a version of **ca** which uses memoization. In this way the calculation of the sizes of the subexpressions is computed at most once.

It is instructive to consider alternative solutions to this problem. In an imperative language one would almost certainly arrange to store the number of atoms in a binary tree in the nodes themselves (as extra fields). We could undertake this in our language by introducing a type:

$$CSexp(\alpha) = (N \times N \times \alpha) + (N \times N \times (CSexp(\alpha) \times CSexp(\alpha)))$$

We will use a colon as the data constructor of the fifth product above, as we do for sexpressions. For the others we use the constructor:

$$\langle \_, \_, \_ \rangle$$

Now we introduce a function, **label**, of type:

$$(\forall \alpha)(Sexp(\alpha) \to CSexp(\alpha))$$

as follows:

> **def label** $(s_1 : s_2) = \langle n_1 + n_2, n_3 + n_4, (cs_1 : cs_2) \rangle$
> > **where** $\langle n_1, n_2, cs_1 \rangle = ($**label** $s_1)$
> > **where** $\langle n_3, n_4, cs_2 \rangle = ($**label** $s_2)$
>
> **def label** $a \qquad = \langle 1, 0, a \rangle$

Given these definitions we can redefine **balance** by first defining **balance1** which is now to have type:

$$(\forall \alpha)(CSexp(\alpha) \to Sexp(\alpha))$$

and then setting:

> **def balance** = **balance1** ∘ **label**

Exercise 6.7(viii)

Define the function **balance1**. Notice how similar it is to our original function **balance**. The main point to observe is that there is a need to redefine the maps **roll** and **unroll** so that they operate over the extended type CSexp rather than Sexp.
∎

This is not an attractive solution because it changes the interface of any functions which manipulate sexpressions that are required by **balance**.
∎

Exercise 6.7(ix) (Hughes)

This program attempts to find the deepest atom in an sexpression. Since many such atoms may exist at the same depth this program returns a list of results.

def deepest $s_1:s_2=(\textbf{deepest } s_1)$
                when (depth $s_1) > (\textbf{depth } s_2)$
def deepest $s_1:s_2=(\textbf{deepest } s_2)$
                when (depth $s_2) > (\textbf{depth } s_1)$
def deepest $s_1:s_2=(\textbf{deepest } s_1) * (\textbf{deepest } s_2)$
                when (depth $s_1)=(\textbf{depth } s_2)$
def deepest a $=[a]$
def depth $s_1:s_2$ $=\textbf{inc (max (depth } s_1)(\textbf{depth } s_2))$
def depth a $=0$

Clearly the repeated calculation of depth information can be overcome by memoing **depth**. An alternative solution, when memo functions are not available, is to *combine the two programs into one*. Obtain a new version for **deepest** (preferably using techniques from Chapter 4) which combines **deepest** and **depth** in a way which avoids the repeated computation. Can this be used to obtain an alternative definition of **balance** [say by introducing a function, **balance2**, of type: $(\forall\alpha)(\text{Sexp}(\alpha) \rightarrow \text{CSexp}(\alpha))$ and then setting: **balance** $=$ **forget** $\circ$ **balance2** where **forget** is a function of type: $(\forall\alpha)(\text{CSexp}(\alpha) \rightarrow \text{Sexp}(\alpha))$ which just *forgets the labels*]?

■

6.8 Bibliographic notes

For general study in the area of programming language implementation the reader might like to consult Bornat (1979) which is very readable, and the excellent and comprehensive text by Aho *et al.* (1986) which includes some details of polymorphic typing.

    For a general overview of LISP implementations Wise (1982) and Sussman (1982) would be good places to start. The more recent LISP-like language SCHEME is described in Steele & Sussman (1975) and the various implementation issues (including the development of RACKs) are expounded in Sussman (1982), and Steele & Sussman (1975, 1978) and Steele (1977).

    For combinatory-based implementations the seminal reference is Turner (1979a) but the more efficient combinators S' are defined in Turner (1979b). Considerations relating to the efficiency of combinatory compilation are developed in Kennaway (1983), Meira (1984) and Burton (1982). Other aspects of combinatory compilation and evaluation are discussed in Hudak & Goldberg (1984, 1985), Hudak & Kranz (1984) and Hankin *et al.* (1985). Issues relating to garbage collection and reference counts (in pointers) were developed by the Cambridge group and this work is reported in Stoye *et al.* (1984) and Clarke *et al.* (1980).

Supercombinators were introduced by Hughes (1982, 1984). Related to this is the work of Johnsson on "lambda lifting" (1985) and Hudak & Goldberg (1985). Machines for evaluation of such graphs have been described by Johnsson (1983) and Kieburtz (1985).

Other approaches to evaluation related more to the SECD machine include Abramsky & Sykes (1985) on the SECD-M machine and Cardelli (1984a, 1984b) which introduce the FAM (functional abstract machine). We have had occasion to mention the work of Curien before; in particular his work with categorical combinators. The machine associated with this work is described in Cousineau *et al.* (1985).

Implementation of lazy evaluation is discussed by Henderson & Morris (1976), Pingali & Arvind (1985) and Georgeff (1984).

Memo functions were introduced by Michie (1968) and the material of Section 6.7 is based on the research of Hughes (1985).

Finally, Peyton-Jones (1987) is an excellent place to continue the study of implementation issue for functional languages.

Abramsky, S. & Sykes, R. (1985) SECD-M: a virtual machine for applicative programming. *Proc. Conference on Functional Programing and Computer Architecture, LNCS*, Vol. 201, pp. 81–98. Springer, Berlin.

Aho, A. V., Sethi, R. & Ullman, J. (1986) *Compilers: Principles, Techniques and Tools.* Addison-Wesley, Reading, Mass.

Barendregt, H. P. (1984) *The Lambda Calculus: Its Syntax and Semantics (Revised), Studies in Logic,* Vol. 103. North-Holland, Amsterdam.

Bornat, R. (1979) *Understanding and writing compilers.* Macmillan, London.

Burton, F. W. (1982) A linear space translation of functional programs to Turner combinators. *Information Processing Letters,* **14**, 201–204.

Cardelli, L. (1984a) The functional abstract machine. *Computing science technical report no. 107,* AT & T, Bell Laboratories.

Cardelli, L. (1984b) Compiling a functional language. *Proc. 3rd ACM Conference on LISP and Functional Programming,* Austin, Texas.

Clarke, T. J. W., Gladstone, P. J. S., Maclean, C. D. & Norman, A. C. (1980) SKIM–the *S, K, I* reduction machine. *Proc. ACM LISP Conference,* pp. 128–135.

Cousineau, G., Curien, P.-L. & Mauny, M. (1985) The categorical abstract machine. *Proc. Conference on Functional Programming Languages and Computer Architecture, LNCS,* Vol. 201, pp. 50–64. Springer, Berlin.

Georgeff, M. (1984) Transformations and reduction strategies for typed lambda expressions. *ACM Trans. Programming Languages and Systems,* **6**, 603–31.

Hankin, C. L., Osmon, P. E. & Shute, M. J. (1985) COBWEB–a combinator reduction architecture. *Proc. Conference on Functional Programming Languages and Computer Architecture, LNCS,* Vol. 201, pp. 99–112. Springer, Berlin.

Henderson, P. & Morris, J. H. (1976) A lazy evaluator. *Proc. 3rd ACM Symposium on principles of programming languages,* Atlanta, Georgia.

Hudak, P. & Goldberg, B. (1984) Experiments in diffused combinator reduction. *Proc 3rd ACM Conference on LISP and functional programming.* Austin, Texas.

Hudak, P. & Goldberg, B. (1985) Serial combinators: "Optimal" grains of parallelism. *Proc. Conference on Functional Programming and Computer Architecture. LNCS*, Vol. 201, pp. 382–99. Springer, Berlin.

Hudak, P. & Kranz, D. (1984) A combinator based compiler for a functional language. *Proc. 11th ACM symposium on Principles of Programming Languages*, pp. 121–32.

Hughes, R. J. M. (1982) Supercombinators, a new implementation method for applicative languages. *Proc. ACM Symposium on LISP and Functional Programming*, Pittsburgh.

Hughes, R. J. M. (1984) The design and implementation of programming languages. D. Phil. thesis, Oxford University, *Technical monograph no. PRG-40*, Programming research group, Oxford University Computing Laboratory.

Hughes, R. J. M. (1985) Lazy memo functions. *Proc. Conference on Functional Programming Languages and Computer Architecture, LNCS*, Vol. 201, pp. 129–46. Springer, Berlin.

Johnsson, T. (1983) The G-machine: an abstract machine for graph reduction. *Proc. Declarative Programming Workshop*, University College, London.

Johnsson, T. (1985) Lambda lifting: transforming programs to recursive equations. *Proc. Conference on functional programming languages and computer architecture. LNCS*, Vol. 201, pp. 190–203. Springer, Berlin.

Kennaway, J. R. (1983) The complexity of a translation of lambda calculus to combinators. Internal report no. CS/83/023/E, School of Computing Studies, University of East Anglia.

Kieburtz, R. B. (1985) The G-machine: A fast, graph reduction evaluator. *Proc. Conference on Functional Programming and Computer Architecture, LNCS*, Vol. 201, pp. 400–13. Springer, Berlin.

Meira, S. L. (1984) Optimised combinatoric code for applicative language implementation. *UKC computing laboratory report no. 20*, Computing Laboratory, University of Kent.

Michie, D. (1968) 'Memo' functions and machine learning, *Nature*, **218**, 19–22.

Milner, R. (1978) A theory of type polymorphism in programming. *J. Computing and System Science*, **17**, 348–375.

Peyton-Jones, S. L. (1987) *The implementation of functional programming languages*, Prentice Hall, London.

Pingali, K. & Arvind, (1985) Efficient demand driven evaluation. *ACM Trans. Programming Languages and Systems*, **7**, 311–33.

Steele, G. L. (1977) Debunking the 'expensive procedure call' myth. *Proc. ACM National Conference*, pp. 153–62.

Steele, G. L. & Sussman, G. J. (1975) SCHEME: an interpreter for extended lambda calculus. *AI memo 349*, MIT AI Laboratory, Massachusetts Institute of Technology.

Steele, G. L. & Sussman, G. J. (1978) The art of the interpreter: the modularity complex (parts 0, 1 and 2). *AI memo 453*, MIT Laboratory, Massachusetts Institute of Technology.

Steele, G. L & Sussman, G. J. (1979) The dream of a lifetime: a lazy variable extent mechanism. *AI memo 527*, MIT AI Laboratory, Massachusetts Institute of Technology.

Stoye, W. R., Clarke, T. J. W. & Norman, A. C. (1984) Some practical methods for rapid combinator evaluation. *Proc. 3rd ACM Conference on LISP and Functional Programming*, Austin, Texas.

Sussman, G. J. (1982) LISP, programming and implementation. In *Functional Programming and its Applications*. J. Darlington, P. Henderson & D. A. Turner (eds), pp. 29–72. Cambridge University Press, Cambridge.

Turner, D. A. (1979a) A new implementation technique for applicative languages. *Software, Practice and Experience*, **9**, 31–49.

Turner, D. A. (1979b) Another algorithm for bracket abstraction. *J. Symbolic Logic*, **44**, 267–270.

Wise, D. S. (1982) Interpreters for functional programming. In *Functional Programming and its Applications*. J. Darlington, P. Henderson & D. A.Turner (eds), pp. 253–280. Cambridge University Press, Cambridge.

Chapter 7

Theoretical foundations

7.1 Introduction

The purpose of this chapter is to introduce some of the mathematics and the techniques which are necessary for understanding the semantics of programming languages and, of course, functional languages in particular.

We have contrasted, particularly in Chapter 3, the operational understanding of programs with a declarative or denotational understanding. In Section 2.4.1 we actually provided a formal definition of a denotational semantics for the lambda calculus, but there we avoided the hard questions regarding the existence and nature of data spaces with rather special properties (in particular a data space V *equal* to its own function space, $V \rightarrow V$).

In this chapter we will pursue denotational semantics more rigorously. In particular we will introduce a theory of data types based on sound intuitions and discover that these are sufficient to ensure that a satisfactory data type, V, for the lambda calculus exists (although we will see that the naïve equality of V and $V \rightarrow V$ has to be weakened to an isomorphism).

In a sense this material is complementary to the previous chapter. Here we expound the mathematics and techniques which are required for the interpretation of programs (and languages) denotationally, that is, in an abstract, compositional, implementation free fashion. In the last chapter we described programs and languages in terms of compilation and evaluation schemes, that is, in an operational manner.

In the next section we will try to explain how programs may be described in terms of abstract mathematical functions. We will see, for example, how they correspond to rather esoteric objects called *chain continuous mappings*.

By Section 7.3 we will be in a position to extend the theory so that we may solve recursive data type equations. We will show, in particular, how a solution to $S = A + S \times S$ can be constructed in such a way that S contains all finite, all partial and all infinite lists of sexpressions over the data space of atoms A. We will also indicate how a model of the lambda calculus can be constructed.

7.2 Order theoretic semantics

We will begin this section with a word about terminology. In order to avoid confusion we will refer to our program texts as *programs* rather than as *functions* which we have used up to now. The reason for this is that we wish to reserve the term function for the *interpretation* of such programs in suitable mathematical domains. Thus, in the next paragraph, we will talk of the *program* **append** (the text in our language) and the *function* it denotes over the domain of lists.

Consider the program **append**, which takes two lists as arguments and returns one as a result. We should like to regard this program as a mathematical entity and in this case we should regard it as some kind of function. If L is the set of lists then presumably the function we intend for the program **append** is a member of $L \times L \to L$ (or $L \to L \to L$). But are programs to be regarded as arbitrary functions? In other words, can all functions be the value of some program? Indeed not; the theory of computability develops the theory of computable functions and the uninformed but interested reader could consult any of the texts mentioned at the end of this chapter. Our purpose now is not to examine the boundary between computable and uncomputable functions but to develop a mathematical theory of computing entities. By entity we refer both to data and to program values. If we are prepared to think of programs (procedures and so on) as just certain kinds of data we can simply ask ourselves questions about the variety of programming data types.

Consider the program:

$$\mathbf{f}\, x = \mathbf{if}\,(\mathbf{eq}\, x\, 0)\,(\mathbf{f}\, x)\, 1$$

At first sight we might expect this to denote a function in the set of functions $N \to N$ from natural numbers to natural numbers. But, intuitively, from an operational perspective, $(\mathbf{f}\, 0)$ never returns an answer so $\mathbf{f}$ is only *partially defined*. We can put this more abstractly: the program is specified by an equation and any function which yields 1 whenever x is not zero satisfies it. The value of $\mathbf{f}$ at zero is, therefore, *unspecified by the equation*. Now in computability theory we should treat $\mathbf{f}$ as a partial function in the set $N \to N$ of partial functions. Here we follow the work of Scott (see Bibliography) and treat $\mathbf{f}$ as a total function in a new space of data values.

The first idea is to place an additional element into the set N which is to stand for a lack of information; an *undefined value* in other words. This, on its own is, perhaps, not sufficient. We wish to capture the idea that this new value is, in some sense, *worse* than all the others since it communicates no information whilst the others do. We shall use the symbol $\perp$ to represent absence of information. This can be pronounced "undefined" or "bottom" (the latter terminology will appear more reasonable later). This might remind the reader of the prototypical non-head normal form of Chapter 2 (see Section 2.2.3), the data structure "hole" of partial induction (see Section 3.11.2) and the undefined value of FP systems (see Section 5.2.1 which includes a critical comment in respect of FP on this issue). The similarity is by no means coincidental. In order to capture how $\perp$ stands in relation to all other values (in terms of information content) we impose an *ordering* on the extended set. This is a partial order on the information content provided by the values in the set. In the example we are pursuing let us be precise:

Definition 7.2(i)

Let $N_\perp = \langle N \cup \{\perp\}, \sqsubseteq \rangle$

Suppose $n, n' \in N_\perp$ then define: $n \sqsubseteq n'$ iff $(n = \perp) \vee (n = n')$
■

Exercise 7.2(ii)

Show that the relation $\sqsubseteq$, defined above, is indeed a partial ordering of the elements in $N_\perp$. In other words, $N_\perp$ is a *poset* (see Appendix).
■

By far the best way of appreciating the order structure of $N_\perp$ is diagrammatically. In the following picture information content of elements (dark dots) increases up the page. Elements which are on the same level are incomparable.

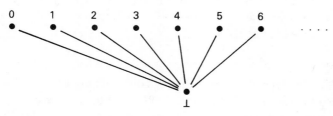

Fig. 7.2(iii)

In general we have:

Definition 7.2(iv) Lifted sets

Let E be a set.

Define $E_\perp = \langle E \cup \{\perp\}, \sqsubseteq \rangle$ where

$$(\forall e,\, e' \in E_\perp)(e \sqsubseteq e' \text{ iff } (e = \perp) \vee (e = e'))$$

∎

It is easy to show that all lifted sets are posets.

Notation 7.2(v)

To avoid cumbersome formulae we will often, ambiguously, write E for $E_\perp$, unless, as above, the context prevents this.

∎

As a second example consider the set {true, false} which may be the intended co-domain of a program which acts as a predicate. The lifted set, which we call T, looks like:

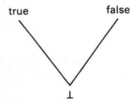

Fig. 7.2(vi)

So far the ordering is rather simple, and indeed may seem overly complicated for the task it is fulfilling. To see the richness and variety that develops from these humble beginnings we now turn to data type constructions.

We have already needed to combine sets together by a variety of set operators. For example, the set:

$$L = \{\text{"Nil"}\} + A \times L$$

constructs a data type of lists by means of a disjoint union, a cartesian product operation and even recursive definition. We need to ask ourselves how these operators ought to be defined when their arguments are partially ordered sets. In particular, how should the ordering on the resulting sets be defined?

For the moment we just provide three constructions for cartesian product, disjoint union and function spaces.

Definition 7.2(vii) Cartesian product

Let $A = \langle A, \sqsubseteq_A \rangle$ and $B = \langle B, \sqsubseteq_B \rangle$ be posets.

$$A \times B = \langle A \times B, \sqsubseteq_{A \times B} \rangle$$

$$(\forall \langle a,b \rangle, \langle a', b' \rangle \in A \times B)(\langle a, b \rangle \sqsubseteq_{A \times B} \langle a', b' \rangle \text{ iff } a \sqsubseteq_A a, b \sqsubseteq_B b')$$

■

This new poset inherits its ordering *pointwise* from the arguments. This operator makes the order theory of the spaces we are considering very much more complex.

Exercise 7.2(viii)

Check that $A \times B$ is a poset whenever A and B are.
■

Consider the set $1 = \{\cdot\}$ a one-element set. Now $1_\perp$ looks like this:

Fig. 7.2(ix)

Now, 1×1 (dropping the $\perp$ as explained above) looks like:

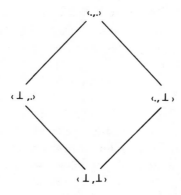

Fig. 7.2(x)

This is already more complicated than a lifted set. Calling this poset 2 we can draw 2×2:

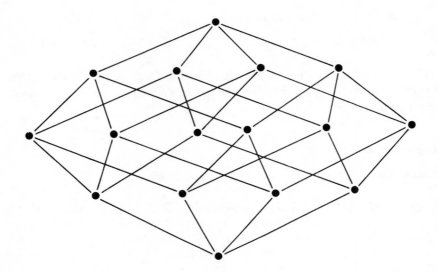

Fig. 7.2(xi)

In the figure above the elements have not been labelled:

Exercise 7.2(xii)

Label the figure with the elements of 2×2.
∎

We next turn to the disjoint union of posets.

Definition 7.2(xiii) Disjoint union

Let $A = \langle A, \sqsubseteq_A \rangle$ and $B = \langle B, \sqsubseteq_B \rangle$ be posets.

$$A + B =_{\text{def}} \langle (A + B) \cup \{\bot\}, \sqsubseteq_{A+B} \rangle$$

(a) $\bot \sqsubseteq_{A+B} v$ for all $v \in (A + B) \cup \{\bot\}$
(b) $\langle a, 1 \rangle \sqsubseteq_{A+B} \langle a', 1 \rangle$ iff $a \sqsubseteq_A a'$ for all $a, a' \in A$
(c) $\langle b, 2 \rangle \sqsubseteq_{A+B} \langle b', 2 \rangle$ iff $b \sqsubseteq_B b'$ for all $b, b' \in B$
∎

Again the definition is more clearly understood by an example shown diagrammatically. Recall the lifted set of Booleans. Figure 7.2 (xiv) shows $T + T$.

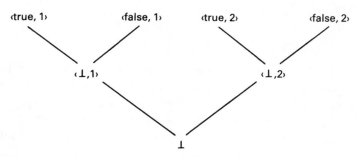

Fig. 7.2(xiv)

It can be seen that the ordering is inherited from the sum components. One rather odd feature of this definition are the three values which include $\perp$. These are the two disjoint copies of $\perp_T$ and the new $\perp_{T+T}$ value. The explanation for these values, and their respective positions in the ordering, runs as follows: $\perp_{T+T}$ represents no information in the space $T + T$. The value $\langle \perp, 1 \rangle$, whilst providing no information regarding truth, does, at least, communicate which of the sum posets it belongs to. Thus it is justifiable that $\langle \perp, 1 \rangle$ should appear strictly above $\perp_{T+T}$.

Exercise 7.2(xv)

Show that $A + B$ is a poset whenever A and B are.
■

Finally, for the time being, we deal with the construction of posets of functions:

Definition 7.2(xvi)

Let $A = \langle A, \sqsubseteq_A \rangle$ and $B = \langle B, \sqsubseteq_B \rangle$ be posets; then:

$$(A \to B) =_{\text{def}} \langle A \to B, \sqsubseteq_{A \to B} \rangle$$

$$(\forall f, f' \in A \to B)(f \sqsubseteq_{A \to B} f' \text{ iff } (\forall a \in A)((f\,a) \sqsubseteq_B (f'\,a)))$$
■

Now *should this set of functions* $(A \to B)$ *contain all the set theoretic functions from A to B* (subject to the inherited ordering on B)? For the moment we shall restrict this set to just those functions which are *monotonic* with respect to the ordering but later we will need a stronger condition than this.

Chapter 7

Monotonicity condition

In the definition above $(A \to B)$ contains just those functions which are monotonic with respect to the ordering. That is, those functions, **f**, which satisfy:

$$\mathbf{f} \in A \to B \text{ iff } (\forall a, a' \in A)(a \sqsubseteq a' \Rightarrow (\mathbf{f}\, a) \sqsubseteq (\mathbf{f}\, b))$$

We must explain why this is imposed. Presumably the result of a function will depend on the information content of the input provided. If we increase the information about the input we would not expect the function to provide *less* information than before. Indeed, we would expect the output to improve, or at least stay the same (this would occur if the input already provided sufficient information for an output to be given).

Example 7.2(xvii)

Let T be, as before, the set of values $\{\perp, t, f\}$ under the ordering discussed above. Let **and** be a function from T^2 to T. The output we give depends on the information content of the input. Occasionally it is possible to provide a defined output even though the input is only partially specified. For example, we could set $(\mathbf{and}\, \langle f, \perp \rangle) = (\mathbf{and}\, \langle \perp, f \rangle) = f$. In other circumstances a partially specified input is not sufficient; consider, for example: $(\mathbf{and}\, \langle \perp, t \rangle) = (\mathbf{and}\, \langle t, \perp \rangle) = \perp$. Now if we improve the input from $\langle \perp, t \rangle$ to $\langle t, t \rangle$ the output improves from $\perp$ to t. On the other hand, if the input improves from $\langle \perp, t \rangle$ to $\langle f, t \rangle$ the output improves from $\perp$ to f. Consider the input $\langle f, \perp \rangle$. If this improves to either $\langle f, f \rangle$ or $\langle f, t \rangle$ the output stays at f. The point is that (on this interpretation) $\langle f, \perp \rangle$ is *sufficient information* about the input to conclude that the output is f. This definition for **and** is given by the following truth table:

and	t	f	$\perp$
t	t	f	$\perp$
f	f	f	f
$\perp$	$\perp$	f	$\perp$

Fig. 7.2(xviii)

which makes the strongest decision it can, based on the information in the argument. A more conservative definition might be:

and	t	f	$\perp$
t	t	f	$\perp$
f	f	f	$\perp$
$\perp$	$\perp$	$\perp$	$\perp$

Fig. 7.2(xix)
∎

Exercise 7.2(xx)

(a) Show that both these definitions of **and** are monotonic mappings.
(b) Find two monotonic definitions for **or**.
(c) Find a monotonic definition for **not**.
∎

It does seem eminently reasonable to require all functions to respect the information ordering in this way. We will, however, return to this later when we will see that we also need to strengthen this requirement.

Rather than attempt to draw a diagram for a function space let us look at an example.

Suppose we define a function called $\mathbf{fac_0} \in N \to N$ which is undefined no matter what its argument is. That is to say:

$$(\mathbf{fac_0}\ n) = \perp \qquad \text{for all } n \in N$$

(note that we have dropped the subscript on $N_\perp$ again). From this let us define a sequence of functions:

$$\mathbf{fac}_m \in N \to N \qquad \text{for all } m \geq 0$$

such that

$$(\mathbf{fac}_m\ n) = n! \qquad \text{when } n < m \text{ and}$$
$$(\mathbf{fac}_m\ n) = \perp \qquad \text{when } n \geq m$$

As the subscript m increases so the functions $\mathbf{fac}_m$ provide more information about the factorial function. More formally, we can write:

$$(\forall n, m)(n \leq m \text{ iff } \mathbf{fac}_n \sqsubseteq_{N \to N} \mathbf{fac}_m)$$

Exercise 7.2(xxi)

Prove this.

∎

Now it is clear that $\mathbf{fac}_n \neq \mathbf{fac}$ for any n since $\mathbf{fac}$ is defined for all integer arguments but $\mathbf{fac}_n$ is undefined when the argument exceeds n. However, it is also clear that the sequence:

$$\mathbf{fac}_0 \sqsubseteq \mathbf{fac}_1 \sqsubseteq \mathbf{fac}_2 \sqsubseteq \ldots \sqsubseteq \mathbf{fac}_n \sqsubseteq \ldots$$

is an *improving* sequence of function and seems to be tending toward $\mathbf{fac}$ as the subscript increases. We should like to be able to claim that $\mathbf{fac}$ *is a summary of all the information in the increasing sequence*. To do this we need to be precise about forming summaries of information.

Definition 7.2(xxii)

Let $A = \langle A, \sqsubseteq \rangle$. $d \in A$ is an *upper bound* for $\mathrm{P} \subseteq A$ if and only if $p \sqsubseteq d$ for all $p \in P$. $d \in A$ is the *least upper bound* of P when:
(a) it is an upper bound and
(b) if d' is any upper bound of P then $d \sqsubseteq d'$.
The least upper bound of a pair of elements p and p' is written: $p \sqcup p'$ ($\sqcup$ is pronounced "join"). The least upper bound of a set P of elements is written: $\bigsqcup P$. We will sometimes refer to $\bigsqcup P$ as the limit of P.

∎

When the relation $\sqsubseteq$ is an information ordering it is easy to see that an upper bound for a set of values contains all the information in the set (and possibly some more). A least upper bound seems to summarize the set without including any irrelevant information.

For example $\mathbf{fac}_4$ is an upper bound for the set:

$$\{\mathbf{fac}_2, \mathbf{fac}_3\}$$

but contains some information:

"the factorial of 3 is 6"

that neither $\mathbf{fac}_2$ nor $\mathbf{fac}_3$ contain. The least upper bound of this set is $\mathbf{fac}_3$. This example is not very revealing for $\mathbf{fac}_3$ is *already* an element of the set. We shall be more interested in cases where the least upper bound is *not* an element of the set like, for example and in particular, the set: $\{\mathbf{fac}_i | i \geqslant 0\}$.

Now, upper bounds do not always exist in our posets for *arbitrary* subsets of values. The set $\{1, 2\}$ of values from $N_\perp$ has no upper bound in $N_\perp$. On the other hand, the set $\{\perp, 1\}$ does. The intuition behind this is that the elements 1 and 2 taken together are contradictory because they are distinct (and irreconcilable) atoms of information. It is possible to include this observation in the theory by adding an element $\top$ (which is pronounced "overdetermined", "contradictory" or "top") to all our sets of values. The space of truth values would then look like this.

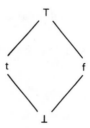

Fig. 7.2(xxiii)

If such a policy is seen through systematically, *all* sets of values have summaries, even if this is only an indication that the set contains irreconcilable information. We shall *not* include such values for the added complexity as this does not provide significant conceptual rewards. However, we must discover or impose a reasonable constraint on our value sets which will ensure that summaries exist when we want them to. The secret is that least upper bounds exist for sets which contain information which is consistent. But we need to make this precise. How can we delineate such sets from others?

Definition 7.2(xxiv)

Let $A = \langle A, \sqsubseteq \rangle$ be a poset. A chain in A is a subset $P \subseteq A$ which is totally ordered by $\sqsubseteq$.
∎

In other words a chain, P, is a subset of A whose elements can be indexed by natural numbers so that:

$$i \leq j \text{ iff } p_i \sqsubseteq p_j$$

It is easy to see that every value in a chain must include all the information introduced by all its predecessors.

Definition 7.2(xxv)

A poset is *chain complete* if and only if it has least upper bounds for all chains.
∎

We impose this as a *requirement* on all value spaces that we are prepared to admit into our theory.

Exercise 7.2(xxvi)

Check that T and N (and indeed all lifted sets) are chain complete.
∎

This exercise ensures that the simple lifted sets are admissible to the theory.

Proposition 7.2(xxvii)

If A and B are chain complete posets then:

(a) $A \times B$ is chain complete.
(b) $A \to B$ (the poset of *monotonic* functions) is chain complete.

Proof.   Let $\langle a_i, b_i \rangle_{i \geq 0}$ be a chain in $A \times B$; then

$$\bigsqcup_{i \geq 0} \langle a_i, b_i \rangle = \langle \bigsqcup_{i \geq 0} a_i, \bigsqcup_{i \geq 0} b_i \rangle$$

Let f_i, $i \geq 0$ be a chain in $A \to B$; then

$$\bigsqcup_{i \geq 0} f_i = \mathbf{g} \text{ where } \mathbf{g}\, a = \bigsqcup_{i \geq 0} (f_i\, a)$$

It is easy to see that the definition of a summary in $A \times B$ is indeed an element of $A \times B$. For the summary of a chain of monotonic functions it is necessary to show that the function $\mathbf{g}$ is monotonic, but this is straightforward.
∎

Exercise 7.2(xxviii)

Show that the disjoint union of two chain complete posets is chain complete.
∎

So providing we base our deliberations on chain complete posets we can combine them and still maintain chain completeness.

We can now return to our sequence of functions $\{\mathbf{fac}_i | i \geqslant 0\}$ which approximate the factorial function. We have already established that this is a chain, and moreover it is easy to see that the elements are all monotonic functions, so it has a least upper bound in $(N \rightarrow N)$ given by:

$$\lambda n \cdot \bigsqcup_{i \geq 0} (\mathbf{fac}_i\, n)$$

This function when given an integer argument obtains the results of $(\mathbf{fac}_i\ n)$ for all $i \geq 0$ and returns the best (most informative) result. Since there exists an m for all n (in fact any $m > n$) for which $(\mathbf{fac}_m\ n) = n!$
we see that

$$\lambda n \cdot \bigsqcup_{i \geq 0} (\mathbf{fac}_i\ n) = \mathbf{fac}$$

At this point we need to turn our attention back to functions, which we have required to be monotonic. How should our functions behave with respect to summaries?

Clearly we do not represent functions like **append** and **factorial** in extension. That is, we do not represent the graph of such functions explicitly (as an infinite lookup table or some other such impractical device). What we do is to provide a *recipe*, or method for generating the graph of the functions and we take just those bits of it that we need. The recipes are our *function definitions* and it is the evaluator or machine which *uses* them to generate portions of the graph. Most importantly, it is quite obvious that *we only ever generate a finite portion of the graph*. For example in running the program factorial with input 6 we actually only generate the information in $\mathbf{fac}_6$ which is just a finite approximation to **fac**.

In general we only manipulate finite portions of our data spaces too, for our space of lists contains the list $[1\ 1\ 1\ \ldots]$ and we can certainly write: $\mathbf{h}(\mathbf{t}(\mathbf{t}[1\ 1\ 1\ \ldots]))$ which give us the third element. Now we represent this infinite list by a recipe like:

ones $= 1 : \mathbf{ones}$

or by a recipe like:

Fig. 7.2(xxix)

but either way, during execution, we only ever produce a finite part of this list.

Exercise 7.2(xxx)

$[1\ 1\ 1\ \ldots]$ is the least upper bound of the set $A = \{(\mathbf{f}^i\bot)|i\geq 0\}$ where $\mathbf{f} = \lambda v \cdot 1 : v$.

    If we adopt a strict **cons** what happens to the least upper bound of A?
∎

This discussion is very important indeed. Our programs and program evaluations only manipulate finite approximations but the theory deals with the infinite values. We have to ensure these two enterprises are related properly. The following example captures our requirements.

Example 7.2(xxxi)

Consider the program **inclist** given as follows:

    inclist $(a:l) = (n+1):(\textbf{inclist } l)$

Consider also the list:

    ones $= [1\ 1\ 1\ \ldots]$

and the program:

    inclist ones

In practice any evaluation of this program only utilizes a finite portion of $[1\ 1\ 1\ \ldots]$ and only generates a partial result. If we set:

$$\begin{aligned}\textbf{ones}_0 &= \bot \\ \textbf{ones}_{n+1} &= 1:\textbf{ones}_n\end{aligned}$$

we can say that during any evaluation **inclist** takes $\textbf{ones}_i$ (for some finite i) to an output. Suppose that we form a set of all *practical* evaluations by setting:

    $\mathbf{R} = \{\textbf{inclist ones}_i | i \geq 0\}$

Now these are the results we can obtain in a finite time. It is easy to show that, for all i:

    $\textbf{inclist ones}_i = \textbf{twos}_i$

where:

$$\begin{aligned}\textbf{twos}_0 &= \bot \\ \textbf{twos}_{n+1} &= 2:\textbf{twos}_n\end{aligned}$$

It is also easy to see that this forms a chain and so must have a summary (least upper bound) since our spaces are chain complete. This summary is the list [2 2 2 . . .]. This value then summarizes the information that can be gleaned from all finite investigations of (**inclist ones**), that is:

inclist ones$_i$ (for all i)

What we cannot actually do is run **inclist** over the summary of $\{$**ones**$_i|i \geq 0\}$ in a finite time. However from the theoretical point of view this is exactly how we wish to view things. Is it the case that:

inclist $(\bigsqcup \{$**ones**$_i|i \geq 0\} =$ **twos**?

We know at least that our functions are monotonic and so we can certainly conclude that, for all $i \geq 0$:

(**inclist ones**$_i$) $\sqsubseteq$ (**inclist** $\bigsqcup \{$**ones**$_i|i \geq 0\})$

since **ones**$_i \sqsubseteq \bigsqcup \{$**ones**$_i|i \geq 0\}$ by the definition of least upper bound. However if this is true for all $i \geq 0$ it will certainly be true of the limit. Thus we may conclude that:

$\bigsqcup \{($**inclist ones**$_i)|i \geq 0\} \sqsubseteq$ (**inclist** $\bigsqcup \{$**ones**$_i|i \geq 0\})$

but the left-hand side we already saw is just **twos**. If all we can say is that **inclist** is *monotonic* then it is possible that the mathematical model of **inclist** takes **ones** to a list containing **more** information than that which we can discover by finite computations. This seems wrong, we would like absolute agreement between theory and practice.

■

In order to force this through we have to impose a stronger condition on the kinds of functions we allow in the space $(A \rightarrow B)$ (A and B are, as usual, chain complete posets).

Continuity condition

If A and B are chain complete posets then the space $(A \rightarrow B)$ is the chain complete poset (we will discover) of chain continuous functions from A to B. This means that if:

f $\in (A \rightarrow B)$ and
$\{a_i|i \geq 0\}$ is a chain in A

then we have:

(**f** $\bigsqcup \{a_i|i \geq 0\}) = \bigsqcup \{($**f** $a_i)|i \geq 0\}$

Note that the two least upper bounds (the first in A and the second in B) both exist. We will often simply say *continuous* for chain continuous.

This really is a stronger condition than monotonicity because monotonicity follows from continuity as we now show.

Proposition 7.2(xxxii)

Let $f \in (A \to B)$ be a chain continuous function between chain complete posets A and B. f is monotonic.

Proof. Let a and a' be values in A such that $a \sqsubseteq a'$. $a \sqsubseteq a'$ iff $a \sqcup a' = a'$ iff (since f is a function) $(f(a \sqcup a')) = (f a')$ iff (f is continuous) $(f a) \sqcup (f a') = (f a')$ iff $(f a) \sqsubseteq (f a')$. Hence f is monotonic. ∎

Before we go on we must return to proposition 7.2(xxvii). Not only do we need to know that $(A \to B)$ (the data type of chain continuous functions) is chain complete but we also need to know that all the primitive operations on our data spaces (projections on products, injections on sums, application and abstraction for function spaces) are continuous functions.

Proposition 7.2(xxxiii)

Let A_1 and A_2 be chain complete posets with typical values, a_1 and a_2, respectively.
(a) $A_1 \times A_2$ is chain complete.
(b) $\text{proj}_i \in A_1 \times A_2 \to A_i$
    $\text{proj}_i \langle a_1, a_2 \rangle = a_i$
    are continuous, for $i \in \{1, 2\}$.
(c) $A_1 + A_2$ is chain complete.
(d) $\text{inj}_i \in A_i \to A_1 + A_2$
    $\text{inj}_i\, a_i = \langle i, a_i \rangle$
    are continuous, for $i \in \{1, 2\}$.
(e) $A_1 \to A_2$ is chain complete.
(f) Application and abstraction are continuous operations.

Proof. (a) and (c) have already been established in proposition 7.2(xxvii) and exercise 7.2(xxviii). The construction of the limit of sequence of chain continuous functions is identical to that given in proposition 7.2(xxvii) except that we need to check that the function **g**, defined there, is a chain continuous function. The continuity of the primitive operations are routine calculations. ∎

We can now return to our example concerning the factorial function and look at it in a slightly different way. From this we will discover a general result.

Recall that $\mathbf{fac} = (\mathbf{h}\,(\mathbf{fac}))$ where:

$$\mathbf{h} = \lambda f \cdot \lambda n \cdot \mathbf{if}\,(\mathbf{eq}\,n\,0)\,1\,((f\,n-1)*n)$$

Now $\mathbf{h} \in (N \to N) \to (N \to N)$ since abstraction is continuous. Let us for the time being write $\bot$ for $\bot_{N \to N}$. Observe that $(\mathbf{h}\,\bot)$ is a function in the space $(N \to N)$ which yields 1 for input 0 but is undefined otherwise. Now $(\mathbf{h}^2\,\bot) = (\mathbf{h}\,(\mathbf{h}\,\bot))$ yields 1 for input 0, 1 for input 1 and is undefined otherwise.

Generalizing, it is easy to see that:

$\mathbf{h}^n(\bot) = \mathbf{fac}_n$ so from our previous result we have:

$$\mathbf{fac} = \bigsqcup_{i \geq 0} \mathbf{h}^i(\bot)$$

Now we can check that $\mathbf{fac}$ is a fixpoint of $\mathbf{h}$.

$(\mathbf{h}\,\mathbf{fac}) = (\mathbf{h}(\bigsqcup \mathbf{h}^n(\bot))) = $ (by the continuity condition)
$\bigsqcup(\mathbf{h}^{n+1}\,\bot) = \bigsqcup(\mathbf{h}^n\,\bot) = \mathbf{fac}$ as required.

This leads to the following general result.

Proposition 7.2(xxxiv)

Let $\mathbf{fix} = \lambda f \cdot \bigsqcup (f^n\,\bot)$. $\mathbf{fix}\,g$ is the *least fixpoint* of g.

Proof. To see that $\mathbf{fix}\,g$ is a fixpoint we repeat the argument above:

$g(\mathbf{fix}\,g) \quad =$
$g(\bigsqcup g^n\,\bot) = $ (by continuity)
$\bigsqcup(g^{n+1}\,\bot) =$
$\bigsqcup(g^n\,\bot) \quad =$
$\mathbf{fix}\,g$

To see that $\mathbf{fix}\,g$ is the least fixpoint we will suppose that d is another fixpoint of g. Then since $\bot \sqsubseteq d$ by definition of $\bot$ and since g is monotonic we have $(g\,\bot) \sqsubseteq (g\,d)$. But d is a fixpoint so this is just $(g\,\bot) \sqsubseteq d$. By monotonicity again we obtain $g^2(\bot) \sqsubseteq d$ and this we may repeat for all n to yield $(\forall n \geq 0)((g^n\,\bot) \sqsubseteq d)$. Hence, by the definition of least upper bound, we get $\bigsqcup (g^n\,\bot) \sqsubseteq d$. Now $\bigsqcup (g^n\,\bot)$ is a fixpoint of g and it is weaker than any fixpoint d. Thus we conclude that $\mathbf{fix}$ generates the least fixpoint.
■

The semantic construction of least fixpoints gives rise to a useful induction principle.

Fixpoint induction

Let D be a chain complete poset. Let $f \in (D \to D)$. Suppose we wish to show that $P(\textbf{fix } f)$ holds for some property P. We need to show that:
(a) $P(\perp)$ holds.
(b) $P(fd)$ holds assuming that $P(d)$ holds.

We need to be very careful, however, because this principle does not work for arbitrary properties P. To see this let us suppose that a property P satisfies the two criteria above. It is easy to see (by numerical induction) that (for all $n \in N)(P(f^n \perp))$ holds. From this we need to be able to conclude that $P(\textbf{fix } f)$, that is, $P(\bigsqcup (f^n \perp))$ holds. We need P to satisfy the following:

$$(\text{for all } d \in A \subseteq D)(P(d)) \Rightarrow P(\textstyle\bigsqcup A) \text{ (where } A \text{ is a chain)}$$

If we arrange our domain of truth values a little differently it is easier to state the condition on P.

Fig. 7.2(xxxv)

It is rather easy to see that *conjunction of truth values* in this ordered set is the *join* operation. This generalizes nicely so that universal quantification ("for all") corresponds to the operator $\bigsqcup$. Moreover, if a and a' are taken from this set then: $a \Rightarrow a'$ (implication) if and only if $a \sqsupseteq a'$.

If we now re-express our requirement for P it becomes:

$$\textstyle\bigsqcup \{P(a) | a \sqsubseteq A \subseteq D\} \sqsupseteq P(\textstyle\bigsqcup A) \text{ (}A \text{ is a chain)}$$

Such a property is called *inclusive*. Note that the inclusive properties include all the continuous ones since a continuous property satisfies:

$$\textstyle\bigsqcup \{P(a) | a \in A \subseteq D\} = P(\textstyle\bigsqcup A) \quad (A \text{ is a chain)}$$

Some classes of properties which are acceptable are easily characterized. In particular *all properties which assert the equality (or even inequality) of chain continuous functions are acceptable.*

An argument like this justifies the partial object induction techniques which we introduced in Chapter 3. However there are one or two steps further we need to take before showing this.

Definition 7.2(xxxvi)

Let D be a data type. $e \in D$ is a *finite* element of D if and only if, whenever $e \sqsubseteq \bigsqcup d_n$ for some chain in D we have $e \sqsubseteq d_i$ for some $i \geq 0$.
∎

This classifies the elements formally whereas, before, we simply discussed at an informal level the distinction between finite and infinite elements.

In lazy induction we show, by a standard structural induction, that a property holds for all finite elements. Providing that the property is an acceptable one [that is, it is an inclusive mapping into the space of truth values shown in Fig. 7.2(xxxv)] we may conclude that the property holds for all limits of finite elements. There is, however, one more step. We claimed that P holds for *all* elements of the data type. How do we know that all infinite elements are limits of chains of finite elements? When data types are generated *inductively* this is so. Such spaces satisfy the following criterion:

Definition 7.2(xxxvii)

Let D be a chain complete poset. D is *chain inductive* if and only if whenever $d \in D$; $d = \bigsqcup e_n$ for some chain of finite elements e_i. Furthermore there are countable finite elements in D.
∎

The cardinality restriction in this definition is important. We will wish to infer properties of infinite elements from their finite constituents. Therefore we will wish to undertake induction proofs over the set of finite elements. This presupposes that the set can be well ordered. No one has ever *constructed* a well ordering for an *uncountable* set so the countability requirement is crucial.

It is necessary to show that all our data type constructors preserve chain inductivity if we wish to impose the requirement that our data types be inductive. It is *not* possible to do this, however, for the function space constructor without imposing further constraints on our data types:

Definition 7.2(xxxviii)

A poset, P, is *bounded complete* if and only if every consistent pair of elements of P has a least upper bound.
∎

A pair of elements, p, p' are consistent providing there is a third, q, so that, $p \sqsubseteq q$ and $p' \sqsubseteq q$; that is, q is an upper bound of p and p'. The requirement that data types be bounded complete is quite intuitive and appealing for it suggests that every pair of values which do not contradict one another (are bounded above) can be extended to an element which contains (just) the information they assert.

We can take bounded completeness as a requirement on our data types. It is easy to see that lifted sets are bounded complete and this suggests:

Exercise 7.2(xxxix)

Let A and B be bounded complete posets. Show that:
(a) $A \times B$ is bounded complete.
(b) $A + B$ is bounded complete.
(c) $A \to B$ is bounded complete.
■

Given bounded complete spaces it can be shown that the function space constructor, along with the other data type constructors, preserves chain inductivity. Under this interpretation our theory requires data types to be bounded complete, chain inductive, chain complete partially ordered sets.

We can now justify the principles of lazy (partial object) induction which we introduced in Section 3.11.2.

Proposition 7.2(xxxx)

The principle of partial object induction is sound. That is:

Let D be a chain complete, chain inductive poset. Let P be an inclusive property. $P(d)$ holds for all elements d of D providing that we can show that, for all finite elements e of D, $P(e)$ holds on the assumption that $P(e')$ holds whenever $e' \sqsubseteq e$.

Proof. If $P(e)$ holds for all finite e of D assuming that $P(e')$ holds whenever $e' \sqsubseteq e$ then $P(e)$ holds for all finite $e \in D$ by structural induction (since the set of finite elements form a well-founded set). Now $P(\bigsqcup e_n)$ holds for all chains of finite elements because P is an inclusive property. However all d of D can be expressed as the limit of a chain of finite elements because D is chain inductive. Hence $P(d)$ holds for all d in D.
■

7.3 Solving data type equations

7.3.1 Inverse limit constructions

In the previous section we explained how data types can be combined to form products, sums and function spaces. We do however need more than this. Many data types are described *equationally*, that is, by recursion, and so we need to find ways of solving such recursion equations as chain complete partial orders. Naturally we want this construction to preserve the property of chain completeness.

In the Appendix we describe an elementary way for solving simple set equations. We remark there that these are simple in two respects. Firstly, only equations involving cartesian product and sums can be handled. The function space construction cannot be utilized. Secondly, the solutions are sets of *finite* elements. We do not obtain either partial elements or infinite elements by this process. Although we do not show this, it *is* possible to obtain solutions of simple equations, in which infinite elements lie, by means of a technique called the *ideal completion*, but this is, for various reasons, not altogether satisfactory.

The method we outline now not only provides richer solutions to those equations we have already considered, but is also capable of solving equations involving the function space constructor. The secret of the success of this method is essentially the restriction to continuous functions which we argued was necessary in the last section. This solves the cardinality problem we first raised in Chapter 2. The problem is that the lambda calculus, by making no type distinction between functions and values, requires a model V for which the function space $V \to V$ is a subspace. But if V contains more than one element then $V \to V$ is always strictly larger (more exactly has strictly larger *cardinality*) than V. It turns out that by restricting $V \to V$ to the *continuous* functions this cardinality problem is solved. There is, however, more to the story than just this.

The technique we describe is due to Scott. Many of his papers, and those of others who have worked on these models are given in the Bibliographic notes at the end of the chapter.

As an example we will outline a solution to the equation:

$$S = A + S \times S$$

in such a way that the solution is a bounded complete, chain inductive, chain complete, partially ordered set. For convenience we will call such spaces *domains*.

The aim of this section is to describe the main elements of the construction and to give the major results. There are a number of propositions whose proofs we omit and some of the detailed but standard technical steps are glossed over. Again, the full details are available in the literature discussed at the end of the chapter.

Example 7.3.1(i)

We find a solution of $S = A + S \times S$ by means of the *inverse limit process*.

We shall suppose that A is a lifted set of atoms. We define for all $n \geq 0$;

$$
\begin{aligned}
S_0 &= A \\
S_{n+1} &= A + S_n \times S_n
\end{aligned}
$$

Note that as A is a partially ordered set the operations $+$ and $\times$ here are those described in the previous section. In view of proposition 7.2(xxxiii) and the comments following exercise 7.2(xxxiv) we can conclude that S_n is a domain for all $n \geq 0$. In the simpler construction described in Appendix A we note that $S_n \subseteq S_{n+1}$ for all n and we take the union of all the S_n to form S_∞. It is clear that the relation between S_n and S_{n+1} is more complex because they are more than just sets. To capture the idea that S_n is in some sense *contained* in S_{n+1} we need to specify an injective map which embeds S_n in S_{n+1}. Furthermore to capture the idea that S_n is a *poorer* version of S_{n+1} we specify a projection from S_{n+1} to S_n which given an element of S_{n+1} gives us the best approximation to it in S_n. These pairs of mappings, which we will now spell out, capture the appropriate relationship between successive data types in the hierarchy.

Definition 7.3.1(ii)

We define:

$$
\begin{aligned}
\phi_0 &\in S_0 \to S_1 \\
\phi_0 &= \lambda a \cdot a
\end{aligned}
$$

In other words ϕ_0 takes every atom to itself in the larger set S_1.

$$
\begin{aligned}
\psi_0 &\in S_1 \to S_0 \\
\psi_0\, a &= a \\
\psi_0 \langle a, a' \rangle &= \bot
\end{aligned}
$$

In other words ψ_0 takes every atom in S_1 to itself in S_0. S_0 is however not rich enough to represent pairs of atoms; so ψ_0 takes each such pair to $\bot$.

∎

Fact 7.3.1(iii)

Let I_0 and I_1 be respectively the identity functions of S_0 and S_1. We have:

$$\psi_0 \circ \phi_0 = I_0$$
$$\phi_0 \circ \psi_0 \sqsubseteq I_1$$

∎

Definition 7.3.1(iv)

It is possible to extend these functions to others in the hierarchy by setting:

$$\phi_n \in S_n \quad \to S_{n+1}$$
$$\phi_n a \quad = a$$
$$\phi_n \langle s, s' \rangle = \langle \phi_{n-1} s, \phi_{n-1} s' \rangle$$

$$\psi_n \in S_{n+1} \to S_n$$
$$\psi_n a \quad = a$$
$$\psi_n \langle s, s' \rangle = \langle \psi_{n-1} s, \psi_{n-1} s' \rangle$$

∎

Proposition 7.3.1(v)

$$\psi_n \circ \phi_n = I_n$$
$$\phi_n \circ \psi_n \sqsubseteq I_{n+1}$$

Proof. By induction.
∎

If we were able (somehow) to take just the *union* of all the S_n we would clearly not produce a chain complete poset. For example, consider the set $\{(\textbf{adda}^n \perp) \mid n \geq 0\}$ where $\textbf{adda}\, x = \text{``}A\text{''} : x$. Each element is in S_n for some S_n (and all S_m with $m > n$ by virtue of the injections ϕ_n and so on). However the infinite sequence this set tends to is in no S_n and so would not lie in their union. A more sophisticated approach is required. First we set up the following mappings:

Definition 7.3.1(vi)

$$\phi_{mn} = \phi_{n-1} \circ \ldots \circ \phi_m \qquad \text{when } m < n$$
$$\phi_{mn} = I_n \qquad\qquad\qquad\ \text{when } m = n$$
$$\phi_{mn} = \psi_{n+1} \circ \ldots \circ \psi_m \qquad \text{when } m > n$$

∎

These maps allow us to move between any pair of levels in the hierarchy with ease.

Definition 7.3.1(vii)

Define $S_\infty = \{\langle s_n \rangle_{n \in N} | s_n \in S_n, \ (\psi_n s_{n+1}) = s_n\}$

This is the so-called *inverse limit* of the domains S_n. Elements of S_∞ are infinite sequences of values, one from each S_n, in such a way that the nth value of such a sequence is the result of applying ψ_n to the $(n+1)$th value.

But this only defines the set of values. S_∞ also has an ordering on its elements. Let $\langle s_n \rangle_{n \in N}$ and $\langle s'_n \rangle_{n \in N}$ be elements of S_∞. We define:

$$\langle s_n \rangle_{n \in N} \sqsubseteq \langle s' \rangle_{n \in N} \text{ iff } (\forall n \in N)(s_n \sqsubseteq s'_n)$$

■

How do we form summaries of information in S_∞?

Fact 7.3.1(viii)

Let $\langle s_{in} \rangle_{n \in N}$ be an element of S_∞ for all $i \geq 0$.

$$\bigsqcup_{i \geq 0} \langle s_{in} \rangle_{n \in N} = \langle \bigsqcup_{i \geq 0} s_{in} \rangle_{n \in N}$$

In other words the least upper bounds are formed *componentwise*.

■

Actually this is not obvious. How do we know that the sequence $\langle \bigsqcup s_{in} \rangle_{n \in N}$ is in fact an element of S_∞? This follows from properties of ψ_n which we will not dwell on here. So we see that S_∞ is chain complete when all the S_n are.

If we return to example set $\{(\mathbf{adda}^n \perp) | n \geq 0\}$ we see that, for all n, $\psi_n (\mathbf{adda}^n \perp) = \mathbf{adda}^{n-1} \perp$ and of course: $\mathbf{adda}^n \perp \in S_n$ for all n. Therefore $\langle \mathbf{adda}^n \perp \rangle_{n \in N}$ is actually an element of S_∞. In a moment we will see that this is, in fact, the least upper bound of the set and is therefore the mathematical value which corresponds to the infinite sequence ["A" "A" "A" . . .].

S_∞ actually contains copies of all the spaces S_n. To see this we extend our mappings to include S_∞.

Definition 7.3.1(ix)

We define $\phi_{n\infty}$ and $\phi_{\infty n}$ such that

$$\phi_{\infty n} \in S_\infty \to S_n$$
$$\phi_{\infty n} \langle s_m \rangle_{m \in N} = s_n$$

$$\phi_{n\infty} \in S_n \to S_\infty$$
$$\phi_{n\infty} s_n = \langle \phi_{nm} s_n \rangle_{m \in N}$$

$\phi_{\infty n}$ just picks out the term of S_n in the element of S_∞. $\phi_{n\infty}$, given an element of S_n, uses ϕ_{nm} for all m to find the representative of this element in all of the S_m. Again we are avoiding some detailed calculation here for we need to be sure that $\langle \phi_{nm} s_n \rangle_{m \in N}$ is indeed an element of S_∞. The keen reader can check this out. [Hint: use definition 7.3.1(vi) and proposition 7.3.1(v).]

We can now construct replicas of S_n inside S_∞ for all n.

Definition 7.3.1(x)

$$S_n^\infty = \{ \phi_{n\infty} s_n \mid s_n \in S_n \}$$

■

To see that this really is a replica of S_n we need to show:

Proposition 7.3.1(xi)

(a) $\phi_{\infty n} \circ \phi_{n\infty} = I_n$
(b) $\phi_{n\infty} \circ \phi_{\infty n} = I_\infty$ (restricted to S_n^∞)
■

For convenience we will write, for any $s \in S_\infty$; $(\phi_{\infty n} s)$ simply as s_n.

Fact 7.3.1(xii)

For any $s \in S_\infty$; $s = \bigsqcup_{n \geq 0} (\phi_{n\infty} s_n)$
■

That is, every element, s, is the limit of a chain of finite constituents. Hence:

Corollary 7.3.1(xiii)

S_∞ is chain inductive.
■

Again there are some details which need to be checked out which we are passing over.

We are now in a position to show that S_∞ is a solution to the equation. If we were simply dealing with sets we would need to show that each side of the equation $S_\infty = A + S_\infty \times S_\infty$ is contained in the other. In our present development the relation between the S_n is more involved. Let us write:

$A \leq B$

if and only if we have two functions $f \in A \to B$ and $g \in B \to A$ so that:

$$g \circ f = I_A$$
$$f \circ g \sqsubseteq I_B$$

Given this we can certainly write $S_n \leq S_{n+1}$ for all n by virtue of definition 7.3.1(iv) and proposition 7.3.1(v). We will now define mappings:

$$\phi \in S_\infty \to [A + S_\infty \times S_\infty] \text{ and}$$
$$\psi \in [A + S_\infty \times S_\infty] \to S_\infty$$

so that $S_\infty \leq [A + S_\infty \times S_\infty]$. However both $\phi \circ \psi$ *and* $\psi \circ \phi$ are identity maps. Therefore the same pair establish that: $[A + S_\infty \times S_\infty] \leq S_\infty$. We can conclude that the two spaces are isomorphic.

Definition 7.3.1(xiv)

(a) $\phi : S_\infty \to A + S_\infty \times S_\infty$

$\langle a \rangle_{n \in N} = a$ when $a \in A$

$s = \bigsqcup \langle \phi_{m\infty}(\text{proj}_1 s_{m+1}), \phi_{m\infty}(\text{proj}_2 s_{m+1}) \rangle$

(b) $\psi : (A + S_\infty \times S_\infty) \to S_\infty$

$\psi_a = \langle a \rangle_{a \in N}$ when $a \in A$

$(\psi \langle s_1, s_2 \rangle)_{n+1} = \langle \phi_{n\infty} s_1, \phi_{n\infty} s_2 \rangle$ for all $n \geq 0$

Proposition 7.3.1(xv)

(a) $\phi \circ \psi = I_{[A + S_\infty \times S_\infty]}$
(b) $\psi \circ \phi = I_{S_\infty}$

∎

This example is a simple version of the inverse limit construction due to Scott who used a similar method to obtain a solution to the equation $V \cong [V \to V]$ a data type suitable for interpreting lambda expressions. Along with the space we obtain the continuous operations of functional application and functional abstraction.

Note that, as in the example we have given, the equations are solved up to isomorphism, not equality. Therefore there is an important sense in which the definition of the denotational semantics of the lambda calculus, given in Section 2.4.1, is incorrect. We need to mark the passages between the spaces V and $V \to V$.

Let $\phi \in V \to (V \to V)$ and $\psi \in (V \to V) \to V$ establish the isomorphism between V and $V \to V$. With these in mind we redefine the lambda calculus semantics as follows:

Definition 7.3.1(xvi)

$$[\ ] \in EXP \to ENV \to V$$
$$[x]\, p \quad = (p\ x)$$
$$[\lambda x \cdot E]\, p \ = (\psi\ f) \qquad \text{where } (f\, v) = [E]\, p[x \leftarrow v]$$
$$[(E\ E')]\, p \ = (\phi([E]\, p))([E']\, p)$$

■

7.3.2 Universal domains and retracts

We will now move on to a remarkable and exciting property of the theory which emerges when we consider the following questions: which other recursively defined data types can be constructed? Furthermore, is it the case that we have to embark upon an explicit inverse limit construction for every data type we require?

Thankfully, the answers to these questions are the best possible. In the first instance we can construct any mutually recursive family of domains built from the product, sum and function space constructors. The answer to the second question is a simple one: no, we do not need to construct the data types explicitly, *provided we have a sufficiently rich universe in which to find them.*

Essentially the technique is to find (or form, by an inverse limit) a *universal domain* and then to extract our desired data types from this. Although this may seem, at first sight, a rather different approach to anything we have considered so far it turns out that we use no more than the machinery already developed to see it through.

We begin by introducing a universal domain, U, which is closed under all the constructors. That is:

$$U \cong D + (U + U) + (U \times U) + (U \to U)$$

for some suitable lifted set D.

Such a domain can be constructed from the hierarchy:

$$U_0 \quad = D$$
$$U_{n+1} = D + (U_n + U_n) + (U_n \times U_n) + (U_n \to U_n)$$

by an inverse limit in much the same way that S_∞ was constructed.

Now, given U, we hope to find other domains of interest as subspaces. For example we would like to find a space $V \cong V \to V$ for the lambda calculus in U along with $S \cong A + S \times S$ (although we have already got this directly) and $L \cong \{\text{"Nil"}\} + A \times L$.

How, though, do we define these subsets of U? One natural way is to define them as the image of some suitable function from U to U. What kind of functions are suitable for this? The following proposition is helpful.

Proposition 7.3.2(i)

Let $f \in E \to E$ be a chain continuous function from a chain complete poset, E, into itself. The set of fixpoints of f is a chain complete poset.

Proof. Let $F = \{e \mid e \in E \land (fe) = e\}$. We know that the least upper bound of the empty chain exists in F by proposition 7.2(xxxiv), that is, F has a least element. Furthermore let e_i be a chain in F. Note that $\bigsqcup e_i$ exists in E since E is chain complete. We want $\bigsqcup e_i$ to exist in F. To see that this is so is a simple calculation: $(f \bigsqcup e_i) = $ (by continuity of f) $\bigsqcup (f e_i) = $ (since every e_i is a fixpoint of f) $\bigsqcup e_i$. Thus, $\bigsqcup e_i$ is a fixpoint of f and so $\bigsqcup e_i$ is an element of F as required. ∎

Definition 7.3.2(ii)

A continuous function $\mathbf{f} \in E \to E$ is a *retract* if and only if, $\mathbf{f} = \mathbf{f} \circ \mathbf{f}$. ∎

Fact 7.3.2(iii)

The image of a retract over a chain complete poset is chain complete.

Proof. If $\mathbf{f}$ is a retract then, for any $e \in E$, we have: $(\mathbf{f} \, e) = (\mathbf{f}(\mathbf{f} \, e))$. That is, $(\mathbf{f} \, e)$ is a fixpoint of $\mathbf{f}$. Conversely, it is easy to see that *every* fixpoint of $\mathbf{f}$ lies in the image of $\mathbf{f}$. ∎

This answers the question we posed above. Retracts are the suitable functions for picking out data types from a universal domain.

Let us define $U(\mathbf{f})$ for the data type specified by the retract $\mathbf{f}$ as follows:

$$U(\mathbf{f}) = \{u \in U \mid \exists \, u' \in U; (\mathbf{f} \, u') = u\}$$

Naturally we will want to formulate an algebra of retracts so that we can construct data types of whatever shape we please.

We will begin by considering cartesian products. An element, $u \in U$ lies in the space, $U(\mathbf{f}_1) \times U(\mathbf{f}_2)$ if $(\text{proj}_i \, u) \in U(\mathbf{f}_i)$ for $i \in \{1, 2\}$. Thus, $\mathbf{f}_i \, (\text{proj}_i \, u)$

$=(\mathrm{proj}_i\, u)$ for $i \in \{1, 2\}$. Consequently:

$$\langle(\mathbf{f}_1(\mathrm{proj}_1 u)),(\mathbf{f}_2(\mathrm{proj}_2 u))\rangle = u$$

That is, $u \in U(\mathbf{f}_1) \times U(\mathbf{f}_2)$ if u is a fixpoint of the following function:

$$\mathbf{f}_1 \times \mathbf{f}_2 = \lambda u \cdot \langle(\mathbf{f}_1(\mathrm{proj}_1 u)),(\mathbf{f}_2(\mathrm{proj}_2 u))\rangle$$

In other words we introduce a *retractional*, x, by:

$$\_\times\_ = \lambda ff' \cdot \lambda u \cdot \langle(f(\mathrm{proj}_1 u)),(f'(\mathrm{proj}_2 u))\rangle$$

Any u which satisfies the fixpoint equation above is a pair and so may be written as $\langle u_1, u_2\rangle$ for some values u_i, $i \in \{1, 2\}$. Thus we have: $\langle u_1, u_2\rangle = \langle(\mathbf{f}_1\, u_1),(\mathbf{f}_2\, u_2)\rangle$ whence: $u_i = (\mathbf{f}_i\, u_i)$ for $i \in \{1, 2\}$. This establishes an isomorphism between the spaces: $U(\mathbf{f}_1) \times U(\mathbf{f}_2)$ and $U(\mathbf{f}_1 \times \mathbf{f}_2)$. Note that $\times$ is, by proposition 7.2(xxxiii), a chain continuous function of functionality: $(U \to U) \to (U \to U) \to (U \to U)$. It also generates retracts from retracts as a simple calculation shows; this is why we call $\times$ a retractional.

We can also introduce retractionals for sums and functions by means of:

$$\_+\_ = \lambda ff' \cdot \lambda u \cdot (\mathrm{inj}_1(f(\mathrm{out}_1\, u))) \sqcup (\mathrm{inj}_2(f'(\mathrm{out}_2\, u)))$$

where the out_i are continuous functions defined as follows:

$\mathrm{out}_i \in (U + U) \to U$
$\mathrm{out}_i(u, i) = u$
$\mathrm{out}_i\, u\ \ = \bot$ **otherwise**
for $i \in \{1, 2\}$

$$\_\to\_ = \lambda ff' \cdot \lambda u \cdot f' \circ u \circ f$$

Both of these do generate retracts from retracts and are, by proposition 7.2(xxxiii) and the definition of the functions out_i, continuous functions in both arguments. Furthermore they establish the following isomorphisms:

$$U(\mathbf{f}_1) + U(\mathbf{f}_2) = U(\mathbf{f}_1 + \mathbf{f}_2)$$
$$U(\mathbf{f}_1) \to U(\mathbf{f}_2) = U(\mathbf{f}_1 \to \mathbf{f}_2)$$

Suppose we had retracts $\mathbf{f}$, $\mathbf{g}$ and $\mathbf{h}$ and we wished to form the data type:

$$(U(\mathbf{f}) \times U(\mathbf{f}) \to U(\mathbf{h})) + U(\mathbf{g})$$

This is just the data type generated by the retract:

$$(\mathbf{f} \times \mathbf{f} \to \mathbf{h}) + \mathbf{g}$$

That is:

$$U((\mathbf{f} \times \mathbf{f} \to \mathbf{h}) + \mathbf{g})$$

This (simple) example does not, however, require the formation of a *recursively* specified data type. In fact we have not yet provided a way to obtain retracts for these. Let us illustrate how this is done by trying to find a retract for the data type:

$$L = \{\text{"Nil"}\} + A \times L$$

Let "Nil" $\in D$ or at least let there be an element of D which we can use to model "Nil". Note that the function:

$$1 \in U \to U$$
$$1 \bot = \bot$$
$$1\, u = \text{"Nil"} \qquad \textbf{otherwise}$$

is a retract and in fact:

$$U(1) = \{\text{"Nil"}\}_{\bot}$$

which is the lifted set consisting of "Nil" alone. Furthermore, let us assume a retract $\mathbf{f}$ so that $U(\mathbf{f}) = A$. We need, for L, a retract $\mathbf{h}$ so that:

$$U(\mathbf{h}) = U(1) + (U(\mathbf{f}) \times U(\mathbf{h}))$$

Now this may be written:

$$U(\mathbf{h}) = U(1 + (\mathbf{f} \times \mathbf{h}))$$

In other words we require a function, $\mathbf{h}$, such that:

$$\mathbf{h} = 1 + (\mathbf{f} \times \mathbf{h})$$

Now this is just an ordinary recursive definition of a function and we should like to solve this by the method of fixpoints as we usually do. In order for this to work we first require some assurances.

Firstly, since all the retracts and retractionals are continuous we see that the abstract:

$$\mathbf{H} = \lambda g \cdot 1 + (\mathbf{f} \times g)$$

is a continuous function [of functionality $(U \to U) \to (U \to U)$] by proposition 7.2(xxxiii). This means that the function:

$$\textbf{fix } H$$

exists in $U \rightarrow U$. But we require more than this; **fix** H has to be a retract and not just any function in $U \rightarrow U$ will do. How do we show that it is?

Note that retracts are themselves specified by a recursive equation:

f is a retract iff **f** $\circ$ **f** = **f**

Consequently, the retracts are the fixpoints of the abstract:

$\lambda f \cdot f \circ f$

Now proposition 7.3.2(i) tells us that the fixpoints of a chain continuous function form a chain complete poset. Thus the retracts form a chain complete poset. This is enough to ensure that (**fix** H) is a retract.

It is quite an incredible feature of the theory that we can use the same techniques for finding recursive solutions to data type equations as we do for recursive function definitions.

Exercise 7.3.2(iv)

Show how mutually recursive families of data type equations can be solved using retracts.

∎

7.4 Bibliographic notes

The first model of the lambda calculus was discovered by Scott in 1969. This model, the so called D_∞ model, is described in Scott (1973) and investigated by Wadsworth (1976). More recently Scott has reworked his basis for a mathematical theory of computation (1970) introducing 'neighbourhood systems' as reported by Stoy (1982) and 'information systems' in Scott (1982). Other models and indeed a characterization of models can be found in Barendregt (1984).

The motivation for the theory of domains came via the lambda calculus from Strachey's investigation of semantics for programming languages. From our perspective this was an attempt to translate arbitrary programming into a more or less stable functional language which had a precise semantics in the theory of domains. We will use some of the elementary techniques in the next chapter.

Tennent's book (1981) does not use semantics explicitly for the most part but is clearly motivated from this perspective. His tutorial paper (1976) is a good place to begin a study of this topic. Gordon's book (1979) is devoted to the techniques of denotational semantics without too much of the underlying mathematics. Stoy's book (1977) is comprehensive and discusses the $P(\omega)$ model of the lambda calculus too. He discusses techniques for relating semantic definitions which we mentioned in passing but did not describe in any detail although our example in the next chapter raises these issues again. Most comprehensive, although not for the faint-hearted (there are no words for the first 168 pages!), is the two-volume work of Milne & Strachey (1976).

Barendregt, H. P. (1984) *The Lambda Calculus: its Syntax and Semantics, Studies in Logic,* Vol. 103. North-Holland, Amsterdam.

Gordon, M. (1979) *The Denotational Description of Programming Languages, an Introduction.* Springer, New York.

Milne, R. E. & Strachey, C. (1976) *A Theory of Programming Language Semantics,* 2 vols. Chapman and Hall, London/Wiley, New York.

Scott, D. S. (1970) Outline of a mathematical theory of computation. *Proc. 4th Princeton Conference on Information Sciences and Systems,* Princeton University.

Scott, D. S. (1971) The lattice of flow diagrams. *Proc. Symposium on the Semantics of Algorithmic Languages.* Springer, Berlin.

Scott, D. S. (1973) Lattice-theoretic models for various type-free calculi. *Logic, Methodology and Philosophy of Science,* Vol. IV. North-Holland, Amsterdam.

Scott, D. S. (1976) Data types as lattices. *Proc. Colloquium in Mathematical Logic.* Springer, Berlin.

Scott, D. S. (1982) Domains for denotational semantics. *Proc. 9th Colloquium on Automata, Languages and Programming, LNCS,* Vol. 140, pp. 577–613. Springer, Berlin.

Stoy, J. E. (1977) *Denotational Semantics: The Scott–Strachey approach to programming language theory,* MIT Press, Cambridge, Mass.

Stoy, J. (1982) Some mathematical aspects of functional programming. In *Functional Programming and its Applications.* J. Darlington, P. Henderson & D. A. Turner (eds), pp. 217–252. Cambridge University Press, Cambridge.

Strachey, C. & Wadsworth, C. P. (1974) Continuations, a mathematical semantics for handling full jumps. *Technical monograph no. PRG-11,* Programming Research Group, University of Oxford.

Tennent, R. D. (1976) The denotational semantics of programming languages. *Commun. ACM,* **19,** 437–53.

Tennent, R. D. (1981) *Principles of Programming Languages.* Prentice-Hall, N. J. Englewood Cliffs.

Wadsworth, C. P. (1976) The relation between computational and denotational properties for Scott's models of the lambda calculus. *SIAM J. Computing,* **5,** 488–521.

Chapter 8

Compiler derivation – a worked example in functional programming

In this final chapter we will undertake a substantial exercise in program development by deriving a correct compiler for an induced architecture for a *small imperative language* (SIL).

The techniques we will require for this are those developed in the previous chapters of the book and range from issues of type, programming techniques, transformations (including our favourite – continuations), verification and also the order theoretic semantics of the last chapter.

The style of this example proceeds in the spirit of that developed by Wand in, for example, (1982a, 1982b).

We have chosen an imperative language for several reasons. Firstly, it allows us to illustrate some of the techniques from the world of denotational semantics, in particular, ways of explaining imperative notions in functional terms. Secondly, it highlights the benefits of modelling relatively unfriendly domains of discourse (imperative languages) in a way which allows pleasing algebraic properties to emerge and be exploited. Indeed we will see that the model of SIL can be expressed in a way which is extremely attractive and which allows us to obtain an induced architecture and a compiler.

8.1 The language SIL and its description

8.1.1 Syntax

The syntax of SIL is based on three *syntactic domains* called *CMD*, *EXP* and *DEC*. These stand for *commands*, *expressions* and *declarations*. We give a description of these sets in BNF notation.

Assume a set *VAR* of *variables* and *NUM* of *numbers*.

$c \in CMD, d \in DEC, e \in EXP, i \in VAR, n \in NUM$
$c ::= `i := e' | `c ; c' | `begin \ d ; c \ end'$
$e ::= `n' | `i' | `e + e'$
$d ::= `var \ i' | `d ; d'$

Commands include assignment statements, sequencing and blocks. Expressions are built from variables and constants by addition. Declarations are sequences of variable introductions.

We will define the syntax of SIL in our language of types.

$$VAR = C$$
$$NUM = N$$
$$CMD = VAR \times EXP + CMD \times CMD + DEC \times CMD$$
$$EXP = NUM + VAR + EXP \times EXP$$
$$DEC = VAR + DEC \times DEC$$

We will use the data constructor, $\_;\_$ for the $CMD \times CMD$ and $DEC \times DEC$ product spaces; begin $\_;\_$ end, for the $DEC \times CMD$ space; $\_:=\_$, for the $VAR \times EXP$ space; $\_+\_$, for the $EXP \times EXP$ space and var$\_$ for the VAR space (in DEC). Variables are just symbolic atoms and NUM is, as expected, just N.

By these definitions elements of CMD (and so on) are *parse trees*.

8.1.2 Direct semantics

We now describe the programs of this language by introducing certain functions which map the syntactic entities into certain other types: the *semantic domains*.

The language SIL has assignable variables and so we need to introduce a type called S, for *store*, which represents the assignable locations and the values which they hold. The syntax suggests that the store holds numbers so we will define the type S as follows:

$$S = \text{List}\,(LOC \times N)$$

where LOC is some type of *locations*. An element, s, of this type is an association of locations to numbers. For simplicity of presentation we will write $(s\ l)$ for the number associated with l in s. We will also need a way to update a store at a certain location. We postulate a (mix-fix) function:

$$\_[\_\leftarrow\_] \text{ of type: } S \to LOC \to N \to S$$

Exercise 8.1.2(i)

$s\,[l \leftarrow n]$ behaves like the store s except that the contents of location l is n. Define this function.

■

A command (for instance an assignment statement) changes the store so it seems at first sight that we should define a type for the interpretation of commands to be:

$$CM = S \rightarrow S$$

That is, the meaning of a command is a store transformation. This is not quite correct because variables occurring in a command need to be linked to the locations in the store which they denote. Note that, since SIL is block structured, there may be several versions of a variable (in different blocks) each denoting a distinct location. We introduce a type called *ENV*, of *environments*, which associate variables to their current location:

$$ENV = \text{List}(VAR \times LOC)$$

An environment, p, is an association of variables to locations. We also need a (mix-fix) function of type $ENV \rightarrow VAR \rightarrow LOC \rightarrow ENV$ in order to extend environments. Again, for simplicity, we access the location associated with the variable i in the environment p by writing $(p\ i)$.

Exercise 8.1.2(ii)

Can you define an operator: $\_[\_ \leftarrow \_]$ of type:

$$(\forall \alpha,\ \beta)(\text{List}(\alpha \times \beta) \rightarrow \alpha \rightarrow \beta \rightarrow \text{List}(\alpha \times \beta))$$

which can be used for updating stores *and* extending environments?
∎

Since commands contain variables they will need the information which the environment provides; consequently we will redefine the meaning of commands to be:

$$CM = ENV \rightarrow S \rightarrow S$$

Expressions correspond to numbers which might suggest that the type, *EM*, of expression meanings should be:

$$EM = N$$

However, expressions also contain variables and these correspond to locations. Moreover each location has a content. This information is provided by the environment and the store. Consequently we are led to define:

$$EM = ENV \rightarrow S \rightarrow N$$

Declarations introduce new variables in a block. A declaration, then, must obtain a fresh location, and record the association of this to the new variable. This suggests that the type DM, of declaration meanings should be a way of altering environments:

$$DM = ENV \to ENV$$

There is, however, one subtlety we overlooked. We will need to record, somehow, the fact that the fresh location is now active so that it is not used again for the next variable to be declared. This should be done in the store and suggests that declarations alter stores as well as environments:

$$DM = ENV \to S \to ENV \times S$$

We will use a colon for a data constructor for this product. We need now to return to the store itself to allow for the mechanics of the declarations:

$$S = \text{List}(LOC \times (N + \text{"unactivated"}))$$

We postulate a function **new** of type $S \to LOC$ which returns the first unactivated location. Moreover, we postulate **activate** of type $LOC \to S \to S$, which replaces the unactivated message with zero.

Exercise 8.1.2(iii)

Define **new** and **activate**.
∎

With all these types at our disposal we can now define the interpretation of SIL by introducing some *semantic functions*:

$$\begin{aligned}
&\textbf{cmd} \in CMD \to CM \\
&\textbf{exp} \in EXP \to EM \\
&\textbf{dec} \in DEC \to DM
\end{aligned}$$

We begin with commands:

$$\textbf{cmd}(i := e)\ p\ s = s[(p\ i) \leftarrow (\textbf{exp}\ e\ p\ s)]$$

We update the store at the location denoted by i to the value of the expression e:

$$\textbf{cmd}(c; c')\ p\ s = \textbf{cmd}\ c'\ p\ (\textbf{cmd}\ c\ p\ s)$$

The meaning of a sequence of commands is to be formed by evaluating the second command in the store which results from executing the first:

$$\textbf{cmd}(\text{begin } d; c \text{ end}) p \, s = \textbf{let } p' : s' = (\textbf{dec } d \, p \, s) \textbf{ in} (\textbf{cmd } c \, p' \, s')$$

The meaning of a block is the meaning of the commands in the block evaluated in an environment and store which have been processed by the declarations:

$$\textbf{exp } n \, p \, s = n$$

The meaning of a numeral is the obvious number it denotes:

$$\textbf{exp } i \, p \, s = s(p \, i)$$

The value of a variable is found in the location to which it has become bound in the environment:

$$\textbf{exp}(e + e') p \, s = \textbf{plus}(\textbf{exp } e \, p \, s)(\textbf{exp } e' \, p \, s)$$

This is self-explanatory:

$$\textbf{dec}(\text{var } i) p \, s = (p \, [\, i \leftarrow (\textbf{new } s)]) : (\textbf{activate} \, (\text{new } s) \, s)$$

The resulting environment binds the new location to i. The new location has been activated in the store:

$$\textbf{dec}(d; d') p \, s = \textbf{let } p' : s' = (\textbf{dec } d \, p \, s) \textbf{ in} (\textbf{dec } d' \, p' \, s')$$

A sequence of declarations is executed from left to right.

This completes the semantic description of SIL. We can view what we have in two ways. The most obvious is that we have specified an interpreter for SIL in a functional programming language. The second viewpoint is more sophisticated: if we treat the functional language as simply a meta-language for specifying values in the types, and if we view the types as *domains* in the sense of the previous chapter, then we can view what we have as a mathematical semantics of SIL. That is, a description of SIL within the theory of domains.

The latter viewpoint is the denotational semantics of SIL. It is mathematically specified, abstract and compositional. The former viewpoint gives us an operational semantics in which we beg the question: what is the semantics of the functional notation?

We are interested in pursuing both these perspectives in what follows for we wish to obtain an implementation of SIL which is *correct*, that is, which agrees with the denotational semantics.

8.2 Deriving a continuation semantics

In this section we will derive an equivalent continuation semantics for SIL from the one we have given above. There are a number of reasons for doing this. Firstly, we will find a continuation semantics particularly useful for obtaining a compiler. Secondly, we might wish to extend the language SIL to include other imperative features, for example, labels and jumps. As it stands these features cannot be added in a simple way and we will see that continuations help to solve this problem.

8.2.1 Continuation semantics

We learnt in the last few sections of Chapter 4 how to introduce new functions which take a continuation as an argument. Our present example is only slightly more complex for we have a family of functions given by mutual recursion whereas our previous examples were all single functions.

   This suggests a natural generalization of the eureka step which we used in Section 4.7. We define three new mutually recursive functions. These are to be continuation versions of **cmd**, **exp** and **dec**. Let us begin informally.

   We want to define functions, **Cmd**, **Exp** and **Dec** so that:

$$\textbf{Cmd } c \, p.q \, s \; = (q \circ (\textbf{cmd } c \, p)) \, s$$
$$\textbf{Exp } e \, p \, k \, s \; = (k \circ (\textbf{exp } c \, p)) \, s$$
$$\textbf{Dec } d \, p \, x \, s \; = (x \circ (\textbf{dec } d \, p)) \, s$$

where q, k and x are continuations. But what are the types of these continuations?

   Note that (**cmd** $c \, p$) has type: $S \to S$ and this is to be composed with a continuation which therefore must have S as its domain. Presumably we do not wish to change the intended co-domain for the interpretation of commands so the co-domain of continuations is also S. From this we infer the type of **Cmd**:

$$\textbf{Cmd} \in CMD \to ENV \to CCON \to S \to S$$

where:

$$CCON = S \to S$$

the domain of *command continuations*.

   Now expressions require a different kind of continuation, *ECON*, the *expression continuations*. It is easy to see that the domain of *ECON* should be N, the value of expressions. This value, along with the store, then determines the future course of the computation. This suggests:

$$\textbf{Exp} \in EXP \to ENV \to ECON \to S \to S$$

where:

$$ECON = N \rightarrow S \rightarrow S$$

Declarations produce altered environments and stores. Consequently, the domain of the type, *DCON* of *declaration continuations* should be $ENV \times S$. We shall curry this as usual and define:

$$\textbf{Dec} \in DEC \rightarrow ENV \rightarrow DCON \rightarrow S \rightarrow S$$

where:

$$DCON = ENV \rightarrow S \rightarrow S$$

This means that we have to alter the eureka step a little:

$$\textbf{Dec } d \ p \ x \ s = \textbf{let } p':s' = (\textbf{dec } d \ p \ s) \textbf{ in } x \ p' \ s'$$

Exercise 8.2.1(i)

Show that the functions **Cmd**, **Exp** and **Dec** satisfy lemma 4.7(x).
∎

Exercise 8.2.1(ii)

Under what conditions is the following true?

$$\textbf{let } x = e \textbf{ in } (\textbf{let } y = e' \textbf{ in } e'') = $$
$$\textbf{let } y = (\textbf{let } x = e \textbf{ in } e') \textbf{ in } e''$$
∎

Armed with these definitions and the exercise above we can undertake the transformation. The fold steps respect the *structural* ordering on the syntax types. Consequently the transformation is correct and amounts to a proof (by simultaneous structural induction) that the continuation semantics we derive is equivalent to the direct semantics. In such a proof the eureka definitions become the criteria used to assert equivalence.

$$\textbf{cmd } c \ p \ s = $$
$$(id \circ (\textbf{cmd } c \ p)) \ s = $$
$$\textbf{Cmd } c \ p \ id \ s$$

$$\textbf{Cmd } (i := c) \ p \ q \ s = $$
$$(q \circ (\textbf{cmd } c \ p)) \ s = $$
$$(q \circ (\lambda s \cdot s[(p \ i) \leftarrow (\textbf{exp } e \ p \ s)]))s = $$

$(q \circ ((\lambda n \cdot (\lambda s \cdot s[(p\ i) \leftarrow n]))(\mathbf{exp}\ e\ p\ s)))s =$
$(q \circ (\mathbf{Exp}\ e\ p(\lambda n \cdot \lambda s \cdot s[(p\ i) \leftarrow n])))s =$
$\mathbf{Exp}\ e\ p(\lambda n \cdot \lambda s \cdot q(s[(p\ i) \leftarrow n]))s$

$\mathbf{Cmd}\ (c\ ;\ c')\ p\ q\ s =$
$(q \circ (\mathbf{cmd}\ (c\ ;\ c')\ p))\ s =$
$q((\mathbf{cmd}\ c'\ p)(\mathbf{cmd}\ c\ p)\ s) =$
$(q \circ (\mathbf{cmd}\ c'\ p) \circ (\mathbf{cmd}\ c\ p))\ s =$
$\mathbf{Cmd}\ c\ p\ (q \circ (\mathbf{cmd}\ c'\ p))\ s =$
$\mathbf{Cmd}\ c\ p\ (\mathbf{Cmd}\ c'\ p\ q)\ s$

$\mathbf{Cmd}\ (\mathbf{begin}\ d\ ;\ c\ \mathbf{end})\ p\ q\ s =$
$(q \circ (\mathbf{cmd}\ (\mathbf{begin}\ d\ ;\ c\ \mathbf{end})\ p))\ s =$
$(q \circ (\lambda s \cdot \mathbf{let}\ p' : s' = (\mathbf{dec}\ d\ p\ s)\ \mathbf{in}\ (\mathbf{cmd}\ c\ p'\ s')))\ s =$
$(q \circ (\lambda s \cdot (\mathbf{Dec}\ d\ p\ (\mathbf{cmd}\ c)\ s)))\ s =$
$\mathbf{Dec}\ d\ p\ (q \circ (\mathbf{cmd}\ c))\ s =$
$\mathbf{Dec}\ d\ p\ (\lambda p' \cdot \mathbf{Cmd}\ c\ p'\ q)\ s$

$\mathbf{Exp}\ n\ p\ k\ s =$
$(k \circ (\mathbf{exp}\ n\ p))\ s =$
$k\ n\ s$

$\mathbf{Exp}\ i\ p\ k\ s =$
$(k \circ (\mathbf{exp}\ i\ p))\ s =$
$k\ (s\ (p\ i))\ s$

Exercise 8.2.1(iii)

Show that:

$\mathbf{Exp}\ (e + e')\ p\ k\ s = \mathbf{Exp}\ e\ p\ (\lambda n \cdot \mathbf{Exp}\ e'\ p\ (\lambda n' \cdot \mathbf{plus}\ n\ n'))$

■

$\mathbf{Dec}\ (i := e)\ p\ x\ s =$
   $\mathbf{let}\ p' : s' = (\mathbf{dec}\ (i := e)\ p\ s)\ \mathbf{in}\ x\ p'\ s' =$
$x(p\ [i \leftarrow (\mathbf{new}\ s)])(\mathbf{activate}\ (\mathbf{new}\ s)\ s)$

$\mathbf{Dec}\ (d\ ;\ d')\ p\ x\ s =$
$\mathbf{let}\ p' : s' = (\mathbf{dec}\ (d\ ;\ d')\ p\ s)\ \mathbf{in}\ x\ p'\ s' =$
$\mathbf{let}\ p' : s' = (\mathbf{let}\ p'' : s'' = (\mathbf{dec}\ d\ p\ s)\ \mathbf{in}\ (\mathbf{dec}\ d'\ p''\ s''))\ \mathbf{in}\ x\ p'\ s' =$
$\mathbf{let}\ p'' : s'' = (\mathbf{dec}\ d\ p\ s)\ \mathbf{in}\ (\mathbf{let}\ p' : s' = (\mathbf{dec}\ d'\ p''\ s'')\ \mathbf{in}\ x\ p'\ s') =$
$\mathbf{let}\ p'' : s'' = (\mathbf{dec}\ d\ p\ s)\ \mathbf{in}\ (\mathbf{Dec}\ d'\ p''\ s''\ x) =$
$\mathbf{let}\ p'' : s'' = (\mathbf{dec}\ d\ p\ s)\ \mathbf{in}\ (\lambda p' \cdot \mathbf{Dec}\ d'\ p'\ x)\ p''\ s'' =$
$\mathbf{Dec}\ d\ p\ (\lambda p' \cdot \mathbf{Dec}\ d'\ p'\ x)\ s$

Note that exercise 8.2.1(ii) is required for this final stage. Check that the conditions you discovered are satisfied in the above.

The derived semantics for SIL is summarized in Table 8.2.1(iv).

Table 8.2.1(iv)

Cmd $(i := e) \, p \, q \, s$	$= \textbf{Exp} \, e \, p \, (\lambda n \cdot \lambda s \cdot (q \, (s \, [(p \, i) \leftarrow n]))) \, s$
Cmd $(c \, ; \, c') \, p \, q \, s$	$= \textbf{Cmd} \, c \, p \, (\textbf{Cmd} \, c' \, p \, q) \, s$
Cmd $(\text{begin } d \, ; \, c \text{ end}) \, p \, q \, s$	$= \textbf{Dec} \, d \, p \, (\lambda p \cdot \textbf{Cmd} \, c \, p \, q) \, s$
Exp $n \, p \, k \, s$	$= k \, n \, s$
Exp $i \, p \, k \, s$	$= k \, (s \, (p \, i)) \, s$
Exp $(e + e') \, p \, k \, s$	$= \textbf{Exp} \, e \, p \, (\lambda n \cdot \textbf{Exp} \, e' \, p \, (\lambda n' \cdot k \, (\textbf{plus } n \, n'))) $
Dec $(\text{var } i) \, p \, x \, s$	$= x \, (p \, [i \leftarrow (\textbf{new } s)]) \, (\textbf{activate } (\textbf{new } s) \, s)$
Dec $(d \, ; \, d') \, p \, x \, s$	$= \textbf{Dec} \, d \, p \, (\lambda p' \cdot \textbf{Dec} \, d' \, p' \, x) \, s$

8.2.2 Extending the language

This section is not directly related to the main thrust of the development but has some independent interest.

Suppose we had a language, like SIL, with a formal semantics and we wished to extend the language for some reason. We would, of course, be duty bound to extend the semantics as well. It turns out that this is not always as easy as it seems because some additions to the language can have serious repercussions that affect everything else.

For example, let us contemplate adding labels and jumps to SIL by extending the syntax of commands with:

$$\textbf{CMD} ::= \, \dots \mid \text{goto } i \mid i : c$$

We model this by altering our syntactic types; we provide two new summands, VAR and $VAR \times CMD$ for this purpose and we use 'goto' and the colon as data constructors as expected.

It is not difficult to see that it is not easy to add these features to the existing direct semantics of SIL. Consider that we have somehow determined how the semantics of jumps should proceed:

$$\textbf{cmd} \, (\text{goto } i) \, p \, s = f \, i \, p \, s$$

for some function, f, of type $VAR \rightarrow ENV \rightarrow S \rightarrow S$. Now consider the following sequence of commands:

$$\text{goto } i \, ; \, i' := 6$$

The semantics of this composite command is:

cmd (goto i ; i' := 6) p s =
cmd (i := 6) p (**cmd** (goto i) p s) =
cmd (i := 6) p (f i p s)

It is clear that, whatever the function f is, we have no way of avoiding the consequences of the command which follows the jump. The semantics of sequencing is inappropriate for a language with jumps.

We need to develop a semantics for sequencing which allows sub-sequents to be *ignored*. This topic was introduced in Section 4.8 and, of course, the solution is to utilize continuations. Note that sequencing in the continuation semantics will allow sub-sequents to be ignored if required. What is the semantics of a label? Presumably the value of a label is the continuation from the labelled point. To put this into practice we alter the type, *ENV*, so that variables can denote label values too:

$$ENV = VAR \rightarrow N + CCON$$

This allows us to introduce the following naïve semantics for labels:

Cmd (i : c) p q s = **Cmd** c (p [$i \leftarrow$(**Cmd** c p q)]) q s

Note that the label is bound to a continuation which includes the labelled command.

A jump is now easily explicated. We just need to replace the current continuation with that bound to the label:

Cmd (goto i) p q s = (p i) s

Observe that q does not appear on the right-hand side of the equation. Furthermore, we assume that the programs are correctly typed; in this case that i is indeed a label (and not introduced by 'var'). The checking can be done explicitly in the equations but we shall not bother with this as the details are fairly obvious.

Let us return to our earlier program fragment and see how jumps now work:

Cmd (goto i ; i' := 6) p q s =
Cmd (goto i) p (**Cmd** (i' := 6) p q) s =
(p i) s

and the assignment command is avoided as required.

We mentioned that the semantics of labels given above is rather naïve. This is because it fails to account for jumps which occur before the label is encountered. The solution to this is to set up the labels when the block in which they appear is entered. This suggests that we introduce two new functions, **Labels** and **Conts**, which form lists of the labels and corresponding continuations which appear in a command:

$$\textbf{Labels} \in CMD \rightarrow \text{List}(VAR)$$
$$\textbf{Conts} \; \in CMD \rightarrow ENV \rightarrow CCON \rightarrow \text{List}(CCON)$$

These are defined as follows:

$$\textbf{Labels} \, (i : c) \quad = i : (\textbf{Labels} \; c)$$
$$\textbf{Labels} \, (c \, ; c') \quad = (\textbf{Labels} \; c) * (\textbf{Labels} \; c')$$
$$\textbf{Labels} \; c \qquad\quad = [\;\;]$$

$$\textbf{Conts} \, (i : c) \; p \; q \; = (\textbf{Cmd} \; c \; p \; q) : (\textbf{Conts} \; c \; p \; q)$$
$$\textbf{Conts} \, (c \, ; c') \; p \; q \; = (\textbf{Conts} \; c \; p \; (\textbf{Cmd} \; c' \; p \; q)) * (\textbf{Conts} \; c' \; p \; q)$$
$$\textbf{Conts} \; c \qquad\quad\; = [\;\;]$$

Notice that we allow commands to be labelled more than once. The only other subtlety is the second equation of **Conts** with ensures that the continuation associated with the first command in a sequence contains the contribution of the second command of the sequence.

Given these we may redefine the semantics of the block:

$$\textbf{Cmd} \, (\text{begin } d \, ; c \text{ end}) \; p \; q \; s = \textbf{Dec} \; d \; p \; (\lambda p' \cdot \textbf{Cmd} \; c \; p'' \; q) \; s$$
$$\text{where } p'' = p' \; [(\textbf{Labels} \; c) \Leftarrow (\textbf{Conts} \; c \; p'' \; q)]$$

Exercise 8.2.2(i)

Define the following mix-fix operator:

$$\_ [\_ \Leftarrow \_]$$

which is the extension of $\_[\_ \leftarrow \_]$ to lists for the second and third arguments. What is its (polymorphic) type?
■

There is an important technical trick in the new equation. Note that the environment supplied to **Conts** is p'' and that this is the function which we are trying to define. Of course there is no problem in defining p'' by recursion but it is the *reason* why it is necessary to do so which is subtle. If we replace p'' on the right-hand side of the definition of p'' by p' then the continuations associated with the labels will be based on an environment in which the labels are not bound. In such a circumstance a second jump will not be treated correctly.

Exercise 8.2.2(ii)

What would be wrong with the following definition of blocks?

> **Cmd** (begin d ; c end) p q $s =$ **Dec** d p'' $(\lambda p' \cdot$ **Cmd** c p' $q)$ s
> **where** $p'' = p[($**Labels** $c) \Leftarrow ($**Conts** c p'' $q)]$

■

In conclusion we observe that changes to the language can have semantic ramifications which prevent the simple extension to the semantics. Often the whole semantic basis has to be altered. In such a circumstance we will need to be sure that the new semantics restricted to the old language agrees with the original semantics. In the example we are pursuing this is the case as we developed the new semantics for the unextended language by a correct transformation.

8.2.3 An algebra of semantic connectives

In this section we will take the continuation semantics and formulate a collection of *semantic operators* or *combinators* which capture certain styles of combination for semantic values. Many of these combinators will be written as various kinds of arrows, some of which we have used for other purposes in the text [in particular, $\rightarrow$ (function space constructor) and $\Rightarrow$ (logical implication)]. Careful reading should prevent any confusion; the intention is always clear from the context.

Let us begin with commands. If we look at the equation for sequences:

> **Cmd** $(c$; $c')$ p q $s =$ **Cmd** c p (**Cmd** c' p $q)$ s

we can abstract the essential details of how the values (**Cmd** c) and (**Cmd** c') are to be combined by introducing the following infix operation:

> $\rightarrow = \lambda m$ $m' \cdot \lambda p$ q $s \cdot m$ p $(m'$ p $q)$ s

The equation can now be rewritten like this:

> **Cmd** $(c$; $c') = ($**Cmd** $c) \rightarrow ($**Cmd** $c')$

The reader may like to calculate the type of this operator in order to see how it is put together. The operator joins two functions which themselves manipulate continuations. We can call values like (**Cmd** c) *continuation transformers* and thus an operator like $\rightarrow$ becomes a way of combining continuation transformers. We do seem to be working at a high functional level!

A similar combination of continuation transforms appears to be at work in the universe of expressions. Consider the clause:

$$\textbf{Exp}\,(e+e')\,p\,k\,s = \textbf{Exp}\,e\,p\,(\lambda n \cdot (\textbf{Exp}\,e'\,p\,(\lambda n' \cdot (k\,(\textbf{plus}\,n\,n')))))$$

In this case the continuations require values as well as stores and it seems that the number of values expected can vary. That is, for example, the external **Exp** is not embedded in any context at all, the next most internal occurrence is embedded in an expression expecting one value, and the expression $(k\,(\textbf{plus}\,n\,n'))$ expects two (n and n'). With this in mind we introduce a family of connectives which we will write, for any n, as:

$$\Rightarrow_n = \lambda r\,r' \cdot \lambda p\,k\,v_1 \ldots v_n s \cdot r\,p\,(r'\,p\,k)\,v_1 \ldots v_n s$$

It is not difficult to see that, given these connectives we can rewrite the equation for the addition of expressions as:

$$(\textbf{Exp}\,e) \rightarrow_0 (\textbf{Exp}\,e') \rightarrow_1 \textbf{ADD}$$

where:

$$\textbf{ADD}\,k\,n\,n'\,s = k\,(\textbf{plus}\,n\,n')\,s$$

Other primitives are needed for the other clauses:

$$\textbf{Exp}\,n\,p\,k\,s = \textbf{PUSH}\,n\,k\,s$$
$$\textbf{Exp}\,i\,p\,k\,s = \textbf{LOOKUP}\,i\,p\,k\,s$$

where:

$$\textbf{PUSH}\,n\,k\,s = k\,n\,s$$
$$\textbf{LOOKUP}\,i\,p\,k\,s = k\,(s\,(p\,i))\,s$$

Declarations can be handled in a similar fashion:

$$\textbf{Dec}\,(d\,;d')\,p\,x\,s = \textbf{Dec}\,d\,p\,(\lambda p' \cdot (\textbf{Dec}\,d'\,p'\,x))s$$

suggests the connective:

$$\rightarrowtail\, = \lambda v\,v' \cdot \lambda p\,x\,s \cdot v\,p\,(\lambda p' \cdot v'\,p'\,x)\,s$$

and then the clause can be rewritten as:

$$\textbf{Dec}\,(d\,;d') = (\textbf{Dec}\,d) \rightarrowtail (\textbf{Dec}\,d')$$

Basic declarations are handled by introducing the primitive, **DECL**:

$$\textbf{Dec}\,(\text{var}\,i)\,p\,x\,s = \textbf{DECL}\,i\,p\,x\,s$$

where:

DECL i p x $s = x$ (p [i←(**new** s)]) (**activate** (**new** s) s)

In order to explicate blocks we require a further connective:

⇒ λv $m \cdot \lambda p$ q $s \cdot v$ p ($\lambda p' \cdot m$ p' q) s

allowing the clause to be written:

Cmd (begin d ; c end) = (**Dec** d) ⇒ (**Cmd** c)

Finally we have the assignment command which allows us to move from the expression to command world. We first introduce the primitives, **ASSIGN**

ASSIGN = λi n p q $s \cdot q$ (s [(p i)←n])

Then we need a connective, ⇸, defined as follows:

⇸ = λr $f \cdot \lambda p$ q $s \cdot r$ p ($\lambda n \cdot f$ n p q s)

to allow us to write:

Cmd ($i := e$) = (**Exp** e) ⇸ (**ASSIGN** i)

This completes the combinatorial rewrite of the continuation semantics of SIL.

Let us take a small program and observe the concrete form that the semantics now takes:

($i := 6$; $j := (3 + 4) + 1$) ; $i' := 2$

Strictly speaking sequencing is a binary syntactic operator and we have shown this in the fragment above. If we apply **Cmd** to this and rewrite the result as far as the primitive combinators we obtain the expression:

(((PUSH 6) ⇸ (ASSIGN i))→(((((PUSH 3)⇒(PUSH 4))⇒ADD)⇒
(PUSH 1))⇒ADD) ⇸ (ASSIGN j)))→((PUSH 2) ⇸ (ASSIGN i'))

This looks suspiciously like a sequence of machine code instructions. We must be careful because as the brackets show, this is *not* a sequence of primitives at all but a *tree*. The reader may like to draw out the expression in tree form to see this.

It may be the case that the tree can be converted to a sequence by suitable transformations. Ideally we would like the expression above to be a right linear list for then we could write it without any brackets. In that case it really would look like a sequence of instructions. In order to find out whether such transformations are viable we have to investigate the algebra of the semantic combinators we have introduced. Here for example is a useful proposition:

Proposition 8.2.3(i)

For all m, m', m''; $(m \rightarrow m') \rightarrow m'' = m \rightarrow (m' \rightarrow m'')$
∎

This is an easy manipulation of the lambda definition of $\rightarrow$. Note that this is the proof we have been waiting for since Chapter 1! There are other such associativity rules which the reader is invited to find.

In order to exploit putative associativity laws we would need to treat the semantic algebra of combinators rather differently. We would need to represent terms in the algebra as data structures. The application of an associativity law would then be realized as a transformation of the terms. Given an arbitrary term (as a tree) and sufficient associativity laws we could *rotate* the terms into a right linear list. Indeed we have seen a program which will do this (although for nodes of one type only) in Section 3.3.

We will not undertake any of the details of this because as it stands there is a serious problem: *there are not sufficient associativity laws.*

To see this, it suffices to examine a simple example. Consider the program:

> begin d ; c end ; c'

This "compiles" into the following expression in the semantic algebra:

> $(d \Rightarrow c) \rightarrow c'$

and we need a way of writing this as:

> $d ? (c ?' c')$

for some pair of connectives, ? and ?'. The obvious choices are:

> $d \Rightarrow (c \rightarrow c')$

Exercise 8.2.3(ii)

Show that, in general, the putative property:

> $(v \Rightarrow c) \rightarrow c' = v \Rightarrow (c \rightarrow c')$

fails to hold.
∎

The reader is encouraged to do this exercise and to observe why the proposition fails. Roughly this happens because the subexpression c' obtains the original environment (the one which preceeds the declarations in d) on the left-hand side and yet obtains the new environment (as altered by the declarations in d) on the right. In other words the bracketing in the semantic term is the semantic equivalent of scope control.

Is there a way around this problem? Not, it seems, directly because a connective, ?, such that:

$$(v \Rightarrow c) \rightarrow c' = v ? (c \rightarrow c')$$

would have to communicate two environments to the subexpression, $(c \rightarrow c')$. The first is the updated environment for c and the second is the original for c'. Without changing the nature of the semantics it does look bleak.

8.3 Adding further structure

The clue is contained in the paragraph above. A little further thought will convince us that in a more complicated example with an arbitrary number of blocks we would have to pass on an arbitrary number of extra environments. Suppose we alter the semantics so that we deal at all times with a *list of environments* rather than a single one. This would give us an opportunity to introduce new combinators called **NEW** and **OLD** which respectively place new layers or remove old layers from this list. We will call these lists of environments, *ensembles*.

However, if we are about to change the semantics we might as well ask if there are any other changes which could be beneficial in making the semantics more conducive to our enterprise of deriving a compiler.

One way is to rationalize the expression connectives which take various numbers of extra values; these could be presented as a *value stack*. The second is more subtle and we will postpone it until the next section.

The new types we require are:

$$z \in STK = \text{List}(N)$$
$$y \in ENS = \text{List}(ENV)$$
$$k \in ECON' = STK \rightarrow S \rightarrow S$$

Informally, accessing an ensemble should provide the value associated with the *first* matching entry. Since an ensemble is a list of environments we proceed as follows. If the target is not in the head environment then search the tail (recursively). Informally, extending an ensemble should cause an alteration to the head environment of an ensemble. We make this precise later.

■

From our work in Chapter 4 we can see techniques for transformations with which we are familiar. The first (adding a stack) is an accumulation strategy (of sorts), and the second (moving from ENV to ENS) is a generalization strategy. We introduce the types of the new interpretation functions:

$$\textbf{Cmdd} \in CMD \rightarrow ENS \rightarrow CCON \rightarrow S \rightarrow S$$
$$\textbf{Expp} \in EXP \;\;\rightarrow ENS \rightarrow ECON' \rightarrow STK \rightarrow S \rightarrow S$$
$$\textbf{Decc} \in DEC \;\;\rightarrow ENS \rightarrow DCON \rightarrow S \rightarrow S$$

It is now possible to describe these new functions in terms of **Cmd**, **Exp** and **Dec**. These, then, are our eureka definitions:

$$\textbf{Cmdd}\; c \; y \; q \; s = \textbf{Cmd}\; c \;(\textbf{repens } y)\; q\; s$$
$$\textbf{Expp}\; e \; y \; k \; z \; s = \textbf{Exp}\; e \;(\textbf{repens } y)\; (\textbf{repecont } k\; z)\; s$$
$$\textbf{Decc}\; d \; y \; x \; s = \textbf{Dec}\; d \;(\textbf{repens } y)\; x\; s$$

We now expound the representation functions used in these definitions:

$$\textbf{repens} \in ENS \rightarrow ENV$$
$$\textbf{repens } lst = \textbf{smooth } lst$$

Recall that an element of ENS is a list of lists. We smooth this to a single environment (most recent entries dominate).

$$\textbf{repecont} \in ECONT' \rightarrow STK \rightarrow ECONT$$
$$\textbf{repecont } k\; z = \lambda n \cdot k\; (n:z)$$

The transformation is, by and large, uneventful. We provide the definitions of some combinators which are usefully introduced.

$$\textbf{ASSIGN} \in VAR \rightarrow ENS \rightarrow CCONT \rightarrow STK \rightarrow S \rightarrow S$$
$$\textbf{ASSIGN}\; i \; y \; q \; (n:z)\; s = q \;(s\; [(y\; i) \leftarrow n])$$
$$\textbf{ASSIGN}\; i \; y \; q \; z = cerror \; \textbf{otherwise}$$
for some $cerror \in CCONT$
$$\textbf{PLUS} \in ECON \rightarrow ECON$$
$$\textbf{PLUS}\; k \; n:n' \; :z = k\; ((\textbf{plus } n\; n'):z)$$
$$\textbf{PLUS}\; k \; z = kerror \; \textbf{otherwise}$$
for some $kerror \in ECON$

$\textbf{DECL} \in VAR \rightarrow ENS \rightarrow DCONT \rightarrow S \rightarrow S$ is defined to be:

$\textbf{DECL}\; i \; y \; x \; s =$
 $\textbf{let }\; y':s' = [(y\; [i \leftarrow (\textbf{new } s)])] : (\textbf{activate (new } s)\; s) \;\textbf{ in }\; x\; y'\; s'$

It is also necessary to define a function **join,** which links environments to ensembles, as follows:

> **join** p $(p' : y) = (p * p') : y$
> **join** p [ ] $= [p]$

After the transformation we obtain the new interpretation for our language SIL given in Table 8.3(i).

Table 8.3(i)

Cmdd $(i := e)$ y q $s =$ **Expp** e y **(ASSIGN** i y q) [ ] s
Cmdd $(c ; c')$ y q $s =$ **Cmdd** c y **(Cmdd** c' y q) s
Cmdd (begin d ; c end) y q $s =$ **Decc** d y $(\lambda p \cdot$ **Cmdd** c (join p ([ ]:y)) q) s

Expp n y k z $s = k$ $(n : z)$ s
Expp i y k z $s = k$ $((s$ $(y$ $i))$:z) s
Expp $(e + e')$ y k z $s =$ **Expp** e y **(Expp** e' y **(PLUS** k)) z s

Decc (var i) y x $s =$ **DECL** i y x s
Decc $(d ; d')$ y x $s =$ **Decc** d y $(\lambda p \cdot$ **Decc** d' (join p y) $(\lambda p' \cdot x$ (join p' (join p y)))))

Recall that the original motivation for making the change in the structure of the environment to ensembles was to obtain an associativity law which would allow us to rotate algebraic terms, which include blocks, into right linear form. We will not undertake this immediately because the next section, for all its complication, allows us to present the semantics in a much simpler form. It is easier to see the benefits of this section then.

8.4 Universal continuations

In this section we address another transformation of the semantics. We left this one until now because it is conceptually and technically the most demanding.

Consider, again, the clause for (say) command sequencing:

> **Cmdd** $(c ; c')$ y q $s =$ **Cmdd** c y **(Cmdd** c' y q) s

and notice how the environment (actually the ensemble of environments) appears twice; once for each subcommand. The semantics is telling us explicitly that *commands do not alter the environment.* Even blocks (which contain declarations which *do* alter the environment) *preserve* the environment; this, after all, is what we mean by *scope.* It would be advantageous to extract the environment from the continuations so that we treat the environment as a data structure, along with the stack and store, which the programs manipulate. By the results we mentioned in Section 4.9 it is then possible to implement representations of these structures which use destructive updating. Another benefit which follows from these decisions is that we *only need one connective* to piece the program together. The complications of interfacing between commands, declarations and expressions disappears.

Unfortunately the connection between the new semantics, we would introduce by factoring out the environment, and the old semantics is not *functional*. It is, in fact, *relational*. The upshot of this is that we cannot write down a functional eureka definition for the new semantic functions in terms of the old. It is a feature of higher-order systems that this occurs and so we will spend a moment describing the general situation.

Suppose we have two spaces A and B equipped with representation functions called **repA** $\in A \to A'$ and **repB** $\in B \to B'$ where A' and B' are the abstract domains corresponding to A and B. Now suppose we have also to represent *functions* over the concrete spaces by functions over the abstract spaces. We then require maps which effect this representation. Presumably, a representation function for the space $A \to B$ in the space $A' \to B'$ is somehow systematically derived from the representation functions of the component spaces. This is almost correct but notice that if we are given a function, $\mathbf{f} \in A \to B$ then its representative, (**repAB f**) which belongs to $A' \to B'$ has to translate in the reverse direction for the domain (input) of the function. That is, we need a map **repA'** $\in A' \to A$ and then we *can* provide a systematic strategy for defining the higher-order representation functions. In this example we would define:

$$\mathbf{repAB} = \lambda f \cdot \mathbf{repB} \circ f \circ \mathbf{repA'}$$

Unfortunately it is not always possible to find maps for arbitrary higher-order spaces and it is in these circumstances that we adopt the relational approach. Note that being a relation is a symmetrical property whilst being a function is certainly not. Thus it is rather rare that we can get away with defining the map, **repA'** to be **repA**$^{-1}$. If we have two relations:

$$=_A \in A \times A' \to T$$
$$=_B \in B \times B' \to T$$

then we can easily define a relation on the function spaces by:
Let $f \in A \to B$ and $f' \in A' \to B'$; we define:

$$f =_{AB} f' \text{ iff (for all } a \in A, a' \in A')(a =_A a' \Rightarrow ((f a) =_B (f' a')))$$

Now the domain T used in these definitions is the chain complete poset consisting of the elements t (true) and f (false) ordered so that $t \sqsubset f$ [we saw this in Fig. 7.2(xxxv)]. This has an important ramification: the semantic analogue of logical implication (which was used in the definition of the higher-order relation above) is the *approximation relation* (we discussed this in Section 7.2). If we treat this as a *function* over our data types then it is *not monotonic*. This is easy to see: let $x \sqsubseteq y$ and let $x \sqsubseteq x'$. If $\sqsubseteq$ is monotonic as a function then we need to be able to infer that $x' \sqsubseteq y$. This is clearly not the case for let $y \sqsubseteq y'$ then we have $x \sqsubseteq y'$ but certainly not $y' \sqsubseteq y$. This non-monotonicity has no impact on our example but it can be troublesome in many cases. We will return to this at the end of the chapter.

We now return to the new semantics, in which the environment is to be factored out. Let us begin with new semantic types:

$$u \in UCON = ENS \rightarrow STK \rightarrow S \rightarrow S$$

This is the type of *universal continuations*. Our programs will be interpreted as *transformations of universal continuations* or *TUCs* (known occasionally in the literature as the *domain of pure code*). This implies that the new interpretation functions have the following types:

$$\mathbf{CCmd} \in CMD \rightarrow UCON \rightarrow UCON$$
$$\mathbf{EExp} \in EXP \rightarrow UCON \rightarrow UCON$$
$$\mathbf{DDec} \in DEC \rightarrow UCON \rightarrow UCON$$

It should be reasonably clear why we call them *universal* continuations.

There is but one sensible way to combine these TUCs. Let $t, t' \in UCON \rightarrow UCON$:

$$\rightarrow = \lambda t\, t' \cdot \lambda u\ p\ z\ s \cdot t\ (t'\ u)\ p\ z\ s$$

We use the arrow introduced in a previous section for combining command values.

Proposition 8.4(i)

For all TUCs t, t' and t''; $(t \rightarrow t') \rightarrow t'' = t \rightarrow (t' \rightarrow t'')$
∎

The proof is a trivial exercise.

How should these new types be related to the earlier ones? This is not an easy question to answer. The relationship is not functional, in fact we introduce a number of relations for this purpose.

We begin with the relationships between TUCs and the earlier inter-pretations for commands, expressions and declarations. Recall that these were, respectively:

$$ENS \rightarrow CCON \rightarrow S \rightarrow S$$
$$ENS \rightarrow ECON \rightarrow STK \rightarrow S \rightarrow S$$
$$ENS \rightarrow DCON \rightarrow S \rightarrow S$$

As before we use the typical elements, m, r and v from these spaces, respectively.

We now wish to establish reasonable criteria for deciding when and whether we should treat a universal continuation and a command (expression) (declaration) continuation as in some sense *congruent*.

Let us begin with universal and command continuations. Two issues stand out: firstly, a command continuation is already relativized with respect to an ensemble whilst a universal continuation is not. Secondly, a universal continuation can take a stack of partial results whilst a command continu-ation does not. These observations suggest a way of comparing the two entities. We will define a three-place relation, written:

$$(\_ = = \_) \, \mathrm{mod} \, \_$$

which asserts the congruence between the two continuations *modulo an ensemble*. Let us be precise:

$$(u = = q) \, \mathrm{mod} \, y \, \mathrm{iff} \, (u \, y \, z) = q \, \mathrm{for \, all} \, z \in STK$$

Note that the relation is based on *equality* in the domain $S \rightarrow S$. In general we overload the symbol, $=$, so that it plays the role of the equality relation for arbitrary types. This is, of course, standard practice. We will, in order to avoid a multitude of different symbols, also overload the symbol, $= =$, which will stand for a relation over one of our types. As is the case for equality, it is easy to determine which relation is intended by careful inspection of the context.

We now move on to the congruence conditions for universal and expression continuations. In this case both expect a stack of partial results but an expression continuation is relativized with respect to an environment. This suggests we define:

$$(u = = k) \, \mathrm{mod} \, y \, \mathrm{iff} \, (u \, y) = k$$

Finally we have the connection between universal and declaration continu-ations. Note that a declaration continuation expects an environment and not an ensemble as an argument. This is because each block constructs just one layer of an ensemble. Thus, a declaration continuation is partially relativized to an ensemble. Furthermore, a declaration does not utilize a stack of partial results. This leads us to:

$$(u = = x) \bmod y \text{ iff } (u \, (\textbf{join} \, p \, y) \, z) = x \, p \text{ for all } p \in ENV, z \in STK$$

These relations allow us to define congruence conditions for the higher-order spaces. That is, the connections between TUCs and the various interpretations of commands, expressions and declarations.

$$(t = = m) \text{ iff (for all } y, q, u) \, ((u = = q) \bmod y \Rightarrow ((t \, u) = = (m \, y)) \bmod y)$$
$$(t = = r) \text{ iff (for all } y, k, u) \, ((u = = k) \bmod y \Rightarrow ((t \, u) = = (r \, y \, k)) \bmod y)$$
$$(t = = v) \text{ iff (for all } y, x, u) \, ((u = = x) \bmod y \Rightarrow ((t \, u) = = (v \, y \, x)) \bmod y)$$

Roughly, these are based on the idea that functions are congruent if they yield congruent results whenever they are supplied with congruent arguments.

It is now possible to provide *eureka constraints* for a new semantics based on these new domains. As in example 4.8(i) the new functions are not functionally related to the old ones. Here we simply express criteria which such new functions have to obey. It might look as though we could be faced with a large degree of freedom in specifying such functions, but in fact the guidance offered by the constraints is quite severe and almost forces us to certain canonical definitions. Here then are the constraints for the new functions, **CCmd, EExp, DDec**:

$$(\textbf{CCmd} \, c) = = (\textbf{Cmdd} \, c)$$
$$(\textbf{EExp} \, e) \ = = (\textbf{Expp} \, e)$$
$$(\textbf{DDec} \, d) \ = = (\textbf{Decc} \, d)$$

Note that these are *forced* on us by the functionalities of the six functions and the congruence relations above. We may expand these constraints to obtain a more detailed perspective as follows:

$$(u = = q) \bmod y \Rightarrow ((\textbf{CCmd} \, c \, u) = = (\textbf{Cmdd} \, c \, y \, q)) \bmod y$$
$$(u = = k) \bmod y \Rightarrow ((\textbf{EExp} \, e \, u) \ = = (\textbf{Expp} \, e \, y \, k)) \bmod y$$
$$(u = = x) \bmod y \Rightarrow ((\textbf{DDec} \, d \, u) = = (\textbf{Decc} \, d \, y \, x)) \bmod y$$

These, of course, follow from the definitions of the relations.

We now demonstrate, by considering some cases explicitly, how the transformation based on these constraints may proceed. The equivalent of the fold steps are those which make use of the constraints and indeed assume that they can be met. Providing that we are careful to fold only when the argument is lower in the well-founded ordering (this is just the syntactic structure in this example) the fold steps are correct. It is not difficult to show that folding in a more cavalier fashion destroys termination properties by an example rather like the one we used in Section 4.4.

We begin with command sequences. Let us assume values u, q and y such that $(u == q)$ mod y.

> **CCmd** $(c\,;\,c')\,u\,y\,z =$
> **Cmdd** $(c\,;\,c')\,y\,q =$
> **Cmdd** $c\,y\,(\textbf{Cmdd}\,c'\,y\,q)$ (*)

Now from the assumption we deduce (a fold step) that:

> $((\textbf{CCmd}\,c'\,u) == (\textbf{Cmdd}\,c'\,y\,q))$ mod y

But if this is the case then we can fold again to obtain:

> $((\textbf{CCmd}\,c\,(\textbf{CCmd}\,c'\,u)) == (\textbf{Cmdd}\,c\,y(\textbf{Cmdd}\,c'\,y\,q)))$ mod y

Thus expression (*) is *equal* to:

> **CCmd** $c\,(\textbf{CCmd}\,c'\,u)\,y\,z$

by the definition of the relation.

The equation we obtain is thus:

> **CCmd** $(c\,;\,c')\,u\,y\,z\,s = \textbf{CCmd}\,c\,(\textbf{CCmd}\,c'\,u)\,y\,z\,s$

It is interesting to see that, in spite of the lack of a functional connection between the old and new interpretations, we are highly constrained in the transformation.

Our second transformation step is probably the most complicated. We tackle blocks. For this we introduce two auxiliary TUC combinators called **OLD** and **NEW** which we promised in the last section. These help to make the final clause that we obtain rather elegant.

> **OLD** $\in UCON \rightarrow UCON$
> **OLD** $u\,(p{:}y)\,z\,s = u\,y\,z\,s$
>
> **NEW** $\in UCON \rightarrow UCON$
> **NEW** $u\,y\,z\,s = u\,([\ ]{:}y)\,z\,s$

Assume that we have y, q, u such that $(u == q)$ mod y.

> **CCmd** (begin $d\,;\,c$ end) $u\,y\,z\,s =$
> **Cmdd** (begin $d\,;\,c$ end) $y\,q\,s =$
> **Decc** $d\,y\,(\lambda p \cdot \textbf{Cmdd}\,c\,(\textbf{join}\,p\,([\ ]{:}y))\,q)\,s$ (*)

Now from the assumption we may deduce (fold) that:

$$(\textbf{CCmd } c \text{ (\textbf{OLD} } u)) = =(\textbf{Cmdd } c \text{ (\textbf{join} } y \text{ ([ ]:}y)) \text{ } q) \text{ mod } (\textbf{join } p \text{ ([ ]:}y))$$

This is quite subtle. Note that u and q are related modulo y so we need to arrange that the ensemble supplied to u is y and not $p' :y$ for some p'.

Now the relation above holds for any environment, p, so by the definition of the relation between declaration continuations and universal continuations we have:

$$(\textbf{CCmd } c \text{ (\textbf{OLD} } u)) = =(\lambda p \cdot \textbf{Cmdd } c \text{ (\textbf{join} } p \text{ ([ ]:}y)) \text{ } q) \text{ mod } [\text{]:}y$$

We can now fold again to obtain:

$$((\textbf{DDec } d \text{ (\textbf{CCmd} } c \text{ (\textbf{OLD} } u))) = =$$
$$(\textbf{Decc } d \text{ } y \text{ } (\lambda p \cdot \textbf{Cmdd } c \text{ (\textbf{join} } p \text{ ([ ]:}y)) \text{ } q))) \text{ mod } [\text{]:}y$$

Thus, the expression (*) is *equal* to:

$$\textbf{DDec } d \text{ (\textbf{CCmd} } c \text{ (\textbf{OLD} } u)) \text{ ([ ]:}y) \text{ } z \text{ } s =$$
$$\textbf{New } (\textbf{DDec } d \text{ (\textbf{CCmd} } c \text{ (\textbf{OLD} } u))) \text{ } y \text{ } z \text{ } s$$

The derived equation for blocks is:

$$\textbf{CCmd } (\text{begin } d \text{ ; } c \text{ end}) \text{ } u \text{ } y \text{ } z \text{ } s$$
$$= \textbf{NEW } (\textbf{DDec } d \text{ (\textbf{CCmd} } c \text{ (\textbf{OLD} } u))) \text{ } y \text{ } z \text{ } s$$

The other clauses can be derived in a similar fashion. Although we do not provide the details of any more steps we will address the question of the induced primitive combinators.

First we will develop a combinator **Plus** which is congruent to **PLUS**. **Plus** is to have type: $UCON \rightarrow UCON$. Assume we have u, k and y such that $(u = = k) \text{ mod } y$.

$$\textbf{Plus } u \text{ } y \text{ } (n : n' : z)$$
$$\textbf{PLUS } k \text{ } (n : n' : z) = \text{ (by assumption)}$$
$$\textbf{PLUS } (u \text{ } y) \text{ } (n : n' : z) =$$
$$u \text{ } y \text{ } ((n + n') : z)$$

Thus:

$$\textbf{Plus } u \text{ } y \text{ } (n : n' : z) = u \text{ } y \text{ } ((n + n') : z)$$

Now we develop a combinator **Assign** congruent to **ASSIGN**. **Assign** is to have type $VAR \rightarrow UCONT \rightarrow UCONT$. Assume that we have u, q and y such that: $(u == q) \bmod y$.

> **Assign** $i\, u\, y\, (n:z)\, s =$
> **ASSIGN** $i\, y\, q\, (n:z)\, s =$ (by assumption)
> **ASSIGN** $i\, y\, (u\, y\, z)\, (n:z)\, s =$
> $u\, y\, z\, (s\, [(y\, i) \leftarrow n])$

Thus:

> **Assign** $i\, u\, y\, (n:z)\, s = u\, y\, z\, (s\, [(y\, i) \leftarrow n])$

The reader is invited to finish the details of this transformation which includes the derivation of other primitives like **Lookup** (congruent to **LOOKUP**) and **Push** (congruent to **PUSH**).

Ultimately we derive the semantics given in Table 8.4(ii).

Table 8.4(ii)

CCmd $(i := e)\, u\, y\, z\, s$	$=$ **EExp** e (**Assign** $i\, u$) $y\, z\, s$
CCmd $(c\, ;\, c')\, u\, y\, z\, s$	$=$ **CCmd** c (**CCmd** $c'\, u$) $y\, z\, s$
CCmd (begin $d\, ;\, c$ end) $u\, y\, z\, s$	$=$ **NEW** (**DDec** d (**CCmd** c (**OLD** u))) $y\, z\, s$
EExp $n\, u\, y\, z\, s$	$=$ **Push** $n\, u\, y\, z\, s$
EExp $i\, u\, y\, z\, s$	$=$ **Lookup** $i\, u\, y\, z\, s$
EExp $(e + e')\, u\, y\, z\, s$	$=$ **EExp** e (**EExp** e'(**Plus** n)) $y\, z\, s$
DDec (var i) $u\, y\, z\, s$	$=$ **Decl** $i\, u\, y\, z\, s$
DDec $(d\, ;\, d')\, u\, y\, z\, s$	$=$ **DDec** d (**DDec** $d'\, u$) $y\, z\, s$

It is possible to write this really elegantly using the arrow combinator, $\rightarrow$, introduced earlier. We make one further simplification; if we form the syntax type:

$$STM = CMD + EXP + DEC$$

we can define a single semantic function, **T**, of type $STM \rightarrow UCON \rightarrow UCOM$ from **CCmd**, **EExp** and **DDec** in the obvious way.

Table 8.4(iii)

T $(i := e)$	$=$ (**T** e)$\rightarrow$**Assign**
T $(c\, ;\, c')$	$=$ (**T** c)$\rightarrow$(**T** c')
T (begin $d\, ;\, c$ end)	$=$ **NEW**$\rightarrow$(**T** d)$\rightarrow$(**T** c)$\rightarrow$**OLD**
T n	$=$ **Push** n
T i	$=$ **Lookup** i
T $(e + e')$	$=$ (**T** e)$\rightarrow$(**T** e')$\rightarrow$**Plus**
T (var i)	$=$ **Decl** i
T $(d\, ;\, d')$	$=$ (**T** d)$\rightarrow$(**T** d')

No bracketing has been shown for complex expressions in Table 8.4(iii) because we know that the combinator, $\rightarrow$, is associative. Moreover, any expression generated by this semantics can be expressed by a right linear tree of primitive combinators.

A program such as:

$$(i := 6 \, ; j := (3+4)+1) \, ; i' := 2$$

can be expressed in the semantics by the expression:

(Push 6)$\rightarrow$**(Assign** *i*)$\rightarrow$**(Push** 3)$\rightarrow$**(Push** 4)$\rightarrow$**Plus**$\rightarrow$
(Push 1)$\rightarrow$**Plus**$\rightarrow$**(Assign** *j*)$\rightarrow$**(Push** 2)$\rightarrow$**(Assign** *i'*)

and this is very much like a sequence of instructions. We must be careful because the semantics is still denotational and is still an interpretation of the language in the theory of domains. Moreover, it is equivalent to the direct semantics we began with.

Finally, we must discuss the relations we utilized for the transformation. We remarked earlier that they are not monotonic (when viewed as functions into **T**). This does not cause us any problem in our example but it would if our domains were recursively specified, for then the relations would become recursively specified. Our method of forming solutions to recursive equations relies on the underlying mappings being continuous (although monotonicity will do). If the relations are non-monotonic, we cannot use this technique. It then becomes an important task to show that solutions of the equations postulating the relations actually exist. The interested reader might consult Milne & Strachey (1976).

8.5 Operational semantics

If we wish to treat the expressions obtained in the previous section as instructions we need to move to operational semantics and we will need to be sure that this operational semantics agrees with the denotational.

Let us define an abstract machine and a compiler by immediate reference to the semantics we have just developed.

8.5.1 Syntax

The syntax of ML (machine language) is based on the combinators we derived in the semantics above. Let *INS* be a syntactic domain of *instructions*. We define the members of this set by means of a BNF description:

$w \in INS$

$w ::= \text{'assign } i\text{'} \mid \text{'decl } i\text{'} \mid \text{'plus'} \mid \text{'lookup } i\text{'}$
$\mid \text{'push } n\text{'} \mid \text{'new'} \mid \text{'old'} \mid \text{'}w \text{ ; } w\text{'}$

It is easy to see how, by suitable choices of data constructor, we can represent this grammar by means of a type in our language.

We can write a compiler for SIL into ML by close examination of the semantics of the previous section.

compiler $\in STM \to ML$

This will utilize a map, **c**, of the same type. We define this first:

Table 8.5.1(i)

c $(i := e)$	$= (\mathbf{c}\ e)$; assign i
c $(c ; c')$	$= (\mathbf{c}\ c)$; $(\mathbf{c}\ c')$
c (begin d ; c end)	$= \text{new}$; $(\mathbf{c}\ d)$; $(\mathbf{c}\ c)$; old
c n	$= \text{push } n$
c i	$= \text{lookup } i$
c $(e + e')$	$= (\mathbf{c}\ e)$; $(\mathbf{c}')$; plus
c (var i)	$= \text{decl } i$
c $(d ; d')$	$= (\mathbf{c}\ d)$; $(\mathbf{c}\ d')$

Now we can define **compiler**:

compiler $stm = \textbf{rotate } (\mathbf{c}\ stm)$

where **rotate** is the program we introduced in Section 3.3.

8.5.2 Semantics

We can give ML a denotational semantics very easily by interpreting every instruction as the corresponding semantic combinator (old as **OLD** and so on) and by interpreting sequencing in ML (indicated by the semicolon) as the binary connective, $\to$. We obtain immediately a *soundness* proof for the compiler by virtue of proposition 8.4(i).

We adopt a slightly different tactic. We introduce some rewrite rules. The meaning of the program is to be gleaned from the state of certain data structures when (if) the program halts.

We start by treating rotated ML programs as lists by setting:

$$MLL = \text{List}(INS)$$

actually we do not intend the compound summand of INS to be included here.

Let ENS, STK and S be the usual data structures. We specify the rewrites in Table 8.5.2(i) for the quadruples $MLL \times ENS \times STK \times S$:

Table 8.5.2(i)

$[\ ]\, y\, z\, s$	$\rightarrow s$
old:ins $(p\!:\!y)\, z\, s$	$\rightarrow$ins $y\, z\, s$
new:ins $y\, z\, s$	$\rightarrow$ins $([\ ]\!:\!y)\, z\, s$
plus:ins $y\, (n\!:\!n'\!:\!z)\, s$	$\rightarrow$ins $y\, ((n+n')\!:\!z)\, s$
(assign i):ins $y\, (n\!:\!z)\, s$	$\rightarrow$ins $y\, z\, (s\, [(y\, i)\!\leftarrow\! n])$
(lookup i):ins $y\, (n\!:\!z)\, s$	$\rightarrow$ins $y\, ((s\, (y\, i))\!:\!z)\, s$
(push n):ins $y\, z\, s$	$\rightarrow$ins $y\, (n\!:\!z)\, s$
(decl i):ins $y\, z\, s$	$\rightarrow$ins $(y\, [i\!\leftarrow\!(\textbf{new } s)])\, z\, (\textbf{activate } (\textbf{new } s)\, s)$

Now this is an operational semantics for ML and there is no immediate reason for assuming that it is equivalent to the denotational. However, there is usually a short-cut that can be employed.

This consists in showing that the rewrite rules are a simulation (a shorthand) for a normal-order reduction of the lambda terms which correspond to the denotational interpretation of ML. This involves removing all the syntactic sugaring (including numerals and arithmetic which we use) in the language used to express the denotational semantics and then checking to see that each combinator rewrite above is a sequence of normal-order reductions of the corresponding lambda terms.

This works because we are basically stealing the result that the normal-order operational semantics of lambda expressions is correct with respect to the denotational semantics of the lambda calculus.

We do, therefore, exploit both perceptions of semantics which we mentioned at the beginning of the chapter. That is, on the one hand, we have mapped the language into values in domains and, on the other hand, we have mapped the language into a meta notation (essentially our programming language but for the purposes of the correctness proof a typed lambda calculus) and the meta notation is then interpreted in domains (or by reduction rules).

Well, is the machine correct? This we leave as a final exercise!!

8.6 Bibliographic notes

Many of the ideas for semantic combinators, rotations and so on are due to Wand. His papers (1982a, 1982b) are good references.

Mosses has worked on semantic algebras with the intention that it should be possible to find some stable notation which can be reinterpreted when languages are altered. See for example (1977, 1983).

Further details of semantics directed compiler generation can be found in Schmidt (1986) and in Jones (1980).

Jones, N. D. (Ed.) (1980) *Semantics Directed Compiler Generation, LNCS*, Vol. 94. Springer, Berlin.

Milne, R. E. & Strachey, C. (1976) *A Theory of Programming Language Semantics*, 2 vols. Chapman and Hall, London/Wiley, New York.

Mosses, P. D. (1977) Making denotational semantics less concrete. *Workshop on Semantics of Programming Languages*. University of Dortmund, Technical report 41.

Mosses, P. D. (1983) Abstract semantic algebras! In *Formal Description of Programming Concepts II*. D. Bjorner (ed.), pp. 45–72. North-Holland, Amsterdam.

Schmidt, D. A. (1986) *Denotational Semantics*. Allyn and Bacon, London.

Wand, M. (1982a) Semantics directed machine architecture. *Proc. 9th ACM Symposium on POPL*, pp. 234–41.

Wand, M. (1982b) Deriving target code as a representation of continuation semantics. *Trans. Programming Languages and Systems*, **4**, 496–517.

Appendix A

Mathematical preliminaries

The purpose of this appendix is to state and develop some of the more elementary mathematics which is necessary for the material we cover in this book. Other mathematical material, including that associated with denotational semantics, has its own place in Chapter 7 and elsewhere. Here we concentrate on the elementary concepts; however, this section may be useful even to the cognisant if only to fix notation and so on.

It is often necessary to use some logical formalism. Quite often we will write: (for all ...) (...) but in some places for succinctness we employ the universal quantifier: $\forall$ (read 'for all'). Likewise we abbreviate logical equivalence: 'if, and only if', most often to: 'iff' (occassionally $\Leftrightarrow$). Implication is written: '$\Rightarrow$'. So, for example: $(\forall a)(P(a) \Rightarrow Q(a))$ is to be read: 'for every value a, if $P(a)$ holds then $Q(a)$ holds'. Once or twice we need the existential quantifier: $\exists$ (read 'there exists'). Logical conjunction and disjunction are written, respectively: $\wedge$ and $\vee$. The reader should be careful to distinguish these from the *programs* (yielding atoms as results) called **and** and **or**.

A.1 Sets and set operations

We use the naïve notion of a set as a collection of elements without restriction. In particular sets may contain sets as elements. We will describe sets in extension like $\{1, \text{Jenny}, \{\text{Jasper}\}\}$ (a set of three elements) and in intension like $\{n \mid n \text{ is an even integer}\}$. This reads: the set of all n such that n is an even integer. We write $\varnothing$ for the empty set and $a \in A$ ($a \notin A$) for the assertion that element a is (not) in the set A. We write $A \subseteq B$ for A is a subset of B. $A \subseteq B$ if and only if for all $a \in A$ we have $a \in B$. Two sets A and B are equal if and only if $A \subseteq B$ and $B \subseteq A$. We write $P(A) = \{E \mid E \subseteq A\}$. $P(A)$ is the powerset of A.

We need some operations on sets. Given sets A and B we define:

$$A \cup B = \{c \mid c \in A \vee c \in B\}$$
$$A \cap B = \{c \mid c \in A \wedge c \in b\}$$
$$A \times B = \{\langle a,b \rangle \mid a \in A \wedge b \in B\}$$
$$A + B = A \times \{1\} \cup B \times \{2\}$$
$$A - B = \{a \mid a \in A \wedge a \notin B\}$$

Two of these are particularly important. $A \times B$ is the Cartesian product of A and B, and consists of all pairs formed from A and B. $A + B$ is the disjoint union. Note that every element of A and of B is uniquely tagged (by 1 and 2) so that the sets become disjoint before union takes place. This ensures that each element from A and B is uniquely represented in $A + B$.

A.2 Relations and functions

We are particularly concerned with binary relations. Given sets A and B a binary relation (henceforth relation) is a subset of $A \times B$. A relation is meant to describe how elements of A and B may be deemed to be associated. For example let $B = A = \{$Ron, Bob, Mary, Norman$\}$. The relation is-the-brother-of consists of $\{\langle$Ron, Bob$\rangle, \langle$Bob, Ron$\rangle, \langle$Norman, Mary$\rangle\}$. Quite clearly this is a subset of $A \times B$.

There are two kinds of relation of particular importance.

Equivalence relations

Let $\equiv \subseteq A \times A$ be a relation on A. We write $a \equiv a'$ if $\langle a, a' \rangle$ is an element of the relation. This relation is an equivalence relation providing:

$$x \equiv x \qquad \text{(it is reflexive)}$$
$$x \equiv y \Rightarrow y \equiv x \qquad \text{(it is symmetric)}$$
$$x \equiv y \wedge y \equiv z \Rightarrow x \equiv z \qquad \text{(it is transitive)}$$

The relation is-the-same-colour-as is an equivalence relation, as the reader may easily check.

Partial and total orders

Let $\leq \subseteq A \times A$ be a relation on A. We write $a \leq a'$ if $\langle a, a' \rangle$ is an element of this relation. This relation is a partial ordering providing

$$a \leq a \qquad \text{(reflexive)}$$
$$a \leq a' \wedge a' \leq a \Rightarrow a = a' \qquad \text{(antisymmetric)}$$
$$a \leq a' \wedge a' \leq a'' \Rightarrow a \leq a'' \qquad \text{(transitive)}$$

This is called a partial order because some pairs of elements are not comparable under this ordering. A total order deems that all pairs are comparable. This kind of relation satisfies the following axiom, in addition to those above:

$$a \leq a' \vee a' \leq a \qquad \text{(totality)}$$

Let $P(A)$ be the powerset of A, that is, the set of all subsets of A. The relation is-a-subset-of is a partial ordering of this set.

Consider the integer Z. This is totally ordered by the relation is-less-than-or-equal-to.

Functions

A function from A to B is a special kind of relation. It is total (if $a \in A$ then there exists a $b \in B$ such that $\langle a, b \rangle$ is in the relation) and it satisfies the unicity condition (if $\langle a, b \rangle$ and $\langle a, b' \rangle$ belong to the relation then $b = b'$). When we view a function in this way the relation (as a subset of $A \times B$) is called the *graph* of the function.

We will write $A \rightarrow B = \{f \mid f \text{ is a function from } A \text{ to } B\}$ that is $\{f \mid f \subseteq A \times B \text{ satisfying totality and unicity}\}$. This is the function space from A to B. We refer to the set A as the *domain* of the function and the set B as the *co-domain* of the function. The set $\{f(a) \mid a \in A\}$ (which is a subset of the co-domain) is called the *image* of the function.

There are a number of special kinds of functions which we need to consider. Let $f \in A \rightarrow B$.

f is *injective* iff whenever $f(a) = f(a')$ then $a = a'$. That is: if b lies in the image of f then there is a unique $a \in A$ which generates it.

f is *surjective* iff the image of f is the co-domain. That is, every element of B is the value of f for some $a \in A$.

f is *bijective* iff it is injective and surjective. That is, the function is a relabelling of elements of A by elements of B.

f is a *projection* iff it is surjective and *not* injective.

Sometimes we need to use functions whose domain and co-domain are ordered sets. Let A and B be partially ordered sets and let $f \in A \rightarrow B$.

f is *monotonic* iff it preserves the ordering. That is, more formally:

$$(\forall a, a' \in A)\,(a \sqsubseteq a' \Rightarrow f(a) \sqsubseteq f(a'))$$

f is an *isomorphism* iff it is a monotonic bijection.

Finally, it is often necessary to combine functions f and g so that the result of g is passed to f. For this to be possible it must be the case that the co-domain of g is the domain of f. Let $f \in A \rightarrow B$ and $g \in C \rightarrow A$.

$$(f \circ g)(c) \text{ (pronounced 'f composed with } g\text{')} = f(g(c)) \text{ for all } c \in C.$$

It is easy to check that $f \circ g$ is a function (check totality and unicity conditions). If A, B and C are partial orderings and f and g are monotonic then so is $f \circ g$.

A.3 Solving simple set equations

In this section we show how simple set equations can be solved. The method we employ can only solve certain kinds of equations. In Chapter 7 the same equations dealt with here receive a more complex treatment. That method is also capable of solving more sophisticated equations.

A set equation for the time being is an expression built from certain sets by means of set operations (including function space construction) and recursion.

For example the set of lists of atoms is specified by the equation:

$$L = \{\text{"Nil"}\} + A \times L$$

where $\{\text{"Nil"}\}$ and A are fixed sets.

In order to solve this equation we define a family of sets as follows:

$$L_0 \quad = \{\text{"Nil"}\}$$
$$L_{n+1} = A \times L_n$$

Note that for all n these are definitions of sets and not equations. Intuitively L_n consists of all lists of length n. We now set:

$$L_\infty = \bigcup_{n \geq 0} L$$

We claim that L_∞ satisfies the equation $L = \{\text{"Nil"}\} + A \times L$. This is easy to see.

$$A \times L_\infty = A \times \bigcup_{n \geq 0} L_n = \bigcup_{n \geq 0} A \times L_n = \bigcup_{n \geq 0} L_{n+1}$$

Now

$$\bigcup_{n \geq 0} L_{n+1} = L_\infty - \{\text{"Nil"}\}$$

hence $L_\infty = \{\text{"Nil"}\} + A \times L_\infty$ as required. Note in this construction that all the sets L_n are disjoint by definition. Since

$$L_\infty = \bigcup_{n \geq 0} L_n$$

and each L_n contains finite lists we see that L_∞ consists of all lists of finite length. As we remark in the text, partial lists and infinite lists only appear in more sophisticated constructions of solutions to the equation.

The other main data structure we require is a solution to $S = A + S \times S$. We attack this in a similar manner, by defining:

$$S_0 \quad = \varnothing$$
$$S_{n+1} = A + S_n \times S_n$$

In this example we have to add in A at each level or we do not get all the elements required. If we just set $S_n = S_n \times S_n$ we do not generate elements like $(a:b):c$; only symmetrical binary trees with 2^n leaves for some n.

Given these sets we set

$$S_\infty = \bigcup_{n \geq 0} S_n$$

and claim that it satisfies the equation. Now in this example the sets S_n are not disjoint but form an increasing sequence $S_0 \leq S_1 \leq S_2 \ldots$.

Now

$$S_\infty = \bigcup_{n \geq 0} S_n = \bigcup_{n \geq 1} S_n =$$

$$\bigcup_{n \geq 1} (A + S_{n-1} \times S_{n-1}) =$$

$$\bigcup_{n \geq 0} (A + S_n \times S_n) =$$

$$A + \bigcup_{n \geq 0} (S_n \times S_n) = \text{(the } S_n \text{ form a sequence)}$$

$$A + \bigcup_{n \geq 0} S_n \times \bigcup_{n \geq 0} S_n =$$

$$A + S_\infty \times S_\infty$$

as required.

A.4 Induction proofs

Central to the theme of program verification is the notion of an inductive proof. Here we shall simply review the proof method known as numerical induction. In Chapter 3 a generalization to induction over well-founded sets is developed and this, so-called structural induction, is then specialized so that inductive proofs can be carried out over the set of finite lists, finite symbolic expressions and indeed natural numbers. Later in Chapter 7 we consider another induction method over the structure of fixpoints.

It is often necessary, or desirable, to claim that every member of a set satisfies some property. If the set is finite then we could simply check the elements one by one. This is just proof by case analysis. Quite often the set will contain an infinite number of elements. No amount of checking of individual cases will produce the desired result. In such a situation induction is often the method to apply. Suppose we wish to show some property of natural numbers (which is clearly an infinite set). One possible example might be the property $P(n)$ which is true if and only if the sum of the natural numbers, from 1 to n is equal to $(1/2)n(n+1)$. To show this is true for all n we use the principle of numerical induction. This states that P holds for all n if we can show that P holds for 0 and P holds for $n+1$ on the assumption that it holds for n. Stated more formally we write.

Principle of numerical induction

$$(P(0) \wedge ((\forall n > 0)\ (P(n) \Rightarrow P(n+1)))) \Rightarrow (\forall n)\ (P(n))$$

So our proof of $P(n)$ for all n has two parts. Firstly a base step, in which we show that $P(0)$ holds, and an induction step in which we show $P(n+1)$ holds on the assumption that $P(n)$ holds.

We may now complete our example.

Proposition A.4(i)

For all $n \in N;\ 1 + \ldots + n = (1/2)n(n+1)$

Proof (by induction).   Let $P(n)$ iff $(1 + \ldots + n = (1/2)n(n+1))$.

Base step $(n=0)$

The left-hand side sum is 0.
Also $(1/2)0(1) = 0$ as required.

Induction step

Assume $P(n)$ holds:

$$
\begin{aligned}
&1 + \ldots + n + n + 1 &&= \text{(by induction)} \\
&(1/2)n(n+1) + n + 1 &&= \\
&(1/2)n^2 + 1/2\,n + n + 1 &&= \\
&((1/2)n + 1/2)\,(n+2) &&= \\
&(1/2)\,(n+1)\,(n+2)
\end{aligned}
$$

as required.

∎

Appendix B

Computational preliminaries

In this short appendix we cannot, of course, do justice to many of the issues surrounding programming languages and computers. There are, however, a couple of basic ideas which the computationally naïve reader ought to be made aware of. The sketches we give are necessarily rather terse. The interested reader can consult the books mentioned in the bibliography below for further details.

The first of these is the *Von Neumann Machine* which is an abstract description of a prototypical computer. Although real computers are much more sophisticated than the Von Neumann machine they are based to a greater or lesser extent upon it. It is only relatively recently that designs have begun to emerge which deviate from it significantly.

The second idea concerns the computer scientists' use of the term *variable* and other terminology associated with this. Students of a mathematical disposition often find particular difficulty because their variables tend to be somewhat different.

B.1 The Von Neumann machine

Essentially, this machine consists of three components. An *input–output unit*, with which the machine communicates with the outside world, a *central processing unit* and a *memory*. These are connected in the manner shown in Fig. B.1(i).

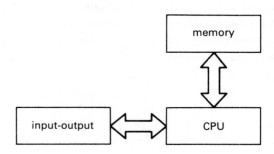

Fig. B.1(i)

412

The input–output unit is not significantly interesting from our point of view and we will not mention it again. The memory (or *store*) consists of a totally ordered set of *locations*. The ordering is effected by giving each location a numeric *address*. Each location can contain a unit of information and it is possible for this information to represent:

(a) data which has to be processed;

(b) the address of another location;

(c) an instruction which the processor can execute.

In fact the value stored in a location can often be treated in any of these ways depending on the context. For example an address can be treated as a number and arithmetic may be performed upon it. The result could then be used as an address.

The central processor can execute the instructions contained in the memory. A program for this machine is a totally ordered set of instructions. These are stored in the memory in some contiguous sequence of locations. The *stored program concept*, that is, the idea that programs reside as data in the memory, is the most fundamental aspect of this machine. Execution is initiated by the processor, once it is provided with the address of a location in which it can find the first instruction. The processor then repeats what is known as the *fetch–execute cycle*.

The fetch consists of obtaining the instruction from the memory. The execute cycle consists of the processor obeying the instruction it has fetched. The next cycle usually fetches the instruction in the next location after the first.

This need not happen because some instructions, when the processor executes them, compute a new address which the processor can then use to find the next instruction.

The sequence of instructions making the program may be totally ordered but the execution sequence rarely is. Indeed the execution sequence is conditional on various data and cannot be predicted in advance. This is not to say it is not deterministic, simply that it is not *computable*.

Because the data and the program reside in the store the connection between the store and the processor is very busy. It is this connection which Backus has attempted to ridicule as we discuss in Chapter 5.

Finally, it is important to note that, under this regime, programs are to be thought of as sequences of commands to be executed. If one treats the store as an element of the set, S, of store states, then an instruction is a way of changing the store, that is, it is a member of $S \rightarrow S$. A program, then, is a way of making large changes to the store by suitable sequences of these small changes. This perception of the semantics of a program is reflected in many programming languages which allow sequences of commands to be formed and *assignments*, which can change the store contents.

B.2 The variable

In mathematics a variable ranges over the values of some set. There are some conventions, however, which tell us, for any occurrence of a variable in an expression, which defining occurrence is intended. For example, consider the following expression:

$$\sum_{i=1}^{i=5} \sum_{j=2}^{j=i} (i+j) + \sum_{i=1}^{i=6} i$$

The mathematically inclined reader will have no trouble in seeing that there are three distinct variables introduced in the expression. The *defining occurrences* are those on the base of each summation. In particular the variable i introduced by the third summation is distinct from those occurring on the left. Moreover the use of i (in "$j=i$" and "$i+j$") in the nested summation refer to the i introduced by the outer summation. It is surely also clear that it would not be meaningful to replace either the term "$i=5$" or the term "$i=6$" by "$i=j$" because, somehow, j would be used outside its *scope of definition* which we take to be just the nested summation.

This happens in programming languages as well. A scope of definition is introduced by a *block* written here as:

begin . . . **end**

Variables are introduced by:

var i, j

Thus a program skeleton whose shape resembles the expression above might be:

begin var i **begin var** j . . . **end end** ; **begin var** i **end**

Computer scientists refer to the *scope* of a variable and mean the block in which it is defined.

Variables are also used in mathematics as formal parameters for functions as in, for example:

$$f(x) = x + 3$$

The scope of the variable is just the body of the function being defined. This happens in computer programs too. We may write:

procedure $f(x : \textbf{integer}) = \textbf{return } x + 3$

Again the variable inside the brackets is being introduced and its scope is the procedure body.

So far we have reasonably similar behaviour but this is short lived. In a program one might write:

$$x = x + 1$$

To a mathematician this is an equation and if we interpret it over, let us say, the real numbers it has no solution. To a computer scientist it is quite meaningful. It is not an equation at all but a *command*:

"replace the current value of x with $x + 1$"

This reveals the major difference between mathematical and programming variables. In mathematics variables are associated to values. That is, there is a mapping at any moment which tells us that, for example, x has value 3 and y has value 4 and . . . for all the variables we are using.

This can be thought of as a function in the set:

$$VARIABLES \rightarrow VALUES$$

In a program things are more complex – take for example the command:

$$x = x + 1$$

The intention is that the *value* of x is to be added to 1 and the result placed in the *location* x. Thus there are two aspects to any variable. In fact *variables in a program denote locations* and locations have contents. The aspect of x we need is highly dependent on the context in which it appears. Functionally we think of the association of variables to values as:

$$VARIABLES \rightarrow LOCATIONS \rightarrow VALUES$$

Breaking this into two parts we have maps:

$$VARIABLES \rightarrow LOCATIONS$$
$$LOCATIONS \rightarrow VALUES$$

Let p be the current function associating variables to locations and let s be the current function which yields the contents of each location. That is, roughly: p explains how variables in the program are mapped onto the locations in the store of the computer and s is a particular state of the store.

$$x = x + 1$$

is a command which will alter the store (the mapping from $LOCATIONS$ to $VALUES$). Roughly, the command generates a new store state, s', (a function

s' from *LOCATIONS* to *VALUES*) which is equal to s in every respect except that location $p(x)$ now contains $s(p(x)) + 1$.

Further details of this are covered in Chapter 8.

This complex relationship between variables and stores has many ramifications. For example, if we define a function in mathematics like:

$$f(x) = x + 3$$

then, in the expression:

$$g(y) = f(y) + 2$$

there cannot be any doubt what $f(y)$ means. If we write $g(4)$ then we bind x to 4 in the definition of f and obtain the result 7 which gets added to 2.

If, on the other hand, these were functions in a programming language we have an ambiguity. When we write $f(y)$ do we intend the *location* associated to y or the *value* in the location associated to y to be bound to x?

In many cases a programming language will have several *parameter passing conventions*. For example, passing the location is "call by reference" and passing the value is "call by value". In fact, call by value is more complicated, in general, because the formal parameter, x, itself has two aspects and the binding causes the value of y to be placed in the *location* associated with x. To see the implications of this consider the program fragment:

> **procedure** $f(x : \textbf{integer}) = \textbf{begin } x = x + 1 \textbf{ end}$
> **begin var** y; $y = 3$; $f(y)$; **print** y **end**

If f adopts call by value then the value 4 gets placed in the location associated with x. This value gets incremented during the procedure. Consequently the print command will write the number 3. If x is call by reference then the location associated to y will be associated to x. The procedure will increment the value in the location associated to y. Thus the print command will write the number 4.

This is usually enough to drive the most even-headed mathematician to the bar! The good news is that functional languages adopt a binding of variables to values just as mathematics does. Consequently, behaviour like that exhibited above cannot occur.

Finally we turn to *free variables*. Suppose we define the function:

$$f(x) = x + y$$

Mathematicians call y a *free parameter*. In:

> **procedure** $f(x:\textbf{integer}) = \ \ldots \ y \ \ldots$

computer scientists call y a *global variable*. The question of *when* a global variable is to be associated with some, globally occurring, defining occurrence of y, gives rise to another distinction. Consider the program:

```
begin
    var x;
    x = 3;
    procedure g( ) =
        begin
            print x
        end;
    procedure f( ) =
        begin
            var x;
            x = 4;
            g( )
        end;
    g( );
    f( )
end
```

This program introduces a new variable x and then sets it to 3. At this point it defines a procedure called g. This procedure makes global reference to x. The reader who cannot see this could usefully write out the definition of g on its own, it should then be clear that x is a free parameter of g. It then defines a procedure f which also defines a variable x (in a different scope to the earlier one). When called, this procedure will set x to 4 and then call g. After the three declarations (of x, g and f) then program executes g which will print the value of x. After this it executes f which will set x to 4 and then execute g, which in turn prints x.

What exactly does the program print? There are two possibilities which arise from the two possible times at which the global reference, which g makes to x, is resolved.

If the binding of x is resolved at the moment the procedure g is *defined* then the x in the outer block is the target. Under this regime (called *static binding of free variables*) the program will print 3 followed by 3. This is because the value of the outer x does not change after it is initially set to 3.

If the binding of x is resolved at the moment the procedure is *called* then the x in the outer block is the target for the first call of g and the x in f is the target for the second call to g. Under this regime (called *dynamic binding of free variables*) the program will print 3 followed by 4.

This issue arises in Chapter 2 when we discuss the lambda calculus. Note that it is completely independent of the complex way in which programming variables are bound through locations to values.

We have, of course, barely touched the surface in this extremely modest appendix. Hopefully the material will be of some use to the computationally naïve reader. Further details can be found in the following texts.

B.3 Bibliographic notes

Tennent (1981) is an excellent introduction to programming languages and takes a semantic perspective: it is likely to appeal to the mathematically inclined reader. Although the book uses little explicit mathematics its style results from Tennent's knowledge of mathematical semantics. The few issues we have mentioned here are dealt with very comprehensively in this book along with many other fundamental ideas.

Tanenbaum (1984) is an introduction to computer architecture and covers processor organization, memory structures, input–output and also a number of specific conventional machines in detail.

Tanenbaum, A. S. (1984) *Structured Computer Organisation*. Prentice-Hall, Englewood Cliffs, NJ.
Tennent, R. D. (1981) *Principles of Programming Languages*. Prentice-Hall, Englewood Cliffs, NJ.

Solutions to exercises

Chapter 1

Exercise 1.2(iv)

The conditional is strict in its first argument and non-strict in its second and third. This non-strictness is crucial; consider the program:

if $x = 0$ **then** print "can't divide by zero" **else** n/x

This is discussed further in Section 5.2.3. Distributivity depends on the semantics of expressions which can follow the **if**. If these can do side-effects then sequencing does not distribute over the conditional on the left.
∎

Exercise 1.3(i)

Arrange for **f** to update (and then return) same global variable.
∎

Chapter 2

Exercise 2.2.3(iv)

See Hindley & Seldin (1986, p. 6).
∎

Exercise 2.2.3(xiii)

(a) This has no normal form. The expression generates an extra $\lambda x \cdot xxx$ at each β-reduction.
∎

Exercise 2.2.5(ii)

(d) Think carefully about 0 raised to any power and the relationship between I and c_1.
∎

Exercise 2.2.5(iii)

(a) Let X be any lambda term. $X = (K\ X\ X) = (F\ X\ X)$ (since we are taking the extra axiom) and $(F\ X\ X) = (F\ X) = F$. So all expressions are equal to F and by transitivity all expressions are equal to each other.

(b) Can you find a general rule for S^{2n+1}?

Exercise 2.2.6(ii)

(a) F is the fixpoint of a well-known combinator ... but which one?

(b) Every expression is a fixpoint of I. $(Y\ I)$ reduces to $\lambda x \cdot xx(\lambda x \cdot xx)$.
∎

Exercise 2.4.2(vii)

(d) The SECD machine does applicative reduction and consequently attempts the following: $(Y\ F\ 0) = F\ (Y\ F)\ 0 = F\ (F\ (Y\ F))\ 0\ \ldots.$
∎

Chapter 3

Exercise 3.3(vii)

The set A is the set of minimal elements of S.
∎

Exercise 3.4.1(v)

$P(l)$ iff (for all $l' \in L$) ((**length** l) + (**length** l') = **length** ($l * l'$))
∎

Exercise 3.4.1(vii) (b)

$P(l)$ iff (for all $l' \in L$) ((**reverse** ($l * l'$) = (**reverse** l') * (**reverse** l))
∎

Exercise 3.4.1(xii)

Show that, for all lists $l, l' \in L$:
sublist ((**comtaillist** $l\ l'$) l) & **sublist** ((**comtaillist** $l\ l'$) l')
∎

Exercise 3.4.2(iii)

Show that, for all sexpressions $s \in S$:

(**smember** a s) iff (**member** a (**fringe** s))
∎

Exercise 3.4.2(vi)

Sequencing and also the conditional command allow the construction of programs which delay the evaluation of their arguments. These constructs allow the PASCAL program to terminate before completely flattening the expressions.
∎

Exercise 3.4.2(xii)

$$\textbf{def srec } h\ g\ (s:s') = h\ (s:s')\ (\textbf{srec } h\ g\ s)\ (\textbf{srec } h\ g\ s')$$
$$\textbf{def srec } h\ g\ a \qquad = g\ a$$
∎

Exercise 3.4.3(v)

Think about the well-founded order over which to perform an induction.
∎

Exercise 3.4.3(viii)

(a) Define an ordering over sexpressions which expresses the complexity of the left (**fst**) subexpression for the program **roll**. Similarly, the right (**snd**) subexpression for **unroll**.
(b) The same orderings are required.
∎

Exercise 3.4.3(ix)

(a) Refer to example 3.4.3(ii) for this.
(b) The same ordering is required to establish these properties.
∎

Project 3.4.4(xiv)

The proof can be found in Robinson (1979).
∎

Exercise 3.5(iii)

Refer to Section 4.7 for a functional program on which to base the PASCAL program.
■

Exercise 3.5(vii)

The best case arises from an sexpression which is right linear and the worst case from one which is left linear.
■

Exercise 3.6(vi)

def length l = **length1** l 0
  def length1 [ ] $n = n$
  def length1 $(a:l)$ $n =$ **length** l (**plus** n 1)
■

Exercise 3.6(ix)

(a) **def ca** s = **cal** s 0
  def cal $(s:s')$ $n =$ **cal** s (**cal** s' n)
  def cal a n = **plus** n 1

(b, c) At this stage **mirror** is not amenable to this technique because **cons** is not an associative operation. We will investigate a higher-order accumulation strategy in Section 4.7 which helps.

(c) Note that under applicative evaluation the accumulator holds a partial result. This is always a list. Under normal order (or more properly, the canonical semantics) the accumulator holds an arbitrary expression (which none the less evaluates to a list). This latter situation is particularly important in later sections of the book.
■

Exercise 3.7(iv)

It is necessary to show a more general statement true, namely:

(for all $l \in L$ and $n \in N$) $(((\textbf{length } l) + n) = (\textbf{length1 } l \ n))$

The required result is obtained by setting $n = 0$ in the above.
■

Exercise 3.9(ii)

The ordering required is developed in the preamble to proposition 3.9(iv).
∎

Exercise 3.9(iii)

(a) **def ca** $s = $ **c** $[s]$
  def c $[\ ] = 0$
  def c $((s:s'):l) = $ **c** $(s:(s':l))$
  def c $(a:l) = ($**c** $l) + 1$

But addition is not a non-strict primitive so this is not yet an iterative form.
The next stage is to add an accumulator:

  def ca $s = $ **cc** $[s]\ 0$
  def cc $[\ ]\ n = n$
  def cc $((s:s'):l)\ n = $ **cc** $(s:(s':l))\ n$
  def cc $(a:l)\ n = $ **cc** $l\ (n+1)$

Exercise to do

Suppose that we work with a strict **cons**. The solution to example 3.9(i) is now
not an iterative form. Obtain one using the solution above as a guide. (There is
a catch!)
∎

(b) Refer to Burstall & Darlington (1975) in the bibliography to Chapter 4.
∎

Exercise 3.12(iv)

The important thing to note is that under applicative evaluation a good deal of
unnecessary work is undertaken because the accumulator is evaluated. Under
the canonical semantics the accumulator is often an unevaluated expression
and this is ignored (in the example) as soon as the atom "B" is encountered.
∎

Exercises 3.13(x) and (xi)

Refer to Wadler (1985) in the bibliography to Chapter 3.
∎

Chapter 4

Exercise 4.2(ii)

This exercise is worked through in Burstall & Darlington (1977).

∎

Exercise 4.5(ii)

fact n m = (**factorial** n) + m EUREKA

∎

Exercise 4.5(v)

f n m = (**fib** n) + m EUREKA

∎

Exercise 4.7(iv)

If we assume that **H** is associative we can classify continuations which occur during the evaluation of **f′** which have the form: (**H** a (**H** b (. . .))) by the atoms they contain (in this case [a b . . .]). This forms the basis of the eureka definition.

∎

Exercise 4.7(viii)

Use numerical induction.

∎

Exercise 4.7(xii)

Possibly the most difficult exercise in the book. The result can be obtained as a corollary of the following lemma:

for all lists l, z and z'; (**R** l ($z * z'$)) = $z * $ (**R** l z')

and this is an easy induction which makes use of lemma 4.7(x). The result we want is now obtained by case analysis over lists; lemma 4.7(x) and the lemma given above are required for the non-"Nil" case.

∎

Exercise 4.9(iv)

The program **goto**$_5$ is **square** ; **inc**.
∎

Chapter 5

Exercise 5.2.3(i)

The apply-to-all functional corresponds to **map** and the insert (right) functional to **reduce** (except the right unit is implicit in FP).
∎

Exercise 5.3.1(ii)

(b) (i) See theorem 5.5(iv).
    (ii) **eq** ∘ [[ ], **id**]
∎

Exercise 5.3.2(ii)

def distr = **null** ∘ 1 → [ ]; **apndr** ∘ [**distr** ∘ (**t1** × **id**), (**1** × **id**)]
∎

Exercise 5.3.2(iii) and Project 5.3.2(iv)

See Backus (1981b).
∎

Exercise 5.3.3(iii)

member is developed in example 5.6(x).
reverse = /(**append** ∘ **swap**) ∘ [id] where **swap** = [2, 1]

Exercise to do

Which insert operators can be used in this function?
Evaluate **reverse** ⟨ "*A*","*B*","*C*","*D*","*E*","*F*" ⟩.
∎

delete = **concat** ∘ **p** ∘ **distl**
p = **eq**→[ ]; [1]
■

Exercise 5.3.3(vi)

def append = /$_L$ **apndr** ∘ **apndl**
■

Exercise 5.6(ix)

Consider the class of programs specified by:
$f = p \rightarrow g$; $Q(f)$ where $Q(k) = k \circ j$. Note that this is a BLF.
■

Exercise 5.7(ii)

Refer to Williams (1982a).
■

Chapter 6

Exercise 6.3.2(iv)

Define $C_:$ as follows:
$C_: x\ y\ z = (x\ z): y$
■

Exercise 6.3.3(ii)

Ensure that the result of every recursive call of abstraction is processed by the optimization rules. Another technique would be to undertake some program transformation so that the abstraction and optimization are combined completely. This way one avoids the unoptimized code ever coming into existence.
■

Exercise 6.4.1(x)

In both cases the head cell must be overwritten to maintain the sharing of subexpressions.
■

Exercise 6.5.2(vi)

It is, of course, advantageous to note repeated free expressions and to identify these in the abstraction process.
∎

Exercise 6.5.4(iii)

Usually the left argument of an application and a **cons** (when it is used to represent lists) is simpler than the right-hand argument. This has an impact on the depth of the stack which is necessary for a rewrite.

Exercise to do

Redefine the compilation rules for application and construction with e_1 before e_2. Recompile the program **intsfrom** and observe the depth of stack which is required.
∎
∎

Exercise 6.6.3(v)

(a) $(\forall \alpha)\,(\text{List}(\alpha) \rightarrow \text{List}(\alpha))$
(b) $(\forall \alpha)\,(\alpha \rightarrow \text{List}(\alpha) \rightarrow \textbf{bool})$
(c) $(\forall \alpha, \beta)\,((\alpha \rightarrow \beta) \rightarrow \text{List}(\alpha) \rightarrow \text{List}(\beta))$
∎

Exercise 6.7(ix)

Refer to Hughes (1985).
∎

Chapter 7

Exercise 7.2(xx)

(b) **or**	t	f	$\perp$
t	t	t	$\perp$
f	t	f	$\perp$
$\perp$	$\perp$	$\perp$	$\perp$

or	t	f	$\perp$
t	t	t	t
f	t	f	$\perp$
$\perp$	t	$\perp$	$\perp$

(c) **not**	t	f	$\perp$
	f	t	$\perp$

■

Exercise 7.2(xxi)

By induction.
■

Exercise 7.2(xxx)

Each element of the set reduces to $\perp$ so the least upper bound is $\perp$.
■

Chapter 8

Exercise 8.1.2(i)

$s[l{\leftarrow}n] = \lambda l' \cdot \mathbf{if}\,(l{=}l')\,n\,(s\,l')$

Exercise 8.2.2(ii)

The label values would be unaware of the local variables declared in the block.

Index

abstraction 14–15, 177, 182
  functional 13–14, 89
  lambda (*see* lambda abstraction)
  multiple 277–8
  over patterns 69, 277
  principle of 14, 22, 39, 279–81
  procedural 89–90
accumulator 105, 113–21, 124, 132–3, 143, 157–8, 189–90, 195, 205, 249, 337, 393, 422, 423 (*see also* parameter—accumulating)
activation record 261–9
  template 262
ADA xiii, 1, 9
ALGOL60 1, 25, 206, 262–3
ALGOL68 xiii, 1, 3, 9, 57–9, 202, 213–14, 262
antecedent 87
antisymmetry 407
application 4, 14
  functional 5, 12–13, 282
  relational 5
  self 36, 44
applications 15
architecture (*see* machine architecture)
argument 15
arithmetic 11, 13
assignment 1, 2, 4–8, 25, 173, 212, 378, 413
associativity 2, 13, 76, 140, 185–8, 191, 206, 226, 258, 391, 422, 424
atoms 57, 215, 366
axioms
  lambda (*see* lambda axioms)
  pairing 31–2

backtracking 161–9
bags 153
balancing 326, 330
BASIC 1
BCPL 202
bijection 408
binding 63, 268
  dynamic 144, 417
  static 144, 263, 417
body 15

bottom 216, 347
bounded completeness 363–4, 365

C 173, 202
callee-saves strategy 268–9
caller-saves strategy 268–9
cartesian product 133, 216, 227–30, 348–9, 365, 372, 407
catch points 159
category theory 129, 169, 257, 259
chain 355, 359, 362
  inductive 363–4, 369
  complete 356, 364–5, 372, 375, 396
  continuity 345, 359, 362, 365, 373, 375
class objects 264
clause (*see* recursion equation)
closure 47, 49, 51, 53–4, 144, 262
COBOL 272
codomain 408
coercions 335
combinator 38, 273–9
  calculus 11, 37–54, 259
  categorical 343
  compilation 261, 271–81, 306, 342
  evaluation 261
  head redex 43
  head reduction 43
  higher order 257
  redex 42, 70
  reduction 42, 109, 281–305
combining forms (*see* form—combining)
command 377, 379, 415
  assignment (*see* assignment)
  blocks 378, 390, 392, 397, 414, 428
  conditional 4, 419
  destructive control 6, 9, 157
  destructive data 6, 9
  jumps 382, 385
  labelled 382, 385
  sequencing (*see* sequencing)
compilation xii, 43, 261, 377, 403, 427
complexity 108–13, 119, 169
  average case 119
  best case 113, 222